POSTNATIONAL IDENTITY

CRITICAL PERSPECTIVES
A Guilford Series

Edited by
DOUGLAS KELLNER
University of Texas, Austin

Postmodern Theory: Critical Interrogations
Steven Best and Douglas Kellner

A Theory of Human Need
Len Doyal and Ian Gough

Psychoanalytic Politics, Second Edition:
Jacques Lacan and Freud's French Revolution
Sherry Turkle

Postnational Identity:
Critical Theory and Existential Philosophy
in Habermas, Kierkegaard, and Havel
Martin J. Matuštík

POSTNATIONAL IDENTITY

Critical Theory and Existential Philosophy in Habermas, Kierkegaard, and Havel

MARTIN J. MATUŠTÍK

THE GUILFORD PRESS
New York   London

© 1993 Martin J. Matuštík
Published by The Guilford Press
A Division of Guilford Publications, Inc.
72 Spring Street, New York, NY 10012

Printed in the United States of America

This book is printed on acid-free paper.

Last digit is print number: 9   8   7   6   5   4   3   2   1

Library of Congress Cataloging-in-Publication Data

Matuštík, Martin Joseph, 1957–
    Postnational identity : critical theory and existential philosophy
in Habermas, Kierkegaard, and Havel / Martin J. Matuštík.
        p.   cm.
    Includes bibliographical reference and index.
    ISBN 0-89862-420-7 (hard) — ISBN 0-89862-270-0 (pbk.)
    1. Habermas, Jürgen.   2. Kierkegaard, Søren, 1813–1855.
3. Havel, Václav.   I. Title.
B3258.H324M316   1993
142—dc20   92-42692
                                                                CIP

For Patricia J. Huntington

Introduction

WHY AN ENCOUNTER BETWEEN CRITICAL THEORY AND EXISTENTIAL PHILOSOPHY?

In the wake of the end of totalitarianism in central-eastern Europe, the president of former Czechoslovakia, Václav Havel, characterized the history-making events of November 1989 in Kierkegaardian terms as an *existential revolution* (i.e., the awakening of human responsibility, spirit, and reason), while others paraded the end of the Cold War as a victory for the New World Order. Where once the communist nomenclatura and free markets competed for the global pledge of allegiance, now nationalist identity and religious and secular fundamentalism fill in the void created on our world-historical stage. By bringing us face to face with this cultural and ideological void, Kierkegaard and Havel make life difficult for totalitarians, fundamentalists, nationalists, and "bourgeois philistines" alike. An urgent new task for a critique of the present age is to harness the experience made by the movements of dissent against totalitarian mentality into critical social theory and democratic politics.[1]

Critical theory and existential philosophy, brought together in this book, engender two forms of suspicion of the present age. The critical social theorist, such as Jürgen Habermas, unmasks the forms in which social and cultural life become systematically distorted by the imperatives of political power and economic gain. Existential critics, like Søren Kierkegaard and Václav Havel, are suspicious of the various ways in which individuals deceive themselves or other people. This study aims to integrate Kierkegaard's and Havel's existential critique of the motives informing human identity formation with Habermas's critique of the colonization of fragmented, anomic modern life by systems of power and money. The move from nationalist or fundamentalist constructions of identity to postnational, open, and multicultural identity represents a critical ideal on which both the existential and sociopolitical suspicions of the present age converge.

Etienne Balibar and Immanuel Wallerstein explain theoretically a hard lesson about nationalism which we have been learning ever since the 19th century: the freedom that nationalism promises is inscribed in a highly ambiguous Faustian pact. The nationalists of liberation not only rightly react to cultural and classist hierarchies, or to imperial hegemonies, but easily emerge as the nationalists of conquest. Along the same lines, Cornel West and bell hooks argue that separatist achievements of new communal bonds, whether in liberation struggles or in some rap music, offer a mixed blessing. The nationalist renaissance recovers the marginalized voices, thereby furthering larger political and economic liberation. Yet by failing to consider the complex historical context for this emancipation, the neonationalists give a false impression that we can harken back to innocent origins. Bell hooks points out that separatism, which lacks democratic political culture, is not self-determination and, moreover, that it reads the white patriarchal power into its own presumed innocence. Balibar and Wallerstein show that nationalists entrench forms of racism and sexism when the past cultural and economic exclusions are transferred to the present ones. Both racism and sexism underpin certain forms of nationalism and all three overlap in distorting any emancipatory or democratic dividend that is expected to arise from the postcolonial freedom movement on nationalist grounds. We can say that this point, made by the African-American theorists of race, nation, and class, has been historically true of the nationally carried revolutions against the Soviet imperial internationalism as well. Thus, while nations remain with us as a reality, nationalism and its excesses in racism and sexism are the forms of ideology that can only problematically become the principle of democratic social integration for which the new spring of the nations of 1989 yearns. Minimally, we need the de-romanticized and political view of nation, which Julia Kristeva appropriately designates *Nations without Nationalism*.[2]

Some thinkers, such as Outlaw, argue for the conservation of races and ethnicities as the basis for sociopolitical philosophy and a radical politics of difference. To be sure, Outlaw wants to eliminate ethnocentrism and racism while preserving the "discernable race- and ethnic-based communities of meaning." Yet he thinks that we continue to need the flourishing of various groups of meaning in order to sustain the well-being of individuals against the modernist forms of humanist universalism.

> "Difference," rather than similarity, has become a significant basis of political mobilization. . . . The celebration of universal principle has often turned out to be the rhetoric—rather than realization—of liberal-democratic, socialist, or communist principles of universality and equality in the midst of the domination of political, economic, and cultural life by a particular race and/or ethnies.

I argue that in order to subvert these hegemonic forms of universalism and sustain (citing Outlaw) "democratically 'multicultural'" institutions, and do both while resisting the romanticist nation–state, and imperial and regional nationalisms, we need to go beyond that politics of difference which is formulated on the basis of the communitarian communities of meaning.[3]

I take it from Balibar that both liberal nationalisms and imperial states oscillate between the ambiguity of homogenizing universalism and communitarian romanticism toward group differences. Since all identities are historically constructed, universalism and particularism are not necessarily radical opposites. The problem with both is that they offer egalitarianism and well-being on a selective basis or only to offset the anomie of sexist and racist societies. The strategic differences that function against colonial or antisemitic racisms can become problematic political and economic forces of integration. "[I]n articulating itself to nationalism, . . . [racism] is, in its difference, necessary to nationalism." Racist difference provides a necessary "internal supplement" to nationalism. If this is so, then neither universalism nor particularism as such offer a refuge from racist and nationalist hatred since both universal discourse and local solidarities can become its accomplices: "supernationalism" supplements discourses of particular differences and "supranationalism" engenders discourses of "racist internationalism" such as the secular "frontiers of an ideal humanity" or those of religious integrations. "Nationalist internationalism" and "internationalist nationalism" are two faces of the same dialectic: the myth of proper origins and the enlightenment and "universalist projects within nationalism." An antiracist and antisexist attitude, not just any preservation of identity and difference, recommends itself as the way out of the universalist and the particularist forms of nationalism.[4]

The question before us, then, is the "how" of universalism and particularism: how is one to embody the particular differences and how is one to communicate, hence to universalize, one's identity without marginalizing that of others? Kierkegaard locates this "how" question in the category of self-choice exercised within the traditions in which one finds oneself already situated and socialized. To support my reading of Kierkegaard, let me cite Kristeva in this connection:

> Beyond the *origins* that have assigned to us biological identity papers and a linguistic, religious, social, political, historical place, the freedom of contemporary individuals may be gauged according to their ability to *choose* their membership, while the democratic capability of a nation and social group is revealed by the right it affords individuals to exercise that choice.[5]

The question for the politics of difference is not only the "what" of tradition but its "how" as well. Any regional or global village can become homogenizing, just as nationalism and fundamentalism can be spearheaded by states and local chieftains alike.

Postnational identity cannot be, then, confused with some ethnic cleansing in either its global or regional forms. On the contrary, because I project this notion, in principle, as a positionality of concretely existing individuals, each in their multicultural diversity, I seek an expression for our communal and individual resistance to oppressive homogeneity. Kierkegaard's category of the individual, not a communitarian or nation–state ethos, is the most radical, and to be sure nonatomistic, expansion of multiple or open unity in difference. With this category, we can rethink democratic multiculturalism from the most extreme standpoint of diversity (self-realization) while still making moral and sociopolitical uses of identity and responsible agency (self-determination). We can envision this individual as a citizen in democratic spaces of multicultural and multigendered positionalities. If postnational means multicultural, then it can be neither super- nor supranational. Identity does not cancel out difference, and yet the call for diversity of all voices does not preclude but, rather, requires some normative notion of agency: we need not exchange abstract rights and goulash socialism for "postmodern pastiche." Identity as positionality can be conflated neither with some group soul nor with the possessive individualist presuppositions of unitary universal human essence. Thus, postnational identity must be different from racist particularism which is only a convex mirror of homogeneous internationalist universalism. Even though nationalist integrations at times play an emancipatory role against colonial hegemony, we have learned about the devastating setbacks of this unholy alliance. By recognizing with Kristeva that we all are strangers, not just to others but also to ourselves, postnational identity admits only an "open-ended," political, "transitional, and cultural nation" without the tribal and herd *Volksgeist* of nationalism.[6]

I define *the existential* as a form of praxis rooted in the attitude of a critical examination of those motives and presuppositions that influence the formations of identity, the parameters of communication, and theoretical ideals. My argument is that existential critique and social critique complement each other and overcome their respective limitations. A Kierkegaardian critic is explicitly focused on the attitudinal orientation that permeates a given sociopolitical critique, yet is only implicitly interested in shaping economic and political institutions. Honesty about motives does not guarantee that we reach the level of material praxis; yet the latter does not deliver the critic into sufficient sobriety about what motivates any emancipatory theory and action. Habermas's critique of the systemic distortions of symbolic orders is explicitly sociopolitical and economic, but it is only implicitly concerned with the ways in which motive informs the very material critique. Thus, the critic of the present age must learn to resist all abstraction from political and economic life, yet also embody radical honesty about critical theory and action. The "existential" stands for a moment in emancipatory praxis that keeps the sociopolitical and economic concretion (the "what") of the theorist or activist pinned down to the concretion motivated by the ways (the "how") one engages material life.

The modern individual is a *crisis individual*—one no longer easily definable by the motives offered through the given traditions and cultures. She becomes a dissenting *existential individual* when she does not try to construct a new ideology in order to flee the anomie and fragmentation of modern life but views the identity crisis of the present age as an occasion for learning to live with an attitude of sobriety about the question of motive. *The critical social theorist* unmasks how systems of economy and political power, which govern the material reproduction of life, coopt the symbolic reproduction of life; *the existential critic* strives with honesty to resist any totalitarian closure of identity formation, communication, and community ideals. The critical theorist and the existential critic thus represent two forms of distinguishable though interrelated concretion.

I view Havel's literary and political posture as highly relevant for carrying through this new task of articulating a thoroughly sincere, sociopolitically and materially relevant critical theory. Havel envisions that deliberative democracy brings the experiences of dissent against totality into professional politics. His writings and activism, both before and after 1989, provide a fitting example for an examination of the proposed encounter between critical theory and existential philosophy. This examination is made in distinctly nondogmatic terms and is in contrast to both the conservative political existentialists of Nazi Germany and some left decisionist existentialists. Havel's opposition to totalitarian politics is in harmony with similar critiques by thinkers like Marcuse, Adorno, and Habermas. This posture does not validate the current celebrations of the conservative status quo that under the rubric of family and democratic values often marginalizes others on the basis of gender, race, and class. Havel's defense of human and civil rights in the context of resurgent hatred in central-eastern Europe is just as groundbreaking as was Kierkegaard's exposure of those who justified nationalism on the basis of the "Christian" moral majority. Havel differs from the market conservative, Václav Klaus, and the left populist, Vladimír Mečiar—both winners in the June 1992 parliamentary elections, the watershed event that has brought a breakup of Czechoslovakia into the Czech Republic and Slovakia—because Havel's personal style in politics embraces a vision of a democratic, multicultural community. We need not push him into a quietist, piously individualistic corner, where Kierkegaard's inwardness is so often placed. I find it more philosophically interesting and socially significant to examine the implications of Havel's Kierkegaardian politics for democratic multiculturalism after 1989.

Considering the theoretical motives for this new task, existential philosophy was attacked by hermeneutics and poststructuralism in continental philosophy on the one hand, and by analytic philosophy on the other. How is one to speak about Kierkegaard or Havel after the failures of both the rightist and leftist existentialist politics, and after the demise of the philosophy of the subject? If there is to be more than an antiquarian interest in teaching survey courses on existentialism, the next generation of thinkers and activists ought also to answer this methodological problem. How can one thematize the questions of genuineness or critical honesty under what Habermas has called the postmetaphysical conditions of the linguistic–communicative turn in philosophy? The challenge of Habermas's theory to the Kierkegaardian position is to rethink the category of the individual within an intersubjectivist theory of identity formation.

EXISTENTIAL HABERMAS OR COMMUNICATIVE KIERKEGAARD AND HAVEL?

Habermas's project of radical democracy and postnational identity emerges from revisionary Marxist and American pragmatist contexts. The central-eastern European experience of what Jan Patočka called "the solidarity of the shaken" draws on resources similar to Mahatma Gandhi's and Martin Luther King's nonviolent resistance. The 1977 formulations of the Czechoslovak manifesto for human rights, *Charta 77*, and Havel's term *existential revolution* borrow from Lévinas's requirement of radical responsibility which one bears towards the other. These historical parallels meet a present theoretical need to bridge the gap between the components represented in Habermas's democratic project and those typical of the politically democratic and ethical appropriation of the Kierkegaardian category of the individual.[7]

The importance of this task then does not lie in having to choose between Habermas's critical modernism and Kierkegaard's or Havel's critiques of one-dimensional rationality and totalitarian society. While neither Habermas's rendition of the Enlightenment Project under the regulative and universalizing theory of communication nor Kierkegaard's insistence that modern sociopolitical life be rooted in the category of the radically honest individual alone would address this new task, an encounter between them need not replay the antagonist relation of Kierkegaard vis-à-vis Hegel. On the contrary, Habermas's fallibilist reason and Kierkegaard's defense of the individual converge in their opposition to the communitarian or nationalist justifications of morality, democracy, and religion. Havel's transformation of the ideals of 1789 and his critique of the new forms of hatred suggest that this timely convergence provides an opening for revising the relationship between critical theory and existential philosophy.

This admittedly ambitious task to rethink a new composite figure of a critical theory eludes even those thinkers and activists who find this possibility attractive. While a bold plan to develop critical theory in this direction was envisioned by the young Herbert Marcuse, the project never got beyond a programmatic sketch. Attempts by other thinkers to integrate the Kierkegaardian critical use of the category of the individual with a sociopolitical critique of the present age have also shipwrecked. The reason for this theoretical and practical failure is that some define the existential under the rubric of subjectivism, thereby opposing it to extreme objectivism, whereas others identify it with a quietist and idealist withdrawal from the material and historical concretion of life.[8]

This book confronts the received view of Kierkegaard as irrational, antisocial, and uncritical. This traditional view of Kierkegaardian apolitical, acommunicative, and acosmic individualism, which is unreflectively copied from one commentary to another, becomes my polemical interlocutor. Again, the importance of the task at hand does not lie in having to analyze the right- and left-wing (ab)uses of existentialism. Rather, my aim is to fill the present gap between the critiques of politics and economy and those of motivated deception. I argue that Kierkegaard, by wielding both a theory and practice of sincere communication, puts equally at risk those who object to and those who exhibit varied intensities of sympathy with his individualist posture. An urgent issue for a critical theory of the present age is to rethink the "existential" in terms of communicative action, and vice versa.

My argument contradicts the received view of Kierkegaard on the one hand, and introduces a greater degree of concretion into Habermas's formal notions of identity formation, communication, and the community ideal on the other. I propose—in spite of the fragmentation, strife, and anomie of the present age—that we imagine the possibility of a communication community whose regulative ideal embodies not only a fallibilism of the critical theorist, but likewise an honest sobriety of the existing individual. This invitation, that individuals and groups harness posttraditional and postnational identity formation in the context of an intensely honest communicative ethics, is thus inspired by the present identity crises and by Habermas, Kierkegaard, and Havel alike.

THE DIFFICULTY OF BEGINNINGS

The first draft of this book was written at the time of the November 1989 fall of the Berlin Wall, the Czechoslovak "velvet revolution," and the February 1991 American-led allied ground offensive in the Persian Gulf. It was completed during the rise of nationalist wars in southeastern Europe, the Los Angeles urban rebellion of April 1992, Havel's resignation from the federal presidency of dissolving Czechoslovakia in July 1992, and his January 1993 election as president of the Czech Republic. These events marked the experiences that brought me to the problems taken up in this study.

Several weeks after I arrived as a Fulbright scholar in Frankfurt, Germany (September 1989), Hungary opened its borders and Prague's overflowing West German embassy organized trains for the westward-fleeing East Germans. November saw the Wall between the divided Germanies crack open. With the rise of unification fever, many Germans, not just leftist intellectuals, became concerned with the growing momentum for a new nation–state. Old national symbols were revived, but it was an uneasy flag waving shot through with the fearful memory of National Socialism, the phoenix rising from the ashes.

At the same time that Jürgen Habermas was musing in Frankfurt about whether German identity would orient itself toward Western constitutional patriotism or engage in historical revisions of its past and become insularly nationalistic, Havel, students, theater artists, and workers in Czechoslovakia authored and acted out a drama that became known as the 'velvet revolution' of 17 November 1989. This was a Western-oriented, progressive, nonviolent movement which, after Dubček's Prague Spring was crushed by the Soviet allied invasion in 1968, emerged in the 1970s out of the human and civil rights struggles of the pluralist grouping *Charta 77*. It was inspired by the phenomenologist Jan Patočka and the playwright Havel. There is nothing equivocal in witnessing national colors displayed by the nonviolent resistance of students against the brute force of hired guns, whether on Tiananmen or St. Wenceslas Square. Such resistance is similar to and as justified as were anti-imperial aspirations in the Baltic Republics or among South Africa's blacks. Yet Czechoslovakia, perhaps more mildly than the former multinational states Yugoslavia and the Soviet Union, also experienced an ambiguous rise of the nationalist politics of identity and difference after the debacle of forty years of the real socialist experiment. Here nationalism becomes the sign of Czecho–Slovak contradiction when it threatens to undermine the very constitutional texture of that nonviolent November: some separatists favor a self-determination through the compromised symbols of the Slovak clerical–fascist state that harken back to the last world war; others, in Bohemia for instance, frustrate constitutional safeguards for the cultural self-realization of all national groups; and still others among the deposed communist mafia use nationalism to obstruct democratic and economic reforms. Regardless of whether the Czechs and Slovaks succeed in splitting Czechoslovakia more peacefully than the warring groups of Yugoslavia, today nationalism already eclipses their revolution, which, by its distance from the traditionalist standpoint, prompted democratic change in November 1989.

Just when Americans discovered a new Hitler in Saddam Hussein, Germany afforded another poignant parallel. America, still sensitive to its defeat in Vietnam and to the Watergate and Iran–Contra affairs, and Germany, divided since the end of World War II, today both long to rally around their flags and celebrate national pride. While Germans were as much stimulated by their World Championship in soccer during the year of their economic and political unification as, in a much more historically naïve and destructive fashion, Americans were by the high technology they employed against Iraq, nevertheless young Germans expressed their new sense of duty by filing more applications for the status of conscientious objector to war after unification and during the allied moral crusade against Iraq than at any postwar time. To the American complaint about Germany's unwillingness to contribute troops to this war effort, Chancellor Helmut Kohl replied: "First the Germans were accused of not taking off their combat boots and now they are being accused of not putting them on."[9] Yet, at present both Europeans and Americans still seem paralysed by the ethnic butchery in the Balkans.

The rise of American nationalism and moralizing fundamentalism, which are mixed with self-doubt about a national, collective identity, is even more puzzling in the aftermath of the Persian Gulf War. The United States is not a nation–state in a European sense, but a constitutional democracy gathered under a leitmotif–idea personified in the Statue of Liberty. Not even the Protestant work ethic exhibits that sense of social and historical togetherness which gives Europeans both justification for their grand systems of social welfare and for the constant shadow of balkanization and disunity which threatens the promise of a European union. So what does all this American flag-waving signify but an imperial construction? Where are the signs that after this military venture the vertigo of forceful victory might soberly translate into a passion for dealing with the problems of the homeless, the disadvantaged, the poor, and the uneducated? Is it not an ambiguous nationalism, whose soldiers include so many African-Americans and whose flag-wavers at home include so many sentimental, and presumably "Christian," white Americans, who do not exhibit equal concern for their cities so plagued with poverty, violence, drugs, ugliness, and environmental decay? Both the police beating of Rodney King and the racially myopic response (exemplified by Pat Buchanan's speech at the Republican National Convention in August 1992) to the Los Angeles urban rebellion show, to paraphrase Kierkegaard's critique of Christendom, that professed nationalist and 'family values' have smuggled the care for the disadvantaged and dispossessed concrete other out of the mainstream culture.[10]

And so I experience a difficulty in how to begin. In confronting these events, the questions of overcoming self and other-destructive nationalism through a deliverance into the posttraditional and postnational identity of which I speak in this book make their claim upon me. I address those European and multicultural American forms of life that today give rise to these questions with a new sense of urgency. Since the contents of the chapters that follow, like the events that accompanied my writing, kept running ahead of the project, I have been relieved from the temptation of becoming what Kierkegaard pins on Hegel, an abstraction of absolute speculation. This piece, while being a serious encounter with theory, was deeply influenced by the events of 1989–92. My study calls neither for a resolution nor an elimination of the difficulty. The conclusions can be revised. But their modifications cannot bypass the difficulty of its beginnings. The postnational identity which I present is not a hypothetical notion but an invitation.

OVERVIEW

In a conversation with Jürgen Habermas (at the World Congress of Philosophy in Brighton, England, 1988), I learned about his renewed reading of the ethical writings of Søren Kierkegaard. After discussing my interest in linking critical theory with existential philosophy, Habermas encouraged me to pursue this relation and invited me to come to Frankfurt. At the Brighton convention, Habermas presented a paper that articulated an intersubjectivist notion of individuality; this piece appeared in the original, much longer form in his 1988 Mead essay. But Habermas's rereading of Kierkegaard had been introduced the previous year in his 1987 Copenhagen lecture where he directly addressed the key questions of posttraditional and postnational identity. During my stay in Frankfurt I discussed several other manuscripts where these themes are mentioned. In his rebuttal to theologians (1989), Habermas appeals to Kierkegaard as his ally against positive theological appropriation of the communication model. In another essay he introduces a new category of "ethical–existential discourse" which he distinguishes from "moral discourse" (1989). This same category pops up in various interviews published together with his latest political essays (1990). All these texts prompted me to ask him several more questions about his use of Kierkegaard. My reconstruction of this conversation (1990) reviews the major themes of this book and is, therefore, included as Appendix A.[11]

In Part I, I discuss how Habermas reads Kierkegaard through Kant and Hegel (Chaps. 1 and 2), Marx (Chap. 3), and Mead, and Durkheim (Chap. 4), and how he thereby translates a Kierkegaardian critique of herd mentality and the nation–state into a democratic project of deliberative postnational identity. The argument begins by showing that Habermas presents a more nuanced and original reading of Kierkegaard than is found in the received, subjectivist or quietist, view of his philosophy. Yet Habermas, despite his sympathy with Kierkegaard's critique of nationalism, objects to the deficiencies in his personal approach, which Habermas claims is in need of socially resolving its crisis identity. He thinks that radically open identity formation, apart from being anchored in communicative rationality, cannot safeguard the conditions of its possibility in complex societies. Habermas aims to complement this crisis individual intersubjectively and to welcome her politically within the regulative community ideal of a radical democratic republic.

In Parts II and III, I argue that Habermas's own use of Kierkegaard to critique nationalism and fundamentalism is wanting. This portion of the book develops a reading of Habermas's communicative ethics from the angle of Kierkegaard's position (Chap. 5). If one faces the task of becoming the individual, then the how of self-choice and the how of communicating one's identity embody a way of life that provides the possibility that one can act morally and communicate ethically. My argument demonstrates how these categories of self-choice and communication mark ordinary language by a certain difficulty of beginnings, namely, pathos (Chap. 6). We can read 'inwardness' in both individual and communal terms, and thus root the new composite categories of radically honest critical theory in a concrete way of life and in a critical theory of the present age (Chap. 7). Overall, I defend Habermas's suggestion that a permanent democratic revolution in constitutional patriotism can cure nationalist and fundamentalist crisis trends. But my argument also appeals to Havel's critique of the new forms of hatred (Chap. 8). From his Kierkegaardian posture, it is possible to derive an invitation to a permanent existential and democratic revolution whereby one is prompted to confront nationalism and fundamentalism by allowing for receptive and self-active, multicultural and egalitarian, nonpatriarchal, and nonauthoritative identities (Chaps. 9 and 10).

In my reading of Kierkegaard's critique of the present age I articulate the philosophical equivalents of his pathos whereby Habermas's formal notions of identity formation, communication, and community ideal undergo qualitative transformations. In a proposed methodological innovation, the book projects a radically honest mode of communication as a corrective and a complement to the formal structures of communicative ethics. Although Kierkegaard does not thematize the social life form that could integrate his category of the individual, and thus leaves himself open to Habermas's objections, Habermas fails to preserve the radically open attitude insofar as this pertains both to the individual and community. If these claims are true, then, what would it mean to read Kierkegaard's attitude communicatively and at the same time read Habermas's communicative turn in a Kierkegaardian mode? With Habermas I ask what type of group identity could integrate one socially without losing the attitude of Kierkegaard's individual. With Kierkegaard I inquire what mode of existence could sustain both the individual and community as envisioned in the ideal of Habermas's communicative ethics. In sum, this book reads the Kierkegaardian corrective into a Habermasian critical social theory. This two-fold movement repeats one key question: can we do for Kierkegaard what Habermas suggests (provide social integration for crisis-identity) in Kierkegaard's temporal mode? In the first movement, Habermas's reading of Kierkegaard facilitates my elaboration of a communicative expression for the category of the individual. The second movement voices the difficulty of beginnings.

ACKNOWLEDGMENTS

I am grateful to friends and colleagues in three countries who witnessed the birth of this project, which began as a doctoral dissertation submitted to the philosophy department of Fordham University in April 1991. In Frankfurt, Germany, Jürgen Habermas was a warm host during my participation in his two research groups: the Monday night colloquium and *theoretische Rechtsarbeitsgruppe*. Among those who discussed the ideas of this project with me were Kenneth Baynes, Martin Löw-Beer, James Bohman, Hauke Brunkhorst, Günther Frankenberg, Josef Früchtl, Klaus Günther, Axel Honneth, Detlef Klee, Bill Rehg, and Lutz Wingert; Seyla Benhabib and Drucilla Cornell (during their guest lectures on critical feminism in the summer semester of 1990); and other international scholars and students in Frankfurt. My research in Europe would not have been possible without two grants from the Fulbright Commission (1989–1990 and 1991), a grant from Fordham University (1990–1991), and generous practical support from Heide Natkin and Reiner Rohr.

In Czechoslovakia, I was warmly received by Ladislav Major, Milan Sobotka, Josef Velek, and Milan Znoj in the philosophy department of Charles University, Prague, where I was invited to give public lectures on "Identity and Power: Habermas and Foucault," "Vertical Identity as a Critique of Power: Kierkegaard, Lévinas, and Havel" (10–11 April 1990), and "Permanent Democratic Revolution as Habermas's Critique of Nationalism" (8 May 1991); by Ladislav Hejdánek and Jednota Filosofická, (the Philosophical Union), where I presented a paper, "Kierkegaard and Existential Revolution" (7 May 1991); by Zdeněk Pinc at "Modré pondělí" (Blue Monday—a continuation of the philosophical evenings at Charles' University that until November 1989 took place in Václav Havel's apartment) where I gave a talk in a panel on "Intellectuals and Power"; and by Ivan Chvatík, from Prague's Central European University, where I gave three lectures on the problem of nationalism (28 February–8 March, 1992). The second paper above became a springboard for the core argument of the last part of my study. During this period I was stimulated in my writing by conversations with Václav Bělohradský, Jacques Derrida (in Prague), Ivo Dubský, Ivan M. Havel, Alžběta Holá, Marie Hošková, Ivo Krobot, Petr Oslzlý, Iva and Mirek Vodrážkovi, and my father Radislav.

In the United States, among those who gave me feedback on the entire manuscript were: at Fordham University, Merold Westphal and James L. Marsh; at the New School for Social Research, Richard J. Bernstein; at the University of Texas, Douglas Kellner; and at The Guilford Press the anonymous reader. Among other critical voices in the United States and Europe were John D. Caputo, Jean Cohen, Peter Dews, Vincent Colapietro, Alessandro Ferrara, Leonard Harris, William McBride, David Rasmussen,

Calvin O. Schrag, and Ivan Vejvoda. I thank Sara S. Penella of the *International Philosophical Quarterly* for copyediting the earlier versions of the text.

I wish to acknowledge the following journals and their publishers for permission to use lengthy quoted material from copyrighted works of which I was the author:

In Chapters 1 and 10, from "Post-national Identity: Habermas, Kierkegaard, and Havel," *Thesis Eleven,* No. 34 (March 1993) 89–103. Copyright 1993 by the Massachusetts Institute of Technology Press.

In Chapter 3, from "Post/Moderní pokoušení, *Tvar,* no. 36 (Praha, 8 November 1990) 1, 4–5. Copyright 1990 by *Tvar.*

In Chapter 8, from "Havel and Habermas on Identity and Revolution," *Praxis International* 10/3–4 (1990/1991) 261–277. Copyright 1991 by Blackwell Publishers.

In Chapter 10, from "Jurgen Habermas's Observation on the 'Spiritual Situation of the Age,'" a book review, *Auslegung* 14/2 (1988) 225–228. Copyright 1988 by *Auslegung.*

In Appendix A, from "Habermas's Reading of Kierkegaard: Notes from a Conversation," *Philosophy and Social Criticism* 17/4 (1991) 313–323. Copyright 1991 by *Philosophy and Social Criticism.*

In addition, I wish to acknowledge the following journals and conferences for the use of ideas I developed under their auspices:

From "Kierkegaard and existenciálna revolúcia" *Kultúrny život* (Bratislava, June 1991) 6–7.

From "Habermas's Reading of Kierkegaard: Post-traditional and Post-national Identity in Communicative and Existential Ethics," presented to the Søren Kierkegaard Society at the American Philosophical Association (New York, 28 December 1991).

From "Kierkegaard on Authoring and Identity from the Perspective of Havel's Existential Revolution and Non-political Politics," presented to the Society for Phenomenology and Existential Philosophy (Boston, 10 October 1992).

Martin J. Matuštík
Purdue University

NOTES

1. Havel, Lp 89.

2. Etienne Balibar and Immanuel Wallerstein, *Race, Nation, Class: Ambiguous Identities* (1988), trans. Chris Turner (New York, London: Verso, 1991) 6, 9, 37f., 45f. Bell hooks and Cornel West, *Breaking Bread: Insurgent Black Intellectual Life* (Boston: South End Press, 1991) 93–95, 100, 102, 104, cf. 108. Julia Kristeva, *Nations without Nationalism*, trans. Leon S. Roudiez (New York: Columbia University Press, 1993).

3. Lucius Outlaw, "Against the Grain of Modernity: The Politics of Difference and the Conservation of 'Race'," *Man and World* 25/3–4 (October 1992, pp. 443–468) 448, 449, 451; see 444, 457, 459, 466. Cf. Outlaw, "Lifeworlds, Modernity, and Philosophical Praxis: Race, Ethnicity, Critical Social Theory," in Eliot Deutsch, ed., *Culture and Modernity: East–West Philosophic Perspectives* (Hawaii: Hawaii University Press, 1991) 21–49. Anthony Appiah, "The Uncompleted Argument: Du Bois and the Illusion of Race" in Henry Louis Gates, Jr., ed., *Race, Writing, and Difference* (Chicago: University of Chicago Press, 1986) 21–37; W. E. B. Du Bois, "The Conservation of Races," in Howard Brotz, ed., *African-American Social and Political Thought, 1850–1920* (New Brunswick, NJ: Transaction Publishers, 1992) 483–492.

4. Etienne Balibar, "Racism and Nationalism," in Etienne Balibar and Immanuel Wallerstein, *Race, Nation, Class: Ambiguous Identities* 50, 53f., 61f.; see 64, and Wallerstein's "Postscript" 228–232.

5. Kristeva, *Nations without Nationalism* 16.

6. Kristeva, *Nations without Nationalism* 41, 45; see 2f. and 42. See Bill Martin, *Matrix and Line: Derrida and the Possibilities of Postmodern Social Theory* (Albany: SUNY Press, 1992), on positionality 75ff., 102, 121, 132, 149; and on Fredrick Jameson's critique of "postmodern pastiche" 162.

7. Let me offer a working definition of Habermas's complex sociological, psychological, and philosophical term *posttraditional rational identity*: The historical designation *posttraditional* (synonymous but narrower terms are *postconventional* and *postnational*) is here coterminous with the systematic meaning *rational*. Part I of the present volume explains that for Habermas both terms refer to the type of postmetaphysical, communicative rationality that represents the unfinished project of critical modernity. Identity in *communicative rationality* supports neither the disencumbered self nor any communitarian concretistic determinations of it. Habermas agrees with Michael Sandel's critique of atomistic identity (*Liberalism and the Limits of Justice* [Cambridge: Cambridge University Press, 1982]) but disagrees with neo-Aristotelians and neo-Hegelians that under the plural and secular, viz., posttraditional, conditions of modernity an adoption of a particular historical lifeform as normative can be morally justified. Parts II and III read identity in an existential mode of thinking and acting. See references to Lévinas by the Latin

Abbreviations used in the notes and bibliography for the works of Habermas, Havel, and Kierkegaard are spelled out in full in Appendix B, pp. 265–271.

American philosopher of liberation, Enrique Dussel, *Ethics and Community*, trans. Robert R. Barr (New York: Maryknoll, 1988).

8. See works by Herbert Marcuse between 1928 and 1933: "Beiträge zu einer Phänomenologie des Historischen Materialismus," *Philosophische Hefte* 1/1 (1928) 45–68; "Über konkrete Philosophie," *Archiv für Sozialwissenschaft und Sozialpolitik* 62 (1929) 111–128; "Transzendentaler Marxismum?" *Die Gesellschaft* 7 (part 2)/10 (1930) 304–326; "Zum Problem der Dialektik," *Die Gesellschaft* 7 (part 1)/1 (1930) 15–30 and 8 (part 2)/12 (1931) 541–557; "Neue Quellen zur Grundlegung des Historischen Materialismus," *Die Gesellschaft* 9 (part 2)/8 (1932) 136–174; and *Hegels Ontologie und die Grundlegung einer Theorie der Geschichtlichkeit* (Frankfurt a/M: Klostermann, 1932). For a good example of the failure to envision a fruitful encounter between critical theory and existential philosophy, see the historical study by Richard Wolin, *The Terms of Cultural Criticism: The Frankfurt School, Existentialism, Poststructuralism* (Columbia University Press, 1992) and my discussion of Marcuse, Schmitt, and Wolin in Chap. 10, section 10.4, below.

9. Helmut Kohl, interview with Austrian national television (16 February 1991).

10. Cf. Kierkegaard's PC and AUCH.

11. See Habermas, ICI, ND, NC/EAS, TuK, EzD, and NR. I show that TCA anticipates Habermas's reading of Kierkegaard. See also AG (Kierkegaard section) and PDM (critiques of Hegel, positivism, and the amoral *ethos* of the present age). Habermas systematically and descriptively (though not normatively) incorporates a Kierkegaardian reflexive category of radical self-choice in his most recent work on law and the democratic theory (FuG 124–135 and HRPS). In 1992 Habermas in KFnT returns to Kierkegaard once again through his dialogue with Theunissen. See Michael Theunissen, *Negative Theologie der Zeit* (Frankfurt a/M: Suhrkamp, 1993) and *Der Begniff der Verzweiflung: Korrekturen an Kierkegaard* (Frankfurt a/M: Suhrkamp, 1993).

Contents

PART I

IDENTITY
IN COMMUNICATIVE ETHICS

CHAPTER 1

Identity Crises
and the Present Age

n his 1991 paper delivered at the Brussels conference on "Identity and Difference in Democratic Europe," Habermas searches for the conditions that can make a social integration of multicultural lifeworlds possible. As civil wars rage in the backyards of European nations and racial tensions mount in sidewalk cafes, one senses a certain urgency in Habermas's query. The events of 1989 marked not so much what Fukuyama calls *The End of History and the Last Man,* but rather, with freshly won political freedom for central and eastern Europe and for the republics of the former Soviet Union, a resurgence of nationalist fervor. The question that in 1944 Horkheimer and Adorno posed in the Introduction to their *Dialectic of Enlightenment* sounded equally timely in the situation of the present age: why do humans, "instead of entering into a truly human condition" sink "into a new kind of barbarism?"[1]

Five hundred years after Columbus inaugurated the conquest of the Americas by European modernity, and only a few years after the dubious New World Order began to replace the Cold War and the Iron Curtain, many people are raising this type of concern. In Germany some question whether or not the celebration of the unified nation–state ushers in a reenactment of prewar history. In Europe mass nationalist and fundamentalist identity aspires to take the place of both the deposed communist nomenclature and of the welfare state compromise. Numerous post-1989 groups opt for nationalist separatism over democratic multiculturalism. Now that the paradigm of "socialism with a human face" of 1968 suffered motivation and legitimation crises together with the disenchantment of communism, a transition to "democracy with a human face" seems uneasy. Finally, in spite of President Bush's assurance in the U.N. that *pax americana* is *pax universalis,* the New World Order functions as a homogenizing principle; its universalism denotes something quite imperially nationalist.

3

It fills the absence of a deliberative political culture with a fundamentalist mission: "making the world safer for democracy" signifies in reality "securing vital national interests." These vital interests construct multiculturalism as a monster of "political correctness," thereby masking their own imperial–nationalist identity born of hatred.[2]

It is after the history-making excitement of those 1989 revolutions—so well captured by Timothy Garton Ash—settled into gray economic and political realities that one can address the theoretical and practical aspects of Habermas's urgency: can the lived appeal of local identity, when promoted on the basis of the nationalist politics of identity and difference, sustain regional communities in their many cultures? To answer this query, I doubt that mere celebration of difference can resist the building of individual and group identities on hate. It is the politics of separatist difference that gives rise to the politics of oppressive identity, and it is the latter that invokes the former. The cycle of blind rage issues from this binary opposition.[3]

The move to *postnational identity* emerges in response to the dead ends of the oppositionally constructed politics of identity and difference. Habermas delimits *nationalism* as "a specifically modern phenomena of cultural integration," a problem that emerges "at a time when people are at once both mobilized and isolated as individuals." Nationalism is, then, a historical construct that fashions from devalued traditions and via mass communication an artificially integrated identity. He proposes that modern multicultural society, which would sustain the rights of individuals and minorities, should be maintained in deliberative democracy. In general, this model would need to be complemented by a political culture that instead of rallying nationalists around flags gathers citizens in more sober procedures of constitutional patriotism. I believe that Habermas's proposal is necessary if we want to institutionalize multiculturalism in deliberative democracy and at the same time prevent destructive identity formation. But in this view of the problem of identity, constitutional patriotism remains too far removed from regional cultures to provide a sufficient resistance to the appeal of nationalist, racist, and fundamentalist awakenings on both sides of the politics of identity and difference. It is too weak to check that hatred, which is typified in the neoconservative myth that gender and multicultural concerns represent a Grand Inquisitor of political correctness.[4]

In Part I, I defend Habermas's critical modernism against a too precocious proclamation of its death. Parts II and III then problematize his notion of a postnational identity operative within deliberative democracy, as well as the contrary claims of the present age about the end of history and human identity through the distinctions that Kierkegaard and Havel draw between honest and leveling modes of identity, communication, and the community ideal. My suggestion is that we strengthen Habermas's model with a critique of that individual and group formation which, in both regional and political cultures, fuels the authoritarian strife of identity and difference. Through an existential critique of nationalism and fundamentalism I point to a type of unmasking of hatred and leveling that I distinguish from Habermas's more formal procedural critique. My argument is that a radically honest critique is a necessary precondition for one's embodying postnational identity in deliberative democracy and mature political culture. I hold that without admitting the distinction between radically honest and leveling modes of identity-formation, critical theory—apart from raising a critique of individual and group forms of hatred requisite to embody its agenda—can resist neither the totalitarian–authoritarian nor the nationalist–fundamentalist outcomes of the politics of identity and difference. I will imagine such new possibilities as multicultural difference without ethnocentrism and nationalism, postnational identity without the modern homogenization of regional differences, and deliberative democracy that can resist both imperial consensus and xenophobic backlash against cultural fragmentation and anomie.

This chapter introduces Habermas's concept of posttraditional identity by way of his reading of Kierkegaard (1.1). Next, I link this concept to Habermas's political notions of postnational identity and constitutional patriotism (1.2). I argue that Habermas's heightened sense of urgency about the loss of meaning and freedom in the present age raises both the question of motivation identity crisis, and issues concerning rationality and legitimation crises in social theory and practice.

1.1. HABERMAS'S QUESTION TO KIERKEGAARD

In his 1987 Copenhagen lecture Habermas poses the following sociopolitical question to Kierkegaard: if the modern individual suffers homelessness in traditionally formed cultures, what is that rational life form which could socially integrate his or her posttraditional crisis identity? Habermas's recent interest in Kierkegaard is timely especially after the revolutionary events of 1989. Addressing the resurgence of nationalism and fundamentalism in Europe, Habermas affirms Kierkegaard's defense of that individual who faces the crisis of modern identity with honesty. He shows how Kierkegaard grows suspicious of an already well socialized citizen, and how he opposes the state with its demand for the conformity of individual moral autonomy to social engineering. Habermas, however, wants to restore a balance in this argument with Hegel on the side of collective identity formation without disvaluing Kierkegaard's resistance to nationalism. Habermas critiques Kierkegaard's failure to resolve the crisis of traditional identity socially.

Indeed, Habermas's question points to a failure to integrate the individual, with his or her admission of the crisis of identity, into modernity on a noncommunitarian, postnational basis:

> [Kierkegaard's] concept of an ego-identity produced through the reconstruction of one's own life history in the light of an absolute responsibility for oneself can also be read in a somewhat more secular way. . . . Kierkegaard had to think under the presupposition of Kantian ethics and wanted to offer an alternative to Hegel's attempt at a dubious "concretization" of Kant's universal morality. For Hegel had wanted to provide support for subjective freedom and moral conscience in the institutions of a rational state. Kierkegaard, who distrusted this objective spirit as much as Marx did, anchored both instead in a radicalized inwardness. In this way he arrived at a concept of personal identity that is clearly more suited to our *post-traditional*, but not yet in itself rational world. . . . *Then, of course, we may ask how intersubjectively shared life contexts must be structured in order not only to leave room for the development of exacting personal identities but also to support such processes of self-discovery. What would group identities have to be like to be capable of complementing and stabilizing the improbable and endangered type of ego identity that Kierkegaard outlines?*[5] (emphasis added)

Only a few months before the November 1989 collapse of "real existing socialism" in central-eastern Europe, Habermas wrote on the revolutionary ideas of 1789. Here he further develops his 1987 Copenhagen query. How is one to think within plural and secular modernity about a radical democratic republic? He notes the paradox of posttraditional ethical self-realization and moral self-determination: social revolutions project contents and forms that in a finite way transcend the revolutionary action, but "revolutionary instrumentalism" shipwrecks the project before it gets off the ground. He proposes that to overcome the "sorrow" and the "melancholy" over the lost revolutionary possibility, one must form posttraditional identities in those life forms that are nurtured by a *"permanent and everyday becoming revolution"*[6] (emphasis added).

In a key essay (1990) that comes to terms with the ideas and revolutions of November 1989, Habermas reiterates his 1987 and 1989 revolutionary proposals. At this historical juncture he addresses the disconsolate leftists who despair over the disenchantment of "socialism." Has "socialism" become an empty phrase and a "ritual oracle," to use Václav Havel's characterization, because it signifies merely the deposed mafia practices of the communist nomenclature? Why are many reformed Western leftists today in a condition of hopelessness that is reminiscent of Christians in the ages that followed the Inquisition, the Thirty-Year War of religion, or Kierkegaard's attack on Christendom? Is the project of nonauthoritarian, open identity formation irretrievably leveled? Habermas stipulates that a post-1989 "noncommunist leftist" translates the projected revolutionary possibility into a concrete life form based on a collective rational will formation. This form of life is a "placeless place," yet it cures revolutionary melancholy by socially integrating posttraditional identity in a radical democratic republic. Such a republic constitutes the sovereignty of the people through its rationally motivated and fallible procedures; their patriotism and pledges of allegiance belong to the democratic constitution that allows for this sovereignty.[7]

I argue that there are actually two apparently contrary assumptions and three distinct critiques operative in Habermas's Copenhagen question to Kierkegaard. These assumptions and critiques color Habermas's proposed cure for identity crisis in the present age.

Two Assumptions and Three Critiques in Habermas's Question to Kierkegaard

The first assumption is that Kierkegaard's individual, who can no longer be socially integrated via immediate culture or sacred authority yet faces the crisis of identity with radical honesty, is well suited to modern societies. Kierkegaard's defense of this critical individuality suspends conventional role identity typical for the nation–state. By his defense of the deliberative individual, Kierkegaard stands in opposition to the communitarian role of nationalist and Christian culture. Habermas appeals to this critique of nationalism in order to foster autonomy, pluralism, and radical democracy.[8]

The second assumption invokes Hegel's perspective that ego continuity can be sustained only by reciprocal recognition. Even though Habermas, along with Kierkegaard, rejects Hegel's move to the nation–state, he argues that group identity is the condition of the possibility of ego identity. Habermas holds that Kierkegaard's honest individual can resolve the crisis of identity and become socially integrated into modernity only in the context of the universal moral point of view.[9]

In spite of the sympathy recorded in his first assumption, Habermas critiques the rationality, the legitimation, and the motivation deficits in Kierkegaard, all of which follow from the second assumption. He finds Kierkegaard's category of the individual *monological*, his either/or self-choice (either drift or choose to become responsible) *decisionistic*, and his language of inwardness or verticality *untranslatable* into the value spheres (science, morality and law, art) of secular modernity.[10]

Note that these three critiques are not one-sided, and preserve Habermas's sympathetic reading of Kierkegaard. First, Habermas argues that Kierkegaard's concern is not with a Robinson Crusoe but rather with a citizen in the context of Hegel's nation–state. Yet, Habermas appeals to

Wittgenstein's private language argument, showing that any position which assumes unsocialized access to meanings and norms is *monological*. If I assume myself to be the private author of my meanings, then I privilege self-relation to social origins. Second, Habermas defends Kierkegaard's either/or self-choice against emotivism (MacIntyre's charge) and against the assimilation of the "existential" posture into communitarian sources of the self (Taylor's attempt). But he objects that giving "rational grounds" for one's choice means raising intersubjectively criticizable validity claims. Habermas, developing Wittgenstein's linguistic turn, defines rationality always as communicative. Thus, any principle of choice whose validity I claim apart from my interaction with others is *decisionistic*. Third, he suggests that given Kierkegaard's attack on the traditionalist forms of legitimating Christendom, it is difficult to sustain religious discourse metaphysically. Yet Kierkegaard's open attitude notwithstanding, Habermas stipulates that either religious claims can be translated into one of the posttraditional cultural spheres, thereby erasing all differences between expert discourses and theology, or that religious claims are *untranslatable* into what can be validly communicated in modernity, and thus their *dogmatic* assertions are not criticizable.[11]

It is imprecise to conclude from these three critiques that Habermas simply adopts a Hegelian position vis-à-vis Kierkegaard by coming down on the side of the second assumption—that the crisis individual is to conform to the nation–state. A more nuanced analysis shows Habermas attempting to find a form of life with a complementary relation between Kierkegaard's existential and Kantian moral identity. The sought social integration for modern individuals cannot be identified with Hegel's national community, but rather must be constituted across national and communitarian boundaries, in deliberative democracy and in the league or the postnational commonwealth of nations.

Next I focus on (A) Habermas's shared ground with Kierkegaard and (B) his communicative translation of the existential attitude. I will pursue aspects of Habermas's critiques of monologism, decisionism, and dogmatism in both by paying attention to his adoption of the hermeneutical standpoint, of the cognitive and performative attitude in identity claims, and of postmetaphysical methodology.

A. Habermas's Sympathetic Reading of Kierkegaard

The positions that Habermas shares with Kierkegaard represent a decisive theoretical departure from the received view of Kierkegaard as the irrational, antisocial, and apolitical individualist. I argue that in his agreements with Kierkegaard, Habermas opens, though does not develop, a path for a new communicative rereading of the existential attitude.

The Hermeneutical Standpoint

Hegel's notion of "spirit" is transcribed by Habermas into an intersubjec-tivist concept of personal identity. Returning to Kant's moral philosophy, Habermas seeks in Kierkegaard an ally against Hegel's absolutization of social ethics, although he depicts Hegel's "spirit" of the people as the cul-turally self-reproducing, lifeworld source of identity-formation. Habermas reads Kierkegaard's either/or, which characterizes self-choice, as a stand-point endowed with a hermeneutical awareness that "the personal self is at the same time a social self and a self that is a citizen."[12]

I offer two corollaries to clarify this reading of Kierkegaard: first, Habermas defends the concretely existing individual against the tendency to submerge her within Hegel's higher level, communal life; second, this defense does not mean that the self-choosing individual is a subspecies of possessive individualist. Kierkegaard's individual, like the participant envi-sioned in moral discourse, requires an intersubjective context. Westphal has in mind this possibility of agreement between Kierkegaard and Habermas when he rejects the view of Kierkegaard as a methodological individualist:[13]

> The first step towards understanding Kierkegaard's politics is to recognize that he shares with Hegel . . . [the] conception of spirit and the dialectical indi-vidualism [spirit is the I that is We, and the We is itself also many I's] con-tained therein. Being dialectical, this individualism is a social theory of human experience, inherently political in a broad sense.[14]

Kierkegaard's individual lives as a situated, embodied, gendered, his-torical, and social self and other-relation. She never begins as an atomic self, but rather always exists as a member of the human race. Habermas affirms that Kierkegaard envisions here a hermeneutically embedded self. If this reading is correct, and I believe that it is, then we cannot legiti-mately use Kierkegaard's focus on inwardness or verticality as a proof of his decontextualized individualism. Kierkegaard commences with a well socialized individual (i.e., a Copenhagen citizen), who is then philosophi-cally cured of the Cartesian, epistemic doubt and of the empiricist, presocial, or prepolitical individualism present in social contract theories. Yet this hermeneutical cure of one-sided individualism in philosophical theory and sociopolitical practice does not grant us an honest way of relating. For Kierkegaard, Hegel's concrete universal is still insufficiently concrete. As I will argue in Part II, Kierkegaard has more to say on the human as "spirit" than either Hegel or Habermas, since he commences with an inter-subjectively socialized individual, but at the same time remains suspicious that individuation through socialization is the whole basis of identity formation.[15]

If a hermeneutical starting point can be attributed to Kierkegaard (this aspect is strongly brought out by Gadamer's appropriation of Kierkegaard's ethic to characterize the continuity of tradition), then the commonly held view of the self-choosing individual as antisocial must appear misconstrued. It will be crucial later that I differentiate Habermas's critique of Kierkegaard's monologism from these received views that identify Kierkegaard's methodology with solipsism. Such received views of Kierkegaard blur care for the individual with methodological individualism. Both these views and the liberal method of possessive individualism de-differentiate the distinction between the content of hermeneutical situatedness and the way one is situated. Because of this oversight, I will argue, Kierkegaard's concern with the "how" of one's existence is interpreted one-sidedly. Yet, he does not dispute Hegel's reflective overcoming of one-sidedness (e.g., in possessive individualism), but rather rejects Hegel's absolutization of the nation–state.

Let me come back to my initial point. Habermas and Kierkegaard agree with Hegel—although not in all respects and in the same way—that the self is spirit. For all three, an individualized ego is neither a Cartesian subject nor a part reducible to mass society. The notion of spirit denies "compositional" and affirms "dialectical" individualism. A composition is a merger of its parts. In a composition, individuals are independent of their participation in the whole. A compositionally formed individual is a convex mirror of the failed marriage, mass society, nationalism, fundamentalism, and totalitarianism. The compositional forms of ego and group identity result from the initial failure to appropriate identity relationally, and thus a failure to conceive of relationships with the other as a higher possibility of freedom. But the dialectically conceived individual partakes in a whole that is a mutually mediating relational unity not reducible to its parts. Individuals find their freedom through the whole; they view themselves embedded within the generalized "we" of society, culture, and history. Unless one is socialized, one cannot deliberately take up relations with the world, self, and others.[16]

Hegel's totality cannot be identified simply with totalitarianism. While dialectical identity grows out of hermeneutical totality—in other words, within the lifeworld—compositional identity produces totalitarianism or nationalist and fundamentalist mass society. It is quite another issue whether Hegel's or Marx's privileging of a particular historical form of life might have misled others and allowed for the rise of totalitarianism. Even if this charge were to be argued historically, the negative outcome would not change the distinction brought out by the Hegelian–Marxist position. Any privileging of a particular life form could sustain an oppressive regime only if it also reproduced compositional individualism. Kierkegaard's corrective to this outcome reflects a warning against an unholy union, in both the individual and community, between social totality and compositional identity.

A conclusion from my two corollaries follows: if neither Kierkegaard nor Habermas promote compositional individualism, then they both reject the higher-level individuality of Hegel's nation–state. Kierkegaard neither cherishes a classical, liberal view that begins with disrelational parts in order to compose a whole, nor a communitarian option that commences with the hermeneutical–ethical whole in order to replace or guide radical self-choice. He confronts the socialized individual for the sake of unmasking the ideology that privileges any historically specific, classical or modern, life form.[17]

Habermas, analogically to Kierkegaard's "yes" and "no" to Hegel, confronts both the possessive individualist and the communitarian methodologies. Yet his is not a strictly personal confrontation of the ideologies that absolutize a social ethic (*Sittlichkeit*). Instead of taking Kierkegaard's path of attacking mass identity, Habermas inhabits Hegel's portrait of the struggle for reciprocal recognition with communicatively transformed Kantian autonomous individuals (*Moralität*). He grounds Hegel's social–ethical whole from within a discursively concretized Kantian moral theory.[18]

The idea behind Habermas's communicative turn is to arrive at the posttraditional condition of the possibility of identity formation wherein concrete individuals are neither sublated into a higher identity of historical *ethos*, nor dirempted like unprincipled atoms. He turns to a pragmatist reading of Kant and Hegel and replies to Hegel's critique of Kant through Mead's thesis that individualization occurs through socialization: "Spirit is the medium, in which the reflexivity of the ego is built at the same time with the intersubjectivity of reciprocal recognition."[19]

Let me note the two points that clarify the intersubjectivist notion of identity shared by Habermas and Kierkegaard: first, both defend the concrete individual against the tendency to lose her in the social whole; second, both distinguish the moral from the possessive individual. Since both promote dialectical rather than compositional individualism, they reject the higher-level individuality of the nation–state. Habermas acknowledges that this hermeneutical embodiment of self-relation avoids the pitfalls of anthropological subjectivism and objectivism: "Kierkegaard certainly does not identify the other any longer with the absolute I as the subject of the primordial act of self-positing." Neither sets self-relation apart from one's socialized capacity to relate, but they nonetheless insist that in defining oneself one cannot take a flight to a ready-made social definition of identity.[20]

The Cognitive–Performative Attitude in Identity Claims

Habermas's performative attitude plays an analogical role to Kierkegaard's "existential posture"; a performing identity claim is made possible vis-à-vis the other since one can never know oneself as a supreme owner of an object in the world. Yet, the identity of the social whole is challenged by this critical, performative self-relation of the individual to the social. National identities are to some degree posttraditional, but their constructed tendency towards sectarian warfare makes them unsuitable for an individual who is to adopt a more open way of life. "It is easy to see that nationalism could not serve as . . . a complement to Kierkegaard's ethical view of life. . . . [The] situation of voluntarily falling into line is the sheer opposite of the 'either/ or' self-choice with which Kierkegaard confronted the individual."[21]

Thus, Habermas affirms the cognitive and earnest dimensions of the either/or pertaining to self-choice. He argues that Kierkegaard's self-choice is not mere foil for emotivism, but rather "has a cognitive side" and "authenticity"; the situated, bodily, gendered, historical, and social individual is to gather fragmented existence and to come under the universal point of view. The act of self-positing, as opposed to aesthetical drift, constitutes one's genuine self-realization and the possibility of autonomous action. The universal under which I resolve to lead my life becomes internalized as my action principle. This resolve allows for my adopting the moral point of view. Self-choice consists not in applying myself to this or that action—particular actions might turn out to be wrong—but in choosing my existence from a universal concern. It is this radical self-choice that makes one's choosing from the moral point of view possible.[22]

Habermas affirms: "I must choose myself in a paradoxical act as that self which I am and want to be." In self-choice I repeat the given communitarian sources of my identity, for which I am, from the ethical viewpoint, responsible. My individual and social life-project becomes a "principle of individuation." "Once the individual has made the existential decision who he wants to be, he assumes responsibility for deciding what will henceforth be considered essential in the life history he has taken on morally—and what will not. . . ."[23]

Postmetaphysical Methodology

The most intriguing aspect of Habermas's third critique (the presumed untranslatability of the language of inwardness or verticality) is his alliance with Kierkegaard against those who seek a *rapprochement* between theology and communicative ethics. Habermas's first assumption, defined above in my interpretation of his Copenhagen question to Kierkegaard, discloses that an open ego-identity could not be portrayed as suitable for modern forms of life if both thinkers did not share postmetaphysical thinking. In fact, there are two arguments where Habermas, in spite of his third critique, affirms that Kierkegaard's methodology is postmetaphysical.

First, Habermas characterizes Kierkegaard neither as a thinker with metaphysical premisses nor as an aesthetical reductionist. A thoroughly open individual can claim her identity neither through a scholastic proof (still typical for the Cartesian doubt) nor through subject-centered modern rationality. Kierkegaard carries on a dramatic experiment with one's nonsubstantively formed identity: How can I appropriate my temporal historicity from an ongoing concern? How can I do it without arbitrariness? Apart from metaphysical frameworks, do I have to fall either into subjectivist emotivism or into the one-dimensionality and objectivism of mass society? This dead end either–or, as distinguished from Kierkegaard's either/or, does not present me with an option of radical self-choice, even though it does define some situations in the present age.

We have seen how Habermas resorts to a cognitive and performative claim to identity: "In the performative posture of the subject, who chooses herself, the metaphysical opposition between what in the individual is essential and what applies to her accidentally loses all meaning." The honest individual cannot be justified directly by any tradition, nor can she justify herself in *foro interno* through a posture of an observer. Because in modernity one is taught the way to self-choice in the schools of anxiety, despair, and the either/or does not mean that existence can be defined by an introspective analysis. The confusion of "existential" with "subjectivist" occurs when one reads Kierkegaard as a complement to an objectivist frame such as value-free scientism. In Part II, I argue that Kierkegaard's focus on concretion is not only postmetaphysical, but in the way that it is so it offers a corrective to both aesthetic subjectivism and functionalist objectivism.[24]

Second, in his reply to those who would like to bring theology and the theory of communicative action (as well as discourse ethics) together, Habermas adopts a deliberately Kierkegaardian angle. Here is Habermas's position in a nutshell. Christian theological discourses after Kierkegaard suffer from identity crises: either one must opt for the "Protestant way" of wholly separating the claims of faith from those of reason; or one must choose the way of "enlightened Catholicism" which participates in scientific discourses to such a degree that it leaves the Judeo–Christian experiential basis of religious discourses untouched; or one must, like Hegel and departments of religious studies, demythologize religious language, and thus on the one hand, entirely bypass religious experience, or, on the other, destroy its integrity. This last way in the end bespeaks "methodological atheism." Theological discourses encounter a two-fold problem: either the distinction between theological and scientific, or moral and aesthetic, expertise breaks down; or the religious claims cannot be validly raised, problematized, or discursively affirmed or denied. We can claim a form of temporary coexistence between the two realms.[25]

Yet from Habermas's three options, I will ask in Part II, does it follow that Kierkegaard is either a religious fundamentalist, or a metaphysician, or a theological activist, or a methodological atheist? Habermas does not draw proper implications from his own critical use of Kierkegaard. Can we reply to the third objection against Kierkegaard (namely, that he imposes untranslatable, communicatively unjustifiable, and unsound claims upon discourse) without disvaluing the lived appeal of his postmetaphysical methodology? If Habermas raises here a valid objection, then Kierkegaard must invoke some other authority than that of existential communication. I believe that Kierkegaard does not.

B. Habermas's Communicative Translation of Kierkegaard

A clue to Habermas's reversal of Kierkegaard's starting point emerges in the question posed in Copenhagen: why would Habermas worry about a social integration of open identity on a noncommunitarian basis if he agrees that this individual is hermeneutically embedded in the social time and space of modernity, that she is morally formed by the imperatives of self-determination and defined by the task of self-realization, and that she would not be "suited for our post-traditional, but not yet in itself rational world" should her identity be formed metaphysically?[26] In spite of the obvious existential elements in Habermas's performative notion of identity, his reception remains ambivalent due to his three areas of doubt, which correspond to the three systematic objections to Kierkegaard's presumed monologism, decisionism, and dogmatism.

Is Kierkegaard Monological?

Habermas portrays Kierkegaardian identity as constituted in relation to some other, but argues that one can sustain this identity only if one turns from inwardness (communicating with the wholly other) to intersubjective communication. I submit that the disputed issue remains even after Habermas managed to translate Kierkegaard's language of inwardness or verticality to the horizontal mode of communication: I agree with Habermas that ego cannot steal away from the grammatical unity of communication in order to determine and realize itself, but I doubt that from this we may immediately conclude that an honest individual judges, chooses, and acts monologically.[27]

Habermas affirms Kierkegaard's dramatization of that individual who complements modern collectivities. Yet Habermas remains skeptical that the individual who confronts repeated upheavals about who he or she is or wants to be can make it in modernity apart from the moral point of view. He suggests that only universal group-identity can socially integrate that radical ego-identity which Kierkegaard projects in ongoing legitimation and motivation crises. Like Erikson in his studies of adolescent crises, Habermas thematizes the regulative ideal that could maintain and stabilize this modern identity not on a communitarian but rather on a morally autonomous basis against personal and social anomie. The point of contest between Habermas and Kierkegaard lies in their identification of the key question. Habermas finds the key in an institutionalization of that democratic collective that could, under idealized but fallible presuppositions of infinite normative consensus, secure autonomous and existential ego-identity. Kierkegaard is suspicious that the social ideal alone and apart from radical self-choice could sustain modern identity against the adolescent and social crises that worry Habermas.[28]

Habermas's more sophisticated objection must be, therefore, distinguished from those insipid portraits that depict Kierkegaard as an antisocial and acommunicative individualist. The distinction from this received view is granted already in Habermas's first agreement with Kierkegaard's hermeneutical starting point, which both share with Hegel. Habermas injects his objection on the reflexive level where one forms ego identity. Despite his agreement with Kierkegaard that self-choice requires a certain critical distance from the hermeneutical horizon of the traditional lifeworld, Habermas insists that this distanciation must itself be projected onto the public forum of the ideal community. It must be socially recognized in order for the individual to be able to sustain identity against possible crises. Habermas objects that Kierkegaard's failure to thematize equiprimordially such a posttraditional social context with radical self-choice is methodologically monological. Kierkegaard appears monological insofar as he allows for self-choice by an already socialized individual without having to appeal for recognition by an idealized forum of the universal community. Kierkegaard considers self-critical identity formation as neither a communitarian nor a generic community ideal. It is itself a locus where a critical measure for every life form is disclosed.[29]

Is Kierkegaard's Either/Or Decisionistic?

Kierkegaard develops a social critique that is suspicious of inward self- and other-relations. Therefore, for him self-choice cannot be replaced by collective choice. This angle problematizes Habermas's reversal of Kierkegaard's beginnings: how am I to participate in discourse? What type of identity is presupposed as complementary to the idealized participant of practical discourse? When Habermas objects to the arbitrary, extreme, and individualist character of Kierkegaardian beginnings, he does not share the received view of an antisocial Kierkegaard. Yet because Kierkegaard does not thematize the ideal collective life form to which the individual can address her self-choice, Habermas is worried about the unchecked, even fundamentalist, claims that one's radical self-choice raises. Hence, Habermas constrains one's (individual) self-realization with moral (universal generic) self-determination. An individual project can be maintained only vis-à-vis the community ideal.

Habermas critiques the decisionism of Kierkegaard's either/or because it lacks the normative force of valid claims of truth, normative rightness, and sincerity; the formal structures of linguistic interaction provide the conditions of symmetry—vis-à-vis these claims and of reciprocity vis-à-vis the participants—that cannot be denied without performative self-contradiction. An ego offers to an alter claims that participants inevitably should consider to be true, normatively right, sincere offers of speech acts. The alter can accept or reject these validity claims; she can demand justification of their validity. This yes–no possibility of justification represents the ground for rational motivation of one's assent. Since the possibility occurs not *in foro interno* of an ego or an alter, but rather within their symmetrical and reciprocal equidistance to confirming or rejecting the claims to validity, Habermas can speak about the collective formation of meaning and will. Nondiscursive forms of convincing the alter violate the reciprocal conditions of discourse. If one raises a validity claim and also tries to convince others by threats, manipulation, unjustified rhetoric, or appeals to authority or tradition, then one's argument becomes entangled in performative self-contradiction. Discourse would become distorted by the asymmetries of power.

Habermas's argument against Kierkegaard's perceived decisionism can be reconstructed as follows: the radical either/or self-choice lacks normativity not only because of its monological attitude. One's basis for choice is decisionist if one's claim to a true, right, and sincere decision constrains the will without rationally and collectively motivating it. On the other hand, the validity claims present enabling as opposed to disabling conditions of discourse insofar as they allow the participants to be guided by the force of the better argument alone. The decisionist modes of affirming or justifying claims, by introducing rationally and collectively unverifiable, asymmetrical appeals, disable every posttraditional ethic of discourse. One's self-choice does not seem to require such a discursive mode of the ideal symmetry conditions. Kierkegaard's either/or is therefore decisionistic; it does not possess the validating, normative force of the better argument.

How Postmetaphysical Is Kierkegaard's Language of Inwardness or Verticality?

Habermas reconstructs the relation between the sacred and the profane through the performative attitude of discourse. He proposes that Kierkegaard's inward or vertical language be profanized. This profanization is to further offset the presumed monologism and decisionism of the either/or that characterizes radical self-choice. In addition to rectifying the insecure status of Kierkegaard's crisis-individual by means of the communicative turn, Habermas translates what he considers to be a dualism between immanent discourse (inner) and transcendent otherness (outer) into an immanent transcendence within discourse itself. What I call Habermas's *immanently horizontal transcendence* is not a misnomer. His thesis reads as follows: since "the inherent telos of human speech" is oriented to reaching an understanding with another about something in the world, all forms of meaningful transcendence must occur on *this* side of the "rational collective will-formation."[30]

Habermas attacks metaphysical and theological discourses as untranslatable (meaningless) claims to transcendence: if one can translate these claims into the culture spheres of modernity, then they cannot be distinct from rational discourses, but must be redeemed or rejected like any other validity claims; or, if one cannot translate them, then they are illegitimate power impositions on discourse. There is no distinct religious value sphere of culture that can claim the status of validity as a modern form of discourse. In making a claim to such a special status in actual discourse, which often occurs under the plural and secular conditions of modernity, one falls into self-contradiction; one appeals both to the force of the better argument alone and to the transcendent force. How is one's validity claim to religious transcendence true, normatively right, and sincere? Is it so by the enabling constraint of the better argument? Does one appeal to the constraints of the transcendent itself? If the latter is justified by the former, then religious transcendence is robbed of its special status in discourse. If the former concedes to the latter, then one distorts the symmetry and reciprocity of communication.

Habermas aims to remove the dualism that unnecessarily permeates much of Kierkegaard's language of inwardness or verticality. The formal–pragmatic conditions of discourse are to provide both a translation of the dualistic language of ahistorical transcendence into historical–social lifeworlds and a nondualistic achievement of discursive, immanently horizontal transcendence in a concrete ethical–hermeneutical context. None of the existing social wholes is sacred, the rational collective will formation cannot be Hegel's God marching on earth, and no consensus is infallible or absolute even if the regulative conditions of discourse may be raised unconditionally and absolutely by the revisable validity claims.

Habermas's Reversal of Kierkegaard's Starting Point

Let me comment on Habermas's translation effort. Kierkegaard's inward or vertical criterion of identity before the other is represented by:

> A cattleman who (if it were possible) is a self directly before his cattle is a very low self, and similarly a master who is a self before his slaves is actually no self—for in both cases a criterion is lacking. The child who previously has had only his parents as a criterion becomes a self as an adult by getting the state as a criterion, but what an infinite accent falls on the self by having God as the criterion! The criterion for the self is always: that directly before which it is a self. . . .

This becomes Habermas's horizontal, regulative ideal of communication community:

> [T]he profane equivalents reverse the meaning of religious justification into a wish to be recognized by the forum of all humans as the person who one is and wants to be.

In this counterexample to Kierkegaard's self-critical attitude, Habermas universalizes a model of profanized inwardness, such as that found in Rousseau's confessions and journals addressed to the reading public. In Rousseau's appeal to the public, religiousness becomes a metaphor for an inwardness bereft of all world transcendence. Rousseau's inwardness needs general recognition since his self-transcendence occurs in front of his reading audience.[31]

For similar reasons, Habermas wants to heal the dualism between the vertical (ahistorical or diachronic) and the horizontal (historical or synchronic) axes of identity formation. This is quite consistent with his communicative translation of the relation between the individual and society. In his own use of the vertical–horizontal metaphor, Habermas tilts the vertical and lets the horizontal carry the weight of existence. In Kierkegaard's inwardly or vertically rooted conversation, I am mindful that the other is wholly other than myself; but Habermas's horizontal language supports both the real and the ideal community under an infinitely projected, consensual rubric of human understanding:

> After *the vertical axis of prayer* has been united to *the horizontal axis of interhuman communication*, the individual can no longer alone redeem the emphatic claim to individuality through the reconstructed appropriation of his life-history; whether this reconstruction succeeds can now be decided only in the relation to the others.[32] (emphasis added)

Habermas relocates Kierkegaard's anchor from an inwardness situated before its vertical–existential other to an individualization oriented to a horizontal–social other. Thus, Kierkegaard's problematization of both positive theology and Hegel's idolized nation–state only provides Habermas with a foil for a move from lived posttraditional identity to the moral and legal constraints of the regulative community ideal.[33]

For Habermas, a methodology that depends on the sacred imposes unproblematized claims on discourse. In modernity authoritative appeals to the sacred other, to tradition, or to a historically concrete community cannot be argumentatively redeemed. Such appeals are often sustained by unverifiable private experience. These recourses are indistinguishable from monological and decisionist positions. Habermas's three critiques aim to develop a critical theory of identity crises in the present age; a Kierkegaardian individual must be viewed from within the communicative turn. This turn explains Habermas's shift in methodology from self-choice to posttraditional group-formation, since it is only the latter that can safeguard the former against the identities of possessive individualism and fundamentalist–patriotic wars.

When Habermas thematizes the incomprehensibility of theology after Kierkegaard, he argues against those who seek a *rapprochement* of communicative theory with religious discourses, or who critique Habermas for excluding such a possibility in principle. Habermas claims that this option is blocked by the modern ascendance of postmetaphysical thought. But Kierkegaard, himself a postmetaphysical thinker, becomes a trouble maker for doing both theological and philosophical business as usual. He positions himself within the religious discourses of his time, yet he does not attempt a Hegelian translation of existential–vertical posture into social–horizontal structures. In this inwardness or verticality, which wants to be historically and socially relevant, Kierkegaard attends to the legitimation and motivation crises of modern cultural value spheres without positing a distinct religious value sphere of culture. Habermas adopts Kierkegaard's problematization of both positive theology and the Hegelian synthesis between social ethics and theism, and he sharply notes that Kierkegaard raises problems rather than helps theological discourse. But he does not concede to Kierkegaard that this occasions sustained crises for posttraditional identity. In spite of his sympathy with the attack on "Christendom," Habermas objects that Kierkegaard imports untranslatable claims into discourse. He protests against Kierkegaard's language of inwardness or of the vertical whereby "Kierkegaard's Either/Or is undeniably posited in the discourse of the individual soul with God." The problem with Kierkegaard, concludes Habermas, is that he did not anchor self-choice in a posttraditional social form of life. Instead of turning to the forum of the ideal communication community, Kierkegaard projects the ethical and moral self into religious discourse. This untranslatable appeal, without a developed critical, social theory, becomes monological, decisionistic, and dogmatic.[34]

Habermas argues with Kierkegaard against Kierkegaard. The cogent reason why Kierkegaard delivers trouble to positive theologies is the difficulty of beginnings. This difficulty lies in my temporal query, which cannot be decided apart from my having begun in performance. The gap between metaphysical recollection and lived repetition remains for Kierkegaard unbridgeable. The individual must learn to edit her life choices, cast her character, and set the stage for the drama of her concretely appropriated life history. Here, Habermas transforms this postmetaphysical portrait of self-choice vis-à-vis the other into a performative claim to identity. There is neither an identity that I may claim prelinguistically, nor one that could be grasped from within the perspective of an aesthetic drifter or observer (e.g., via herd mentality or the nationalist attitude). Habermas remains existential in the limited sense that one cannot appropriate identity apart from engaging the other.[35]

But in the process of transcribing the vertical language of inwardness into the horizontal language of the performative attitude in communicative interaction, Habermas, to his satisfaction, resolves Kierkegaard's difficulty of beginnings in a non-Kierkegaardian fashion. As I will show in Part II, Habermas's ideal of the communication community, unlike concrete humans, no longer seems to be troubled by any such difficulty. The language of inwardness or verticality is translated into the pragmatic terms of communicative interaction. In contrast to Habermas's regulative ideal, Kierkegaard's pathos signifies equally, for any individual and for any community in any age, an interminably postponed resolution of the difficulty of beginnings and a permanent openness to that which is not yet, to the wholly other.[36]

I seek a margin for my argument between theological uses of Kierkegaard, found philosophically uninteresting by Habermas, and Habermas's objections to Kierkegaard's untranslatable self-critical attitude, which are critiqued later by my communicative reading of Kierkegaard. My examination of Kierkegaard's language of inwardness or verticality, or of Havel's existential revolution, need not import theology into communications theory. I remain on Habermas's grounds and follow through the implications of his use of Kierkegaard to face the present identity crises under the post-metaphysical condition of the present age.

1.2. POSTNATIONAL IDENTITY AND MULTICULTURALISM

Despite Habermas's critiques, his reading of Kierkegaard is productive in that it sets the self-choosing individual against the present age with its herd (nationalist and fundamentalist) mentality. We get a better glimpse of the philosophical notion of posttraditional identity, and its political counterpart, postnational identity, by asking: how does one form individual and group identity after catastrophes such as Auschwitz and Gulag, the killing fields of leftist terror, "Desert Storm," or in the midst of the nationalist bloodletting for "God and the country?" Let me first draw sociopolitical implications from Habermas's Copenhagen question to Kierkegaard (A), and then return to his Brussels proposal for a postnational, multicultural league (B).

A. Habermas's Kierkegaard: Against Nationalism and Fundamentalism

Habermas shares with Kierkegaard and Havel an insight that no collective guilt (e.g., for the totalitarian past of one's nation) can be ascribed to individuals, yet he argues that we share responsibility to the present age: "the way we continue the traditions in which we find ourselves is up to us." In an apparent echo of Lévinas's ethic after Auschwitz and from exile, Habermas depicts the lifeworld sources of identity in "a deep layer of solidarity among all who have a human face."[37]

This solidarity emerges from shaken traditions. The communitarian womb of meanings was irretrievably violated: "a bond of naïveté has been torn to shreds—a naïveté from which unquestioned traditions drew their authority, a naïveté that as such had nourished historical continuities. Auschwitz altered the conditions for the continuation of historical life contexts—and not only in Germany." The obverse side of responsible confrontation with one's own origins is the sense of shame for having escaped the "moral catastrophe." This shame places all of us under the stricture of "an intersubjective liability . . . for distorted life circumstances."[38]

Modern nationalism already exhibits limited posttraditional aspects: it appropriates traditions reflexively, it is at home in a democratic nation–state, and it lives in the tension between particular cultures and the universality of the republic. Nationalism wins over those anomic, fragmented individuals who, having emerged from the processes of societal modernization without resisting the oppositional politics of identity and difference via radical self-choice, become "susceptible to manipulative misuse by political elites." Thus, nationalism conflicts with both constitutional sovereignty and the rights of multicultural groups and individuals. Paradoxically, the artificial construction of the nation–state, which is based on the fiction of a homogeneous culture, itself produces the nationalist strife of the groups within it.[39]

From Nationalist to Constitutional Patriotism

Habermas envisions "a transformation in the form of national identity" which would shift "the self-assertion of national forms of life through power politics" to the "universalization of democracy and human rights." This proposal is legitimated by the catastrophic leveling of traditions in modernity, and occasioned by conflicts among these same traditions. He assumes that cultural nationality can be redeemed postnationally by a "nationality in the sense of citizenship in a [state]." Cultural identity must allow "for political identification with what the population considers worthy of preserving . . . at any given time." Constitutional patriotism is more "sober" than nationalist gore and heroic sentimentality. One does not get readily co-opted to die for its procedural symbols, since its "political identity has detached itself from the background of a past centered on national history." Habermas envisions integrating isolated modern individuals into a radical republic, itself sustained by constitutional patriotism, not by homogenizing or xenophobic nationalism.[40]

Habermas's political sobriety is today a welcome cure for the resurging habit of nationalist and racial strife in the post-1989 world: it presupposes a world order not based on imperial peace; it would not uncouple the marginalized voices of the poor from the rich worlds; and it offers pride in the American pragmatist roots of multicultural democracy rather than in the manifest destiny of North American imperial interests. This universalist, sobered-up patriotism is anchored in concrete communities and cultures, but its multicultural life form "is no longer pledged to continuities filled with victories." Constitutional patriotism must in its formal structure resist gaining a new "quasi natural character" for its allegiance. If the flag is not sacred, then its burning cannot be a sacrilege, though it may signify an act against perceived injustice. A postnational patriot honors the democratic constitution for which the flag stands, not the worshipped sacral symbol. One must be aware of "the deep ambivalence of every tradition . . . [of] the barbaric dark side of all cultural achievements to the present day." Can these "beginnings of a post-national identity . . . develop and stabilize?" Can these detoxicated patriots stop getting high (e.g., on the know-how in the patriot missiles)? Can they offset the balkanization of modern life or the fundamentalist trends in world religions or politics, and yet allow repressed cultures to rise to their self-determination? Habermas offers four excellent points.[41]

First, referring to Hegel's *Philosophy of Right* (par. 324), he notes that today it is easier to justify morally one's objection to military service than to find any "ethical moment of war" in one's dying for the fatherland. The warrior's identity lags behind our technical capacity to destroy our own living theater. It would seem, then, that a contest such as that between Iraq and the United States ought to be decided along structural trends towards postnational identity rather than on the ideologized rationality of their respective traditions. Second, citing Hannah Arendt, Habermas reads in the twentieth-century detention, death, migrant, and refugee camps the political and economic pressure on all countries to adopt universalist rather than communitarian rationality. The population shifts of our century "constrain one to relativize one's own form of life, and they represent a challenge to take the universalist bases of one's own tradition seriously." Third, communication and travel disrupt homogeneous cultures by laying them open to heterogeneous life forms. There is "the unsettling presence of a society that has expanded to include the world as a whole." The structural pressures of economy, administration, and ecology mount toward a retrieving of racial, gender, profane, and religious traditions under the point of radical equality. Fourth, the human and social sciences have become open to various strata of society and to the international community. "The fallibility of knowledge and the conflict of interpretations promote the problematization of historical consciousness rather than identity formation and the creation of meaning."[42]

Existential Crisis Identity and Postnational Political Identity

Habermas's descriptive account of these structural trends toward universalism raises a normative issue: "how are we to understand the relationship between a historical consciousness that has become problematic and a post-national state identity?" It is at this juncture of grounding social critique that he approaches Kierkegaard. Habermas argues positively that Kierkegaard's resistance to cultural idolatry and anomie alike allows the individual to emerge on the basis of radical (posttraditional and postnational) self-choice. Kierkegaard offers this resistance to nationality and tradition fetishism, which at the same time allows for the formation of meaningful identity. Habermas's Copenhagen question offers, then, not only a communicative corrective to Kierkegaard, but also marks Habermas's search for a normative basis that would ground his critique of nationalist and fundamentalist group identity. It is for this reason that Habermas argues, negatively, that if one's critical self-choice does not occur in an intersubjective context, then it lacks the criticizable character of validity claims.[43]

Habermas desires a meaningful "complementarity" between the structures of personality (the either/or required for posttraditional self-choice) and those of culture (group identities presupposed in postnational constitutional patriotism). As will become apparent later in Part I, Habermas finds that only the posttraditionally differentiated lifeworlds admit an emergence of that postnational patriotism which finds a home in deliberative democracy. In the contexts of rationalized lifeworlds, particular identities cannot meaningfully appeal to an Archimedean (nationalist or fundamentalist) point. Yet this need not condemn the individual to the Weberian iron cage, with its nihilistic loss of meaning and a systemic loss of freedom. "[T]he abstract idea of the universalization of democracy and human rights forms the hard substance through which the rays of national tradition—the language, literature, and history of one's own nation—are refracted."[44]

Analogically to Kierkegaard's editing of a life choice, Habermas suggests that postnational public spheres, rather than the herd "public," can form a fitting counterpart to the existential individual:

> In the public process of transmitting a culture we decide which of our traditions we want to continue and which we do not. The debate on this rages all the more intensely the less we can rely on a triumphal national history, on the unbroken normality of what has come to prevail, and the more clearly we become conscious of the ambivalence of every tradition.

On the one hand, he shies away from translating individual self-choice directly into the terms of public debate; on the other hand, he presents the political question of forming national identity after Auschwitz in the language of self-choice, "either to explicitly problematize a past that we no longer shunt aside, or to affirm, still a little defiantly, continuities that extend on through the Nazi period." Habermas's either/or comes down to a radical self-choice between the uncritical traditionalism of some German historians and the postnational engagement of the radically honest attitude in the public debate about the dark or disputed side of national traditions. Closer to home, to become a good American it seems insufficient to pledge allegiance to America or to celebrate national heroism. We cannot check nationalism in what is Hegel's "rhetorical both/and" (i.e., both begin postnationally and evade the choice in an abstract, semantic gymnastics): "Kierkegaard's *Either/Or* is concerned with the way responsibility for a piece of history is assumed *consciously*. Nor should our postwar history be abandoned to hollow lip service in its decisive point, the renunciation of our disastrous traditions"[45] (emphasis in original).

B. From National to Civic Identity

Habermas argues that national coexistence in the multicultural context of the present age is neither possible by means of ethnic, regional patriotism nor through the construction of some supernational state. To be sure, while accepting Habermas's move, I need not critique here communitarian identities per se. I want to stress that in his opposition to communitarians Habermas goes after the nationalist, quite Eurocentric Western principle, the mark of which is to privilege the lived appeal of ethnic or regional culture as normative for the social integration of complex modern societies. To some suggestions that a democratic country needs a common ethnic identity in order to unite in any political action, he rejoins that the nationalist–communitarian identity offers an anachronistic model for such a normative union.[46]

Habermas distinguishes the lifeworld of national or ethnic identity, to be sustained in complex modern societies, from the constructed nationalist principle, which is normatively insupportable. Nationality and citizenship need not be identical terms. (To speak of American nationality on a USA passport is a misnomer, given that America is a multicultural, multinational state.) Whereas citizenship allows for the self-determination of culturally and ethnically differentiated individuals and nations, nationalist identity promises autonomy through a legitimation in some common collective. Since citizenship (political culture) differs from ethnicity (regional culture), Habermas differentiates constitutional patriotism from the love of one's nation. Nationalism elevates national identity by constructing a homogeneous public sphere into a normative principle of social integration. Because the nationalist principle bypasses deliberative democratic procedures, it is the nationalist determination of identity, not national or communitarian identity as such, that contributes to the weakening of cultures through their ethnic strife.[47]

From Ethnic to Political Culture for Multicultural Identities

Habermas's critique of nationalism does not render national identities obsolete; on the contrary, it aims to preserve their regional integrity in a multicultural context of political culture. He rejects an instrumental universalism of the nationalist principle. This position can be clarified on the basis of his two-pronged formal–pragmatic argument. Pragmatically speaking, one begins with the problems that face us. The national aspirations of different cultures cannot be met on the normative basis of the nationalist principle. Habermas addresses three such concrete problems: first, the national conflicts arising in unified Germany and emancipated central-eastern Europe problematize any easy celebration of the nation–state. Nationalism is too weak to resolve national conflicts without destructing its own regional identity. Second, these nationalist upheavals, because they render economic and democratic reforms impossible, threaten the plan for the financial union of Europe. Nationalism fails to integrate economy with national identities from the global, or even the ecological perspective. Third, given the expectation that in coming years millions will migrate into Europe from Africa, Asia, and Latin America, the idea of "Europe" as a cultural fortress of self-enclosed homogeneous cultures appears to be anachronistic. Nationalism gets stuck in the myth of the homogeneous public and cultural sphere, and thus it fails to provide any ground for an integration of the migrating nations. In sum, pragmatically, one part of Habermas's question—can national identity in itself sustain human communities in their multicultural differentiation?—must be answered negatively.[48]

The formal part of the argument gives us a criterion that provides an answer to the normative aspect of Habermas's question: what would a nonoppressive social and cultural integration look like? Habermas claims that the criterion for this integration is operative in a formally universal notion of political culture. By being differentiated from substantive cultures and from the concrete lifeworld, formal universalism admits a multicultural unity in difference. Habermas builds his formal argument on the thesis that between one's citizenship in a constitutional republic (republicanism) and one's national allegiance to a cultural community (nationhood) there exists only a historically contingent but not a strict conceptual link. Not only do we not need to share a national background in order to promote universal rights, but political multiculturalism requires that we learn to subject our interests to critical reflections in order to be motivated rationally by deliberative procedures. Learning to live in political culture is occasioned by certain historical conflicts among regional interests.

Deliberative democracy, then, problematizes that substantive hold which national cultures wield over the formation of common identity and action. Political culture abstracts from the lifeworld, yet is translated back into the lifeworld since it relates to those problem contexts from which it arose. The formal character of citizenship is a condition for integrating regional identity constitutionally. Precisely because it is a formal and minimal cognitive requirement (e.g., for the political and historical socialization of the immigrant), its overlapping consensus does not postulate some supranational ideal. Constitutional democracy is not understood simply as the heritage of our Western culture, but rather as a normatively grounded procedure. Habermas's neo-Kantian vision of Europe and world citizenship emerges as a multicultural federation with a common political sphere that safeguards universal rights across national and regional boundaries.[49]

There is one question raised by those who want to go further than Habermas in their critique of communitarianism: does the notion of overlapping consensus, just as in any nationalist principle, betray a Western bias and perhaps even inflict injuries and violence on other lifeworlds? Habermas answers by asking what could it possibly mean to integrate socially fundamentalist immigrants who want to join multicultural societies. What could it mean, pragmatically and formally speaking, to postulate pluralism without some overlapping consensus about the nonabsoluteness of different life forms? If this consensus is not forced upon other lifeworlds, but rather if it emerges either from mutual encounter or from a common problem area such as the ecology, then we cannot privilege a constructed innocence of traditions to their decentering vis-à-vis one another. Postnational identity differs from the nationalist principle, since the former does not exclude otherness on the basis of regional identity, and thus does not universalize some substantive framework. Fundamentalism refuses to relativize its own lifeworld vis-à-vis other lifeworlds. Immigration into any pluralist political culture inevitably problematizes all such absolutist claims. Thus, any decentering of lifeworlds "injures" the insularity of traditions. Yet it would be premature to equate this decentering with colonization. The presumption of innocence cannot be dogmatically granted to substantive traditions and then withdrawn from posttraditional public discourse. One is not more innocent than the other since both ethnic traditions and political procedures may fall into dogmatic self-assertion. But the responsible recovery of traditions appeals to a regulative ideal within the multicultural crisis conditions of complex modern societies. In this urgent sense of the present age we can grasp why Habermas rejects democracy based on a national–communitarian consensus, and why he argues for a radical democratic republic as a self-relativizing, fallibilist, and regulative principle of consensus-forming constitutional patriotism.

> Only within the constitutional framework of a democratic legal system can different ways of life coexist equally. These must, however, overlap within a

common political culture, which again implies an impulse to open these ways of life to others. Only democratic citizenship can prepare the way for a condition of world citizenship which does not close itself off within particularistic biases, and which accepts a world-wide form of political communication.[50]

CONCLUSIONS

I offer two preliminary conclusions. First, I find plausible Habermas's critical use of Kierkegaard in order to reject any absolutization of social ethics, for this enables him to confront the current nationalist and fundamentalist trends in politics and culture. Habermas suggests that a permanent democratic revolution, which enlivens postnational constitutional patriotism, could cure these destructive crisis trends. Second, in Part II with Kierkegaard and in Part III with Havel I will argue that this cure is necessary yet insufficient lest we adopt a posture of existential revolution. A sober resister must confront nationalism and fundamentalism by allowing, in principle, for the development of receptive and self-active, and thereby multicultural and radically egalitarian, nonpatriarchal and nonauthoritative identities.

I agree with Habermas about the necessity of sustaining multicultural communities postnationally. But I want to indicate an insufficiency of Habermas's postnational political culture in at least two regards. In the first place, deliberative democracy requires, yet does not in principle produce, radically honest individuals and open forms of regional culture. It requires this because not every mode of local culture fits with political multiculturalism. It does not produce such a fit, since, as Habermas admits, public debate remains too weak to do this job through the rational motivation of argumentation. The procedural critique of nationalism as the principle of postnational culture begs the question of providing a sufficient motivational backing without also inhabiting an existential critique of nationalism. To give an example from our present age, we see in central and southeastern Europe, in the former Soviet Union, and in the Los Angeles rebellion of 1992, that constitutional patriotism fails to be an integrating motivation for those who emerge from years of ethnic, racial, and economic oppression. I miss in Habermas's principle a more thoroughly sincere critique of nationalism and of religious or racial fundamentalism. Without an honest distance from the motives that color the grasp of one's origins, the procedural approach is too abstract to check the appeal of identities built on hatred.[51]

In the second place, without admitting the distinction between open and leveling modes of identity, communication, and the community ideal, the procedural principle begs the additional question about safeguarding its overlapping claim to sincerity. Without this distinction, I will show in my discussion of Kierkegaard and Havel, even a sincerely achieved consensus cannot resist the possibility that its rationally motivated procedure might engender a new authoritarian politics of identity and difference. Critical theory must resist the possibility that imperial indifference could seep into the universal standpoint; it must, in principle, articulate how to check the leveling trends towards homogenizing the consensual aim and procedure. I will argue that a thoroughly honest critique of nationalism and oppression affords a lived corrective to such an indifference by addressing marginalized, neglected, and suffering peoples in their concretion. Before proceeding with my Kierkegaardian rejoinder to Habermas, however, I will further illuminate Habermas's proposal for socially integrating the modern crisis individual by examining Habermas's reading of Hegel and Marx through Kant, Mead, and Durkheim.

CHAPTER 2

Ethics, Morality, and Identity

In this chapter, I lay out how Habermas's moral theory aims to answer the perceived deficits in Kierkegaard, such as the issue raised in Habermas's Copenhagen question: how to integrate socially that individual whose identity crisis can be no longer stabilized by appeals to communitarian frameworks. Let me introduce two clues that clarify how the concept of identity relates to ethical and moral questions. In his first clue, Habermas, like Kant and Hegel, distinguishes two types of questions: ethically, I ask what is good for me or for us in respect to this particular life form; morally, I ask what is normative or right universally. A norm must be valid not just for me or for a particular life form, but rather ought to be agreed upon by all in practical discourse. Morality is to compensate for one's fragility inherited through identity development. Habermas's first clue indicates that the moral point of view reconstructs intuitions shared with ethics: individualization via socialization makes identity a precarious achievement. Ethics and morality, in different ways, compensate for one's vulnerability to identity crisis. Fragile human identity becomes socially integrated in modernity through one's capacity to accept and reject discursive validity claims.

The second clue occurs in Habermas's performative adoption of the *"maieutic* method." *Maieutics* stands originally for a Socratic way of teaching through questioning, and later for Kierkegaard's mode of indirect communication. Habermas thematizes those pragmatic conditions of speech that one can access, practically, only in concrete discourse, in a *maieutic* engagement with the value skeptic, or, theoretically, in a reconstruction of these discursive conditions. His argument remains performative in the Socratic sense of engaging the other in discourse; if the skeptic deliberately evades communication, then he falls, practically, into self-contradiction. This vulnerability to a lived performative conflict in the core of practical discourse bespeaks what I call a clue to the existential elements in Habermas's integration of modern identity.[1]

My last point may be challenged by those who argue that Habermas is either quasi-transcendental or formally communitarian. But his Copenhagen question fits neatly neither the liberal defense of a decontextualized subject nor the communitarian attempts to cure modernity via national or ethnic communities. Thus, it is appropriate to read his intention (to heal Kierkegaard's crisis individual) by situating it in a tension between Hegelian and Kantian quests: How does Habermas ask a Hegelian question? Does he search for a life form which sublates the self-choosing individual into a concrete universal of modern ethical life (*Sittlichkeit*)? How does he raise a Kantian question? Does he want to justify the moral point of view (*Moralität*), ground one's inner conviction rationally, and thus harmonize individual autonomy with that of all? I will reconstruct Habermas's question to Kierkegaard, anachronistically, via Habermas's reading of Hegel through Kant (2.1), and systematically, in his regulative ideal of communicative ethics (2.2).[2]

2.1. HABERMAS'S READING OF HEGEL WITH KANTIAN MEANS

Hegel reconciles modernity with itself by sublating Kant's formal view of the moral individual into the substantive view of an ethical community. This moment of "sublation" places Hegel within the communitarian camp; the moment that preserves the principle of moral subjectivity makes him an uncanny modernist antagonist of neo-Aristotelian communitarians. Hegel begins with a critique of ethically deficient identities, thereby taking the liberty to do something for which Sandel cannot forgive Rawls: he commences with the minimal, abstract, disencumbered self, and by drawing out the unacknowledged normative presuppositions of the liberal standpoint of a contractor, arrives at a nonliberal alternative—the fraternal self in rational community. Hegel's argument has a developmental character; it educates the possessive individualists—the Nozicks, Hayeks, and Hobbesians of his day—to the freedom of ethical life.

Habermas, leaning as much on Kant and Marx as on Kierkegaard, reacts against Hegel's emphatic institutionalism. Three steps outline Habermas's reading of Hegel: he pits the early, "existential" Hegel of love and life against the later Hegel of the absolute knowing; he interprets Hegel's notion of affective and dialogic reciprocity within the linguistic–communicative turn; and finally he "redeems Hegel's intentions with Kantian means." I will take up the first two steps by commenting on Habermas's agreements with Hegel (A) and continue the second and third steps through his agreements with Kant (B). I leave open the question of whether and how Habermas's Kantianized Hegel succeeds in integrating socially and securing Kierkegaard's self-critical individual against modern identity crises. In the next chapter this problem will occasion my examination of Habermas's reading of Marx and critical social theory.[3]

A. Habermas's Agreements with Hegel

Habermas targets four Hegelian objections to Kant. First, Hegel questions the *formalism* of moral reasoning. Can a formal principle generate moral contents or does it lead to tautologies? Can questions of justice be separated from those of the good life? Second, he objects to the *abstract universalism* of Kant's moral imperative. The categorical imperative, if it wants to universalize a maxim for morally obligatory action, must abstract from particular contexts. Must not, then, practical reason resign itself to the fortune and pure cleverness of its conceptuality? Third, Hegel finds the *pure ought of morality* powerless to guide action in practice. Moral imperative demands that the ought be separated from what is. How, then, can insights gained in the moral point of view, if they are radically severed from their origins in the lifeworld, bear upon practice? Fourth, Hegel warns against the *terror of the ethic of pure conviction*. Because moral imperative separates itself from the processes of education and historicity, it remains open to political abuse. One is in danger of falling into an action that is itself justified by an abstract goal. How can political action be justified, how can it win for itself moral insights?[4]

Habermas's affirmation of the early Hegel aims at unresolved problems in Kant's critical philosophy, and yet, in considering these agreements, we must keep in mind that Habermas raises a two-edged argument. He argues against communitarians and against both the impotence of mere ought and the terrorism of pure conviction. His question—how to integrate socially a crisis identity—must be read against his critique of the monological senses of Kantian autonomy and against his critiques of the attempt to determine Kant's perceived monologue through the recourse to a substantive life form. I will focus on the agreements with Hegel through Habermas's intersubjectivist reading of *identity*, his *communicative* translation of the moral point of view, and his rendition of the community *ideal* in the figure of world-immanent, horizontal transcendence.[5]

An Intersubjectivist Reading of Identity

Habermas wants to secure Kant's moral autonomy by anchoring it in social origins. For this, he returns to an intersubjectivist model of identity formation found in the young Hegel. Habermas argues that in this model, the notion of ethical life is bound to a contextual, not absolute, dialectic of love among single individuals. Following this path, he interprets Hegel's notion of spirit, without its later adjective "absolute," as communicative interaction.[6]

Loving and living cannot be fetishized or commodified as objects; they cannot be elevated to an absolute. Community takes place among those who live for one another. Loving does not collect atomic experiences. In loving the two are separate, but they come together as a unified life principle. Loving means taking and giving in mutual reciprocity. The only thing that divides lovers is their mortal being. Hegel attempts here to overcome the perceived formalism, abstractness, powerlessness, and arbitrary assertiveness of the Kantian position. This model of loving conjoins inclination and rationality through a binding and bonding feeling that is the motivating factor for action. One individuality does not occur in formal and abstract distance from another. It is not a powerless ought imperative, and it cannot be sanctioned by an inward conviction, but must occur within a community.[7]

The mature Hegel expands the feeling of love into a struggle for recognition among the members of the social whole, rather than among presocial contractors. His notion of ethical totality provides measures of "false" identities and of every deficient social whole. This totality is spirit:

> A self-consciousness exists *for a self-consciousness*. Only so is it in fact self-consciousness. . . . *Spirit* . . . is—this absolute substance which is the unity of the different independent self-consciousnesses which, in their opposition, enjoy perfect freedom and independence: "I" that is "We" and "We" that is "I."[8] (emphasis in original)

Westphal interprets this view of "spirit" as the fulfilment of the earlier intimations of love: by being a self-conscious unity, spirit provides subjective and substantial reciprocity. We have to do with concrete, desirous, and linguistic individuals, not with disencumbered and contractarian selves. Spirit is a linguistic whole, yet language does not express a super-subject, but rather a middle ground that constitutes intersubjectivity. Spirit means here neither something one-dimensional or identical with the world nor the world-transcendent, the "wholly Other."[9]

Habermas understands Hegel's conception of spirit as the grammar and the universal medium of intersubjective relations. Language is the medium of individualization through socialization. The notions of grammar and medium embody "the dialectic of the 'I' and the 'other' within the framework of the intersubjectivity of spirit, in which the 'I' communicates not with itself as its 'other' but instead with another 'I' as its 'other'." The relation between the I and the alter does not occur within subjective self-relation or self-knowledge, but rather in "the complementary relationship between individuals who know each other." I am individualized through the same reciprocal medium, linguistic competence, and communicative action that socialize me. I learn to take both the universal and the individual perspective, and become self-determined and self-realized.[10]

Human experience transpires in interaction with another. Hegel's "theory of spirit" depicts mutual recognition as the origin of ego identity:

> The spirit is not the fundament underlying the subjectivity of the self in self-consciousness, but rather the medium *within* which one "I" communicates with another "I," and *from* which, as an absolute mediation, the two mutually form each other into subjects. Consciousness exists as the middle ground on which the subjects encounter each other, so that without encountering each other they exist as subjects. (emphasis in original)

Self-relation is tied to the mode of interaction with the alter. I learn to experience myself through the experiences communicated to me by others. "The consciousness of myself is the derivation of the intersection of perspectives." Inwardness is permeated by my ability to take the attitude of the other. There is no self-recognition without mutual recognition.[11]

Habermas notes that "spirit" serves Hegel by expressing a very specific experience of transcending "solitary self-consciousness" in the larger whole of an epoch, nation, or team. Spirit is "the ethical totality" comprising individual and universal perspectives. Spirit is the lived "identity of the I with an alter who is not identical with it." Habermas defines Hegel's spirit as "the communication of the individuals in the medium of the universal." He focuses on this medium as the normative framework of communication. "[Spirit as communication] does not place the moment of universality before that of individuality, but instead allows the proper connection among them." Habermas applies this definition of spirit to the problem of human development. Since identity exhibits a unity of universal and individual perspectives, we can explain the process of individualization via socialization: "socialization may not be thought of as adaptation to society of an already given individuality, but as that which itself produces an individuated being." The lifeworld is the "concrete universal"; the domain wherein identity is constituted and reciprocal recognition can be further maintained.[12]

"Spirit" defined as linguistic intersubjectivity still does not clarify what sort of whole it expresses. There are at least three ways in which Hegel's "spirit" can be read: descriptively speaking, as finite humans we form the sense of our "I" on the basis of the "We" that gives us linguistic and cultural tools. Further, sociologically viewed, the social whole is actually determinative of the normative frameworks into which we are socialized and through which we develop identity. Finally, normatively evaluated, none of the many historical forms of culture is an absolute spirit of history. We cannot get norms for a critical social theory from the fallible hermeneutical horizons of history. Habermas argues that no society owns the final measuring rod; thus we cannot abandon ourselves to a simple trust in history. We need a theoretical standpoint that admits a normative, yet revisable, critique of the concrete societies in which the critic happens to find herself. Hegel holds the ultimate normative priority of the "We" to the "I"; Habermas inhabits the middle position with an achieved normative priority of the consensual "we" to the individual "I." These three ways—descriptive, sociological, and normative—build upon one another: Hegel holds the third along with the first two; Habermas holds the first two but his fallibilism denies the third; and Kierkegaard, I will show, while sharing the hermeneutical (first) and sociological (second) relations to the present age with Hegel and Habermas, in denying the communitarian normativism (third), argues for spirit as an existential category of identity formation.[13]

Habermas sets the early Hegel against the mature one. He critiques the latter's sublation of morality into the subjectivity of the nation–state. Nagl objects that one cannot reconcile the finite judgment of Kant's moral individual with Hegel's absolute communitarian priority. He suggests that the young Hegel does not afford Habermas the needed categories; he merely allows him to defend Kant against the mature Hegel by an intersubjective transformation of moral autonomy. But should Habermas extract from the early Hegel a clue to such an existential and also intersubjective concretization of Kant, then, despite Hegel's perceived deficits, much has been accomplished. Nagl's point should not distract us from Habermas's innovative move. I consider to be more serious Nagl's claim that the concept of intersubjectivity cannot account for the moral fact of individual judgment to which Habermas in the last instance still appeals.[14]

A Communicative Reading of the Moral Point of View

Following Hegel, Habermas claims that Kant's moral principle, which categorically bids us to act only according to those maxims for action that admit of becoming universal law, presents three problems: it is derived monologically, it is abstractly universal, and it is applied strategically and not communicatively. First, Kant assumes a preestablished harmony of agents, thereby bypassing the moral problematic of communicative interaction:[15]

> The intersubjectivity of the recognition of moral laws accounted for *a priori* by practical reason permits the reduction of moral action to the monological domain. The positive relation of the will to the will of others is withdrawn from possible communication, and a transcendentally necessary correspondence of isolated goal-directed activities under abstract universal laws is substituted.

Second, Kant's principle has "the abstract form of universal validity" because its universality does not result from reciprocal recognition of the problematized claims to validity in real, practical discourses. It presupposes a priori such an agreement:

> The moral laws are abstractly universal in the sense that, as they are valid for me, *eo ipso* they must also be considered as valid for all rational beings. There-fore, under such laws interaction is dissolved into the actions of solitary and self-sufficient subjects, each of which must act as though it were the sole existing consciousness; at the same time, each subject can still have the certainty that all its actions under moral laws will necessarily and from the outset be in harmony with the moral actions of all possible other subjects.

Third, monologic and abstractly universal aspects of Kant's morality fall under what Habermas distinguishes as strategic, not communicative action. I will discuss later in this chapter the difference between communicative and strategic action in relation to validity claims. It suffices now to state that strategic action is goal-directed, rather than oriented to understand-ing: strategically, I can decide between conflicting moral choices in my privacy without having to engage in argumentation and reach an agree-ment. Such a decision can be called neither rational nor moral because rational grounding of moral maxims can occur only within the domain of communication and mutual recognition. An ethic of conviction eliminates the communicative, hence rational and moral, possibility of such a ground-ing: here, "the *a priori* validity of the moral law is guaranteed by practical reason on the transcendental level in Kant's moral doctrine."

Reciprocal recognition, freed from Hegel's march towards absolute reconciliation between the individual and the universal, provides Haber-mas with that model through which he transforms Kantian ethics into a concretely operative communication ideal. Habermas anchors Hegel's struggle for recognition in a procedural–moral point of view. Moral rela-tions result from the mutual recognition "that the identity of the 'I' is pos-sible solely by means of the identity of the other, who in turn depends on my recognition, and who recognizes me." Habermas draws a parallel between Hegel's critiques of abstract self-consciousness and the moral will abstracted "from the moral relationships of communicating individuals." He argues that the young Hegel's critique of Kant's moral philosophy shows both notions to be untenable. One cannot, like Kant, presuppose autono-mous moral self-possession of the law-giving subject (e.g., the liberal judge). Just as we are not in private possession of our identities, so we do not own or oversee the domain of morality.

The Horizontal, World-Immanent Regulative Ideal

Kant's transcendental postulates—the preestablished harmony of duty and happiness, hope, and God's providence—are meant to maintain individual trust in the moral universe within. This might encourage a conceptual mythology about and a quietist stance towards the social status quo. Without moral engagement with others in the lifeworld, an inward claim to moral autonomy is at best illusory and at worst dangerous to others. Hegel critiques the impotence and terror of an autonomous ethic of conviction. Habermas defines autonomy as one's capacity to raise, accept, or reject criticizable validity claims in conversation.

Kant's inward ethic presupposes the validity of universal moral law. His presupposition calls on a moral metaphysic of the two worlds: the world of empirical living and the intelligible world of freedom. The individual is a member not of one ethical totality, as in Hegel, but lives dual lives in these two worlds. While his moral theory has a Kantian rather than a Hegelian character, Habermas does not share this metaphysic of the two worlds. He argues that communicative rationality provides the ground of moral obligation. This ground admits a transcendence on this side of the world, a communicative transcendence towards the other in the world. He retrieves this normative ground in the formal–pragmatic presuppositions of communication. The ideal communication community—what he earlier articulated as the ideal speech situation—provides the interactive medium of identity formation. Habermas chastises Kant for categorically separating duty and inclination, reason and sensibility. An ought which depends on such splits is rendered powerless. Because Habermas gives up the dual standpoint, his moral theory need not oppress the inner nature for the sake of duty and universalizability; it can deal with all of the interests of participants in practical discourse. If moral autonomy means free development of personality, then one becomes autonomous only in the mutual recognition of freedom.[16]

Against Kant's world-transcending ground of morality, Hegel incarnates universal moral norms in institutional life. Since Habermas links ethics and morality with the vulnerability found in identity formation, he agrees that the motivational weakness of moral insights must be compensated for not merely by education and socialization processes but by social institutions and law. Hegel's claim is that through rational means our Western institutions already contain the requisite process of moral justification for the realization of basic rights. With Marx and Kierkegaard, Habermas rejects Hegel's optimism, and thus redeems his claim without an emphatic institutionalism. Rational ground exists neither in the structure of institutions nor in our present world as such, but only within the procedure of the rational collective will formation.

The terror of an inward ethic of conviction arises from the confusion between the discursive grounding of norms and their actualization, between insight and action. Habermas does not fall back on morality to mystify the problem of social structures; only political ethics can realize suitable conditions for the moral point of view. He distinguishes political ethics from morality, yet depicts the implications of the latter for the former. The material conditions of human interaction can prevent any actualization of the demands for universal morality. Political ethics and law aim at a transformation of the concrete forms of life in order to sustain conditions for practical discourse.

B. Habermas's Agreements with Kant

Habermas's defense of multiculturalism against Hegel's communitarian standpoint in ethical totality does not contradict his critique of possessive and disencumbered identity. He describes identity within the hermeneutical plurality of ethical totalities, thereby sustaining the individual against her absorption into the higher-level subjectivity of the nation–state. Further, he rejects any normative recourse to an ultimate substantive justification of morality in ethical life. Finally, adopting postmetaphysical thinking, he appeals to the formally regulative ideal of communication community.[17]

Identity and Ethical Totalities

Hegel's nation–state ends up in the same aporias as the self-assured and self-estranged epistemic ego that Hegel attempted to reform. Hegel's state, Habermas argues, carries on a monologue. From the standpoint of totality it boasts that it knows itself in its individuality and universality. If the solitary self cannot know itself as spirit, then it attains itself as object; alterity is not needed for self-knowledge or for the reciprocal recognition of the absolute by the absolute. Hegel's self-knowledge and envisioned totality of ethical relations remain a private Cartesian affair of the subject in love with itself. In place of the "higher-level subjectivity" of the nation–state, Habermas recovers the moral point of view within the paradigm of "higher-level intersubjectivity."[18]

A common communitarian objection is that Habermas holds an atomist–contractarian view of the individual. Yet he develops an intersubjectivist reading of the Kantian turn to the subject. Concrete discourse admits individuals into the moral point of view as having context-relative ego and group identities. Individuals within their lifeworlds are so many ethical totalities with shared, fused, and differentiated forms of life: "the ethical–existential" questions (Who am I to be? or Who are we to be?) to which one ascribes one's identity are not subjectivist. This questioning individual is hermeneutically embedded and rationally motivated by the answers relative to her lifeworld. "A hermeneutical clarification of one's identity and self-understanding relies also on reasons, and it requires a self-referential interpretation that is capable of being authentic or not."[19]

Communitarians make it too easy for themselves by attacking the monological versions of the moral point of view. If Habermas does not support atomic individualism, then the reasons for posttraditional and postnational questioning differ from what communitarians would like them to be. Moral questions of universal justice and right abstract from ethical questions concerning the particular good life because these latter questions can no longer motivate resolutions of substantive conflicts. That questions of moral justice and right arise at all bespeaks the historical and personal emergence of posttraditional and postnational identity, even though in our societies this possibility co-exists with multiple views of the good. Posttraditional questioning and the need for a postnational form of life arise not because academic philosophers thought these up, but because in our societies today there is no alternative ethical totality that provides an unquestioned horizon for the whole culture. Against Hegel, Habermas, not unlike Kierkegaard, doubts the good of having or even seeking such a totality.

Habermas answers his own question of how to integrate socially Kierkegaard's crisis individual by preserving Kant's principle of subjectivity within the communicative turn. Habermas conceives of identity formation in a post-Cartesian sense but without the backdrop of ethical totality: "Public spheres can be conceived of as higher-level intersubjectivities. Identity-forming self-ascriptions can be articulated within them." A commonly shared life form operates with "the polycentric projections of the totality [that] generate competing centers." Modernity can achieve within "the polyphonous and obscure projections of the totality" a common consciousness. Yet "common" does not mean "communitarian" because it does not simply occur on the hermeneutically given ground of "the traditional forms of representative self-presentation," but rather must be appropriated "in the higher-level, concentrated communicative processes of a public sphere." The differentiated value spheres open up to one another and point to both "a comprehensive public sphere" and "the higher-level intersubjectivity of public spheres." One need not assign the sovereign authority of self-management to this communicative interaction.[20]

The Normative Standpoint of Morality

Habermas's view that ethics and morality compensate for the constitutive vulnerability of human identity informs his intersubjectivist interpretation of the moral point of view. Linking the individual social constitution with ethics and morality reflects as much an Aristotelian and Hegelian–Marxist as a pragmatist insight. Moral intuitions come neither from philosophy nor from speculative constructions but from the process of socialization. This process contains the core of ethical and moral intuitions.[21]

But the issue for Habermas is how to offer an interpretation of "the primacy of ethical life over morality, an interpretation that is immune to neo-Aristotelian and neo-Hegelian attempts to ideologize it." He agrees that moral discourse is always embedded in the lifeworld. "All morals circle around equality of action, solidarity and general well being; these are ground images that reach back to the symmetry conditions and reciprocity expectations of communicative action." This link between morality and the lifeworld, however, does not confirm the positions of the contextualist, the radical value skeptic, or the communitarian. Habermas wants to unify two elements: autonomous individuals who can come under the universal principle and take moralized positions towards problematic value claims; and the solidarity of the single person who is receptive to the attitude and situation of the other. Without these two elements no common moral solutions can be built.[22]

Habermas explicates the moral point of view on the experiential basis of individualization through socialization. First, with regard to Kantian moral duty, norms are internally tied to justified grounds. The binding and bonding force of moral obligation precedes the use of sanctions. The notion of duty arises from this binding and bonding mode of ought sentences. The performative mode expresses the view of participation in discourse (i.e., the enabling force of the better argument). In this perspective of participation the ego binds the alter communicatively by offering justified claims to normative validity.[23]

Second, Habermas reinterprets the Kantian autonomy and respect for moral law as something achieved only via the process of reciprocal recognition. Moral self-determination occurs within a community of moral actors. Habermas insists that moral autonomy does not certify the ego as an owner of itself. The self-possession of either the male, mostly white, breadwinning capitalist entrepreneur or the real socialist "future man" depict currently problematized ideals for men and women alike. Nor can one gain autonomy through a revolutionary fight. The struggle unto death projects a heroic self-image onto the universal notion of freedom in history. This male imaginary was codified in Hegel's dialectic of the desire to be desired, and variously perfected by Marx's notion of the class struggle, Sartre's dialectic of alienating gazes, and Lacan's dialectic of jealousy.[24]

I will not go into these themes here, but it seems that the figures of both possessive individualism and of the master and slave struggle for recognition are derivative modes of integrating society. From the normative angle of the moral point of view—that is, not from an empirical and sociological observation of the lifeworld—possessive individualism and the fight unto death present "false" either–or options for socially integrating the modern forms of life. Here I call decisionistic either–or any limiting options that block one's responsible choice. The either–or of asocial atomism and emphatic communitarianism is targeted by Habermas in his reformulations of the moral point of view. Liberal autonomy and the image of struggling totality are sociological generalizations of the observer's perspective on modern life. In that sense they remain mere normative fictions. Habermas argues that one cannot instrumentalize moral self-respect, but must appeal instead to the reciprocal conditions of communication. What, then, is the ground of respect for the moral law? I respect in the alter both that she can act deliberately and that she can come freely under the universal principle of validity claims. Only then she can motivate me rationally and bind me morally. The key to the moral point of view is that one cannot possess this competence in self-choice fully alone. What makes one worthy of respect is that one can take yes and no positions towards validity claims in discourse. The ground of self-respect is never monologic and decisionistic, since it cannot lean on a choice of one's private values.[25]

From these reinterpretations of the moral point of view, I can sum up Habermas's defense of Kant against Hegel's four objections introduced at the outset of this chapter. First, Habermas need not accept the objection that formal procedures can arrive only at tautologies. The substantive contents that are examined in moral discourse arise from daily communication in the lifeworld. They are not made up by liberal philosophers who write undergraduate textbooks on moral problems. Rather, the contents of discourse are constituted by its participants. Consider the value range represented by the cultures of the former Soviet Union or Yugoslavia: the participants cannot resolve their differences except by recourse to principles of formal justice. No unified framework of the good allows for transcending intercultural differences. No communitarian renewal can offer a plausible resolution for such conflicts.

Again, philosophers did not make up the distinction between formal justice and the substantive good. Rather, they explicate principles that are already operative in practical discourse where problems preclude that the participants have some alternative other than drawing the above distinctions. In practice, questions of the substantive good and of procedural right are never transparently distinct. Most practical discourses are about negotiating the line between what is the substantive question of the good and what the procedure of right. If the problems themselves give rise to certain types of questions, we can expect that discourses themselves must also negotiate this difference. It cannot be dictated to them a priori by moral philosophy. The differentiation of moral from ethical discourses is exhibited by their questioning.[26]

Second, Habermas need not accept the objection that moral universalism, because it abstracts from particular contexts, leads to the oppression and disregard of concrete interests. Habermas accepts the negative aspect of Hegel's attack on conceptual mythology and the methodological illusion of the categorical imperative. Yet Habermas does not split off abstract and formal universalism from its application to historical and hermeneutical contexts. Still, he rejects the prioritizing of substantive communal norms in moral deliberation. Discourse considers the interests of all participants and, in a nonutilitarian sense, the consequences of accepted norms. Justified norms under which the interests of all are met admit of greater universality than the interest-laden views of the substantive good. In addressing the discontinuity between evaluative contexts and questions of right, Habermas distinguishes the justification of norms, their application, and the actualization of moral insights. Without denying questions of application and actualization, he objects to the reductionism of the first two levels (justification and application) to a prudential ethic of virtue. Juristic examples show that virtuous application of norms must also appeal to the universal presuppositions of practical reason.[27]

Third, Habermas does not lean on a powerless ought. He need not accept the objection that insights gained in the moral point of view, if they are abstracted from their origins in the lifeworld, cannot be institutionalized or motivate practice. Morality must unite with the socialization and education processes that enter into one's identity formation; it must be sustained by practical discourse. Further, Habermas conjoins his reconstruction of the pragmatic presuppositions of argumentation with a developmental argument. The Hegelian point: our Western institutions already contain the formal structures of universal justification; thus, in them one can actualize basic principles of justice. A Kantian rebuttal: this process of justification is merely a regulative and thus fallible achievement. Habermas's reformulation: the regulative ideal is operative in actual discourse.[28]

Fourth, Habermas need not be guilty of totalitarianism. The categorical imperative does not separate itself from the processes of education and historicity. He argues against decisionism, both in the ethic of conviction and in communitarianism, and he seems to be in no danger of falling into immoral action as justified by the (individualistic or utopian) terror of virtue. The real problem is how to actualize moral insights. "The conditions which are necessary for all participants to take just part in practical discourse are not fulfilled by discourse itself." Now, what fail any actualization of moral insights are institutions, the process of education, and material conditions. Habermas considers this a question of political ethics: how moral and political practice, which aims at the recovery of the necessary conditions of human communication, is itself justified. Procedurally, politics aims at that transformation of the shared form of life that admits the practice of a moral point of view.[29]

Habermas shows that there is an internal link of both civil disobedience and law to morality because democratic institutions derive their legitimation from the collective will formation. In cases where institutions destroy the conditions of collective life, actions of nonviolent civil disobedience that respect the moral intuitions anchored in democratic institutions are justified. The positive law, which represents complete procedural rationality, compensates for the "motivational weakness" and the "cognitive uncertainty" of posttraditional and postnational, necessarily incomplete and fallibilistic, moral procedure. There is motivational weakness since morality "guarantees neither the infallibility nor the unambiguity of the outcome, nor a result in due time." There is cognitive uncertainty because moral insights do not warrant the enactment of or guarantee that justified norms have "effective bindingness" on all participants. Habermas insists that we cannot expect from moral insights such general adherence to justified norms by all participants.[30]

In his recourse to law, however, Habermas bypasses Kierkegaardian resources of radical self-choice to deal with the problem of the motivational weakness and cognitive uncertainty of morality. This being the case, then, on Habermas's grounds, modern identity remains doubly insecure: one is in need of the communicative turn in morality, and one also needs help from political ethics, civil disobedience, and positive law, in order to overcome the weakness and uncertainty of practical discourse. Habermas argues that morality must be complemented by positive legal warrants. Yet he also argues that the legitimating force of the legal enactment of power lies in the internal link of law and morality.[31]

The Ideal of Communication Community

I can now consider Habermas's reply to Hegel's question concerning whether it is possible to make the moral point of view independent of a lived vision of the good. Habermas argues that we can give only an indirect expression for a life form commensurate with morality. Quite consistently with the main tenor of critical theory, he invokes the Judaic prohibition on making picture idols of ideal life forms. In the aftermath of Gulag, Auschwitz, and Hiroshima, thinking can offer recourse to the positive, if at all, through negative methodology, rather than by a direct ontology of the substantive good. Habermas limits his claims to the argument that there are no alternatives to the presuppositions of communication: one can socially integrate modern crisis identity only through a concrete yet fallible intimation of the damaged form of life.[32]

Habermas distills these alternatives in the skeptic's refusal to converse. He too, if he is to communicate, cannot but throw at least a linguistified tantrum. "By refusing to argue [the skeptic] cannot, even indirectly, deny that he moves in a shared socio-cultural form of life, that he grew up in a web of communicative action, and that he reproduces his life in that web." Unless one commits suicide or goes crazy, one cannot reject the lifeworld in which one must take positions vis-à-vis others:

> [I]nsofar he is alive *at all*, a Robinson Crusoe existence through which the skeptic could demonstrate mutely and impressively that he has dropped out

of communicative action is inconceivable, *even as a thought experiment*. . . .
[T]he radical skeptic's refusal to argue is an empty gesture. (second emphasis
added)

Note here that elsewhere Habermas applies this same distinction prior to
his concern for the social health of the modern crisis individual: "Yet
Kierkegaard was completely aware of the fact that the personal self is at
the same time a social self and a self that is a citizen—for him Robinson
Crusoe remained an adventurer." Thus, we neither need to identify the
"existential" with the "subjectivist" nor agree with the received view of
Kierkegaard as an irrational, acommunicative, and uncritical individualist.[33]

Therefore, the radical skeptic is not to be confused with the radically
self-choosing, posttraditional, and postnational individual whom Habermas
considers in his thought experiments. The skeptic thinks that he has an
option, besides that of refusing to argue, to evade communication. This is
a skeptical myth, not a Kierkegaardian posture. One does not have at hand
such an option. "From the perspective of the lifeworld to which the actor
belongs, these [communicative] modes of action are not matters of free
choice." Open identity does not arise from the skeptic's two-fold refusal
to argue and to act communicatively. Contemporary skepticism is a self-
evading stance within posttraditional and postnational contexts, unlike the
thoroughly self-critical attitude that emerges from the reflexive distance
towards traditions wherein one communicates and acts. An honest posture
is that of self-choice:

> Individuals acquire and sustain their identity by appropriating traditions,
> belonging to social groups, and taking part in socializing interactions. The indi-
> viduals have a choice between communicative and strategic action only in an
> abstract sense, i.e., in individual cases. They do not have the option of a long-
> term absence from contexts of action oriented toward reaching an understand-
> ing. That would mean regression to the monadic isolation of strategic action,
> or schizophrenia and suicide. In the long run such absence is self-destruc-
> tive. . . . [It] leads to *an existential dead-end.* . . .[34] (emphasis added)

To sum up: Habermas finds in the regulative ideal of a communication community a horizontal possibility of transcendence (i.e., on *this* side
of the world). Yet one must not absolutize this world or elevate ethical
totality above existence. Reason ceases to be practical when it seeks metaphysical legitimation. In this two-fold move, Habermas argues against the
dualism of the world-transcending and world-absolutizing frames of Kant
and Hegel without adopting the ethos of the present age, which prefers
the skeptical posture of an observer. Performance cannot appeal to absolute grounding, but critique cannot flee the pragmatic context of communication.[35]

2.2. THE REGULATIVE IDEAL OF COMMUNICATIVE ETHICS

How does Habermas's reading of Kierkegaard express the intuitions of *communicative action* that are explicitly thematized in *communicative ethics*? I limit my examination to modern identity crises resulting from the historical and ontogenetical differentiation of criticizable claims. Communicative action clarifies the intersubjectivist notion of identity (A). Communicative ethics inherits from the structures of communicative action the hermeneutical–social beginnings of identity formation (B). Kantian morality, interpreted through communicative ethics, maintains the pragmatic presuppositions of communication reflexively. This interpretation gives us the moral point of view. I will define Habermas's postmetaphysical thinking within communicative ethics: the questions of normative right take methodical precedence over those of the good life because there is no overlapping life form to which all in practical discourses can appeal rationally. The ideal of a communication community need not specify a good or perfectly rational social form of life.[36]

A. Communicative Action

Habermas claims that not only moral but every discourse appeals to "the ideal conditions" of an action oriented towards reaching understanding. Actors rely on certain operative presuppositions of communication, and these, in turn, project the figures of "an ideal speech situation" or what Apel, following Peirce, envisions under "an unrestricted communication community." Both communicative action and argumentative discourse, ideally, presuppose openness, sincerity, noncoerciveness, and the symmetry among the participants.[37]

The Ideal, Formal–Pragmatic Presuppositions of Communication

We should understand the "ideal communication community," in neither a concretistic nor a transcendental a priori sense: the ideal is not a correlate of Aristotle's good life, Hegel's rational present, or Marx's future historical life form, nor does it pertain to Kant's world-transcendent standpoint.

> The normative fundament of discursive understanding is *both the anticipated and effectively anticipating ground....* Insofar is the concept of the ideal speech situation not a pure regulative principle in Kant's sense; we must always with the first speech act factically take into account this imputation. On the other hand, the concept of the ideal speech situation is not an existing concept in Hegel's sense: no historical society coincides with the form of life that we anticipate in the concept of the ideal speech situation. (emphasis added)

What is anticipated and anticipating in the concept of this ideality is merely "the formal idea of a society in which all potentially important decision-making processes are linked to institutionalized forms of discursive will-formation." This is not an ideal of a perfectly rational life form. "[W]e cannot undertake to appraise forms of life centered on communicative action simply by applying the standards of procedural rationality." We may judge a life form against the "model of sickness and health," against the balance among the differentiated cognitive, moral, and aesthetic aspects of rationality and its value spheres. We may not deduce from the decentered worldview of modernity an idea of the good life. Without recourse to substantial rationality, we can only critique modern societies against passing traditional values or expose colonizations of the lifeworld by one aspect of modern rationality.[38]

Habermas describes this ideal in terms of pragmatics as "the general and undeniable presupposition of concrete communication which every competent actor and speaker must make if she genuinely wants to take part in argumentation." Such an ideal operates in both the therapeutic discourse and critiques of social pathologies. The ideal is to restore freedom to the crisis individuals and let them resume autonomy towards others and vis-à-vis validity claims.[39]

In everyday communicative action we make validity claims, but these remain undifferentiated and unthematized. When claims are questioned, that is, made problematic, we must redeem them through an argumentative discourse. Our naïve attitude changes into a hypothetical one, and communicative action becomes discourse. Argumentatively, we adopt a hypothetical attitude to problematized claims. This shift from the naïve to a decentered world, from preconventional to conventional to posttraditional attitudes, occurs both historically and ontogenetically. The shift transpires between life forms in the passage from conventions to one's appraisal of their claims on us. Contested norms are validated in the attitude that we assume towards them in discourse.[40]

A decentered attitude differentiates communication from the following of a strategy. The latter aims at eliciting an effect on the other by appealing to a nondiscursive force or authority. Openness, sincerity, noncoerciveness, and the symmetrical conditions of communication lie in the orientation of all participants to the validity claims of truth, rightness, and sincerity. Communication relies on the reciprocal recognition of the claims to validity, not on a nondiscursive strategic force. Dialogic reciprocity allows for an enabling force of validity claims, the noncoercive "force of the better argument." "Participants in argumentation cannot avoid the presuppositions that the structure of their communication . . . rules out all external and internal coercion . . . and thereby also neutralizes all motives other than that of the cooperative search for truth." I cannot deny validity claims without falling into self-contradiction, Habermas argues. I may not truthfully, rightly, and sincerely deny these pragmatic presuppositions that guide my very performance of this denial. Either it is true and I am sincerely correct that one cannot justify such validity claims, or the contrary is true. This contrary state of affairs also presupposes the counterfactual fulfillment of the pragmatic presuppositions of communication. All attempts to level communication into strategic and instrumental rationality seem performatively self-refuting.[41]

Habermas's Thought Experiment with Existential Crisis Identity

Habermas dramatizes this shift from a naïve to a decentered world, from traditionalistic to crisis identity. He engages in a thought experiment: what occurs in the "single critical moment" of the attitudinal change from the "quasi-natural" security one has in the lifeworld to a loss of it in the hypothetical attitude assumed towards its validity? He shows how cultures and individuals undergo disenchantments with ethno- and egocentrisms[42]:

> If the adolescent cannot and does not want to return to the traditionalism and unquestioned identity of her past world, she must, on penalty of utter disorientation, reconstruct, at the level of basic concepts, the normative orders that her hypothetically unveiling attitude destroyed.

No matter how sympathetic Habermas might otherwise be towards communitarian values, he knows, just as well as Kierkegaard, that modern cultures and adolescents cannot or will not unquestioningly accept tradition. If for no other reason than practical pedagogy, in modernity one must adopt the priority of a decentered, rebellious attitude towards ethical claims over the communitarian assumption of metaphysical goods. Decentering, disenchantment, and postmetaphysical thinking stand for an existential attitude in which one no longer appeals to, or is incapable of claiming, unproblematically valid goods. Habermas's text could describe crisis identity in the wake of modern religious, ethnic, and imperial wars, as well as after the fall of totalitarianism:

> Using the rubble of devalued traditions, traditions that have been recognized to be merely conventional and in need of justification, she erects a new normative structure which must be solid enough to withstand critical inspection by someone who henceforth distinguishes soberly between socially accepted norms and valid norms, between actual recognition of norms and the norms that are *worthy* of recognition. (emphasis in original)

What results from this breakdown of fundamentalism, nationalism, and traditionalism? Habermas recognizes one further difference between an identity based on rational principles and that which does not have any such Archimedean ground left to lean on:

> At first it is principles that inform her plan for reconstruction; these principles govern the generation of valid norms. Ultimately all that remains is a procedure for rationally motivated choice among principles that have been, in turn, recognized as in need of justification.

The growth into the procedural viewpoint is the moment of the qualitative change from a traditional to a posttraditional and postnational attitude. Habermas remarks that there is "something unnatural" about this breakdown of traditionally and nationalistically anchored identity: "it means a break with the naïveté with which the claims to validity are raised [and] on whose intersubjective recognition the communicative practice of everyday life depends." This breakdown is a rupture, a crisis, and a discontinuity. Posttraditional and postnational identity carries "an echo of the developmental catastrophe that once devalued the world of traditions historically and thereby provoked efforts to rebuild it at a higher level."

I dwell on this dramatization because it helps us to understand why Habermas finds Kierkegaard's individual the modern case in point for this thought experiment. Further, we can grasp here the link of Habermas's ideal to his proposal for stabilizing the perpetual crisis of a Kierkegaardian ego identity. First, this individual is a surviver of a developmental catastrophe, which Kierkegaard exemplifies in his attacks on bourgeois Philistinism, on mass culture, and on Christendom. A Kierkegaardian open attitude emerges within the Habermasian rubble of traditions. Second, identity crisis is stabilized neither at a new level of communitarian life in modernity nor by a flight to value skepticism. Kierkegaard neither bows to the metaphysical goods nor drifts: both communitarianism and value skepticism are maieutically exposed by his posture as forms of self-forgetfulness.

Habermas's question to Kierkegaard—how to integrate socially the modern adult or adolescent crisis individual—implies that these upheavals oppose both options. Kierkegaard debunks the communitarian and the value skeptical evasion of radical self-choice alike. The self-critical attitude bespeaks a single critical moment of qualitative change. Habermas argues that such an attitude itself makes one receptive to modern forms of life, even though Kierkegaard failed to articulate this in social terms. Thus, in spite of his own strong personal tenor to depict the concept of posttraditional and postnational identity, Habermas worries whether or not Kierkegaard provides an alternative to Hegel's concretization of Kant's moral identity. One way in which, I claim, we might want to understand entire Habermas's project is to grasp how he seeks such an alternative. Kierkegaard's individual is invited to enter the moral and sociopolitical ideality of public discourse.[43]

Let me conclude Habermas's experiment by explaining the two alternatives that he finds facing both adolescent cultures and individuals. By maintaining a hypothetical distance from conventional modes of thinking, identity crisis is not automatically restored to a higher ethical life or elevated to a moral point of view. First, one can try to preserve the meaning of having valid norms in the postconventional/contextual manner of Hegel's moral subject. This stage is what some feminists, following Gilligan's critique of Kohlberg, call the ethic of the concrete other, or the other morality. In this stage one "must reconstruct the basic concepts of morality without giving up the ethical perspective." In spite of his Kohlbergian view that this is a deficient resolution of the crisis, Habermas claims that it admits a transition to postconventional–formal, procedural discourses. Second, one can maintain a hypothetical distance from tradition and yet fail to stabilize sincere self-critical thinking. This path not only disallows a reconstruction of ethical life, but also blocks one's adoption of Kant's moral point of view and embroils one in value skepticism or emotivism. Habermas explains that both alternatives accomplish a transition from conventional to posttraditional reasoning, but the breakdown of tradition results at this juncture because theoretical distance from conventions stops short of universal morality.[44]

Habermas's argument applies to concrete discourse. This means that the collision with the skeptic must show maieutically that rules of speech do not favor merely some ideal communication, that they "are not conventions but inescapable presuppositions." The argument is a "maieutic method" because confirmation of its hypothesis "must be checked against individual cases."[45]

> The presuppositions themselves can be identified only by convincing a person who contests the offered hypothetical reconstruction how he is caught up in performative contradictions. . . . We must appeal to the intuitive preunderstanding which every subject competent in speech and action presumably brings into a process of argumentation.

Habermas's method stands closer to Socratic and Kierkegaardian maieutics than to deductive or ultimate–transcendental justification of the ideal communication. I will not do injustice to Habermas if in this regard I stylize his critique of deductive methods, as well as his own adoption of maieutics, in terms of an open attitude. Maieutics is analogical to induction: just as one cannot prove one's identity, even though one cannot take leave of oneself in discourse, so one may not transcendentally justify that preunderstanding that is presupposed in the argumentative context itself.

> The maieutic method . . . serves . . . to make the skeptic who presents an objection aware of presuppositions he knows intuitively; . . . to cast this pretheo-

retical knowledge in an explicit form, and so enabling the skeptic to recognize his intuition in this description; . . . and to corroborate through counterexamples the interlocutor's assertion that there are no alternatives to the presuppositions he has made explicit.

B. Communicative Ethics

To motivate rationally means to ground practical judgments. *Grounding* enables a resolution of substantive conflicts in normative discourse. Discursive formation of the collective meaning and will gives us the definition of "being on a rational ground." Grounding of claims is expressed by the principle of communicative ethics (D): "only those norms can claim to be valid that meet (or could meet) with the approval of all concerned in their capacity as participants in a practical discourse." (D) embodies the basic intuition of communicative ethics as a moral theory. "(D) presents the main assertion that the philosopher as moral theorist seeks to justify."[46]

Principles of Communicative Ethics

For moral justification, Habermas argues, one must win from the normative content of discourse presuppositions apart from both (D) and the substantive subject matter of argumentation. This is the procedural rule of practical discourse. Communicative ethics uses this rule by adopting the impartiality of judgment in the moral point of view, such as in Mead's principle of the ideal role-taking that prompts all concerned to take the attitude of all others. This "universal exchange of roles" is expressed in the argumentation principle (U):

> [E]very valid norm must satisfy the condition that *all* concerned can accept the consequences and the side-effects its *universal* observance can be anticipated to have for the satisfaction of *everyone's* interests (and these consequences are preferred to those of known alternative regulative possibilities).[47] (emphasis in original)

Habermas speaks about communicative ethics because moral deliberation does not begin in a private standpoint. Just as in the encounter with the skeptic, Habermas adopts a maieutic method, so formalization and abstraction occur in actual moral discourses. Communicative ethics projects normatively the structures of intersubjectivity inherited in communicative action. (U) "precludes a monological application." It "regulates only argumentation among a plurality of participants [and] suggests the perspective of real-life argumentations in which all concerned are admitted as participants." The universalization principle (U) expresses the idea of the moral theory (D):

> Communicative ethics does not set up substantive orientations. Instead it estab-
> lishes a *procedure* rich in prerequisites designed to guarantee the impartiality
> of the process of judging. As a procedure, practical discourse tests the validity
> of hypothetical norms; it does not produce justified norms. (emphasis in
> original)

Habermas argues that this proceduralism sets communicative ethics apart
from other moral theories of this type. All contents are made subject to
real discourse; there are no specific normative contents that are protected
from problematization. "(D) makes us aware that (U) merely expresses the
normative content of a procedure of discursive will-formation and must
thus be strictly distinguished from the substantive content of argumentation."[48]

To sum up the derivation of communicative ethics: every discourse
invokes undeniable, pragmatic presuppositions. One can be made aware
of them in a concrete maieutic encounter. Everyone who discursively
redeems normative validity claims appeals to the logic of practical discourses—the conditions specified in the universalization moral principle
(U). When (U) is grounded on the pragmatic presuppositions of argumentation, then the basic intuition of communicative ethics (D) can be stipu-
lated. (D) presupposes that with the help of the inductive principle of moral
argumentation (U), we can justify the resolution of substantive conflicts.
(U) is a bridging principle that makes (D) possible. The above points are
linked with learning and with the attitudinal change from one's naïve to a
decentered attitude:

> Communicative ethics . . . conceives discursive will-formation (and argumen-
> tation in general) as a reflective form of communicative action, . . . [and in
> moral development] it postulates a *change of attitude* for the transition from
> action to discourse.[49] (emphasis in original)

Justice, Care, and Existential Identity in Communicative Ethics

Under one of the clues introduced in this chapter I noted that communicative ethics inherits and develops the pragmatic presuppositions of communicative action. Like Aristotle, yet postmetaphysically, Habermas retrieves
the moral implications of the socialization process: morality maintains the
structure of communicative action and compensates for the vulnerable core
of socialized identity. Could it be that this reconstruction of the moral point
of view allows us to read an intersubjectivistic, posttraditional, and postnational reply to communitarian critiques, on the one hand, and the recovery
of Kant within the communicative turn on the other as shorthand for
Habermas's cure of modern identity crises?[50]

Habermas finds the origins of solidarity and justice in human vulnerability: "No person can assert her identity for herself alone." We are interdependent. "[T]he person forms an inner center only to the extent to which she simultaneously externalizes herself in communicatively produced interpersonal relationships." Both ethics and morality compensate for this "chronic susceptibility" and danger to human identity. Both build and stabilize identity by protecting not only an ego identity, but the lifeworld which sustains the fragile individual through group-identity. Experiencing solidary help and equal respect for individuals links both ethics and morality with identity formation. That the core of adult identity remains vulnerable is anchored in the ethics of mercy. Solidarity bespeaks care for the intersubjectively shared life form and the integral identity of others; justice is to secure equal rights for everyone. The moral viewpoint maintains both these intuitions through the reflexive insight into how we should act given the fragility of human identity.[51]

For Habermas, modernity comprises two levels of this solidarity: particular and general. Solidarity with my tribe, church, city, or country secures a vulnerable identity in a particular ethic of care. Modern identity is sustained by justice that abstracts from particular contexts and reciprocities. Solidarity is "extended" so that the community ideal includes all past, present, and future beings capable of speech and action. This posttraditional and postnational sense of solidarity converges with justice. "Justice conceived deontologically requires solidarity as its reverse side. It is a question not so much of two moments that supplement each other as of two aspects of the same things." While the notions of equal treatment and general welfare are implicit in the pragmatic presuppositions of communicative action (and are present in all cultures), they transcend the frontier of ethnocentric solidarities when they are extended without limitations. Not every particular solidarity, as well as not every politics of identity and difference, is just from the moral point of view. Habermas notes from his experience that the formula, "all for one, one for all," is compatible to the formula, "command us, Führer, we will follow you." For example, in Eichmann's "traditionalist sense of solidarity," fellowship was identified with followership. It is not surprising that he perverted the meaning of justice and interpreted the categorical imperative as a conventional imperative to follow Hitler. Similarly, while Iran, as a republic, acknowledges universal justice, it did not transcend its intra-Islamic solidarity when it declared the death sentence on Rushdie, a Moslem and a British citizen. Rushdie's writing problematizes substantive points in Islam. Both Eichmann's and Rushdie's cases show the distinction between marginalizing and all-inclusive solidarity, between closed and open identity.[52]

Inclusive solidarity is defined by justice, which does not permit arbitrary destructions of lifeworlds and identities. Open, postnational solidarity cannot rest on substantive lifeworld grounds, but is willing to problematize all marginalizing claims, such as Khomeini's sentence on Rushdie, Bush's crusade against Iraq, or the racist legitimation of the police brutality against Rodney King. This questioning places any pretence to impartiality (e.g., world order) under a moral rubric. Habermas insists that universal justice, unlike the false universality of exclusive traditions, allows one to transcend exclusive ego and group identity boundaries. One can assume moral obligation (e.g., towards the blacks in South Africa or Koreans in one's neighborhood; towards members of another religious or national persuasion; towards differences in gender and in sexual orientation, etc.), even though one does not experience their particular lifeworlds. By a feat of abstraction from one's centered to a decentered worldview, one need not destroy the plurality and asymmetry of concrete life forms. Habermas envisions vulnerable identity within the multicultural conditions of reciprocity. On the basis of universal justice, one can share symmetrically in what otherwise remain many asymmetrical lives.[53]

Habermas argues that in justifying moral discourse, the principle of solidarity is expressed by justice. In the moral discourse of application, the collision of prima facie valid norms is resolved in a moral judgment of their appropriateness to a particular context.

> [O]ne must understand that deontological approaches separate questions of justification from questions of application. The abstraction from contexts of the lifeworld, from the concrete circumstances of the individual case . . . is unavoidable in answering the question whether contested norms and modes of action are morally rights and deserve the intersubjective approval of those concerned. In the impartial application of well-grounded principles and rules to the individual case . . . this abstraction is reversed . . . [V]alid principles must be weighed against one another, and exceptions to accepted rules justified. There is no other way to satisfy the principle that like is to be treated in like manner and unlike in unlike manner.

The impartiality of the moral point of view must be interpreted in these two movements of justification and application: universal justice grounds moral norms in discourse that does not consider concrete applications; impartial solidarity with particular times and places occurs in discourse that must justify the appropriate norm from among those that were already found valid.[54]

Habermas coins a rather aggressively "masculinist" metaphor to separate the motives of solidarity and justice: (U) "acts like a knife that makes razor-sharp cut between evaluative statements and strictly normative ones, between the good and the just"; between the "ethical–existential" question (what is good for me or our group) and the moral question (what is good or right universally). Not only conservative communitarians but also feminists suspect that he disregards the posttraditional dimension of concrete solidarity and care while privileging universal justice. Benhabib, following Gilligan, and Fraser, among others, argue that impartial morality is partial to the male perspective; it privileges the generalized other yet excludes the concrete ethics of solidarity and care, and it fails to address a posttraditional ethic of gender asymmetry. Thus, some critics replace the presumed impartiality of white male heads of households with an ethic of care found in the mother–child model.[55]

Therefore, if communicative ethics is to welcome all those voices that are now excluded from discourse, it should address not only race and class but also gender differences. Habermas treats the question of gender as just one among many such differences. He argues that his position neither excludes family from moral discourse nor relegates women and children to the private domestic sphere, while itself inhabits the public male sphere. Practical discourse is not, even though a German academic seminar might be, in principle, dominated by fathers and sons. We can still ask if Habermas's model blurs gender asymmetry, not as just one among many, but rather as a qualitatively individual difference.

Here, I can only outline a reply. Universal justice can, but need not, become partial to the patriarchal world order. The binary link of solidarity and justice ought to be reconstructed so as to avoid male bias. This is possible, since the ethic of solidarity is implied in the intersubjectivist reading of (U) and in the moral discourse of application, both of which attend to the concrete other. Further, against Habermas and differently from the above feminist objections, I argue that a posttraditional and postnational ethic of gender asymmetry, like Kierkegaard's self-critical posture, should qualify the communicative turn itself. The significance of gender asymmetry, insofar as it is raised as a claim to individual difference, is that it should avoid the charges of being monological, decisionistic, and dogmatic or untranslatable. Lest it suffer the fate of Kierkegaard's individual—judged to be irrational, acommunicative, and uncritical—a critical feminist perspective which does not seek essentialist definitions of gender identity but rather an action mode or gender positionality needs a communicative articulation. Otherwise one cannot in discourse distinguish a gender mode from arbitrary power asymmetries that with feminist claims seek equal consideration.

CONCLUSIONS

Reciprocal recognition is the noncommunitarian basis whereby Habermas is to cure that identity which he adopts from civilizational adolescent or adult crises. He claims that the ideal community is not a metaphysical postulate. While the ideal confronts factual empirical communities, it neither absolutizes ethical totality nor privileges one historically concrete form of life. Habermas's two clues disclose that both ethics and morality inherit the vulnerable core of identity formation, and that the maieutic reconstruction alone gives us access to the pragmatic presuppositions of communication. The existential elements in both clues allow us to declare Habermas and Kierkegaard allies where Hegel and Kierkegaard were antagonists. The mature Hegel appeals to emphatic institutionalism of the nation–state, whereas Habermas adopts a regulative community ideal within concrete but fallible discourse. Next, I will turn to Habermas's yes–no to Marx's social critique. Habermas rejects, along with Aristotle's privileged polis ethics and Hegel's nation–state, Marx's metaphysic of historical progress. This is a recognizably sobering Kantian move, which is now politically radicalized in the formal–pragmatic reformulations of the normative basis of critique, or better, of what is meant by the regulative ideal.

CHAPTER 3

Identity and System

Habermas's complaint that Kierkegaard fails to thematize that life form which could sustain open individuality translates into the following view: while sharing with Hegel hermeneutical–ethical beginnings, with Kant the universal moral point of view under which an already socialized individual considers herself, and with contemporary thinkers' postmetaphysical methodology, Kierkegaard leaves himself open to the charges of irrational individualism, antisocial decisionism, and dogmatism. He is vulnerable to these charges not because of what he does but because of what he omits. Kierkegaard fails to elaborate the sociopolitical conditions of the possibility of nurturing "the improbable and endangered" modern identity. Habermas claims to fill this gap.[1]

After examining Habermas's moral theory, I now need to follow his question to Kierkegaard from sociological and critical social angles. Can communicative ethics hold a socially relevant role? Can it maintain social integration against the intrusion from the systemic imperatives of economy and administrative power upon modern life? This line of questioning links Habermas's moral theory and his reading of Kierkegaard to his revision of Karl Marx. If Habermas is to make good on his promise to integrate socially the self-critical individual, he must resolve two systematic problems. Kant's world-transcendent anchor renders the moral standpoint abstract and its convictions absolute. Hegel's world-immanent anchor in the historical life form absolutizes the social ethic of the nation–state. Both omit Marx's critical question: Kant's moral anchor and Hegel's identification of the real with the rational mystify the status quo. They resolve the crises of identity and of the present age at the price of reifying the lifeworld and alienating the self.[2]

Habermas adopts the social aspect of Hegel's objections to Kant. If there is no rational life form that nurtures existential identity, then the imperative of moral autonomy remains an abstract monologue and a leap.

Just as Habermas disagrees with Aristotelians, so he critiques Hegel's concretistic and Marx's utopian subsumption of morality under a historically particular albeit modern form of life. Habermas's critical theory offers the following challenge: how is crisis identity integrated in posttraditional and postnational forms of life, given Hegel's critique of Kant's abstractness, Marx's objections to Kant's and Hegel's mystification about reconciled ethical life, and Habermas's rejection of communitarian nostalgia or Marx's material utopia?[3]

There is an ambiguity in Habermas that some radical leftists point out: what is the use of the regulative community ideal if it can neither maintain me concretely nor envision a material transcendence of existing social injustice? How can this ideal be critical of the status quo beyond the Kantian and American pragmatist senses of critique? Habermas limits critical theory to what can be validly argued: the capacity to make moral judgments, to determine the formal conditions of the possibility of justice, and, thus, to derive an affirmative, normative basis of critique. This basis differs from formal ethics by reaching back to rational structures of the lifeworld, and from material ethics since one cannot read off the lifeworld the valid norms of ethical life.

Honneth modifies the radical left critique: communicative ethics implies a concept of material justice. But if Habermas's theory is to have social relevance, it must show how it can be applied in existing conditions. Reflections on the conditions for ethical behavior cannot be handed over to political ethics, law, or civil disobedience. Rather, they must be introduced within the action norms of material justice. Generally, Honneth defines material justice by those conditions that allow communicative ethics to take place. The problem with this definition is that it remains just as undetermined as revolutionary praxis is bereft of normative checks and balances. Yet Honneth's approach attends first to the need for a qualitative, not merely generic, notion of justice, and second to the necessity of it being a normative not merely an activist notion. By arriving at generic and qualitative conditions of its own possibility, communicative ethics acquires social and personal relevance.[4]

Honneth's sympathetic critique inspires my further reflection. There are resources in communicative ethics to act inclusively with all those voices that have been barred from the community, and to act critically against all obstacles that are in the way of the communicative ideal. In theory Habermas comes close to the ideal conditions that define this task, yet only praxis carries on the job of reciprocal interaction. The task dictated by theory is to call for those material conditions under which just and caring conversation could occur. The interest of critical theory is to define those elements (poverty, male-domination, racism, etc.) that disable dialogic reciprocity.

What is the condition of the possibility of resistance to distortions of the lifeworlds, and thus of the individual's critical judgment? If revolutionary ethics remains blind to this problem by presupposing a historicized *finis ultimis,* and if communicative ethics, *pace* Honneth, can lay out only the weak conditions of the possibility of material justice, can and does Habermas protect the self-critical individual against the distorting power of which Foucault presents such a masterly drama? These questions arise from the core of my concerns in this study, and they present their own ambitions toward a highlighting of Kierkegaard's critical social relevance. Kierkegaard would find Habermas's critique of Hegel incomplete for analogical reasons, as do the radical leftists. Habermas operates with a weak notion of concretion, and thus leaves the communication community open to the Foucauldean possibility of self- and other-deception. The individual, who in the communicative model remains for Habermas the last court of moral judgment, is provided with insufficient resources to confront oppressive economic and political systems.

My reasons for placing Habermas in the company of his leftist critics and for pointing in the direction of Foucault's objections is to situate Habermas's reading of Marx as a reply to these types of problems. While I cannot now take up these objections, I want to examine the place of radically honest identity in Habermas's two-track model of social and system integration. I will not reconstruct the young Marx's critiques of Kant's morality and Hegel's ethical totality. I want to follow Marx's critique of the capitalist form of life insofar as it pertains directly to Habermas's reading of Marx through Western Marxism and the Frankfurt School of Critical Theory (3.1). I will then preview two readings of the present age: Kierkegaard's existential and Habermas's legitimation crises (3.2).

3.1. HABERMAS'S READING OF MARX

Communicative ethics without a critical social theory cannot decipher "the paradoxes of societal rationalization." We must ask whether Marx's critique of capitalism provides Habermas with the desired integration of existential crises. While Habermas remains faithful to Marx in exposing the disruption of the lifeworld by the systems of economy and state (A), what counts as an undistorted social form of life in Habermas's post-Marxian critical theory (B)?[5]

A. Habermas's Agreements with Marx

Normatively, Habermas speaks about the lifeworld with some idealizations in mind. He distinguishes those rationalized components of the lifeworld that linguistically constitute our worlds: understanding, normativity, and undistorted communication. Pragmatically, there are the normatively understood resources of the lifeworld that are reproduced via communicative action and maintained in communicative ethics: background knowledge, solidary relations, and individual capacities. Ideally, one can differentiate between strategic and communicative action, even though sociologically both types of action belong to the lifeworld of actual societies. Empirically, there is no basis for reducing ideal action types to actual integration types, or of explaining communicative action by sociologically describing the lifeworld. Sociologically, one can describe lifeworld as culture, society, and personality.[6]

Habermas portrays the diremption of modern life as the uncoupling of system from lifeworld: Hegel, Marx, and other nineteenth-century thinkers bemoaned the disenchantment with and crisis of traditional life forms. The expression "posttraditional and postnational lifeworld" means, sociologically, that normative structures in modernity emerge as does the ability of individuals to raise validity claims in discourse. With this ability occurs specialized, expert cultures that accentuate one dominant validity sphere. Expert discourse is institutionalized in the distinct value spheres of science, morality and law, and art, which are represented by the university, legal structures, and the museum. With cultural rationalization, societal rationalization systems of money and administrative power create their own distinct dynamics.[7]

By allowing functional autonomy to the subsystems of money and power, does Habermas merely present liberalism in a more sophisticated dress? If both lifeworld and system operate with a certain autonomy, what impact does communicative ethics have on system at all?

Habermas's Marxist Defense of Existential Identity against System

Habermas brings Marx's critique of the capitalist life form into a two-track analysis of social (lifeworld) and systemic integration. He remains at the core of his social theory a Marxist, committed in theory and practice to an analysis of the concretely material and historical conditions of human life. Following both Marx and Kierkegaard, he critiques the colonization of the lifeworld and the individual by systems of money and state power.

The difference between Marx and Habermas lies in their theoretical imaginary: Marx focuses on limiting or dissolving the system and emancipating lifeworld imperatives. His move overlooks the irreducible relation between material (economic, administrative) and symbolic (cultural) reproductions of the lifeworld. Habermas argues that the systemic media of economy and state are in modern societies made possible, paradoxically, not by the economic base, but rather by the emergence of modern lifeworlds. One can neither explain nor critique this paradox of the two-fold societal rationalization from a monistic perspective. Habermas differentiates between communicative structures appropriated in modernity and the

uncoupled steering media of system, and exposes the pathological colonization of the lifeworld's symbolic reproduction through systemic imperatives. Habermas, however, preserves Marx's intent:

> The paradox . . . is that the rationalization of the lifeworld simultaneously gave
> rise to *both* the systematically induced reification of the lifeworld *and* the
> utopian perspective from which capitalist modernization has always appeared
> with the stain of dissolving traditional life-forms without salvaging their com-
> municative substance.[8] (emphasis in original)

Given Habermas's reading of Marx, Kierkegaard's open identity cannot be socially integrated in the capitalist or state socialist forms of life
because these do not transform traditional life forms "in such a way that
the intermeshing of cognitive–instrumental with the moral–practical and
expressive moments [three validity claims], which had obtained in everyday practice prior to its rationalization, could be retained at a higher level
of differentiation." Further, this identity cannot be complemented and
stabilized by nostalgically longing after or futuristically projecting towards
"the images of traditional forms of life." Contrary to Taylor's recent effort,
modern life cannot retrieve in a posttraditional manner the lost unity of
traditional life.[9]

Yet Habermas rejects the bourgeois cultural ascription of modern
pathologies either to secularization or to the system complexity of social
organization. He denies that alienation is a structurally necessary condition of freedom. He does not need to generalize the paradox of modern
rationalization—the loss of meaning and freedom in modern life—nor
parade Kierkegaard's individual as a complement to a totally administered
society.

Instead of melancholy skepsis, Habermas retrieves the structural possibilities of emancipation made historically and personally available in the
present age. He argues that neither the rationalization process nor the
growth of systemic complexity are pathologies per se; nor are secularization or differentiations pathologies per se. Modern pathologies occur, first,
when elitist expert cultures split off from the structures of communicative
action, and second, when material imperatives colonize symbolic reproductions.[10]

Habermas's Sympathetic Revision of Marx

Habermas's normative theory positively builds upon his revision of Marx.
The two-track model of system/lifeworld revises key elements in the monistic paradigm of society. First, Habermas gives up the "devalued concept
of totality," including Hegel's ethical totality and Marx's class struggle to
be reconciled within the fully rationalized social totality. The role of the

dual description of society is to depict distinct modes of social and systemic integration without reducing one to the other. The "steering-media" of money and power cannot be assigned under action structures. Social integration, on the other hand, cannot be reduced to systems. The lifeworld secures the inner stability of ego and group identities; system maintains the outer stability between subsystems and their different environments. These two orders can be analytically distinguished even though they describe the same society.[11]

Second, it follows that the basis of a critical social theory cannot lie in a revolutionary change that would transform the dual character of lifeworld and system into a higher totality. Social criticism occurs, on the descriptive level, in two forms of rationalization of the lifeworld and system. Normatively, the critic unmasks the pathological forms of social and system integrations on the one hand, and the domination of systemic imperatives over validity claims on the other.

This same society undergoes both identity and system crises. While all phenomena can be described under both aspects, there are differences that disallow any reductionism of communicative to functionalist reason. The rationalization of the lifeworld itself is not responsible for modern pathologies; the lost classical life form based on the good life can no longer be normative of health. The one-sided rationalization of system and the domination of functionalist over communicative reason are the objects of most conservative communitarian attempts to discredit critical modernity. Habermas does not find it helpful to evade modernity. Social pathologies must be understood for what they are—"systematically distorted communication."[12]

Habermas's analysis is both descriptive and critical of the consequences that emerged from the split between system and lifeworld. The descriptive element does not reify a norm-free sociality or a power-free lifeworld. It analytically differentiates two integrations that are otherwise concrescent. The difference between the two aspects lies in the justification of their integration: in communication, integration is justified by the normative force of validity claims; in systems, it is effected by steering-media and formal rules. Systemic action is integrated asymmetrically; it splits the steering-media (even if not the whole system as such) from the lifeworld. The lifeworld, which ideally operates on a basis of communicative symmetry, suffers when steering-media dominate the lived integrative dynamism. One cannot reduce love and communication to the value of exchange media such as money and political power. "One can . . . define the lifeworld, *negatively*, as the whole of action regions which escape the description of the steering-media subsystems"[13] (emphasis in original).

The normative force of the distinction between system and lifeworld is the critique of functionalist reason. A problem arises with the subsystems of money and administrative power when their strategic action loses all checks-and-balances through its relation to the lifeworld. In such cases morality and law are reduced to the public administration of legal rules; democracy becomes mere party politics; education and art are made to serve the military–industrial complexes of economic and technocratic school administration; and technology promotes system expansion oblivious to the lived ecology. What differentiates, then, the romantic critic of capitalism from his more sober kin is a different descriptive basis. Habermas objects to Marx in that one cannot critique the rationality of system as such, and then translate this functionalist reason within the sphere of communicative action into its opposite. One cannot critique the rationality of money and administrative power from the viewpoint of action systems.

The social problem occurs, for the first time, in the interaction between system and lifeworld. Habermas grounds this post-Marxian thesis on two points: contra Parsons and Luhmann, the concept of steering-media cannot be transferred into the spheres of culture, social integration, and socialization; contra Marx, these structural elements of social integration can be reproduced and fulfilled only via action oriented to understanding, not via the steering-media of money and power. "Meaning can be neither bought nor forced." Pathologies occur not in subsystems of money and power as such, but when system inequalities and crises begin to overwhelm lifeworld reproduction. An imperialist colonization of the lifeworld by systemic imperatives must be resisted by an ongoing limitation of these tendencies via the principles of the lifeworld.[14]

Third, the implication of these descriptive and normative analyses is a more sobering yet no less politically biting agenda for the social activist, ethician, or lawyer. The goal is no longer an activism on behalf of an earthly paradise with a fully rationalized, ideal life form, a rejectionism of modern life, or a communitarian skeptical nostalgia for the past. Modern life forms do not seem to be conceivable apart from the functional rationality of systems such as money, administrative power, or even technology. This is not an apology for systems of money and power as such. We may ask what a healthy life form, socialization, or individualization would be like. On the basis of descriptive analyses, we can critique pathologies. We can strive for a balance among the value spheres and cultural forms that emerged in modernity. Operative conditions for the possibility of social integration call for a critique of the systemic integrations by economy, power, and technology where these destroy the lifeworld resources and structures.

B. Habermas's Communicative Translation of Marx

We have seen how Habermas argues that Marx's critique of Hegel is incomplete insofar as it takes over the normative monism of ethical totality. Yet this antitotalitarian theoretical point should not implicate Habermas in a liberal apology. He does not uncouple the first world from other poor countries, and he does not defend the welfare state compromise as a crisis-free scenario. His account of the modern world—under its de-colonized community ideal—is more nuanced and socially relevant than either of the following extreme options: one cannot dissolve all traces of system from a participatory view of the lifeworld (Marx) or reduce all social integration to the observer who views society as systems of functionalist rationality (Luhmann). Marx's critique of wage labor analytically presupposes a lifeworld/system distinction, but he ties his critique of alienated labor to the Hegelian identity logic that congeals both developments under the concept of totality.[15]

This normative deficit does not allow Marx to evaluate the integrating advantage of media steering subsystems. Habermas is not an apologete for the status quo because systemic imperatives, per se, cannot be viewed as class based. They provide no direct insight into any real abstractions of the lifeworld. "[T]he young Marx conceives of the unity of system and lifeworld as did the young Hegel, on the model of a ruptured ethical totality whose abstractly divided moments are condemned to pass away." For Marx, subsystems of money and administrative power are simply "the mystified form of a class relation." Habermas admits the possibility of systemic imperatives in the economy and state as "*also* a higher and evolutionary advantageous level of integration by comparison to traditional societies" (emphasis in original). System organization cannot be explained by institutionalized class relations alone. Thus, if we could envision a possibility of a system-free modern life form, this would not necessarily deliver us into the socially emancipatory ideal.[16]

Luhmann's systems theory would not integrate Kierkegaard's individual, but rather would transform existence into a media-steered subsystem; this individual then falls from communicative action to the self-regulative imperatives of systems. Marx would help Kierkegaard by that social revolution which is to free "the realm of freedom" from the imperatives of "the realm of necessity." Marx's aim is to recover an unrestricted spontaneity of the lifeworld: he "projects a *practical–political* perspective for action, which, in its assumptions, stands opposite of the perspective tacitly adopted by systems functionalism" (emphasis in original). Habermas calls this Marxist view of social revolution "the triumph of the lifeworld over the system," but he refrains from a total revolution against the system.[17]

Habermas is too much a Kantian student of Weber and Adorno to imbibe in Marx's social optimism; nonetheless, he draws affirmation from the lifeworld sources of communicative action. "Marx's error" lies in his yielding to "the temptation of Hegelian totality-thinking." An abolition of the system of money and state power does not by itself represent that structural condition of the possibility that would allow emancipation in highly complex capitalist and state socialist societies. Against social pessimism, Habermas separates an analysis of "the level of system differentiation" in modernity from "the class-specific forms" of its institutionalization. A sobering self-limitation results: a life form that could socially integrate Kierkegaard's individual can be neither a media-steered subsystem nor the totality usurped from within the assumed "untrue whole," the system/lifeworld.[18]

Further, Habermas asks how Marx can differentiate between the social evolution that led to the emergence of modern identity formation and "the reification of posttraditional lifeworlds." He critiques the descriptively and normatively undeterminate character of Marx's concept of alienation. Marx's concept of alienation points either to a past Aristotelian or to a projected Hegelian ideal of ethical life. Later, Marx translates the Romantic ideal of self-realization into the formal ideal of distributive justice. Yet his theory of value is, says Habermas, unable to treat separately real abstractions (reification of posttraditional lifeworlds) and differentiations of the lifeworld's symbolic structures.[19]

Marx's concept of alienation applies to the uncoupling of life forms from their traditional contexts and to structural injustices due to systemic transformation of concrete into abstract life. But modern identity and differentiated systems cannot be equated with alienation:

> At the stage of post-traditional forms of life, the pain that the separation of culture, society, and personality *also* causes those who grow into modern societies and form their identities within them counts as a process of individuation and not alienation. In an extensively rationalized lifeworld, reification can be measured only against the conditions of communicative sociation, and not against the nostalgically loaded, frequently romanticized past of premodern forms of life.[20] (emphasis in original)

A revised Marxist critique of real abstractions (the reification of exchange equivalents into use values, the alienation of concrete labor into wage, the commodification of human relations) cannot be read directly off the economy and state. Habermas, therefore, reconstructs both social evolution and the developmental competencies of contemporaries in modern societies. He wants to account for both the crises in individuation and those due to system-induced alienation. Marx's theory of value attends to the economic base directly from a global theory, yet the base can become only an object of empirical research projects. His value theory presupposes a philosophy of history, and thus remains both uncritical and insufficiently empirical. It is uncritical in that it identifies every systemic imperative with real abstractions; it suffers from scientism by inferring distortions of life forms from an economic theory alone.

Finally, Habermas objects to Marx's generalization of the specific class conflicts. The contradictions of a capitalist form of life cannot be reduced to a fundamental class conflict, or, further, to economic subsystems. Habermas exposes Marx's oversights of reifying administrative power, of distortions in private spheres of justice, and of both consumer and vocational

roles. Marx's theory of value reduces an analysis of the systemic colonization of the lifeworld in modern societies to a class specific domination of
concrete labor by the media of money. Because of this reductionism in
description and in normative criteria, Habermas concludes, Marx can
explain neither the ecology, peace, or women's movements in late capitalist life forms, nor the rise of dissent in parallel public spheres and their
nonpolitical politics.[21]

Marx, by limiting his analysis to a critique of political economy, cannot account for late capitalist and state socialist life forms. Habermas does
not seem to refute Marx's labor theory of value, but rather its one-sided,
reductionist economism of base and superstructure. While one can assign
developmental primacy to economy in the rise of modern societies, it is
misleading to stylize the subsystem of state power as a superstructure.
Habermas fills this gap in Marx by offering a two-media concept of money
and administrative power in both public and private domains where colonization of lifeworld *may* occur.[22]

Habermas's Innovations in Critical Social Theory

Critical theory comprises several interrelated moves: it is an epistemologi-
cal critique, thereby exposing contradictions within a dominant social theory;
it is a social critique, which aims at conceptual dilemmas by unmasking
their origin in a particular form of life; and it critiques the status quo, since
utopian possibilities emerge when one confronts the present age. My lead
question is: how can one articulate the conditions of the possibility of a
nonoppressive life form that could integrate Kierkegaard's nonrepressive
identity ideal? Habermas enhances Marx's critical hermeneutics of capitalist modernization. He offers the formal conditions of the possibility of
communication in which one exhibits nonauthoritarian and receptive ego
boundaries. He claims that studying society from these two angles—the
participatory view of the lifeworld (language media) and the observer view
of system (the steering-media of money and power)—allows the theorist
of society to become "critical" in the senses of epistemicly, socially, and
concretely engaged critique. One must expose social sciences and the contemporary reality these disciplines grasp, as well as the system induced
pathologies that in modern societies prevent life forms from developing
potentials for learning.[23]

Habermas ambitiously offers his revisionist posture as a basis for the
new feminist, peace, and ecology movements. I say ambitiously because
all these currents likewise occasion specific problems for Habermas's formal model. We might arrive at a consensus in which we could decide not
to worry about future generations, either from the perspective of our global
environment or on account of the consequences of a justified war. We could
also arrive at a consensus that would manifestly include feminist voices in

communication, and yet would prevent the gender perspective from entering the very theory of this consensus. These temporal and gendered dimensions seem to be bypassed in Habermas's theory, which longs to assign practical relevance to these movements. I am not sure that the communications model cannot be challenged to take these problems into account, but I do not think that Habermas has addressed them sufficiently.

So where can we legitimately affirm the strong social relevance of Habermas's model? Unlike Marx and the early critical theory, Habermas does not identify real abstractions with the modern rationalization of the lifeworld as such. His social theory retrieves Marx's critical hermeneutics in "an analysis that at once traces the rationalization of lifeworlds *and* the growth in complexity of media-steered subsystems, and that keeps the paradoxical nature of their interference in sight" (emphasis in original). Modern rationalization is paradoxical. It frees the structural possibilities of the lifeworld to move towards posttraditional and postnational identity-formation and yet allows for a distinct system rationality to destroy these very possibilities. Real abstractions of the lifeworld give rise to two sets of problems. Pathologies occur imperceptibly within lifeworlds: "communicatively intermeshed interaction can get caught because deception and self-deception can gain objective power in an everyday practice reliant on the facticity of validity claims." Systems can dominate communication in modern life and split it off from any substantive contexts.[24]

Wanting to integrate socially Kierkegaard's radicalized individual, Habermas moves beyond that historical materialism that follows Marx's concretism and the early critical theory's image of "the totally administered society." This two-fold move results from Habermas's rejection of the normative role of totality thinking, whether in terms of Hegel's ethical life, Marx's life totally free from system imperatives, or Adorno's negatively material utopia.[25]

While the lifeworld figures as a horizon of communicative action, the critical theory based on this communication–theoretic concept can account for the devaluation of traditions and the colonization of the lifeworld by system. Habermas's social critique has two aspects: it articulates the normative criteria of communicative rationality (i.e., "the possibilities of a rational conduct of life)"; and it carries a sobered up utopian view that jettisons mixing up "a highly developed infrastructure of *possible* forms of life with the concrete historical totality of a *successful* form of life"[26] (emphasis in original).

Both aspects provide a check on the two-fold illusion of reifying and utopian thinking. Reifying thought totalizes one aspect of rationality, one validity claim to the exclusion of others. Uncritical utopianism is tempted by the deducing of a wholly rational life form "directly from the concepts of a decentered world understanding and of procedural rationality." This utopianism is the obverse side of communitarianism and a complement of reified, scientistic rationality: "[i]t would be senseless to want to judge . . . as a whole, *the totality of a form of life*, under individual aspects of rationality"[27] (emphasis in original).

The two aspects of critique that I have outlined guard against positing a concretistic ideal. Habermas counsels sobriety; one cannot seek a grand narrative that would unify or eliminate modern value spheres. One can balance cognitive, moral, and aesthetic rationality. "But the attempt to provide an equivalent for what was once intended by the idea of the good life should not mislead us into deriving this idea from the formal concept of reason with which modernity's decentered understanding of the world left us."[28]

A theory of communicative action and ethics, in cooperation with the social sciences, ought to clarify "the normative foundations of a critical theory of society." The developmental, reconstructive, fallibilist, and coherent character of several of Habermas's strategies safeguards his normative basis against foundationalism. Habermas's theory does not generate but rather responds to the problems that claim our understanding. "The theory of communicative action can explain why this is so: the development of society must *itself* give rise to the problem situations that *objectively* afford contemporaries a privileged access to the general structures of the lifeworld" (emphasis in original). Marx's "basis" cannot be limited to the economy. A pragmatically understood basis provides all the problems that structure our questions.[29]

Toward a Social Form of Life for Kierkegaard's Existential Individual

Habermas argues that the cognitive development of competent individuals in modern societies can be reconstructed by abstracting from "historical dynamics of events" and from "the historical concretion of forms of life." The formal–pragmatic reconstruction of communicative competencies offers, thus, the normative criteria for evaluating life forms. Critical theory commences neither with traditions nor with positively or negatively material utopias because one can be materially concrete (i.e., socially existential), without being reductionistically materialistic:

> [Critical theory] must orient itself to the range of learning processes that is opened up at a given time by a historically attained level of learning. It must refrain from critically evaluating and normatively ordering totalities, forms of life and cultures, and life-contexts and epochs *as a whole*.[30] (emphasis in original)

Let me sum up the conditions of the possibility of that life form for Kierkegaard's crisis identity, which Habermas envisions in this developmentally and empirically testable hypothesis: *if* worldviews complement and socially integrate identities, *then* the process of ego and world decentration gives us the *structural* possibility of "open worldviews" that would integrate posttraditional and postnational identity by forming nonauthoritarian and receptive ego boundaries. Even though Piaget's and Kohlberg's developmental logics quite possibly overlook gender specifics, yet, unlike in Hegel and Marx, they do not prejudice, in principle, the necessity of certain developments. From his retrospective glance at the stages of cognitive and moral development, Habermas reconstructs and makes available for intersubjective testing the dynamics of learning processes. He hopes to retrieve from this test the criteria of critique that have become available in modern lifeworlds.[31]

3.2. THE PRESENT AGE IN EXISTENTIAL AND LEGITIMATION CRISES

Habermas defines the individual as a locus of identity with competencies for communication, interpretation, and criticism. This definition is broad enough to accommodate preconventional, traditional, and posttraditional identities; it allows for variations in development and for cultural invariants; and it prevents concrete life forms from forming a supertotality.

> The complementary concepts of communicative action and lifeworld introduce a difference that . . . is not reabsorbed into a higher unity of its moments. . . . Otherwise, we would hypostatize the process of mutual understanding into an event of mediation . . . and inflate the lifeworld into the totality of a higher-level subject. . . .[32]

The outcome of this complementarity between communicative action and lifeworld is what I called ethical totalities: each individual is a whole, each arises out of the common pool of communicative resources, and each is an embedded, not disencumbered, self. An individual is never fully identified with a lifeworld because one is an interpretative and a critical whole. One uses the resources and structures of the lifeworld to keep one's distance from it and from other individuals, even though this is never an absolute distancing. Just as there is no totality that could free us from the task of self-choice, so there is also no self-transparency that would make this task risk free. The character of this risk becomes apparent in Habermas's thought experiments with the structural variations of the lifeworld and with cultural rationalization (A). They develop his concern with identity crisis and our age; they are likewise in the backdrop of his critical social question to Kierkegaard (B).[33]

A. Habermas's Thought Experiments in Critical Social Theory

The Structural Variations of the Lifeworld

Habermas wants us to imagine an undistorted lifeworld with healthy communication. What, then, would happen in the structures of the lifeworld if healthy reproduction lost the security of traditions and had to be maintained "by a risky search for consensus"? One may also ask: how is an unrepressed and open identity at all possible without such a security?[34]

Habermas argues that from concrete linguistic and cultural horizons we would arrive at abstracted "universal lifeworld structures." First, from devalued traditions and nation–states we could retain two clues: one's vulnerable identity, whose intersubjective dispossession is to be compensated for by posttraditional morality and law; and maieutical tie to an unobjectifiable a priori of language and culture that serve as resources for reproducing the symbolic life of knowledges, solidarities, and competencies. Both clues are retrieved in the presuppositions of communication and argumentation. Second, forms of legitimation and the moral point of view would be differentiated from particular solidarities. Third, individual competencies would be less tied to "concrete thinking" and accept more operational variability. This growth in freedom does not distill an abstract, minimal, and disrelational self. An ability to abstract from concrete operations of thought, from particular solidarities, and from conventional identities suggests a rich individuality. Habermas enumerates the structural conditions that are applicable to this lived possibility:[35]

> [F]or culture, a condition of the constant revision of traditions that have been unthawed, that is, that have become reflective; for society, a condition of the dependence of legitimate orders upon formal and ultimately discursive procedures for establishing and grounding norms; for personality, a condition of the risk-filled self-direction of a highly abstract ego-identity.

We have here posttraditional and postnational lifeworlds:

> There arise structural pressures towards the critical dissolution of guaranteed knowledge, the establishment of generalized values and norms, and self-directed individuation (*since abstract ego-identities point toward self-realization in autonomous life projects*). (emphasis added)

Habermas's proposal for complementing and stabilizing Kierkegaard's self-choosing individual presupposes that posttraditional and postnational identity emerges along with the structural conditions of its possibility only in decentered lifeworlds. Kierkegaard's honest attitude requires an intense distancing from culture, even if he does not address the social condition of identity integration. Yet, Habermas ignores that this latter requirement makes it impossible to explain this radically open attitude as a form of ideology.

I come back to this point in the next thought experiment. Here I note that for Habermas an individual is stabilized not by "an intensification within the dimensions of the subject's relation-to-self," but "under conditions of an ever more extensive and ever more finely woven net of linguistically generated intersubjectivity." But Habermas's abstract ego identity should be read from Kierkegaard's angle as "abstracted from" traditional contexts, and thus, intensified existentially. The honest individual is sustained in the same measure as

> [T]he rationalized lifeworld secures the contexts of meaning with the discontinuous tools of critique; [as] it preserves the context of social integration by the risky means of an individually isolated universalism; and [as] it sublimates the overwhelming power of the genealogical nexus into a fragile and vulnerable universality by means of an extremely individualized socialization.

To emerge with posttraditional and postnational identity means that one has no other means for sustaining concrete life than these "abstractly differentiated structures of the lifeworld."

Posttraditional or postnational abstraction and lived concretion are therefore internally related. One can appropriate only what one already is in tradition. The "post-" lies in the fact that one must appropriate oneself and one's culture or tradition. "In the structurally differentiated lifeworld, we merely acknowledge a principle that was in operation from the beginning: that socialization takes place in the same proportion as individuation, just as, inversely, individuals are constituted socially." The rationalization of the lifeworld, paradoxically, strengthens the continuities of traditions, solidarities, and identities. I say paradoxically because I have in mind the misplaced communitarian worry that by becoming posttraditional and postnational one must disregard traditions, cultures, and community values. Yet, we have seen that the problem of the value skeptic differs from that of someone with an honest attitude. The outcome of this difference delivers us to Kierkegaard's paradox: in the present age traditional and national continuities are available only through sustained acts of self-appropriation.

The shared lifeworld provides the resources of communication. But these resources give one not only a self-generation of conventions. Radical self-choice calls for a deepening reflexive and hypothetical distance from tradition. Harnessing the universal lifeworld structures admits, then, a plurality of life forms because open identity embodies an abstractly impartial and existentially partial attitude towards traditions:

> [T]here are family resemblances among the plurality of totalities of life forms; they overlap and interlock, but they are not embraced in turn by some super-

totality. Multiplicity and diffusion arise in the course of an abstraction process through which *contents* of particular lifeworlds are set off ever more starkly from the universal *structures* of the lifeworld.[36] (emphasis in original)

Cultural Rationalization and Ideological Distortions of Communication

In this thought experiment Habermas studies how ideological legitimation sacralizes the domains of culture. The paradox of rationalization shows those conditions in social evolution that must be satisfied for the colonization of lifeworld by system to take place. One condition is the "secularization of the bourgeois culture." If "culture loses just those formal properties that enabled it to take on ideological functions," then system can no longer hide behind the forms of understanding that distort communication, Habermas argues.[37]

The forms of understanding viewed from the level of contemporary communicators give Habermas a muster of historical–ideological formations. Ideology is, then, that legitimation which systemically restricts communication. In the forms of understanding this restriction is depicted as a structural violence. By prejudging worldviews in a predefined manner, symbolic reproduction takes on a character of objectively legitimated deception.[38]

Habermas explains this possibility of hidden structural self- and other-deception by the rationality differential between sacred and profane culture. He identifies all "religiosity" with metaphysics, sacred culture, and ideology:

> The mode of legitimation in civilizations is thus based on a form of understanding that systematically limits possibilities of communication owing to its failure to differentiate sufficiently among the various validity claims. . . . If we further consider that between *the sacred and the profane domains* there are differentials in authority and rationality . . . we have then the points of view relevant to ordering the forms of understanding in a systematic sequence.[39] (emphasis added)

Analogically to Marx's critique of the political economy for legitimating the systemic distortion of the bourgeois lifeworld, Habermas examines religious–metaphysical worldviews. He extends beyond Marx's economistic reductionism. Marx was optimistic that the spontaneity of the base market, freed from the legitimating superstructure of capitalist ideology, can deliver us to a deception free lifeworld. This optimism has proved wrong in both liberal and socialist markets. Therefore, cultural critique in the early Frankfurt School aims at democracy in both the market and the public spheres. By describing late capitalism and the parallel cultures of dissent in state socialism, Habermas's communications theory can descriptively and normatively fill this gap in Marx.

I want to raise two related problems. First, if modernity can bridge the differential between sacred and profane realms, would a communicative mode of legitimation, while necessary, provide a sufficient resistance to the distortions of modern life forms? Second, if the secularization of bourgeois culture is the structural condition of the possibility of forming an open identity, how could Kierkegaard's self-critical view play an ideological role? If in principle it cannot, then either it should be accounted for in Habermas's muster, or his need to profanize Kierkegaard does not fit the case.[40]

The first issue is how to resist the distortion of posttraditional identity, how to create public spheres of nonviolence. Habermas gives us structural, not existential, conditions for this possibility. In capitalist and state socialist societies the reification of modern lifeworlds is not class specific, but rather occurs via mass culture. Secularization leads both to rationalized identity formation and to the rise of "the second generation of ideologies" (e.g., nationalism and fundamentalism). These ideologies offer consolation in the face of modernization effects on alienated traditions via deliberately modern means: they moralize claims to autonomy and to political participation; and they aestheticize claims to authenticity and to expressive self-presentation. These second-generation ideologies appeal to "totalizing conceptions of order" across the spectrum from political left to right. When "the communicative practice of everyday life no longer affords any niches for the structural violence of ideologies," then fragmented and anomic individuals struggle against the systemic colonization that wants to assimilate all to its totality.[41]

Constructed systemic totalities, via a fragmented identity that has become incapable of multicultural co-existence, replace the sacred role of tradition. Habermas unmasks this as Western ethnocentrism: "When stripped of their ideological veils, the imperatives of autonomous subsystems make their way into the lifeworld from the outside—like colonial masters coming into a tribal society—and force a process of assimilation upon it." He abandons Marx's ideology critique for an analysis of fragmentation and anomie in cultural modernity. He no longer calls for global revolutionary praxis, but for empowering modern culture with resources of communicative action.[42]

Habermas's options for cultural over ideology critique and for democratic rational procedures over revolutionary activism leave vague how the resistance to colonization can come from the individuals who in modernity may be integrated on the basis of rationalized identity formation alone. How can an open identity sustain against new ideologies? Habermas appeals to autonomous action, yet he must support the motivational weakness and the cognitive uncertainty of communicative ethics by the positive law. How can the law, albeit legitimated by rational procedures and morality, assist individuals to resist any institutionalization of deception? Marx's strength of resistance comes from substantive–utopian contents; communitarian strength comes from traditionalist contents; and system–theoretical strength lies in bypassing the problem by reducing the lifeworld structures to systemic self-steering. Habermas shows the danger in both material utopias and system reductionism: his critical ideal offers a structure of concrete resistance to system in communicative action, morality, and law. Yet I argue in Parts II and III that this ideal does not provide the mode of resistance applicable to that endangered self-choosing identity which is to be integrated in modern life. It does not articulate that lived condition of possible resistance to new ideologies and anomie which is necessary for modern identity formation when lifeworlds have lost their structural ideological function.

My second question suggests why Habermas's muster of ideological forms of understanding cannot accommodate Kierkegaard's case. The problem does not lie in a Kierkegaard who imposes untranslatable claims on discourse, but rather in a Habermas who structurally prejudges concretion. From what standpoint in the muster can Habermas view Kierkegaard as his ally against nationalism and fundamentalism? Do Kierkegaard and Habermas interpret the same experience of secularization differently? For both, modern culture has lost its traditional capacity for ideology formation. In Habermas's muster this is marked by the total reduction of language and culture to the "transparent" validity basis of communicative rationality and a reduction of the sacred to the profane. But Kierkegaard marks this cultural modernity by attending to the ongoing identity crises, which do not afford any such decisive transparency. His existential crisis individual is already stripped of ideological veils, and so would not encounter in the structural possibilities of communicative action and ethics a sufficient way of resisting fragmentation, anomie, and the emergence of new ideological forms of understanding in the present age. This scenario poses a serious problem for Habermas's project, thereby frustrating his social integration of Kierkegaard's individual.[43]

B. Habermas's Proposal for a Permanent Democratic Revolution

In Chapter 1 I introduced Habermas's permanent democratic revolution with an aim to integrate Kierkegaard's vulnerable crisis identity into deliberative democracy. I will discuss here how this proposal learns from the foregoing communicative translation of Marx. Habermas reformulates social revolution and links his reading of Kierkegaard to the thesis of legitimation crisis.

Habermas's Communicative Rendition of Social Revolution

Habermas's democratic revolution sobers up from the theoretical and historical failures of Marxism: it cannot resolve the riddle of history; it can be neither a limiting concept nor a private regulative idea; and it may not embody a utopia that idealizes the past or the future. "In this *concretistic reading* socialism is no longer a goal, it was never realistically [such a] goal" (emphasis in original). This sociopolitical sobriety does not diminish the angularity of a critical imaginary. True, Habermas shifts from the macro-subject of emancipation (class, self, people) to a reciprocal structure of communication. But this move both revises and sustains Marx's core intuition about the radically egalitarian character of political and economic democracy. This "placeless place" of equality—the sovereignty of the people—lies at the heart of a permanent democratic revolution that remains positively permanent (while concretely operative it cannot rest in a particular life form), democratic (since it occurs in institutional, cultural, and public spaces), and always a revolution (because practical questions cannot be solved ontologically or metaphysically).[44]

While Habermas's theoretical sobriety matches his political asceticism, it nevertheless commits him neither to a one-dimensionally negating skepticism nor to quietism. His self-restraint, however, makes him seem unattractive to those leftists who have critiqued Stalinist regimes in theory but have experienced neither the fascist nor the red terror. It is difficult to fault Habermas for not wanting to venture beyond a sociopolitical practice of fallibilism. To the charges that he does not develop the substantive implications of his communicative model, nor does he fill in the imaginary of radical democracy with a clear and distinct path to material justice, one can apply that Ockham's razor that guards against dangerous historical naïveté. In his refusal of leftists icons, Habermas follows Adorno's negative thinking after Auschwitz.[45]

What then deserves the name of social revolution if Habermas's project for a radical democratic republic shies away from a substantially specified imaginary? A nuanced reading requires that we ask what Habermas's formal position implies, even though this is not specified in any economic and political action programme. I limit myself here to Honneth's derivation of substantive justice among the concrete implications of communicative ethics.[46]

Habermas retrieves the meaning of social revolution under a normative projection of those solidarities that are found in the lifeworld and applied to complex modern societies. In cases of ruptured relations, the solidarity among the shaken who are excluded from communication becomes the revolutionary, projected project. The conditions of the possibility of communicative action structurally imply that in order to sustain dialogic reciprocity there ought to be social, political, and economic reciprocity. Communicative ethics grounds the critical social analysis of distorted life forms. The revolutionary role of solidarities among the excluded (whether through class, race, or gender differences), or ecology or peace groupings, cannot be predestined since it arises from practice. Habermas's communicative rethinking of political and economic egalitarianism seems to accommodate, or at least not to exclude, some form of democratic multiculturalism; yet it would not be defined by any of its historical versions. The criterion of emancipatory critique lies neither in existing socialist regimes nor in the complex market economy but rather in the determinate negation of both. The morally normative measure consists in the principle of social integration, which may banish from communication no one and no generalizable need.

Since Habermas gives social revolution a new semantic through communicative and sober criteria, the revolutionary events of 1989 change nothing in the radical projection of lifeworld solidarities upon complex societal structures. If anything, the revolutionary resilience emerges from the crises of state socialism. Habermas concludes with the biblical metaphor of the ever narrower passage that leads through the "eye of the needle." For those who became the shaken victims of history the way of solidary relations leads through the radical–reformist self-critique of capitalist identity. For Habermas, today's socialism passes into something else not with the revolutions of 1989 but with the change in the principle of capitalist social integration.

Existential and Legitimation Crises

To account for the recent ruptures in both welfare state capitalism and state socialism one can turn to Habermas's radicalized thesis of crisis. The notion of crisis implies a normative criterion. Because in Habermas's revisionist Marxism the state is an autonomous steering medium parallel to the autonomous media of the economy, crisis is possible to detect beyond the economic distortions of political and sociocultural life. He envisions that identity crises in complex societies result from failures in systemic integration. This crisis theorem is retained in the thesis that the rationalization of the lifeworld leads both to the splitting off of system from the lifeworld and to the colonization of the lifeworld by system. The noneconomic effects of this colonial hegemony by money and technocracy are rationality, legitimation, and motivational crises.[47]

Modern politicians are stuck between catering to economic bosses and to common welfare. The welfare state may no longer disregard public needs and take the side of the capital. (This was even less possible for the communist–bourgeois class in state socialism.) The failure to reconcile the demands of the market with lived solidarities leads to a *rationality deficit* that satisfies neither party. Moreover, the modern state, such as the United States during economic recession or Germany after its unification, lives under the constant threat of identity breakdown, since it can neither exist without revenues from the capital nor without the mass loyalty of its citizens. With the withdrawal of popular support, the state experiences a *legiti-*

mation deficit. Finally, when the bourgeois elite or communist nomen-clature fail to generate meaning for action, then social integration exhibits an anomie of *motivation deficit*.

Habermas indicates that this legitimation crisis is intrinsically linked to an identity or motivation crisis, and the motivation crisis occurs because of the leveling of traditions. These crises emerge in rationalized forms of life. Kierkegaard meets the early signs of these crises with a resolve that neither legitimizes political, educational, media, and religious establish-ments, nor supplies them with culturally ideological motives. Kierkegaard's individualism neither falls into anomie nor leaps to counterfeit utopianism; one is to remain, in Habermas's words and in Kierkegaard's thoroughly honest praxis, metaphysically disconsolate. When in Chapter 10 we meet Kierkegaard's unmasking of the leveling in the present age, we will find a striking analogy to Habermas's crisis theorem.

Habermas argues that the intuition of communicative ethics and expe-rimental countercultures already determines to a large degree today's socialization and individualization processes. This rather Hegelian projec-tion of rationality into our not so rational world is intelligible as a descrip-tive account of the emerging trends to postnational identity. I do not think that Habermas is justifying any particular status quo. The formation of postnational identity and constitutional patriotism is both a fallible prob-ability pacesetter and a revolutionary–moral imperative. If communicative ethics anticipates an undistorted life form, then being socially integrated on its basis projects a future that conflicts with the present systems of politics and economy. Habermas expects two nonconventional and counterinsti-tutional outcomes of the motivational and legitimation crises: either indi-viduals become alienated and withdraw, or they become protesting radi-cals who refuse to be integrated into the present age.

Did not Habermas encounter these two crisis outcomes in Kierke-gaard's endangered individual, who emerged from despair into protest and a postnational attitude? Habermas's Copenhagen question about how the self-critical attitude could be socially integrated under the present condi-tions of modernity must be read with a freshness indicating an entirely different angle from the received view of Kierkegaard! The question implies not so much an objection to Kierkegaard as to the present age: Kierke-gaard's radicalized individual, just as in communicative ethics, comes into confrontation with the nonpersonal, antisocial, and uncritical imperatives of economy and state power.

CONCLUSIONS

I sum up Habermas's reading of Marx on the backdrop of six interpreta-tions of the ideas of 1989. Habermas depicts two symmetrical relations:

the first group is positively oriented towards Marx; the second negatively. In the first he critiques the Stalinist, Leninist, and reform communist readings. The Stalinist lacks resources for evaluating the destruction of secret service and state technocracy. The Leninist designates 1989 as a "conservative revolution" that sets back the communist orthodoxy. The reformed communist continues Dubček's socialism with the human face of 1968, but is unable to revolutionize state socialism into a democratic one before its shipwreck. The options of the socialist–market economy and the fallible reform communism are bypassed by the events of 1989. In the second group, first, the prevalent ethos of the present age co-opts the events of 1989 and proclaims the end of all revolutions and critical rationality, but it overlooks how modern revolutionary ideas and classical schemes strip the totalitarian regimes of power. In place of the celebrated *posthistoire*, 1989 revives the sovereignty of the people, human rights, and democratic institutions, on the one hand, and nationalist strife on the other. Second, the anticommunist finds in 1989 the endpoint of 1917, but falsely generalizes the Cold War era onto the entire present age. Third, the liberal depicts 1989 as the end of the last totalitarian domination, the end of ideology, and a return to law, the market, and pluralism. The liberal overlooks the present unwillingness to move towards radical democracy. Against the first group and the anticommunist Habermas raises his critique of Marx. In the second group he both rejects the claim of *posthistoire* as precocious and corrects the lukewarm liberal stance. A radical democratic republic with a permanent democratic revolution is to cure the leftist melancholy skepsis.[48]

How can modern identity be socially integrated without appealing either to concrete traditions or to a material utopia of justice? Habermas formulates a theorem with a two-pronged structural condition of possibility:

> [O]nly that universal morality can be defended with good grounds which honors as rational the universal norms and universalizable interests; and only that concept of ego-identity can offer today an appropriate orientation for learning processes which secures in complex role-systems at the same time freedom and individualization of single individuals.

He identifies this condition by three characteristics. The reflexive model of equal participation in communication—not simply in a territorial, nationalist, church, or party organization—allows for a continuous identity formation. Further, neither ego identity nor morality is integrated via concrete worldviews, but in fallible procedures. Finally, identity is not stabilized by traditions or material utopias, but rather by the rational motivation of discourse.[49]

Next, I will discuss Habermas's thesis that qualitative, existential identity requires for its integration the generic identity of the generalized other. In Part II, I will address one problem that emerged in this chapter: Habermas wants to resist every totalizing perspective, self- and other-deception, and system colonization. He provides the necessary structural conditions for this task in his revisionary, formal reading of Marx—in communicatively retrieved posttraditional and postnational lifeworlds. Yet Habermas's formal notions of moral autonomy, communication, and the projected emancipatory ideal remain insufficiently concrete unless they are harnessed by the radical honesty of both the individual and the community.

CHAPTER 4

Self-Realization
and Self-Determination

W hat happens to Kierkegaard's individual who is socially integrated in Habermas's communicative model? Does the intersubjectivist view of identity preserve this individual as someone capable of resisting the system and transcending the collective? Does the model privilege the generalized over the concrete other? Does communicative ethics project the ideal of a communication community, and yet not an ideally honest mode of communication?

There are no explicit Kierkegaard references in Habermas's *Theory of Communicative Action*. Yet I will highlight that when he speaks of the qualitative continuity of self, Habermas aims not only at generalized but also the concrete self- and other-relations. In the discussion of self-realization in the Mead section, Habermas adopts that same "existential mode of expression" that he later uses in his commentary on Kierkegaard. This qualitative aspect of Habermas's theory is often overlooked by the critics of its formalism. I developed the origin of this critique in the context of both Hegel's objections to Kant, and Habermas's reading of Hegel with Kantian means. I highlighted Habermas's appropriation of Kierkegaard as a form of resistance to nationalism and fundamentalism. Some communitarians, Marxists, and feminists, however, object that Habermas privileges the generalized, regulative ideal of the other to the encounter with the concrete, multicultural, lived other.[1]

Here I note two types of such objections: first, some communitarians and Marxists critique the abstractness of the modern conception of selfhood and the lack of concretion in the procedural moral theories inspired by Kant. They attack as fiction autonomous morality because it builds upon the notion of an unencumbered self.[2] Second, some critical feminists argue that Habermas attends to the generalized other of morality but neglects the concrete other of needs. The articulation of gendered identity provides the key strategy for reversing patriarchal, hegemonic relations. Habermas's generic impartiality seems partial to the male viewpoint insofar as it excludes from the formal architectonic of moral discourse considerations of participants qua gendered.[3]

I situate my Kierkegaardian rejoinder to Habermas on the backdrop of his rebuttal to these types of objections. My reading of Habermas is both a "yes" and a "no" to these criticisms: it is a yes insofar as I find Habermas inadequately articulating qualitative identity within moral theory; it is a no insofar as, on the one hand, I find resources within his account that he has not tapped, and on the other, as I will show in Part II, because his reply to the above critiques cannot bypass Kierkegaard's challenge to Kant's formalism and Hegel's communitarianism as Kierkegaard hits upon the core of Habermas's model.

I want to engage the Habermas–Mead thesis that individualization occurs through socialization in terms of the task of self-realization: I will discuss Habermas's explication of Hegel's notion of spirit not only with Kant's but also with Mead's means; and, inversely, Habermas's reading of Mead through both the early Hegel and a communicatively reformed Kant (4.1). I will then examine the Habermas–Durkheim thesis that the linguistification of the sacred explains why the secularization of bourgeois culture is the condition of the possibility for forming one's identity posttraditionally and postnationally (4.2).

4.1. HABERMAS'S READING OF MEAD: INDIVIDUAL AND COMMUNITY

I discussed how Hegel's conception of spirit, when understood as a grammar of intersubjective relations, enhances the Habermas–Mead thesis that individualization occurs via socialization. One is individualized through the same medium that socializes. One learns to take both universal and individual perspectives, thereby becoming self-realized and self-determined. "Membership in the ideal communication community is, in Hegelian terms, constitutive of both the I as universal and the I as individual." I will develop Habermas's reading of Mead's genetic account of identity by commenting on spontaneous and social identity in Mead (A), and then evaluating Habermas's privileging of the generic self-determination over the qualitative self-realization of identity (B).[4]

A. Mead: The Spontaneous and Social Aspects of Identity

In "Fragments on Ethics" Mead discloses the key concern that inspires Habermas's communicative ethics. He wants to work out "an ethical theory on a social basis" in order to give Kant's categorical imperative "its social equivalent." Mead explains that the categorical imperative is possible because "we take the attitude of the entire community," and because the identity, form, and content of moral judgments are social. Not only the form but the content can be universalized, because if the individual is an end in itself and society a kingdom of ends, then one need not sacrifice one's narrow self-interest to formal duty but can become "a larger self." This larger self is not to be understood monologically in Hegel's emphatic institutional sense. Mead's concern parallels Habermas's reading of Hegel with the Kantian means: "When we reach the question of what is right . . . the only test we can set up is whether we have taken into account every interest involved." To introduce contents into the categorical imperative means to work out "a social hypothesis."[5]

Expanding the Individual Spontaneity into a Community Perspective

What is the link between the individual and community? Does communicative ethics operate with too weak a notion of the individual who can neither resist systemic imperatives nor transcend the community? How could Mead limit himself to a behavioral study of self-direction and speak for one's creativity?

Mead's own account of the social genesis of meaning and of the self, unlike Hegel's, admits strong notions of innovative and spontaneous individuality: "A . . . [human] has to keep . . . [her] self-respect, and it may be that . . . [she] has to fly in the face of the whole community in preserving this self-respect." Against the monologism and decisionism recorded in the received view of the self-critical attitude, Mead expands the notion of identity: an individual can resist system or transcend community "from the point of view of what . . . [she] considers a higher and better society than that which exists." If we reject the biologism through which Mead, like Freud, reads this spontaneity of a socialized individual, we can view his method of morality as both social and existential:

> Both of these are essential to the moral conduct: that there should be a social organization and that the individual should maintain . . . [herself]. The method for taking into account all of those interests which make up society on the one hand and the individual on the other is the method of morality.[6]

Mead adopts and reformulates the Hegelian definition of the spirit, and sustains a strong sense of the Kantian individual. Identity comprises two aspects: the hermeneutical, social aspect contains attitudes of others internalized in the self. This is the "me," one's given community (*Sittlichkeit*), which can explain neither creativity nor the ability of a reflexive role distance from tradition. But self-direction allows for both moral action and self-realization. This critical self-direction and reflexive role distance is the "I." For Mead this capacity for spontaneous action arises from the anarchy of biological drives. Its spontaneity is thus never absorbed by society.

With this two-pronged capacity for identity formation one can expand one's horizon through generalizations of the attitude of the other. One relates to others and self by internalizing such social activities as play, games, and symbolic interactions; one transcends *Sittlichkeit* by projecting one's self-relation onto the generalized other. Mead envisions that a social universal can expand individual identity by making it into a moral self within an ideally democratic society. The moral self maintains and stabilizes the spontaneous one. Unlike Hegel's absolutized state that legitimates the unethical and immoral surd of abstract international relations, Mead allows for a resisting and transcending of the aporias of the nationalist politics of identity and difference in the League of Nations. Not only atomic individualists but warring groups are prompted to expand their provincialism. Taking the attitude of the generalized other does not lead to the death of the individual or of national identities and traditions, but rather to their expansion into a pluralistic community.[7]

Social and Existential Dimensions of Self-Relation

Personal identity exhibits a "social structure." I communicate with myself insofar as I respond to and internalize that which is addressed to me. Let me apply this, Mead's insight, to my reading of Kierkegaard. We can reconstruct an existential mode only by an explanation of the genesis of self-relation together with other-relatedness. Phenomena such as gesture communication, inner speech, and indirect communication presuppose an audience. Habermas adopts this explanation when he notes that both Kierkegaard and Rousseau address their journals and writing to the general community.[8]

One's self-relation is affected via an expected response from the other:

> One separates the significance of what he is saying to others from the actual speech and gets it ready before saying it. He thinks it out, and perhaps writes it in the form of a book; but it is still a part of social intercourse in which one is addressing other persons and at the same time addressing one's self, and in which one controls the address to other persons by the response made to one's own gesture.[9]

The geneses of the self and of meanings are coextensive. Significant symbols are those gestures or meanings that arouse a response in us and the other. Speaking and hearing audible communication best satisfies this possibility of self-correcting response. The "meaning" of my communication is secured by the other's expected completion of it. "Communicative rationality" and "thinking" imply "that the type of response which we call out in others should be so called out in ourselves. . . ."[10]

The following consideration is crucial in viewing Habermas's communicative translation of Kierkegaard: one becomes monological and decisionistic when he or she assumes that self-relation is possible apart from other-relation, and that self-choice can occur without projecting a certain type of the ideal other. These are the charges parroted from book to book in the received view of Kierkegaard. I argue that this is not exactly what Habermas means when he proposes to integrate socially the crisis individual. He balances Kierkegaard's corrective to Hegel's privileging of the "me" over the "I," and by utilizing Mead's genetic dialectic of "me" and "I" complements Kierkegaard's objection to Hegel's loss of the individual.

Mead focuses on the social genesis of the self and the transition from play to game to communicative interaction. In play, children learn social roles by calling out the responses of others in themselves. In games, a child learns through rules the generalized attitude of all the participants. In communicative interaction, one learns to take the attitude of the generalized other, of the whole community. "The organized community or social group which gives to the individual . . . [her] unity of self may be called the generalized other." The mature self acts on levels of particular social roles and of the capacity to think. The latter is based on the projected identity of the generalized other.[11]

The difference between the "me" and the "I" covers the two levels: a "me" arises through taking the attitude of others; one reacts as an "I" to the given identity of a "me." "As given, it is a 'me,' but it is a 'me' which was the 'I' at the earlier time." Mead admits, in what could be both a Hegelian and a Kierkegaardian claim, that the "I" can be retrieved only indirectly, since it is never given to the immediate experience. The immediate self is the hermeneutically given "me." The "I" responds to these organized sets of attitudes in an unpredictable way since it is "not given in the 'me'."[12]

Mead distances himself from a Hegelian claim when he preserves the "I" as a qualitative surd that cannot be sublated into a generic "me." He confronts Hegel's privileging of the "me" over the "I" without venturing Kierkegaard's risks of not being able to justify rationally the incommensurability of the "I" with the "me." Remember that in this reading of Mead, "rational" means communicative. While the "I" is not directly communicable, its spontaneity can be reconstructed and discussed. Mead depicts the individual's reply to the attitude of the other as a creative, qualitative act. "The 'I' gives the sense of freedom, of initiative." That the "I" is never subject to calculative thinking shows its separability from the "me." Without this capacity of individual resistance and transcendence, one could not articulate critical social theory. Mead insists on sustaining both moves: "The self is essentially a social process going on with these two distinguished phases. If it did not have these two phases there could not be conscious responsibility, and there would be nothing novel in experience."[13]

Reading Kierkegaard through Mead's Pragmatism

If we reject the biologism of this incommensurability, by which Mead approximates both Freud and Nietzsche, we can give a pragmatic rendition of the either/or characteristic of self-choice. Such spontaneity can be interpreted communicatively. Reading Kierkegaard through Mead need not reject the possibility of a radical self-choice. Mead pragmatically expands individual identity into a communicative perspective. Seen from this angle, Kierkegaard is a far cry from being an irrational, acommunicative, and uncritical individualist. A self-choice is necessarily always a social act; it is a socially critical act by an individual whose resistance to systemic imperatives on behalf of the lifeworld and whose transcendence of culture are inconceivable without a projected community ideal. By thematizing a personal confrontation of community in pragmatic parameters, we can preserve a rather strong notion of individuality within communicative ethics.

Given the hypothesis of a rational (communicative) possibility of freedom on a basis other than instinctual, how is the Kierkegaardian individual a social critic and an activist? Mead explains that creative imagination is eminently social and critical; in it we bring to bear our own attitudes to stimulate different situations in the community. How can individual imagination stimulate community? The socialized individual recalls and projects in her imagination the anticipated responses of the community. Inversely, she can change the attitude of the entire community through her own responses to it. The emancipatory ideal, thus, occurs in the very resisting and transcending capacity of communication—in the ability to appropriate the internal attitude that the other maintains towards me. Therefore, the community ideal is always set by the expanding of the individual's identity, not by the given life form of family, nation, or church. Mead demonstrates that this resisting and transcending identity does not speak Kant's or Hegel's monologue.

In my critical elaboration I appeal to Mead in order to defend Kierkegaard and critique Habermas. Habermas's question to Kierkegaard overlooks that aspect of Mead's insight that gives priority to the qualitative "I" over the generic "me." Habermas doubts that self-realizing identity already exhibits a type of communicative rationality. He therefore condemns any individually critical standpoint, in principle, to monologism, decisionism, and irrationalism. Yet Mead shows convincingly that it is not the community but rather the individual who relates to it and who grounds the very possibility of resisting system and of transcending the status quo. In accord with Mead's insight, which is downplayed by Habermas, I argue that Kierkegaard does not merely set an individualist identity ideal, but that he projects a type of a life form suited for it. While I suggest that Habermas ought to examine Kierkegaard's own ideal, whereby the radically honest individual at extremity projects an existentially communicating community, my proposal is articulated from Habermas's communicative turn.[14]

I offer two examples that powerfully underscore my communicative reading of Kierkegaard's individualism. The first example of the dialectic between individual and community occurs in Mead's pragmatic understanding of scientific practice: hypotheses push beyond the conventions of the community. The individual researcher, while sustained by the rules and data of the scientific community, is often a unique source of qualitative change in community. "The attitudes involved are gathered from the group, but the individual in whom they are organized has the opportunity of giving them an expression which perhaps has never taken place before." One may understand Kierkegaard's literary and philosophical portraits of personal health along the lines of the experimenter at the limits of her own times. That Kierkegaard attacked Hegel for privileging Mead's "conventional individual" over "a definite personality" makes Kierkegaard, from the perspective of scientific creativity, quite rational. Such reason fits a self-critical attitude:

> The demand is freedom from conventions, from given laws. . . . [S]uch a situation is only possible where the individual appeals . . . from a narrow and restricted community to a larger one. . . . One appeals from fixed conventions which no longer have any meaning to a community in which rights shall be publicly recognized, and one appeals to others on the assumption that there is a group of organized others that answer to one's own appeal—even if the appeal be made to posterity. In that case there is the attitude of the "I" as over against the "me."[15]

The second example comes from Martin Luther King, Jr. In January 1963 eight white Alabama liberal clergymen published a letter in which they stylized King's call to nonviolent resistance as extremist. In response to these "white moderates" King argues that activists like the prophets, Socrates, Jesus, Paul, Martin Luther, John Bunyan, Abraham Lincoln, Thomas Jefferson, and others were all extremists who had a vision of another, more just world. In confronting the racist status quo King gives himself the title of extremist. He would agree that the African-American struggle might be a domain deemed monological, decisionistic, and untranslatable to the safe discourse of the white mainstream, which will not wake up from the marginalizing, dogmatic slumber on its own:

> Just as Socrates felt that it was necessary to create a tension in the mind so that individuals could rise from the bondage of myths and half-truths to the unfettered realm of creative analysis and objective appraisal, we must see the

need of having nonviolent gadflies to create the kind of tension in society that will help men to rise from the dark depths of prejudice and racism to the majestic heights of understanding and brotherhood.

King finds the key issue in the mode of one's action:

> So the question is not whether we will be extremist but what kind of extremist will we be. Will we be extremists for hate or will we be extremists for love? Will we be extremists for the preservation of injustice—or will we be extremists for the cause of justice? . . . So, after all, maybe the South, the nation and the world are in dire need of creative extremists.[16]

Mead implies that the "peculiar individuality" is a surd, which cannot be sublated into the "me." He adopts a perspectivism that does not result in either untranslatable claims of windowless monads or in the death of the individual. He asks what the self is like in "the widest community which we can present, the rational community that is represented in the so-called universal discourse." The transformations of communities are due to the "I," not to the "me," aspect of identity.[17]

For this reason a Kierkegaardian identity cannot be witnessed reflectively apart from action. Kierkegaard would admit that one begins as a "me," but one becomes a self, qualitatively, by choosing oneself. Like Mead, he agrees that qualitative self-choice cannot be communicated directly. Mead holds that one has reflective access to the "me," but one cannot get hold of one's "I" hypothetically or by report from another: "it is this living act which never gets directly into reflective experience." When Mead argues that self-realization must be recognized by others, he does not subsume the "I" under the "me." The individual project is always already projected in social terms. To go beyond Mead and appropriate oneself qualitatively one must do more than harness instinctual spontaneity. Instincts offer only the quantitative condition of the possibility of change. The qualitative transformation that informs Kierkegaard's identity formation is a modal possibility of relating to one's psychosomatic and social lifeworld.[18]

Nationalist and church identifications do not necessarily project identity in a concrete way. Mead argues that genuine superiority has no need of herd triumphalism. Freedom returns to its creative—resisting and transcending—function from which it takes its origin. His idea for resolving nationalist and religious fundamentalist identifications is today more appropriate than ever. Mead suggests retrieving the functional, noncommunitarian sense of patriotism and collective identity formation. His functional patriotism, like Habermas's constitutional patriotism, projects a community idealization of the League of Nations that transcends substantive conflicts while preserving the rich reservoir of particular contributions. "One nation recognizes certain things it has to do as a member of the community of nations."[19]

From Vitalist to Existential Spontaneity

I doubt that Mead's vitalist resources of spontaneity can tame instinctual outbursts of mass hysteria and violence. The following summary confirms several such misgivings. Bernard Waldenfels raises three questions concerning Mead's social genesis of the self. What is the relation of the "I" to the biological individual? What is the concrete relation between I and Thou? What is the relation between the two aspects or moments of the self, the "I" and the "me"? Mead's replies give an unsatisfactory account of individuality.[20]

Waldenfels claims that Mead cannot explain how that which can relate to self and others spontaneously can emerge through taking the attitude of the other. The "I" and the biological–instinctual singularity are either barely distinguishable or they lead to a paradoxical dualism: "The I which should lead the dialogue between dialogical instinctuality and social adherence to rules is, on the one hand, a biological resource and, on the other, a moment within a rationally governed whole. It is either undersocialized or oversocialized." Moreover, instinctual biological behaviorism cannot explain the doubled spontaneity of the dialogue. Waldenfels refers to Merleau-Ponty's account of primordial bodily intersubjectivity, which the subject inherits as the core of her vulnerability. Bodily co-existence with others, rather than presocial instinctuality or the generalized other, provides a needed social basis for subjective spontaneity. Finally, depicting the "I" and the "me" in quantitative Hegelian terms as stages or phases of the self cannot account for the qualitative unity of the self. The directly incommunicable "I" cannot be secured on the basis of the generalized other. Waldenfels argues that only a temporal mode of individual existence can explain the difference between the genesis and unity of these two aspects.

When I later address Kierkegaard's individual, I will present this category without relying on an instinctual theory of freedom or on a psychological equilibration between oppression and repression. This category can provide the sought basis for resisting system and for critiques of nationalism and of mass religiosity because a communicatively interpreted, honest, identity ideal promises the richness of concretion without driving individuals and groups to the self-lacerating frenzy of power.

B. Habermas: Qualitative and Generic Identity

Habermas goes beyond merely numeric identity by integrating Henrich's generic and Tugendhat's qualitative identifications. By defining identity communicatively Habermas aims at a performative rendition of Kierkegaard's self-critical attitude. Yet, Habermas subsumes qualitative identity (self-realization) under a generic or generalized sense of it (self-determination).

Habermas's Concept of Human Identity

Habermas justifies the sociopsychological term identity within a linguistic theory: identity designates "the symbolic structures constitutive for the unity of the collective and of its individual members." Linguistically, identity refers with personal pronouns to ourselves and others.

> The unity of the collective is the point of reference for the communality of all members which is expressed in the fact that they can speak *of themselves* and each other in the first-person plural. At the same time, the identity of the person is a presupposition for members being able to speak *with one another* in the first-person singular.[21] (emphasis in the German text)

Habermas clarifies his use of the term identity by juxtaposing it to Henrich's and Tugendhat's discussions. Henrich distinguishes between the problem of *numeric identity* as studied by analytic philosophy and "the social–psychological concept of identity." Numeric identity does not require that we take recourse to some quality or pattern. Thus, a person who does not follow any behavioral scheme and is quite unpredictable can nevertheless exhibit numeric identity. Here identity means singularity. One cannot acquire or lose numeric identity. The notion of numeric identity in analytical philosophy must be distinguished from the sociopsychological sense of acquired and changing *generic identity*. By acquiring generic identity the numerically singular person sets herself free and exhibits a competence for autonomous action. Henrich stresses the generic, self-determination aspect of Mead's concept of ego identity. Tugendhat focuses on the qualitative, self-realization aspect. Here Habermas sides with the latter: "the question of who one wants to be has the sense not of a numerical but of a qualitative identification."[22]

This agreement can be further illustrated by Charles Taylor's polemic with Derek Parfit. Parfit argues that one does not need to depict identity as a unity of life. I am several persons in one life: an adolescent who grew up in Czechoslovakia, a young American, and an old man to be. Taylor objects to Parfit's Lockean and Humean impoverished notion of self. It is impoverished because, as in numeric identification, it has but thin empiricist categories of self-awareness. We cannot think of selves as "punctual objects," Taylor concludes. An identity of selves "exist[s] only in a certain space of questions, through certain constitutive concerns." Taylor, like Tugendhat and Habermas, speaks of qualitative selfhood: "we grasp our lives in a *narrative*." "In order to have a sense of who we are, we have to have a notion of how we have become, and of where we are going"[23] (emphasis in original).

Tugendhat argues that the ability to remain consistent with oneself in contradictory roles occurs in conventional behavior, but it is secured through moral self-determination. The ability to organize one's life project and present it to others is neither a problem of numerical identity nor of the epistemic domain of self-consciousness; rather, it exhibits a propositional structure of qualitative relation to one's existence. Neither my relation to others nor my historical continuity is a numerical issue; the numerical is presupposed in that I win for myself an identity in a qualitative sense. In choosing myself, I reply to the question, "what kind of human am I and what do I want to be"; "I win an identity in a mode of permanence."[24]

Habermas's recent work thematizes both qualitative and generic identity. He distinguishes the Greek term atom, which designates any numerical individual as a singular object, from the qualitative identifications of individuality. Numerical identity expresses, besides the single term (*atomon*), the individual soul or substance in the entire metaphysical tradition. Substantive identification, however, prescinds from the consideration of development and language, both of which express qualitative identity. Habermas argues for the shift from the substantive to the relational understanding of the individual.

> While the *singularity* of an object can be explained in sense of a determined numerical identity, I would like to speak about *individuality* of an existing being only then, when this allows for a differentiation from all (or at least most) other things through qualitative determinations. . . . The individual can no longer be identified only *numerically* through its connection with matter, but rather *qualitatively* through manifold differences in form.[25] (emphasis in original)

By qualitative identification, he means not a thin, disencumbered self but a communicative–ethical identity formation.

> [T]he meaning of "individuality" should be clarified in the ethical self-understanding of a first person in relation to a second person. Only that [person] can embody the concept of individuality, which goes beyond pure singularity, who knows, who she is and wants to be before herself and others.[26]

The performative use of the first person singular is to be differentiated from two other meanings in language analysis. The performative use of "I" denotes neither a grammatical self-reference through which a speaker numerically objectifies the "I" as an object, nor a privileged access to one's subjective world in an epistemic self-relation and in expressive sentences. It denotes the self of practical self-relation in performative sentences. "The

'I' stands, then, for an actor of a speech act, who in a performative attitude with a second person . . . enters into an interpersonal relationship."[27]

Habermas's Performative Transcript of Existential Identity

Habermas distances himself from both Mead's ties to the philosophy of consciousness and his biologism. The genesis of qualitative and generic identity cannot be explained by an interplay between a numerically singular, instinctual individual and given conventions. Internalizing the attitude of the other, when conceived *in foro interno*, generates a higher-level individuality rather than self-relation before the other. Taking the attitude of the other is a mutual self-relation with consequences that change the whole: communication of an ego with an alter leads to a higher-level intersubjectivity.[28]

With Wittgenstein, Habermas speaks about the intersubjective character of meaning conventions; with Mead and Austin, he extends this thought to a performative notion of all identity claims. From this complex of positions, to which I cannot attend singly here, emerges Habermas's communicative turn. Along with Wittgenstein's and Austin's linguistic turns, and on the basis of Mead's and Peirce's pragmatist projections of the community ideal, Habermas argues for the normative bond between the onto- and phylogeneses of claims, on the one hand, and their validity on the other.

What is it to take the attitude of the other? The yes–no responses of alter to ego's communication and the competence to follow rules in order to bring about certain consequences are internalized in the ideal role taking: one learns the attitude of the other as hearer, speaker, and observer. An ego internalizes the significant reaction that an alter assumes to an ego's communicative gesture; it learns to address the alter with communicative intent by offering something to be interpreted and understood. Participants in communication learn to ascribe identical meaning conventions to the same gesture. Competence to follow rules and to critique the validity of claims could not be learned and carried out by solitary subjects.[29]

Developing Mead, Habermas explains: a socialized individual unites, beyond her numerical singularity, two levels of identity, role and ego identity. On both the hermeneutical and the self-directed level, the thesis holds: "the process of socialization is at the same time one of individuation. . . . [I]n the socialization process an 'I' emerges equiprimordially with the 'me,' and the individuating effect of socialization processes results from this double structure." Role identity already exhibits a competence for self-determination (that generalized perspective of the other on me that ego takes vis-à-vis alter) and self-realization (the aspect of I that is spontaneous and never calculable). Roles are primarily acquired through ascribed predicates of traditions. Role identity remains conventional, quantitative, and past oriented. Note, now, how far from Mead's instinctual spontaneity is Habermas's notion of self-direction! Ego identity, whether self-critical or future-oriented, is qualitatively distinct from conventionally ascribed predicates. This biologically nonreducible capacity contains both an ethic of the concrete other and the capacity for the moral point of view, which allows for distancing from Hegel's *Sittlichkeit* without needing Kant's two worlds. Ethical and moral types of reciprocity are formed through reflexive relation to particular and universal perspectives. Under the universal aspect of identity, the individual becomes self-determined. In that aspect one can be reflexively distant from traditions and local contexts. Self-determined ego identity is projected unto the generic social space and historical time of the ideal of communication community. One socially integrates self-realization on the basis of self-determination.[30]

Habermas argues that open identity exhibits not only the generic competence for moral self-determination but also for ongoing concrete self-realization. "An autonomous conduct of life depends in turn on the decision—or on successively repeated and revised decisions—as to 'who one wants to be'." Habermas's Kierkegaardian language of self-choice shows that Gadamerian lifeworld contexts carry deep but never final "decisions." Habermas cannot be viewed as a possessive, individualistic liberal since, along with a rationality of right, he holds a rational theory of self-realization. These two "rationalities" bespeak the difference between Gadamer and Habermas: both agree, along with Hegel and Kierkegaard, that by inhabiting certain traditions we have already adopted some decisions. These do not result from discourse and are not transparent. Habermas argues, with Kierkegaard and against Gadamer and the communitarians, that qualitative decisions can be critiqued. His concession to hermeneutics is that I cannot critique all at once, since I am unable to abstract absolutely from my context. From the role of self-realization follows another implication for the concrete conditions of moral discourse. If in modernity ego continuity is formed performatively, then posttraditional and postnational forms of life must solicit not only the counterfactual but likewise the existential conditions of their own possibility: *"[E]xistential 'decision' is indeed a necessary condition for a moral attitude towards one's own life history, but is not itself the result of moral reflection"*[31] (emphasis added).

Habermas's analysis of reciprocal recognition implies that a fully socialized individual in complex modern societies comprises levels of role and ego identity. One's moral action and self-realization occur in the latter, self-directed identity. Reading with Kierkegaard, Habermas anchors the spontaneous, narrative aspect of identity in repeated acts of self-choice. One becomes a self through responsible choices of ever new but continuous qualitative identities. This characterization fits well with Kierkegaard's so-called ethical sphere of existence. An individual who is identified only by culturally ascribed predicates has not yet taken a self-determined and responsible posture towards socialized identity, even though such an individual is formed intersubjectively (i.e., by the grammar of spirit in Hegel's sense.) Both Kierkegaard and Habermas find that Hegel did not articulate sufficiently this two-fold capacity for self-direction. He subsumed Kant's moral identity under the substantive imperatives of social ethics, and determined inwardness through the nation—state. I argue that implicitly, even if not in deliberate terminology, Habermas makes more than a Kantian point against Hegel's emphatic institutionalism and Mead's biologism. Posttraditional and postnational identity must comprise both of the levels required by communicative and existential ethics. Without either, one cannot sustain reciprocal participation in moral discourse and ethical community.[32]

A Kierkegaardian aesthete—a religious or secular Philistine—lives in modernity but is incapable of moral deliberation and self-realization. He is defined by social roles (church goer, flag-waving patriot, breadwinner), but he has not resolved to be a self. A person who wants to defend against intrusions by the systems of money and political power and maintain a critical distance from traditions ought to become capable of moral and ethical reciprocation with another. Only "an ego-identity of this kind simultaneously makes possible self-determination *and* self-realization"[33] (emphasis in original).

Habermas reads as if he were a Kierkegaardian when he affirms that one becomes an ethical and moral self in acts of radical self-choice:

> To the extent that the adult can take over and be responsible for his own biography, he can come back to himself in the narratively preserved traces of his own interactions. Only one who takes over his own life history can see in it the realization of his self. Responsibly to take over one's own biography means to get clear about *who one wants to be*, and from this horizon to view the traces of one's own interactions as *if* they were deposited by the actions of a responsible author, of a subject that acted on the basis of a reflective relation to self.[34] (emphasis in original)

Without this personal narration—without an attitude of distancing and self-choice vis-à-vis ascribed gendered, cultural, religious, and sociopolitical origins—one remains incapable of the critical posture of solidarity and justice. Yet Habermas never draws out this radical Kierkegaardian implication from his self-ascribed "existential mode of expression." Nevertheless, Habermas clarifies the implications that he draws from American philosophy. "It is . . . the merit of American Pragmatism to have provided the conceptual means for saving this thought [of individual moral judgment] while transcending the frame of contractarian individualism."[35]

Habermas argues that the relation between the "I" and the "me" constitutes a consistent key to identity formation, even though the relation between both in modernity is changed. In traditional identities, the "me" pertained to concrete life forms, and thus could be grasped neither directly nor reflexively. Modern self-determination and self-realization alike must be addressed by an idealized perspective of the generalized other that comprises all future and previously socialized others. Habermas speaks about a projected social form of life that not only makes possible self-determination, but that also "first makes it possible . . . [taking] earnestly my life-history as a principle of individualization and consider[ing] this life-history *as if it were* a product of my responsible decisions" (emphasis in original). Both the reflexive self-direction ("we") and self-choice ("I") of one's life history remain, without the "forum of unlimited communication community," mere undetermined notions. Thus, Habermas concludes, I need to address my life history to this ideal forum. I ought to take the attitude of this ideal forum on *me*—where *I* react and relate to this *me* as if it were "my whole existence in concretion and breadth of its identity-forming contexts of life and learning"[36] (emphasis in original).

An Unfruitful Ambiguity between Qualitative and Generic Identity

How can an ideal community socially integrate open identity? Habermas agrees with Kierkegaard that the "I" of self-realization emerges in a "projected project" that cannot be derived from appeals to the conventional "me" of a tradition, nation, or authority. Yet he disagrees that one's self-choice can be the conditions of its own possibility. Human existence is a "Janus-faced" relation of the normative ego ideal, the "I," to the hermeneutically given contexts, the "me." Individual existence is shot through with a social dimension of communication. Self-direction and self-transcending life projects occur from within the projected unlimited communication community, which confirms moral autonomy, the I-in-general, and my individuality, the existential I. Self-appropriation relates back to these doubly original forms of hermeneutically given and context-transcending identity.

> The "me" that corresponds to the "I" is here possible no longer through an *antecedent* interactive relationship. The "I" itself *projects* every context of interaction and makes possible for the first time the reconstruction of broken conventional identities on a higher level. . . . Although the latter can be thought of only as socially constituted, there exists no social form of life that corresponds [to this project].[37] (emphasis in original)

Let me comment on the disagreements between Habermas and Kierkegaard. In his sympathetic reading of Kierkegaard's open identity, Habermas tackles not only several objections to the perceived abstractness of an intersubjectivist concept of identity. He also keeps at bay the contrary claim that he submerges the individual in collectivism. Yet, as I indicated in Chapter 1, there is an unfruitful ambiguity produced by Habermas's two assumptions (underpinning likewise his three critiques) concerning Kierkegaard: he leaves ambivalent the link between the qualitative mode of self-choice and the generic universal of self-determination, and, in fact, he absorbs the existential into the generic.

In his communicative translation of the qualitative and generic aspects of identity, Habermas is disturbed by the aporia of substance and subjectivity in metaphysical and phenomenological traditions. For this reason he rejects both approaches: "individuality . . . [must be] thought of not . . . as singularity, not as an ascribed sign, but rather as an achievement; *individualization* [must be thought of] as the self-realization of the individual" (emphasis in original). An intersubjectivist reading of individuality does not merely build on a "subject-philosophical transformation of the basic metaphysical concepts," but it highlights the "merit of Mead in taking up the motifs to be found in Humboldt and Kierkegaard."[38]

The link between Mead and Kierkegaard emerges in Tugendhat's analytic reading of existential self-relation. Tugendhat and Habermas ask how self-relation to one's existence can become a basis for universal moral self-determination. Tugendhat follows first Wittgenstein (he replaces the representation "I think" with the personal pronoun "I"), then Heidegger in his ontological reading of Kierkegaard (self-relation is not epistemic self-reflection but rather a relation to existence), and finally Mead (one relates to oneself insofar as one interacts with the other). Habermas continues this line of inspiration and works Kierkegaard into the communicative model:

> [T]he individuation of self-realizing individual cannot be imagined in aloneness and freedom of an indpendently acting subject, but only within a linguistically mediated process of socialization and at the same time within a constitution of self-conscious life-history. *The identity of socialized individuals is formed at the same time in the medium of linguistic understanding with others and in the medium of life-historical and intrasubjective understanding with oneself. Individuality is formed in relationships of intersubjective recognition and intersubjectively mediated self-understanding.*[39] (emphasis added)

Habermas's disagreement highlights an untenable ambiguity that I find in his reading of Kierkegaard. Kierkegaard's radicalized individual vanishes rather than become socially integrated: first, in Habermas's reconstruction of the relation between qualitative and generic identity, and second, between ethics and morality. To begin with the concept of posttraditional identity, Habermas holds two contradictory points. He affirms that, in principle, one's qualitative identity provides the condition of the possibility of generic and numeric identification:

> Rather than leaving things with the demarcation thesis of Henrich and Tugendhat, I will use Mead's concept of identity as a guide in illuminating the semantic interconnections between these three kinds of identification. *I*

> *argue the following thesis: the predicative self-identification that a person undertakes is in certain respects a presuppositions of others being able to identify him generically and numerically.* (emphasis added)

Again, he affirms the primacy of the qualitative over the generic:

> A person satisfies the conditions and criteria of identity according to which he can be numerically distinguished *from others* only when he is in a position to ascribe to himself the relevant predicates. In this respect, the predicative self-identification of a person accomplished at an elementary level is a presupposition for that person's being identifiable by others as person in general—that is generically—and as a specific person—that is numerically.[40] (emphasis in the German text)

I identified this primacy as an "existential mode of expression." Yet this primacy is in tension with another repeated claim that subordinates qualitative identity under generic self-determination. Habermas subsumes the existential elements inherited by communicative ethics under the perspective of the generalized other:

> Corresponding to the ideal communication community is an *ego-identity that makes possible self-realization on the basis of autonomous action.* This identity proves itself in the ability to lend continuity to one's own life history.[41] (emphasis in original)

Since a well-socialized individual can claim total freedom neither from concrete life forms and institutions nor from her own biography, she can gain reflexive role distance and self-realization only on the basis of autonomous action:

> Mead works out the aspects of self-realization and self-determination. Under these aspects of I-as-individual and I-in-general, the moments of the "I" and the "me" return in reflected form, as we can now see. Ego-identity enables a person *to realize herself under conditions of autonomous action.*[42] (emphasis in the German text)

Moreover, this same unproductive ambiguity results from Habermas's linkage of the "existential" to his distinction between ethics and morality. He subordinates Kierkegaard's radical self-choice to the moral questions of justification and application, which generalize interests and rationally evaluate and apply justified norms. Yet this is an unwarranted move. True, there are cogent reasons for subordinating in certain instances particular ethical questions (what am I/what are we/what ought we to become) to the universal moral question, what ought I/we do? Ethical questions are initiated with regard to concrete life projects, while moral questions raise universal claims since in modernity these alone can settle such substantive conflicts as the nationalist strife in former Yugoslavia. But one cannot follow Habermas and equate the category of self-choice with the domains of *Sittlichkeit*—the Aristotelian clinical or the Hegelian ethical questions of the good or happy life:

> If we define practical questions as those of "good life" (or of "self-realization") which relate to the totality of a particular life-form or the totality of an individual life-history, respectively, then is ethical formalism indeed incisive: the universalizing principle functions as a knife, which cuts between the "good" and the "just," between evaluative and strictly normative claims.[43]

Habermas's moral knife might strike the feminist as particularly disclosive of the masculine moral judge. Yet this cutting between the good and the right leaves Kierkegaard's sincere questioning unscathed! The ground for Habermas's analytical distinction between the evaluative questions of the good life and the normative ones of justice is the same as that which differentiates between traditional and posttraditional identity formation. For Habermas, however, the "existential" remains only an ambiguously posttraditional expression: he reasons that we cannot maintain a hypothetical–reflexive distance from the life form in which we were socialized. "Nobody can reflectively *choose* as a norm whose validity one has justified that life-form in which one has been socialized"[44] (emphasis in original).

I affirm Habermas's communicative use of a Kierkegaardian self-choice against fundamentalism and nationalism. I also find his reading of Kant's moral self-determination through Mead's pragmatism appropriate as a response to communitarians. But Habermas is a vacillating reader of Kierkegaard, and thereby disregards the radically self-critical individual as the vantage point for resisting totalitarian thinking and acting. He stresses a kind of primacy of qualitative over generic identity, yet privileges universal self-determination to existential self-realization. He leaves vague the nature of the complementary relation between the generic and the qualitative aspects of identity. I derived this vagueness from his Copenhagen disagreements with Kierkegaard. We are now faced with this same ambiguity in the relation between the existential and moral senses of identity, communication, and the community ideal: either self-determination depends on radical self-choice, or generic identity not only describes quantitative individualization through socialization but makes possible one's qualitative identity. By establishing a relation of dubious complementarity, Habermas leaves us with an untenable resolution. He assimilates qualitative self-realization into the Aristotelian question of the good life. Having, in effect, converted Kierkegaard into a neoHegelian like Taylor, Habermas subordinates his own communitarian–existential understanding of self-realization (his new hybrid category of "ethical–existential" discourse) under that of universal moral self-determination. Habermas welcomes Kierkegaard into modernity and yet he subsumes him under the communitarian concerns of the good life. Rather than socially integrating Kierkegaard's individual on a noncommunitarian basis (this is Habermas's Copenhagen promise), Habermas's generic consensus abstracts from qualitative identity, communication, and the ideal.[45]

Since Habermas categorizes the radically self-critical attitude as communitarian, it is understandable (although wrong because Kierkegaard is anything but a communitarian) why only moral questions can problematize those identity claims that are based on the integrated, hermeneutical horizons of ethical life. The rationale for Habermas's conclusion lies in the thesis that even qualitative self-realization requires the perspective of the generic other in order to sustain identity in modern lifeworlds. It is the generic perspective that in rationalized lifeworlds structurally allows for the integrating of the qualitative perspective, even though qualitative self-identification is a presupposition for the possibility that others can identify one generically and numerically. How this latter assumption is possible—how one can become qualitatively a posttraditional and postnational individual— is untreated by Habermas.

Kierkegaard and Habermas agree with Hegel and the communitarians that hermeneutical embeddedness is presupposed in one's having any identity whatsoever. The argument of the preceding chapters showed that in rationalized life forms one can justify norms not from within ethical–hermeneutical domains, but at the level of a moral validity domain. This is so because there is a basic inability to maintain absolute reflexive distance from one's hermeneutical origins and become ethically self-transparent. This inability is recorded in Merleau-Ponty's thesis about the impossibility of arriving at a total reduction of the conditions of the possibility of experience. For this reason there are unproblematized hermeneutical residues in every value choice of a life project. Therefore, such choices lend themselves to a degree of arbitrariness.[46]

My claim is that Habermas misclassifies the "existential" with the "ethical–hermeneutical." This occurs, I suspect, because the mode of temporal existence disappears completely from Habermas's communications theory and becomes translated into the atemporal structure of the validity domains. Yet I find such a translation unnecessary for effecting the communicative turn, and, moreover, harmful for making this turn without the loss of the temporal mode of both the individual and community. (My manifest reasons for objecting have already been stated: Habermas absorbs a Kierkegaardian self-choice into Aristotelian clinical questions of the good life.) My derived objection points to an omission of temporal analysis in Habermas's communicative model (i.e., a study of the triple "how" of identity, communication, and the community ideal.) Habermas projects qualitative identity onto generic autonomy, communication, and the ideal of communication community. He misapplies the Kantian–Hegelian distinction between morality and ethics to temporal dimensions of qualitative identity. But one cannot retrieve an existential–temporal mode from within generic validity domains. In sum, Habermas's reading of Kierkegaard is compromised by a category mistake. He confuses the ethical valuations of the good life with an existential a priori, or better, with a radical self-choice of oneself as someone motivated by valuating good and evil.

I offer here a preliminary, negative assessment that Habermas's reading of Kierkegaard covers a case that can be treated either in hermeneutical–ethical or critical–moral validity domains, but not in a study of a temporal–existential mode. Kierkegaard's open identity does not fit neatly into an Aristotelian ethic of the good, Kant's aesthetic rationality, or Hegel's social ethic. If, then, an existential mode fits neither a communitarian ethic nor an expressivist validity domain, it cannot be classified under the communitarian–existential category of "ethical–existential discourse." We need not blur Kierkegaard's temporal existing with Aristotle's polis ethics, or even with Hegel's ethical life in the nation–state, and then subsume both, to Habermas's satisfaction, under a generic universal of Kant's moral self-determination.

4.2. HABERMAS'S READING OF DURKHEIM

Habermas secures more firmly Mead's thesis that individualization occurs through socialization. He turns to Durkheim's sociology of religion, thereby deriving a missing phylogenetic support for Mead's account of ontogenetic development. A mythic experience of the sacred provides a missing link between the genesis and the normative validity of claims, on the one hand, and identity claims on the other. The need for this move arises from the following problem: how can socialization also be individualization? Habermas does not think that Mead's explanation of ideal role taking satisfies the phylogenetic view. Mead's thesis helps heal the split between the inner and the outer but not between immanence and transcendence. The former split bespeaks a monological standpoint; the latter relegates the normative grounds of discourse to an untranslatable transcendent claim, and thus becomes a foil for both decisionism and monological postures, regardless of whether this transcendence is articulated religiously or not. Let me comment on Habermas's reading of Durkheim (A) and then argue that Habermas fails to explain the nonideological, critical character of the self-choosing attitude (B).

A. Identity and the Linguistification of the Sacred

Taking a yes–no position to criticizable claims presupposes that an ego can bind an alter by a speech act—that there is a communicative bond among speakers. This internal normativity requires, on the level of ontogenesis, the phylogenetically available conditions of the possibility of intersubjective orientation to validity claims. Here Habermas joins Durkheim's sociology of the sacred to Mead's explanation of ontogenesis and Austin's speech act theory.

How did the possibility of normative validity originate within group-identities? Habermas argues that the profane possibility of the illocutionary effect of speech must be traced to the sacred origins of obligation. He then moves behind the linguistic turn to the linguistification of the sacred within speech acts. Even though Mead presupposes the genesis of speech competencies, he does not make clear the very possibility of normative consensus.[47]

Durkheim's thesis about the sacred completes the puzzle inherent in Mead's thesis about individualization via socialization. The sacred stands for the authority ascribed to symbols and ritual enactments. The normative root in taking the attitude of the other is traced phylogenetically to the ambivalence and consensus that individuals and collectives exhibit vis-à-vis the sacred in traditional societies. Why is the betrayal of another generalized as that of oneself? Habermas notes how Yahweh's covenant with Israel operates with "the dialectic of betrayal and avenging force." Each individual is bound by a covenant membership—its ambivalent relation to the sacred, its prohibition of betrayal, and its consensual ritual practices—against the breakdown of fidelity.[48]

How are these relations exercised by sacred authority on the formation of ego and group identities? Habermas, in a thesis of the linguistification of the sacred, explains how the illocutionary core of validity claims gains its normative force in discourse. In rationalized lifeworlds all that remains of the sacred is the authority incarnate in language. Kierkegaard's language of inwardness, viewed by Habermas as the untranslatable voice of God, becomes profanized; indeed, it is identified with the voice of Rousseau's people, his secular audience.[49]

In modern societies sacred authority is split off from covenants into the formal elements of speech, into communication itself. Such splitting off is called the rationalization of the ordinary form of life. If lifeworlds stand for the unproblematized resources of individual and group identities, then their rationalization leads to a formation of identities based on decentered forms of life. The difference between the two types of life forms lies in the authority from which one claims recognition. The phylogenetic link, required for the transition from symbolically mediated to the normatively guided communication, is the social dissolution—the linguistification—of sacred authority. Habermas claims that the phylogenesis of ego's internalization of alter's responses to ego's offer of speech acts lies in human ambivalence towards sacred authority. This authority is something set apart. It is an impersonal force, which inspires one's devotion and self-renunciation, attraction and fright, and enchantment and terror. This ambivalence expresses what Kierkegaard modally analyzes under "a sympathetic antipathy and an antipathetic sympathy" of anxiety's possibility of freedom. Although in traditional societies a concrete retrieval of this possibility is not yet structurally available, Socrates attains a high degree of critical distance from Athenian conventions, and becomes both Habermas's and Kierkegaard's ally. But in Socrates's polis traditional forms of understanding structurally limit the practical range of such transcending possibilities.[50]

Moral obligation internalizes sacred authority and mediates it in taboos and ritual practices. Ritual provides a traditional form and content for the consensual enactment of authority and embodies the relations between the individual and society. Because it makes consensus actual, ritual forms both group and individual identities. Individualization through ritual socialization broadens Mead's original thesis: the content of ritual action determines group-identities; one's formal participation in ritual consensus secures one's individual identity. Ritual action provides the paradigm for resolving the key issue: "how can we at one and the same time belong wholly to ourselves and just as completely to others? How can we be simultaneously within ourselves and outside of ourselves?" Ritual consensus reconciles the inner and the outer through "sacred semantics." Symbols bond ego and alter through their intersubjectively shared roles vis-à-vis one another. The sacred drama provides an immanently horizontal transcendence, thereby remaining "still this side of the communicative roles of first, second, and the third persons." The semantic character of ritual practice discloses that nondualistic transcendence (sought by Habermas in his profanization of Kierkegaard's inwardness or verticality) which is not opposed to immanence but rather is translatable on "*this side*" of the community ideal (emphasis in original). Ritual action maintains individual and group through its collective repetition of identity:

> It can be seen in ritual actions that the sacred is the expression of a normative consensus regularly made actual. . . . Nothing is depicted in ceremonies of this kind; they are rather the exemplary, repeated putting into effect of a consensus that is thereby renewed. . . . Because the basic normative agreement expressed in communicative action establishes and sustains the identity of the group, the fact of successful consensus is at the same time its essential content.

This phylogenetic rejoinder completes my reconstruction of Habermas's question of how to socially integrate Kierkegaard's crisis individual. The ritual repetition of group identity, like the core of communicative action, already contains the form of normative consensus that becomes structurally available in communicative ethics. "[T]he identities of individual group members are established equiprimordially with the identity of the group."[51]

B. Does Existential Identity Need Linguistification?

Habermas notes how the sacred elements of mythic consensus immigrate into the regulative conditions of discourse: ritual maintains identities via its group repetition of sacred traditions, but within rationalized lifeworlds individuals repeat their identity claims in reciprocal recognition. They socially integrate their fragile posttraditional identities by projecting them onto the ideal community forum. Two types of objections can be raised against Habermas. First, the Durkheim-Mauss School of the French Collège de Sociologie develops a reading of the holy which problematizes his linguistification thesis. Second, this very thesis makes it difficult to categorize Habermas's Copenhagen question to Kierkegaard. Habermas does not think of the possibility that an individual who in modernity beholds her identity via risky acts of repetition already embodies a nonideological and critical social form of life, and thus is in no need of further linguistification of her critical attitude.

Ulf Matthiesen, following the French sociology of the holy, argues that Habermas cannot secure the obligatory nature of validity claims by a sociology of the numinous. But if he cannot transpose love and dread of the holy into the normative bond of communicative action, he then he fails to prove a strong link between the genesis and the validity of claims. This is so because we are unable to explain away the ambivalence of a Kierkegaardian anxious "antipathetic sympathy"/"sympathetic antipathy" towards the numinous without accounting for the body. Matthiesen shows that embodiment motivates this very ambivalence. He argues that Habermas's linguistification thesis reifies the somatic dimension of experience, and hence abstracts from the ambivalent relation itself. Habermas bypasses the lived body as a discursively unredeemable aspect of communication. Ambivalent love and dread cannot be first desexualized and then rendered unproblematic in the formal–pragmatic structures of communicative action. The attraction and terror of sexual power remain diffused in reciprocal relations. Matthiesen concludes that communicative action alone cannot take on combatting colonizations because system is not their unique source. Distorted communication occurs via the lived body, which is an incommensurable field of both speech and flesh.[52]

One serious consequence emerges from Matthiesen's argument: if the body is an integral aspect of lived identity, of the ambivalent love and terror of the numinous, then no total reduction of the sacred into the profane is possible, no transcript of the radically honest individual into reciprocal recognition can be complete. The impossibility of total reduction was painfully learned after Husserl by Heidegger and Merleau-Ponty. Habermas rejected phenomenology because of its purported unredeemable solipsism; yet, did he learn its lesson prior to advancing his trimmed, disembodied account of the lifeworld? Matthiesen thinks that he did not. Habermas's attempt to get to the transparent structures of linguistic interaction suffers a Husserl-type crisis within the very foundations of his communicative theory. The celebrated outcome of the linguistification of the lifeworld is frustrated at the outset by the modern "sacralization of the social"—let us say, by nationalism and fundamentalism. If the body cohabits with the sacred, then there is no boundary between the profane and sacred realms. If the rationality differential between them therefore cannot be reduced to a transparent illocutionary force, then "the holy is the social." Both sacred and profane performance has to do with this bodily ambivalence. From potlatch rituals (expenditures of goods) to modern symbolic activities, humans desire an endurance of the body. Humans need to sacralize the social.[53]

Ernest Becker argues a similar point from a position sympathetic to critical theory and post-Freudian analysis. In his unfinished posthumous work he claims that formally there is no difference between sacred and profane domains. Every culture is sacred insofar as it is in the service of the supernatural. Culture consoles for death as much as any explicit religious ideology. If the "sacred" is defined not by theistic contents but rather by any activity oriented to both a heroic death denial and an expiation for an ambiguous guilt of the body, then societies can be studied as successive immortality ideologies, heroic systems, and scenarios of sacrifice. Social criticism must expose cultures and empires which, in the process of their heroic escape from and expiation for disease and death (apparently morally or religiously justified), unleash humanly made destruction. Therefore, rationalized lifeworlds do not lose their capacity for ideology formation so long as their culture, economy, and public are unconsciously driven by a denial of bodily finitude.[54]

This analysis creates a problem for Habermas. Systematically, a distinction between sacred and profane domains made on the basis of the rationalization of cultural lifeworlds breaks down. Descriptively, military and church parades, the debate about flag-waving or flag-burning, shining paths to revolution, celebrations of the New World Order or of patriotic wars, or trust in the force of the better argument, all equally fulfill some "sacred" function vis-à-vis the body. Habermas gives a false impression that in communicative rationality sacred dissolves into profane. The linguistification thesis notwithstanding, even rationalized culture and society could become sacralized. Critically, he articulates no resources for resisting the new formation of immortality ideologies within socially differentiated rationalized lifeworlds. Given the broader sociology of the holy, I submit that insofar as people remain embodied, the rationalized lifeworlds will not necessarily refrain from ideological motivation and legitimation. If Habermas fails to account for this source of crises in the immortality striving of human identities, then his critical theory of society remains just a naïve heroic project that lacks the conditions of its own sobriety.

I aim at a problem other than that identified by Matthiesen. I find within communicative ethics a need for articulating nonauthoritarian and open yet embodied identity. Perhaps in this concrete locus of resistance lies a check on the destructiveness of the heroic, death-denying immortality ideologies in rationalized forms of life. This brings me to the second problem that I promised to discuss. The linguistification of the sacred effects historically the same dissolution of the sacred into the transparent structures of communicative action that Habermas proposes for a contemporary translation of Kierkegaard's language of inwardness or verticality. I discussed how Habermas tilts the vertical mode of existence onto the horizontal axis of communication. In doing this he runs into systematic difficulties with classifying Kierkegaard. Habermas affirms that, against Hegel and parallel to Marx, Kierkegaard arrived at a concept of personal identity quite suited for the critical vision of posttraditional and postnational age. He also argues that Kierkegaard's language needs to be further profanized and linguistified.[55]

What can Habermas's linguistification possibly do for Kierkegaard's already decentered identity which bespeaks the modern individual in crisis? How is Kierkegaard's vision posttraditional and postnational if he suddenly requires Habermas's linguistification therapy? Habermas cannot have his cake and eat it too! The linguistification thesis notes that modern culture has lost its capacity for ideological forms of understanding. The need to profanize a discourse must be, then, occasioned by the residual, ideological rationality differential between the sacred and profane domains. If Kierkegaard is in this need, then, in principle and on the basis of Habermas's theoretical model of social evolution, Kierkegaard promotes some such residual ideological form of understanding. I find that this consequence follows directly from Habermas's model, yet, I deem it self-contradictory and untenable.

Habermas's explanation is self-contradictory insofar as it does not cover Kierkegaard's case. The linguistification thesis gives us merely the structural conditions of the possibility of emancipation from ideology. Not even the supposedly rational core of the U.N. consensus on the legitimacy and morality of the 1991 U.S. allied intervention against Iraq secures cultures from becoming the devastating sacral dramas of heroic victory and expiation for the body.[56] Consensual procedures betray a blind spot when they fail to recognize how the critique of ideology, anomie, and unfreedom must be embodied in the self-critical attitude. Here Kierkegaard occasions legitimation and motivation crises for all drives to heroism and for the lack of sobriety in the consensual ideal as such. These systematic and critical gaps become even more untenable within Habermas's explanation when, as I have discussed in Chapter 1, he positively uses Kierkegaard against the theological critiques of communicative ethics. My objection is not to such a critical application of Kierkegaard's posture vis-à-vis dogmatic theology, but rather to the impossibility of doing so from Habermas's standpoint in the argument. If Kierkegaard is to be saved from a surd of ideological forms of understanding, then he cannot become Habermas's ally against positive theology. Contrary to Habermas's classification, Kierkegaard could become such a critic because his discourse cannot hide behind the rationality differential between sacred and profane culture. Yet, it cannot hide for reasons other than those given by Habermas. I will explain these reasons in the next chapter by attending to the difference between communicating in an existential mode and within the validity domains.

There are systematic reasons for Habermas's ambiguity: he does not examine the temporal mode of communication. Moreover, we cannot assume that Kierkegaard's language of inwardness or verticality represents an ideological form of legitimation that needs further linguistification. On Habermasian formal grounds, there is no vanishing point beyond a thoroughly honest identity formation where such additional linguistification of Kierkegaard could be followed rationally and argued for validly. Therefore, Habermas cannot redeem his claim against Kierkegaard by a valid argument.

A note of caution: if my reading of Kierkegaard should bring theology into communicative ethics, then Habermas's move to profanization would make very good sense. Yet my argument and use of Kierkegaard's self-critical attitude do not rely on Kierkegaard's Christianity. I am asking whether or not the philosophical equivalents to Kierkegaard's posture are best articulated in Habermas's use of Peirce's secularized theological model of the ideal, horizontally communicating community. Does not Kierkegaard's critique of the heroic–nationalist–fundamentalist motives in modern ego and group identities require an inward mode or verticality (albeit this is not decided by theistic or atheistic domains), thereby qualifying the very projection of identity, communication, and the regulative community ideal?

CONCLUSIONS

Along with Kantian moral self-determination, Habermas adopts a view of individual self-realization: the self-choosing individual cannot rely on ascribed role identity and substantive life forms, but must learn to project every possibility onto some ideal. Habermas fears that Kierkegaard's way of doing this—via a prioritizing of individual over group-formation—is monological, morally decisionistic, and socially conservative. Habermas absorbs existential questions into communitarian–ethical ones, and then subsumes both as ethical–existential questions of the good life under the moral point of view. He is right in wanting to articulate some sense of complementarity between qualitative and quantitative identity. While some qualitative aspects of identity correspond to what Taylor names the sources of the self, this is not so for Kierkegaard. The difference between a qualitative mode and the validity domains of ethical and moral identity does not call for a simple primacy of one over the other. An existential mode qualifies how I determine myself in moral discourse and realize individual and collective life projects in ethical discourse. In Habermas's model, Kierkegaard's individual vanishes as the locus for an ideology-critical resistance to distortions by heroic, nationalist, and pseudoreligious culture and identity formation.

I will show that there is pseudoconcretion in another sense that is neither covered by communitarian, feminist, and leftist critics of Habermas nor by his rebuttals to them. He attends to the structural conditions of the possibility of ethical communication but does not articulate the need of communicative self-transformation (i.e., the triple "how" of identity, communication, and the community ideal). The "how" indicates that one is to choose oneself as that individual who is capable of complementing the moral point of view of communicative ethics. True, Kierkegaard does not thematize the social life form that integrates the open individual and, by nurturing the individual at the extremity of perpetual legitimation and motivation crises, leaves himself open to the charges of monologism, decisionism, and dogmatism. Yet Habermas shortcircuits this Kierkegaardian crisis identity and fails to preserve the radically honest attitude in both the individual and community. My alternative to Habermas's translation of Kierkegaard's inwardness or verticality into the horizontal–generic community ideal entails an examination of what it would mean to read Kierkegaard's critique of herd mentality and nationalism as a communications theory, and, conversely, to appropriate Habermas's communicative turn and postnational deliberative democracy from an existential mode of communication. Kierkegaard read from a pragmatist expansion of identity projects an ideal of the honestly communicating community. A relevant critical question, that corrects and complements Habermas's Copenhagen question, in this context is: what is that mode of existence whose projection admits nondeceptive, nonauthoritarian, and open social forms of life?

PART II

IDENTITY
IN AN EXISTENTIAL MODE

CHAPTER 5

The Performative Mode
of Identity

At the end of April 1847 Kierkegaard outlined lectures on the dialectic of communication. These journal sketches reflect the rereading of his authorship from the years 1841–1846. He abandoned the idea of the lectures in May, but carried out this task with a matured self-understanding after the revolutionary events of 1848, from 1849 to 1850. During this period he authored two texts about communication, and ultimately attacked the establishment.[1]

In these unfinished lectures Kierkegaard apologizes for the manner in which he uses the first person pronominal "I." He jests that in his time it had become accepted usage to get rid of the personal "I." Our twentieth century does not differ from Kierkegaard's age: many a freshman in college learns that to argue or write in the first person means that she has not learned to think "objectively." Academics often judge their students' written usage of the "I" to be a sign of intellectual if not moral immaturity.[2]

Kierkegaard similarly comments in two other entries. He complains that "all communication of truth has become abstract: the public has become the authority, the newspapers [pamphlets] call themselves the editorial staff; the professor calls himself speculation; the pastor is meditation [contemplation]; no . . . [human], none, dares to say *I*." He wonders whether or not one does not venture to become an "I" from fright of the other. To flee such dread, one strives to become something anonymous and impersonal, to appear as a thing or a speculative principle. One abdicates one's performative participation in communication for the third person perspective of the observer.[3]

This abstract theory and practice of communication within the domains of the public sphere, the communication media, educational institutions, and institutionalized churches is rooted in their social forms of life. Anonymity in a herd democracy shelters one from tyranny by the many. Yet to sustain one's nonpersonality is both a comic and strenuous task. In order to protect oneself from others one seeks not to be alone, not to be an "I." One maintains identity by not being discovered by anyone, least of all by oneself. Anonymous existence becomes a modern tyranny that establishes itself in mass communication and replaces traditional forms of oppression.[4]

Why does this age praise aloof identity, communitarian identity, or the death of identity altogether? In all three strategies of self-evasion, one becomes an anonymous "nobody" in order to flee oneself, and thus, the need to relate to others. Our age judges responsibility to be oppressive to one's freedom. Why should an age which disclaims any responsibility for authoring its identity be so concerned about an ethic of freedom? Yet if all concrete freedom is personal, the ethical "can only be communicated from an *I* to an *I*." "[T]he first prerequisite for the communication of truth is personality. . . ." The core of miscommunication lies in the impersonality that has been entrenched in modern life-forms by the anonymous public, the media, academia, and the churches.[5]

Kierkegaard reflects on the revolutionary period of 1848: what good is victorious nonpersonality? What good is storming the bourgeois "castle in Paris" if one does not have a clue as to *how* one is and wants to be? The measure of progress cannot be a revolution which by abstracting from honest communication becomes "untruth, a forgery, a retrogression." Abstract revolution achieves quantitative change. Instead of establishing a permanent opposition within the mode of its democratic governance, this revolution idolizes its achievement, it "worships itself."[6]

Lest one mis/read Kierkegaard as justifying a conservative status quo, one should note his revolutionary passion for equality. In line with his critique of anonymous communication and of the social form of life that justifies it, he acknowledges that modern social revolutions disempower every form of traditional tyranny, from dictators, to church hierarchy, right down to "money tyranny." The fear of self and others, as signified by today's ethnic and religious hatred, is now the most insidious form of tyranny that distorts human relations because it is not directly detectable. Kierkegaard, without jest, parallels his project to social revolution: "The communists here at home and in other places fight for human rights. Good, so do I. Precisely for that reason I fight with all my might against the tyranny of the . . . [human] fear."[7]

Kierkegaard turns from revolution qua strategic, violent strife to a radical egalitarianism of communication. He practices open forms of communication, recorded in the promise of nondoctrinaire Christianity, as the vehicle of this radical human equality. My argument neither rejects nor relies on the substance of Kierkegaard's Christian religiosity. I am concerned with how his communicative theory and practice offset the dread of oneself and of the anonymous moralizing majority.[8]

Kierkegaard begins with himself and takes responsibility for his own anxiety. He uses pseudonyma not because he fears personal danger: in a world that is not accustomed to hearing an "I," he cannot begin to speak in his own voice. The purpose of his "author-personalities" is, therefore, to reaccustom the public "to hearing discourse in the first person." Through these pseudonyma he communicates indirectly both the theoretical content and the practical mode of radically honest communication.[9]

I began my story with Habermas's question: how can Kierkegaard's crisis individual be socially integrated within a collective form of life? I depicted how communicative action and ethics ground a critical social theory, since both open up the possibility for self-determination and self-realization. Freeing identity and community from their ideological forms of understanding facilitates radical democracy and constitutional patriotism rather than herd nationalism. In this radical democratic republic is found that homecoming sought by Habermas for vulnerable modern identity; herein lies a cure for the melancholy emerging from shipwrecked traditions and from the post-1989 exhaustion of revolutionary possibilities.

Habermas argues that posttraditional and postnational identity can be integrated into community performatively. The performative mode is defined by him as a generic self-determination of identity in communicative action and ethics. I provisionally linked the performative with identity claims, since Habermas vouches to have adopted an "existential mode of expression" as "a necessary condition for a moral attitude towards one's own life history." But if his claim can be accepted as valid, then I would be bringing wood to the forest by introducing at this point a discussion of an existential mode of identity. His communicative ethics would comprise an existential ethic, and the self-critical individual would be integrated into it via a projected complementary form of life. I have been raising suspicions about this conclusion for some time.[10]

Thus, I wish to elaborate the notion of the performative (5.1), and then develop its further transformation (5.2). In the first instance I will follow Tugendhat's (A) and Habermas's (B) views of self-relation. In the second, I will derive a distinction between an existential mode and the validity domains of the performative (A), begin to reverse the charges against Kierkegaard (B), and pose Kierkegaard's question to Habermas (C).

5.1. THE PERFORMATIVE NOTION OF THE INDIVIDUAL

A. Excursus: Tugendhat on Self-Relation

Tugendhat articulates the formal semantic conditions of the possibility of self-relation: just like all utterances, self-consciousness exhibits a propositional as-structure. In relating to myself, I take up a relation of predication that p is or is not so. The optical metaphor of I's knowing as looking and questions of intentional states of affairs are replaced in Tugendhat's study of self-relation with the analysis of one's propositional attitudes to self.[11]

Tugendhat, like Habermas, points out in the opening passages of Kierkegaard's *Sickness unto Death* the decisive break with the substance model of self-relation. Instead of retrieving from this text ontological or anthropological structures, Tugendhat formulates a linguistic transcript that accounts for the possibility of self-relation. It is no longer the substance–subject that relates herself to herself, but rather relation itself is considered self-related. How does one get out of a subject–object dualism into a nondualistic self-relation? Tugendhat wants to overcome "a reflexive relation of a to a," since "a" can stand both for the subject and for the relation that relates to itself.[12]

He correctly identifies that in Kierkegaard the posited relation to which one relates is not a self-relation, but a tensed synthesis of infinitude and finitude, eternity and temporal existing, possibility and necessity. How can one have a relation to this synthesis if all one encounters is one's self-relation? Tugendhat objects that Kierkegaard's depiction of the reflexive structure of self-relation leaves linguistically undetermined the structural link between the synthesis and self-relation. The poles of the synthesis at times appear as the constitutive elements of a relation that relates itself to itself. To clear up the residue of dualistic language, Tugendhat argues that the aspects of the synthesis are not subsisting somethings, but rather determinations of a lived human existence.[13]

Tugendhat intervenes with a linguistic transcript of Kierkegaard. What do possibility and necessity or eternity and time stand for if they are neither substantive nor the anthropologically fastened predicates of a subject? They are "second order predicates which qualify existence, a person's life." With this second order predication, one may speak of self-relation apart from the anthropological structure of reflexivity. In self-relation one relates neither to an entity nor to a manifold of predicates of this entity. One's self-relation to the synthesis means that one relates to one's signification as an existing, living being. This analytical transcript of self-relation preserves Kierkegaard's phenomenology of existence in the propositional structure of self-relating: "my relation to that, that I exist."[14]

Tugendhat raises a question pertaining to my query: how can one read the "existential" communicatively and qualify the communicative existentially? "[H]ow can one understand this self-relation, and how can one linguistically render this existing in its concretion?" But he only intimates the performative in the practical and activist character of self-relation. My concrete self-relation to my existing consists of practical possibility and necessity. The active mode of language in which I say yes or no to that—that I exist—is not the same as the assertoric proposition of factual existence, "it is the case that p." The second order predicate, the self-relation to one's existing, is not equal to the assertoric meaning of "existence."[15]

Habermas shows that the yes–no answer to the question "Is it the case?" differs from the yes–no given from first-person-speaker perspectives vis-à-vis second-person-hearer perspectives. The assertoric yes–no depicts the perspective of the observer; the active perspective belongs to the participant in dialogue. Habermas makes it clear that only existing individuals in the performative attitude can take such yes–no positions on criticizable validity claims, and only then can we also speak about a self-relation or an identity claim in the practical meaning of the term "existence." Tugendhat does not develop an analysis of speech acts, but his distinction between the two modes of self-relation to one's being/nothingness, the two semantic modes of yes–no answers to existing, prefigures Habermas's analysis of performatives.[16]

Tugendhat insists that the modalization of assertoric sentences does not split them off from their propositional structure. In Habermas's analysis, this means that even though performative claims about practical existence do not possess that cognitive truth value which pertains to the affirmation or denial by the constatives, they are still deemed to be validity claims analogous to truth claims. The "existential," or to "exist," means one thing in epistemic self-relation, another in practical self-relation, and still another in expressive self-relation. Habermas argues that in the overlapping performative modalization of claims their validity must be grounded and redeemed by participating subjects.[17]

Tugendhat seeks a linguistic transcript for self-relation. Unlike Habermas, he does not attempt a generic translation of Kierkegaard, but rather asks how language links up with existence. This is not the abstract question "To be or not be?" but "How do I want to be, how do I want to live?" How does language enter my concern for determinate possibilities and activities, for the words with which I must choose and do certain things? Tugendhat shows that a personal mode of language resides in the very structure of self-relation: I relate myself to myself in that I am concerned with my existing, not with the subject–object or any reflexive self-relation. He poses for himself a question that also worries Habermas: is it grammatical to speak of one's relation to one's existing? Do we not understand self-relation on the basis of one person's relation to another person? Tugendhat returns to his analytical transcript of Kierkegaard: self-relation is a practical, not assertoric proposition. I relate to a proposition, which is my existing. The propositional content is modalized by "affective–voluntative" self-relation. The second order proposition of self-relation does not lay out the fact of my existence but bespeaks a practical necessity and possibility of how to be.[18]

As a consequence of Tugendhat's analysis, there is introduced a mode of identity that operates within communication and is more concrete than the one suggested by Habermas's own claim to have harnessed the "existential mode of expression" to communicative ethics. First, Tugendhat offers analytically grounded conditions of the possibility of practical self-relation. Second, he shows how, in all action, one is always self-related. Third, in order to maintain and stabilize self-determined identity, one must choose oneself. Fourth, the qualitative possibility and necessity of self-relation provide the necessary if not the exhaustive conditions for the possibility of generic self-determination.[19]

But Tugendhat shortcircuits the move to the performative "I" when he claims that Kierkegaard's analysis of self-relation before God has no equivalent in self-relation to others. My own argument does not appeal to Kierkegaard's God-relation. Yet I am concerned precisely with that which is bypassed by Tugendhat: Kierkegaard's view of self-relation directly before the other. All practical self-relation to the self-relation of the alter must exhibit a propositional structure of the grammar by which I say "yes" or "no" to the other's existing. I relate neither to an entity nor to this or that predicate, but to my and alter's existing. In self-relation I relate to a self-relation of the other.[20]

The propositional reading of self-relation prefigures Habermas's performative rendition of identity claims. Nevertheless, Tugendhat's analysis of the yes–no relation to existing theoretically stops short of the performative attitude of the participants who can take yes–no positions on criticizable validity claims, and who thereby claim identities via the reciprocal exchange of perspectives. What frustrates Tugendhat's insights is the lack of a performative analysis of an existential mode of self- and other-relations. I am convinced by his original and largely untapped linguistic–analytical intervention into Kierkegaard's lived phenomenology, but I side with Habermas's argument against Dieter Henrich. This argument carries the following implications for Tugendhat: self-relation can neither precede nor be constitutively co-equal with one's language capacity in originating identity. If Habermas is correct here, then one's self-relation in Tugendhat's transcript of Kierkegaard must be worked out communicatively. It must be shown how, within the individual's linguistic competence, it is meaningful to speak about an open mode of identity as the condition of the possibility of generic self-determination. I want to preserve Tugendhat's insight into second order predication of the "existential," but, relying on Habermas's analysis of the performative, jettison Tugendhat's precocious claim that Kierkegaard's portrait of self-relation has no equivalent in one's self-relation to others.[21]

B. Habermas on Self-Relation

Tugendhat eliminates one problem ascribed to the self-critical attitude by the received view of Kierkegaard and by Habermas: Wittgenstein's private language argument, while applicable to Cartesian and Husserlian phenomenology and to the received view in analytic philosophy, need not disqualify responsible self-relation. The paradox is that Tugendhat wins a participatory perspective for self-relation but fails to expand it to a communicative praxis. He shows that the self-choosing attitude cannot be apprehended as a subject–object relation, but rather as a propositional relation to one's existing. Yet he does not extend the yes–no attitude from oneself to the other.

Habermas does not expand Tugendhat's path for noted theoretical reasons: the "*communications–theoretic turn*" transcends "the *linguistic turn* of the philosophy of the subject*" (emphasis added). The former "relates the analysis of linguistic meaning to the idea of participants in communication coming to an understanding about something in the world." Within the linguistic turn, he critiques the theories that privilege one function of speech at the expense of another. Referring to Bühler, he distinguishes three such functions. Communication discloses the intentions of the speaker, refers to facts in the world, and facilitates the communicator's relation with the addressee. These three functions comprise the formal structure of language usage: I come to an understanding about something with the other. The point of Habermas's critique is a common oversight of the reflexive, self-relating character of communication. Thus, he adopts the path of linguistifying the existential, thereby also absorbing temporality, along with debunked sacred traditions, into the structural conditions of the possibility of communication.[22]

But it is misleading to read Habermas's critique as his celebration of the death of identity. If this were true, then it would be difficult to place his defense of the moral individual against the amorality of our age. On the other hand, while this individual is at home in communicative ethics, Habermas never makes clear how one is existential, or how the community ideal would be affected should it become a life form for radically honest individuals. Does not he, in linguistifying an ambivalent yes–no attitude to one's existing, inadvertently eliminate an open mode of the self- and other-relation? Let me reconstruct three possible lines of defense that he might offer.

Habermas, in one line of defense, might argue that taking the attitude of the other is the condition of the possibility of self-relation. Performatively, a speaker and a hearer address one another in a reciprocal take-over of perspectives. Self-relation results from an internalization of this perspective switch. Speaking of Kierkegaard: "The self of the existing human is to such a degree derived [and] posited relation, so that in self-relating it relates itself to another."[23]

Habermas would defend here the "original mode of language use" (i.e., the performative orientation to reaching understanding) against the derived mode of reaching effect or success. This original mode is a way of communication; the derived one is a means to something else. The original mode is reached by analytically differentiating between propositional content and the mode of speech acts. Austin distinguished between locutionary and illocutionary speech acts. To say "that p" is to utter a locution; to say "I promise that p" is to act in saying something, that is, to exercise an illocutionary force of the basic mode (Mp) of speech. The purpose of perlocutionary speech acts is to produce an effect upon the hearer rather than to come to an understanding with her. Perlocutions intervene in the world and bring about something through assimilating speech acts into actions oriented to success. Wittgenstein rejected the conception of language as a private, intention-fulfilling tool. Austin discovered that with acts of speech we actually do something. The former insight is the use theory of meaning; the latter lays out the illocutinary character of speech acts. Habermas articulates a self-relating, reflexive structure of communication that links meaning with the illocutionary force of validity claims.[24]

The risky nature of communication is apparent in all claims because they come under the reflexivity or the double contingency of speech: every speech act can be critiqued by the recipient under one or all three of the validity aspects that the communicator introduces by what she says. "We understand a speech act when we know the grounds which a communicator could introduce in order to convince the recipient, that under the given conditions she is justified to claim validity for her saying—shortly: when we know, *what makes them acceptable*" (emphasis in original). The original mode of speech is self-relating; it lets actors know how to apply what is said, and it does so performatively.[25]

In a second line of defense Habermas might extend the analysis of validity claims to identity claims. What he means by reflexivity need not be identified with speculation. There is an outright anti-Hegelian dimension to the performative attitude: it overcomes the abstractions of the subject–object model of self-knowledge; it provides a "profane rescue of the non-identical"; it maintains integrity and a freedom of choice by all communicators; and it is a way, not a means, to stabilize identity. By reflexivity Habermas means that from the perspective of an observer (a third person) one cannot determine what is meant, but must rather take a perspective of a participant, the second person, vis-à-vis the communicator, the first person. Inversely, I can relate to myself in that I am related to the other. I sustain my self-relation in that I am recognized by the other. I am recognized as a participant with a competence to take a yes–no position in communication. I cannot communicate myself as if ahead of myself (speculatively) because I relate to myself in that I relate to the other. With validity claims I raise my identity claim. The performative attitude guarantees that both types of claims can be satisfied without deception.[26]

In a third line of defense Habermas would argue for the primacy of practical self-relation over epistemic and expressive ones. He admits that there is no metadiscourse overarching the three basic modes of speech acts and the corresponding three types of discourse governed by one of the validity claims. But he argues for an "overlapping performative attitude." Performatively, I, in "a dominant basic attitude" of the speaker, always relate through basic and combined "intermodal invariances of validity" to something objective, social, and subjective. The performative unity is sustained by culture-specific variations of speech acts and variable, indirect, transposed, or nonstandard forms of communication.[27]

The competence to take yes–no positions on claims is identified by Habermas with the Socratic posture. I gain reflective self-relation through my capacity to offer reasons for my saying yes–no. When I internalize the critical attitude of communicative action, I develop self-critical identity. I can critique either my communications, my actions, or my aesthetic expressivity. That which Tugendhat determined in the second order predication of one's existing becomes in Habermas the overlapping performative attitude—one's basic mode of self-relation. "It is this attitude of a first person towards a second that guarantees the unity in the changing modes of language use. . . ." Practical self-relation governs epistemic and expressive ones. Does this performative attitude refer to the same category as Kierkegaard's? One clue to the disappearance of the existential attitude from Habermas's performative mode lies in the phylogenetic argument and its implications. He shows that through linguistification, self-critique unifies in the performative mode what ritual consensus or tradition assigns to the authority of the sacred. He aligns the performative with the moral validity domain, not the existential mode, from the beginning: "From a genetic standpoint, the performative attitude can be understood, perhaps, as the result of a secularization and generalization of that emotionally ambivalent attitude towards sacred objects that originally secured the recognition of moral authority." So, "if it is the performative attitude that secures unity through changes in mode," then the priority he gives to the responsible actor's accountability "is at a bottom a moral–practical category," not an existential one.[28]

New questions emerge: can the linguistification of an ambivalent relation to the sacred account for the reflexive character of language, or is this reflexivity, when appropriated as one's capacity, linked with self-relation to possibility and necessity? Again, can the phylogenetic attraction to and terror of the sacred explain the active root of one's performative capacity, or do we need to explain how one takes a yes–no position in both ritual repetition and personal identity formation when one can no longer be identified with sedimented contents of sacred traditions but must learn the way of open communication? *Ergo*, would not a self-critical attitude, the "how", qualify the basic performative mode?

The dubious implications of the phylogenetic argument vanish if we posit an existential mode as the condition of the possibility of "that emotionally ambivalent attitude towards sacred objects that originally secured the recognition of moral authority." Even if the ideological differential between sacred and profane traditions is bridged, one continues to live under an attraction to and a terror of temporality. This existential–temporal mode becomes available in rationalized societies because of the linguistification. Tugendhat's linguistic account of Kierkegaard severs self-relation from a communicative relation to the other. Habermas's reading of Kierkegaard, however, subsumes self-choosing self-relation under the perspective of the generalized other. It is this nuance between Tugendhat's and Habermas's views that I want to emphasize in order to gain a margin for my argument. Two paths, then, present themselves: first, Habermas's domestication of the individual crisis as a communitarian "ethical–existential" affair pacified under the generic universal; second, the path not taken, a communicative reading of existential crisis identity.

5.2. A KIERKEGAARDIAN TRANSFORMATION OF THE PERFORMATIVE

A. Habermas's Validity Domains and Kierkegaard's Mode

Under my proposed Kierkegaardian transformations, an existential mode is distinguished from validity domains, and therefore from the basic performative mode of speech acts: the existential–performative mode is not defined by something in objective, social, and subjective worlds, but rather by the way in which I relate to myself and the alter. Communicating existence does not raise validity claims but imparts a capability. Capability is not about something but is the manner in which one cares about something. Communication in validity domains differentiates strictly among the roles of the communicator, the addressee, and the content; equality is sustained by the dialogic reciprocity envisioned in the ideal of communication community. In an existential mode, equality is sustained by respect for the temporal existing and actuality of the participants. The medium of communicative ethics is the yes–no orientation to validity claims. The medium of an existential mode is the yes–no attitude in the self- and other-relation of temporal existers. An existential mode cannot be imparted structurally, "for to teach it didactically is to communicate it unethically." While the conditions of communicative ethics are fulfilled directly in symmetry and reciprocity, an existential mode is harnessed indirectly by attending to the asymmetry of contemporary existers. The basic performative mode can be read directly from speech acts and their use-meanings; an existential–performative mode is disclosed in communication indirectly.[29]

To ask, as did Meno, "What is virtue?" would be, says Kierkegaard, "asking unethically about the ethical." Socratically, I learn that every participant can appeal to the ethical in communicative action. We encounter this insight in the two clues to communicative ethics—the thesis of individualization via socialization and in the maieutic verification of the performative. Yet, Kierkegaard goes behind these clues and experiments with the maieutic situation: I ask unethically about the ethical not only because by taking the third person perspective of the observer I abstract from the perspective of a participant in discourse, but because I abstract from radical self-choice, communication, and the temporality of the ideal. Kierkegaardian maieutics differentiates indirect from direct communication: "an attempt to communicate the ethical directly would mean to deceive." That the ground of existing can authentically be neither directly communitarian nor transcendental but only temporal means that "ethically there is no direct relationship." Referring to "the dialectic of communication" and to the revolutionary strife of 1848, Kierkegaard argues that the authentic communication of the ethical lies in that education which edifies, thereby training experimentally and artfully. Edification is neither the rote method that Meno desires from Socrates, nor the nation–state in which the ideal is moulded by an elite for the people, nor the mass action that misidentifies actuality with revolutionary possibility. Kierkegaard determines his maieutic task in something like an existential manifesto: to edify the "I" so that it will once again constitute the center of living.[30]

There is a radically honest questioning that is bypassed by Habermas in his maintaining of a nonhypothetical distancing from one's lifeworld and tradition. While Habermas transcends contexts horizontally via problematized validity claims, Kierkegaard does not need to forge a Cartesian doubt of tradition. Such a Cartesian, subjectivist reading of a Kierkegaardian self-choice represents a false alternative to Habermas's hypothetical attitude toward the claims of tradition. Therefore, we ought to articulate Kierkegaard's existential alternative to Habermas with a greater nuance. Kierkegaard distances himself from tradition by the "how" of raising claims or inhabiting validity domains. He transcends through a mode: the triple "how" question of identity, communication, and the ideal. I limit my argument to this difference in mode.

It is wrong to blur the authenticating question with the neo-Aristotelian ethical–hermeneutical question of the good life. Even though both clinical and existential questions are hermeneutically situated in some context, the latter allow for that distance from ascribed identities that make them distinct from both the therapeutic concerns of ethics and the normative self-determination of morality. An existential mode, unlike questions about social ethics, presents a nonabsolutist possibility of distancing from one's own substantive origins. This is a distance which does not rely on a hypothetical problematization of the claims within validity domains. Self-choice confronts me neither with the question "What am I to be?" nor with "Why am

I to be this or that?" but rather with the questions "Am I to be an identity?" and "How am I to be an identity?" What is of great advantage in the moral point of view turns out to be a handicap when applied to existence. Here one cannot sit back and problematize the validity of claims without at the same time being exposed to a possibility of a radical change in one's identity. This change wakes from a hypothetical slumber that participant in discourse who rests comfortably behind the perspective of the generalized other but has not yet problematized his or her hypothetical attitude projected within it.

Maintaining a radically honest distance from one's origins in a tradition does not call for a Cartesian solipsistic or a Hegelian absolute pinnacle. Rather, a crisis attitude provides a disjunctive basis for being delivered into the ethical and moral spheres of existing in multicultural lifeworlds. This distancing from an ascribed "me" calls for the self-choice of an "I": drawing closer to another requires going home to myself; growing nearer to tradition demands my exodus from its substantive claims. My repeated exile from tradition means that the "I" must die away to its immediacy, the received "me." Distancing prompts self-choice, which, in turn, calls for both an ego- and ethno-decentering. An open homecoming leads to an exodus from tradition; the repetition of homecoming engenders a permanent exiling from the ascribed immediacy of conventional identities. Habermas's hypothetical distancing from tradition alone cannot socially integrate an actuality of one's earnestness. The hypothetical provides the structural conditions of reciprocity; a more radical openness, however, allows for both the ethical and the moral by calling on me to reexamine the status quo. Morality does not secure the earnestness of radical self-choice: hypothetical role distancing offers me a possibility, not my actual transformation of identity and will formation.

Posttraditional and postnational identity viewed from Kierkegaard's angle presupposes this thorough distance from historical life forms. I am to choose neither this substantive happiness nor that *telos* of my life project, but learn to change the mode of my self- and other-relations. The term "existential mode" implies, just as in music, that my self-choice affects the key (how), and thus the given lifeworld contexts (what). Self-choice does not occur in decontextualized leaps apart from validity domains. The arbitrariness of life projects questioned by Habermas pertains to value choices in life projects. It is wrong to characterize as arbitrary self-choice that transpires by the "how" rather than the "what" of life projects. A Kierkegaardian self-choice, unlike communitarian *sittliche* or even some textbook existentialist choosing, does not raise validity claims. Rather, it invites all substantive claims and forms of life to pass through the category of an individual mode of life.[31]

Kierkegaard raises this question: what would it take to transgress every conventional bridge and begin to learn from existence? To be sure, this is not a question of some existentialist leap *ex nihilo*. We would best consult with the undergraduate who emerges malnourished from a syllabus confined to epistemic doubt alone. This student would certainly agree with Kierkegaard's observation that "we confuse the existential problem itself with its reflex in the consciousness of all the generations of the learned." The task is to relate identity questions to temporal existing. A mode, by being open, does not bespeak the private and abstract language of a solitary "I think." Kierkegaard begins with an embodied, historical, linguistic, and social exister. Attacks on objectivism must avoid introspective fallacy:

> There is nothing more dangerous for a . . . [human], nothing more paralyzing, than a certain isolating self-scrutiny, in which world-history, human life, society—in short, everything—disappears, and like the . . . [navel-gazer] in an egotistical circle one constantly stares only at his own navel.[32]

This edifying experimentation involves a well-socialized individual (e.g., an undergraduate torn between traditional values and modern epistemic doubt, between communitarian identity and the twentieth-century leap that proclaims as good news the death of identity). To this individual is addressed the following consideration: "It is undeniably the safest and most comfortable thing to join up thoroughly with tradition, to do as the others, to believe, think and talk as the others and prefer to go out after finite goals." Every generation ought to allow for a "reexamination of the fundamental." One ought to recover "primitivity," the courage to examine tradition. "Primitivity" manifests a nonhypothetical distance from one's substantive origins—a position bypassed by Habermas. A primitive mode does not evaluate norms. Hence it never produces "something absolutely new." The radicality of self-choice does not reside within value choices (go with the resistance or stay at home; go to the hairdresser or go shopping, etc). The aestheticizing examples of either–or choices "lack primitivity." What differentiates an open self-choice from a strategic either–or is "honesty in the deepest sense":

> Completely to lack primitivity and consequently reexamination, to accept everything automatically as common practice and let it suffice that it is common practice, consequently to evade responsibility for doing likewise—*this is dishonesty*. (emphasis in original)

The main task, after a radically honest distancing from tradition, lies in the repeated self-choosing and decentering of one's identity. The courage for this task consists in intellectual and moral humility. Herein lies Socrates's second naïveté—its ignorance harnesses a mode, a way of life, not a validity domain.[33]

B. Kierkegaard against Monologism and Decisionism

I can now address why Habermas conflates communitarian ethics with existential questions: he de-differentiates between an existential mode and the ethical or moral validity domains of self-choice, and between an aesthetic either–or and an existential mode of either/or.

Is Existential Self-Choice Monological and Decisionistic?

Habermas secures personal decisions by public discourse. Since the "self of an ethical self-understanding" does not absolutely belong to "an inward possession of the individual," this public context is to remove the monological and the "decisionistic conceptual framework" of self-choice. Individual ethical continuity rests on the recognition by the public forum which alone can confirm or problematize the claims to authenticity.[34]

Habermas's charges can be handled in two ways. In the first place, I have argued that Kierkegaard's self-choice is not a substantive one of a particular life style, church, party, ethic, or nation. It is suited to the posttraditional and postnational life forms that Habermas projects in a radical democratic republic. Yet while communicative ethics in its open-ended form provides a necessary type of universalization (Habermas and Kierkegaard agree in their critique of Hegel's abolutization of the *Sittlichkeit*), it is not sufficient unless it transpires in an existential mode. In addition to the distinction between ethical and moral questions, the good and the right, and their communitarian and deontic domains, I distinguished between the hypothetical distancing that one maintains from the ethical–hermeneutical domains in moral–critical discourse and the existential distancing harnessed in authenticating self-choice.

I can distance myself from my substantive contexts—family (ascribed gender predicates), flag, market, and beliefs. I am delivered to a movement on the spot, to concretion. The more I find myself decentered from tradition, the more concretely I can take up my dwelling within it. Because the distance I must traverse is not within a validity domain but rather in a mode, I can retrieve all of my tradition but in a transposed key. This distancing, which is at the same time an intensification of my existence, carries the meaning of Kierkegaard's repetition. Through repetition I become what I already am (and this must include tradition), but then become myself in a decentered, posttraditional, multicultural manner. Someone might say that such a Sisyphus-like effort is quite meaningless: how can I become through exile what I already am through enculturation? How is retrieving myself within a tradition posttraditional, postnational, or even multicultural? These liberal and communitarian concerns overlook the gap between being myself in tradition primitively, *simply*, and being myself through a humbling second naïveté and a decentering courage of primitivity.

I must become through repetition what I am socially and hermeneutically by birth and socialization. My existence becomes a journey on the spot rather than a forward or backward shuffle through validity domains. Freedom "avenges itself" on me if I establish a hypothetical but not a self-critical distancing; if, in despair, I move beyond myself without being pinned down to radical self-choice. Standing aloof throws me into a "hysteria of the spirit." The hysteric spirit "binds" me "in the chain of depression." In hypothetical flight, I deceive myself and the other: I seem to participate in discourse under reciprocity conditions but do not "will deeply and inwardly." But in willing sincerely, I meet my possibility of becoming decentered in my actuality offered by another.[35]

An argumentative distance from substantive conflicts admits the impartiality in moral discourse; an existential distance provides a check on the impartiality claim itself insofar as this claim excludes the problematization of one's own living. Interdependent open identity cannot be flattened into moral autonomy. Nor can this identity be associated with an unproblematized social ethic. In self-choice, I do not yet opt for either a good or for a norm that resolves conflicts of goods. I become a self-activating principle on the move. I embody a changed self-relation to traditional and normative contexts.

In choosing either/or I do not ask, primarily, which of the values can bring me the good and happy life, but rather how I must choose myself in order to inhabit value spheres as an individual capable of sustained ethical life and of judgment under the moral point of view. I do not choose a what or a why but myself from the view of a certain how. I choose myself as a person capable of distinguishing between ethical goods and of evaluating moral norms. The mode of the how qualifies the what. I choose to exist as a self. Self-choice does not refer to contents but to an activity of my identity. The mark of earnest either/or is not a choice between good and evil, but rather is the instant modally a priori to value conflicts: I am "choosing to will." Without such self-choice, the rational collective will formation catches me unprepared, unless I have become the person who is both fit to determine and realize the moral right. If I do not choose myself with this consistency, the anonymous structures of communicative ethics will not deliver me into ethical life or the moral point of view. Choosing myself, I need to transform my possibility, and consequently the structural conditions of the ideal possibility of communication, into an actuality. I do not become someone else but find myself, where I have been all along. "[T]he greatness is not to be this or that but to be oneself. . . . "[36]

Self-choice is beyond, or better, prior to good and evil; values are not entities preceding my self-choice, but exist by my willing them. Here is affirmed modernity's priority of freedom over the good. Yet Kierkegaard is not a methodological individualist; he does not console the individual with a communitarian resolve. And lastly, self-choice is not reducible to morality on Habermas's middle road between Kant and Hegel. "The earnestness of the spirit" is not found in the debate between communitarians and liberals, on the one hand, and gained through Habermas's communicative ethics, on the other. These are debates among validity domains.[37]

Kierkegaard's either/or presents me with an absolute choice, but it does not make me into Hegel's absolute spirit. I am pressed to choose absolutely neither in ethical nor in moral validity domains as such. There, my will is subject to communally embedded or rationally motivated constraints; hence, I cannot learn whether I deceive myself and an alter, or whether I have chosen to be what I think and claim to be. Nothing in hermeneutical or hypothetical constraints alone obliges me to choose myself. If there were such an obligation, then it could never happen that I participated in collective will formation, yet failed to become a self. Hypothetical imaginaries impose no such obligations on me, unless they become invitations to self-choice. The absolute in self-choice means that I cannot hold back, that there is nothing in me, literally no thing, which I could objectify and also adore to ease the difficulty of self-choice.[38]

In the second place, when a mode of choosing is distinguished from the validity domains of choices, then self-choice falls under identity rather than validity claims. Habermas argues that these two types of claims ought not to be confused, but that identity claims are always presupposed when we raise validity claims:

> The self of practical self-relation makes sure of itself through that recognition by which its claims are received by an alter ego. These *identity claims*, which are dependent on the presence of intersubjective recognition, *must not be confused with the validity claims*, which the actors redeem by their speech acts. . . . The one must have recognized the other as an actor who is of sound mind insofar as the one expects the other to take a "yes" or "no" position to the offer of his [ego's] speech acts. Thus, in communicative action, one recognizes in the other his own autonomy.[39] (emphasis added)

By absorbing open, self-critical identity into social ethics and then both under moral autonomy, Habermas assimilates the mode to the validity domain. He critiques self-choice as decisionistic, but, on his own grounds, one may not treat identity claims as if they were validity claims. Calling honest either/or "decisionist" means to treat it as if it pertained to a validity domain or a cultural value sphere because decisionism applies to normative validity domains, not to a mode of domains or cultures. Habermas's critique is correct when applied, for instance, to existentialist value choices. But the yes–no position towards the how of one's temporal existing does not have to do with the choice of values. To worry about a decisionism or monologism of radical self-choice is, then, a category mistake.

This leveling results from Habermas's link of an Aristotelian–Kierkegaardian category, the "ethical–existential," with the aesthetic domain of a sincerity claim. To be sure, Kierkegaard admits no accommodation between honest self-choice and aesthetical image management. Moreover, while a sincerity claim is supposed to guarantee one's truthfulness, it does not carry a tag that tells the alter that one either means it and is really at home or only bluffs. I have access to the other indirectly through her manifested possibility and directly through my own homecoming in the argument. These qualifications do not violate dialogic reciprocity but qualify the structural equality by an equality of radically honest communication.

An Existential Mode of Either/Or versus Aestheticizing Either–Or

Let me intensify my argument through an immanent critique: in spite of his critique, Habermas cannot but assume a self-critical attitude when he pits earnest against amoral postures in discourse. In lectures on the amoral *ethos* of our age, he seeks to steal the thunder from the discourse that was sparked by Nietzsche's suspicion of the Enlightenment and continued by Adorno, Heidegger, Derrida, Bataille, and Foucault. He wants to free philosophy from subject-centered reason, from monological anthropology or decisionist morality.[40]

He rejects the following arbitrary either–or: there is a dogma of possessive individualism which claims that I can recover my identity in my own privacy and thus be able to forge some form of community. There is a mirror-image of this dogma in the overt *ethos* of our age which claims that since the subject of modernity is a fiction, we have no basis for dialogue and community. Any talk about ego and group identity constitutes violence. Habermas argues that both options get caught in a decisionist circle. The celebration of the death of identity deliberately practices the forgetfulness of existing. Here one forgets in a dual fashion; first, in a search for oneself among the objects; second, in making the futility of this search into a dogmatic norm for self-appropriation.

Habermas's critique often employs Kierkegaard's images of the age's despair and self-deification. Modernity, from its Cartesian, rational grounding of knowing and Hume's skepticism about it, to Kant's Copernican revolutionary turn towards the subject, to Hegel's absolute self-consciousness, struggled with the aporia of the subject as an object. The monological subject oscillates among the false either–or of extreme positivism and skepticism. The "double status" ascribed to knowing pivots between subject as an empirical object and subject as a transcendental object. Epistemic doubling demands that the finite subject transcend itself into the infinite. Kierkegaard identifies such demands as despair, not doubt: spirit's infinite possibility and finitude present one with an invitation to self-choice, not with hypotheticals. Habermas portrays the failures to evade self-choice: "the knowing subject raises itself up out of the ruins of metaphysics in order, in the consciousness of his finite powers, to solve a task requiring infinite power." The subject's doubly infinite demand shipwrecks. The search for self among objects is "the attempt to evade the unhappy alternatives [which attempt] ends in the snares of a self-deifying subject consuming itself in acts of vain self-transcendence."[41]

This rejection of lived self is dogmatic in that the amorality of the present age levels the problem of identity as such. It does not differentiate between a decisionistic self-relation in the identity claim conceived of as an object, and, to use my transformed language, an existential–performative claim to identity. The present age adopts the view of the observer who parades the possessive individualist's certainty by endowing its basic conceptuality with "transcendental generativity *and* . . . empirical self-assertion"[42] (emphasis in original).

Habermas unmasks the present age with its amoral ethos of aesthetic reductionism, just as Kierkegaard discloses the spiritlessness of his times. Our age, like Kierkegaard's aesthete, lacks earnestness. Both imagine possibilities and hide behind them, but frivolously refuse to take a responsible stance. For both, self-choice either makes no difference or effects a policing action; either everything goes or choosing is a form of violence. The despair of choosing reduces existential either/or to an arbitrary either–or: by abstracting from existing, both "either" and "or" present now a nonchoice.

I have argued, immanently, that these main theses in Habermas's lectures admit a restatement in Kierkegaardian terms. The proposed transformation of communicative ethics is warranted in the distinction between an earnest either/or and arbitrary modes of the either–or. I will argue in the following chapters that in order to sustain this distinction within communicative ethics one is to learn, along with raising validity claims, to communicate existence.

C. A Conclusion: Kierkegaard's Question to Habermas

Habermas retrieves performative identity in a thought experiment with adolescent and cultural crises. Qualitative change occurs in a single critical moment of disenchanted traditions, but is subsumed as a mere stage under generic development. While Habermas distinguishes qualitative and generic identity, he privileges the generalized over the concrete other. He critiques the concept of totality but fails to maintain that individual resistance to it which is operative in identity formation. He does not thematize the difference between a decisionist either–or choice within various validity domains or cultural value spheres and an earnest self-choice. To offset the cognitive uncertainty and motivational weakness of the moral point of view, he takes recourse in law. But both legal discourse and political ethics, as well as civil disobedience, as complementary forms of the moral point of view, remain doubly unprotected against possibly institutionalizing a deceptive consensus. Habermas intimates that one can be relevantly material without having to project either a positive or a negative material utopia, yet his community ideal does not satisfy the question of an exister.

My present analysis draws different presuppositions than those introduced through Habermas's question to Kierkegaard in Chapter 1. I cannot assume to be successful with merely an external *rapprochement* between communicative and existential ethics. Kierkegaard poses a question to Habermas about what constitutes the necessary and sufficient conditions of ethical communication. Kierkegaard's question leads to the following triple revision: Habermas rightly privileges the descriptive primacy of the social universal to individual differences. Yet considering identity, Kierkegaard correctly overrides the primacy of the generic other with self-relation to the concrete other. Further, Habermas is right in showing that egalitarian access to raising validity claims in discourse presupposes dialogic reciprocity. Yet this structural symmetry does not in itself require of each participant that he or she learn to communicate earnestly. Finally, pragmatically, Habermas demonstrates that the community, if it wants to reach an understanding, must admit as its regulative ideal the possibility of reaching genuine consensus. But without a qualitative constraint upon such a generic horizontal ideal—without Kierkegaard's language of inwardness or verticality—the procedure can fail to resist a possibly totalitarian consensual outcome. Kierkegaard's how question—what is that mode which is required of identity in communication under the projected ideal of communication community?—does not raise objections from the standpoint of material utopia or eudaemonistic happiness. It asks something that stands prior to the communitarian–liberal controversy that has invaded communicative ethics. This question implies neither monologism nor decisionism nor a metaphysical leap, but an attitude that is to inhabit the structural conditions of the possibility of communicative ethics in order to sustain their actuality. Habermas does not inquire how the exister, in principle, can sustain an opposition to system and transcend the status quo, or how an earnest attitude can be concrete without a drivenness to heroic culture. He neglects the critical function of an existential questioning and fails to detect the sacralization of validity domains. Without the how of identity, communication, and the ideal, consensual procedures are too anonymous to protect projected possibilities against totalitarian results.

If we are to have a communicative ethic that is to be established as an existential ethic, the reverse must be likewise true. That radical self-choice, and that Kierkegaard's dedication of his edifying discourse to the single individual reader, should result in charges of monologism, decisionism, and dogmatism mirrors to the accuser a jest of Kierkegaard's incognito in which he remains the most marginalized among modern social critics and activists. He brings a theoretical corrective to certain types of critical social theory and to the forms of life that legitimate such theories. In that task—not unlike Marx's critique of political economy and capitalism as a form of life or Habermas's critique of the colonization of the lifeworld by system—he exposes ideology, anomie, and fragmentation. I proposed to read Kierkegaard through Mead's analysis of the individual who against the theoretical and practical status quo projects not only a new possibility but a novel form of life. Through such a pragmatic analysis we can read Kierkegaard's communicative action as an experiment in self-realization and self-determination.

Kierkegaard is, then, a lived corrective to critical social theory as well! To answer Habermas's initial question of how to integrate socially the modern crisis individual: that which Kierkegaard communicates is not a withdrawal from social forms of life but rather indirectly a way of action. Misreadings of Kierkegaard's individualism are, thus, self-misreadings. Therefore, I find it wise not to begin my reading with the anthropological, ontological, and theological language of Kierkegaard's authorship, but with his performative mode of authoring. Other entries into Kierkegaard pose a danger of a self-misreading. Identity can be claimed in the first person and reconstructed from the reader's second person participant perspectives, but never from the third person perspective of the aesthetic observer of Kierkegaard's texts. I propose another beginning by reversing Habermas's question. How are we to envision that one's identity can facilitate, through its positively harnessed attitude of personal crisis, the formation of open, multicultural, and solidary forms of life? This transformation of Habermas's question confirms the need to integrate posttraditional and postnational identity without authority, in a temporal openness of communication, and under a decentered community ideal.

CHAPTER 6

Communicating Existence

Is it not probable that in our fundamentalist and nationalistic age, in which one claims to be ethical, or even religious, but shrugs at authoring one's identity, and wherein one worships new sacral authorities, one has her hands full with the single task of becoming an individual? Is not Kierkegaard's invitation that one become a responsibly communicating self a form of offense to such an age? Thus, I am not leaping ahead of myself in order to become contemporary with Kierkegaard's passion for existing as a Christian. I am not in a hurry to be attracted and repelled by the offense of Christian religiosity communicated by Kierkegaard's pseudonym, Johannes Climacus, under the topic of religiosity "B." I am content to take up my residence in the risky business of facing the difficulty of beginnings recorded under Climacus's topic "A" as intensified pathos.

How can one live like the "ice-bird" and "build [her] nest upon the sea?" Can one "achieve" this in a mode of sober, meaningful, and responsible "tranquility"? Can such living be maintained and made socially relevant in resistances to the new idols of family, flag, market, and sacralized culture? To sustain normative discourse without deception, need not one learn to live like Kierkegaard's water bird upon the turbulent sea? The refugee in flight, thrown into decisive self-choice while searching for a new homeland, permanently split between the old and new dwelling, offers a portrait of such an honest distancing from ethnocentrism, nationalism, and fundamentalism. Perhaps this experience of being reduced to mere boat existence admits one to multicultural traditions with an ever more renewed passion of critique and belonging.[1]

Climacus's intensified pathos invites the reader to learn how to think and thereby inhabit one's identity in radical openness (6.1), how to communicate self-choice through one's way of living (6.2), and how to expand self-choice and communication to the community ideal qualified by the permanent difficulty of beginnings (6.3). Because these are not concepts but invitations to communicative self-transformation, I find it wise to become contemporary with them by way of their performative retrieval, and only thus derive the implications of a transformed model of communication for Habermas.[2]

6.1. EXISTENTIAL IDENTITY AND SELF-CHOICE

The difficulty of beginnings lies in existing—in a doubling of contrasts, such as possibility and necessity, infinity and temporality. Climacus refuses to resolve this difficulty by reading off the rules of life from an anthropology or an ontology of existence. The exister cannot transfer self-transformation "away from himself unto existence, or unto the one who placed him in existence." Lest I proceed abstractly, as a speculating self-misreader, it is nonsensical for me to adopt at the outset the view that treats Climacus's invitation to earnest thinking (A) and choosing (B) as either monological or decisionistic.[3]

A. Existential Thinking

Let me begin with several of Climacus's texts:

> To subjective reflection, truth becomes appropriation, inwardness, subjectivity, and the point is to immerse oneself, existing, in subjectivity. . . .
> *An objective uncertainty held fast through appropriation with the most passionate inwardness, is the truth*, the highest truth there is for an *existing* person. . . .
> [I]f inwardness is truth, results are nothing but junk with which we should not bother one another, and wanting to communicate results is an unnatural association of one person with another, inasmuch as every human being is spirit and truth is the self-activity of appropriation, which a result hinders. (emphasis in original)

Evans comments: having objectives differs from inhabiting a mode.

> The basic idea is that a distinction can be drawn between objective knowledge, which can be communicated directly from one person to another as a "result," and a type of self-knowledge that can only be communicated "artfully."

Again, objective communication is useful in building roads but quite useless when I want to disclose my understanding.

> There is a type of self-knowledge, however, that cannot be communicated merely as a "result." This self-knowledge is not acquired simply through gain-

ing more information about oneself, particularly not more information in which the self is viewed from an objective, "third-person" perspective.[4]

I cannot be satisfied with locating Habermas's distinction between strategic and communicative action in Climacus's communication. Climacus means more than switching from observation to participation in arguments:

> [T]he question is about the subject's acceptance.... And here it must be regarded as perdition's illusion (which has remained ignorant of the fact that the decision is rooted in subjectivity) or as an equivocation of illusiveness (which shoves off the decision by objective treatment in which there is no decision in all eternity) to assume that this transition from something objective to a subjective acceptance follows directly of its own accord, since precisely this is the decisive point and an objective acceptance is . . . thoughtlessness. (emphasis added)

Evans notes Climacus's "first-person-present perspective," which indicates nicely the transformation of Habermas's model at which I aim here. Climacus inhabits a "perspective of an exister," without which the structural conditions of communicative ethics are formally necessary but concretely insufficient.[5]

Let me reconstruct Climacus's communication with caution: his stress on "subjective acceptance" should not be read as "subjectivist." The mode of acceptance is an important qualifier of the grounds, meaning, and validity of claims. The "what" of the validity is qualified by the "how" of one's orientation to the criticizability of the claims. The "how" question offers an invitation to earnest thinking and inserts it into Habermas's structural, formal–pragmatic presuppositions of ethical communication. This thinking is articulated in such a way as to avoid both the idealistic philosophy of the subject and the obverse of idealism in a one-sided privileging of social ethics. One cannot account for communication when one reduces the individual to the objective structures of linguistic interaction. Thus, it is necessary to distinguish a subjective mode of acceptance from validity claims that can be objectively accepted or rejected. The subject's acceptance signifies the existential–performative mode of receptivity. This mode, however, might not satisfy someone who is longing for a more substantive description of the individual. Yet Kierkegaard's single most important edification is not an anthroplogy or an ontology of human nature but an experimental use of the first person pronominal "I." We have seen that the fuzzy character of both personal identity and of the concrete other remains a critical deficit in Habermas's communicative theory. I argue that the "how" question articulates a stronger possibility of the self- and other-critical attitude. Without an advertence to this active mode of one's receptivity, we would be unable to explain in what sense the individual communicator is the last resort of practical judgment, which remains Habermas's key affirmation.

If communication has to do with humans, it must pass through radically honest thinking. But there is no Kierkegaardian cookbook on open identity. The difficulty of beginnings is always my own. To level accusations of monologism, decisionism, and dogmatism at this difficulty is to implicate oneself in a lived abstraction. The view of Climacus's invitation to existential thinking as subjectivist reveals objectivism and an introspective fallacy: both self-misread the subjective thinker as a navel-gazer.

Climacus means by the first reflection a form of objective communication that, formally, requires no self-critique. The second reflection establishes, however, an existential mode of communication; it transpires indirectly in order to respect the other as an active recipient of it. This double reflection is occasioned not by the indirectness of the pseudonyma alone. Every reading of Climacus's *Postscript*, and in fact Kierkegaard's entire authorship, invites the reader to this second mode of thinking. We need not conflate the indirection of pseudonymity with that of open identity formation.[6]

B. Toward a Critique of "Masculinist" Rationality

Replying to Habermas's charges against Kierkegaard's language of inwardness or verticality, I want to verify Climacus's claim about the "how" of identity—*"truth is subjectivity"* (emphasis in original)—by performatively inhabiting his invitation to radical self-choice. Is Climacus's claim a serious jest vis-à-vis the public which, fearing responsible self- and other-relations, celebrates the death of self, reader, and author? Climacus cannot directly convince anyone whose celebration signifies self-evasion. Such a person resembles the one who sets fire to an entire city and delights in the scene, like Nero watching Rome burn: no sooner does he strike the self-disclaiming match than it is apparent that his own house is burning down. To argue that self-erasure in conversation is performatively self-contradictory one is prompted to move, like Climacus, beyond Habermas's argument from logical inconsistency and make the interlocutor experience this self-violation. One can dramatize, then, that the self-evading fire inflames the arsonist's entire living room (i.e., that this one has become a self-arsonist). One would need to engage in dialogue the poor patriot who has left the gas-mask on the roof while waging chemical warfare in his own house.[7]

Climacus's jokes, thus, protect Kierkegaard's earnest incognito. Climacus adopts a deliberately self-referential manner of proceeding while remaining shielded by irony and humor. How can I, the reader of Climacus's "truth claim," claim and performatively inhabit its meaning? "Truth is subjectivity" might mean that a *true*, Kierkegaardian way of teaching Kierkegaard is not to teach him. One may apply his texts as occasions, as footnotes for the primary text that one is. One ceases, then, to be a "reader's digest" and commences, rather, in dramatic authoring or self-reading.[8]

But is it true that truth is subjectivity? How can communicative ethics show me grounds that make this claim acceptable or not? This claim cannot be falsified from a third person perspective: Climacus points out how an observing thinker remains in the sphere of existence where insight into subjectivity does not exist for him or her. Habermas's rule for redeeming validity claims, while necessary, is not sufficient for me to become contemporary with the mode ("how") of this claim about subjectivity.

Many a critic of Kierkegaard promotes an objectivist reading of Climacus's claim while really meaning subjectivism. Yet objectivism–subjectivism are doubly nonsense. Both fail to be valid even as methods of communication of objective facts, not to speak of the indirect character of communicating subjectivity. Babble gives away the sign that the critic is out to lunch. The claim is not objective information to be grasped, had, and stored on a 3½" floppy disk. I can gain insight into the claim if and only if I can verify or falsify in my self-activity that I am a subjectively existing thinker, and if and only if I can find in a mode of my existing how I can accept or reject the truth of Climacus's claim about truth.

Any contemporary of Climacus might get a clue to my ignorance from my direct assault on the truth of the claim that truth is subjectivity. The metaphor of a rape assault on truth is not inappropriate: truth transpires in disclosure, openendedness of communication, and con/temporaneity with another. Climacus's critique of objectivism offers his corrective delimitation of such male-dominated—let me say "masculinist"—notions of truth as possession, penetration, hurrying to the point, and getting oneself clear and distinct about.

Climacus's truth lies in its indirect but active mode of the subjective acceptance of claims. Without reducing self-choice to some essential gender predicates, I wish to show that this second order receptivity calls into question the "masculinist" strategy of self-choice. I call as the the first order "masculine" any direct strategy of validating claims. To be sure, this critique of "masculinist" self-strategy does not make either Climacus or Kierkegaard into protofeminists. The related terms "feminine" and "masculine" are not to be associated with the historical predication of the female and the male. Rather, they stand here for distinct types of self-positionings. These terms define the ways in which, mostly in the West, we have made available and valorized gendered identity through certain modes of self-choice. I am a male, but I am not limited to "masculinist" self-positioning. I can learn indirect receptivity just as any female can either choose herself in direct receptivity or learn to behold herself indirectly.[9]

In the second order of receptivity, I learn to dwell in my self-activity; I do not pursue it head on. These are not only two orders of receptivity but also two kinds of activity. The first is oriented to reaching an understanding by directly grasping the grounds. In the latter, I learn to become active in a nonactivist manner. "Pathos" is not "passivity" or, as MacIntyre misidentifies it, an emotivist drift. Learning to dwell in subjectivity involves passionate activity. Pathic activity comprises affective life but does not reduce to it. The self-critical attitude comprises aesthetic–expressive life but does not reduce to it.[10]

In learning to dwell, I become a way. Climacus says that self-discovery is a *kinesis* on the spot. I am invited to live under an imperative, to act in that way which is not a direct way to somewhere, which is an active nonactivity, the Chinese wu-wei! I discover in this critique of my strategies for self-appropriation a dimension of temporal existing. The secret of Climacus's claim is, then, the "nonmasculinist" character of truth as disclosure.

I can now verify Climacus's claim about the truth as subjectivity when I discover and choose myself as an existing knower. When I understand that to understand involves my experience, understanding, and an affirmation of my capacity to accept or reject claims, then I can know myself as such a concrete self-activity. When I affirm that I cannot deny this self-activity without becoming a living joke, then I affirm myself as such a concrete self-activity. Self-critical thinking means that every acceptance of validity claims involves these two levels of reflection: the first reflection grasps the grounds or reasons that allow one to accept or reject a criticizable validity claim; the second reflection affirms how one accepts this claim in the temporal mode of subjectivity as an experiencing, understanding, and affirming self-activity. The second reflection qualifies the "what" of the first reflection.[11]

I am puzzled, however, about how my performing radical self-choice is validated in communication. If an existential mode is something like that Kantian "in-itself" which cannot be communicated, then how is my self-choice accountable to the other? If the "existential" seems to be that trace which dwells in the indirect, metaphorical rift between concepts and anagogical language, that temporal existing which in discursive symmetry remains noncontemporaneous, and that verticality whose otherness cannot be manifested within horizontal dialogic reciprocity, how can I speak about the possibility of a communicative and existential ethic? Are not these the reasons for Habermas's irritation with the dogmatism of all this temporal and vertical mode talk?

I would agree in part with his objection. I cannot communicate with that type of otherness to which there is no order of receptivity possible. The judgment of irrationality in Kierkegaard, sometimes accepted unawares by him to set the earnest attitude over and against the "masculinist" discourse of the Hegelian system, assaults the indirectness of the mode from the direct viewpoint of rationalized validity domains. What, however, appears untranslatable and communicatively irrational in validity domains admits of another order of receptivity. A question nags me: does an existential mode pertain to intersubjective linguistic communication? Can the "how" of self-choice communicate with the "how" of the alter?

6.2. EXISTENTIAL COMMUNICATION

Existing prompts one to become consistent with oneself and to communicate self-choice in one's concrete way of life. In this invitation, Kierkegaard provides a way, or path bypassed in Habermas's own Copenhagen question "how" to integrate socially the modern individual. The point of contrast between the two thinkers elucidates the transformation of the notions of identity and communication—both basic concepts in communicative ethics. Let me performatively retrieve Kierkegaard's concern with existence by expanding the "how" of self-choice to communication (A) and to a concrete way of living (B).

A. "Truth Is Subjectivity": An Intersubjective Communication

Existential Uses of Language

Kierkegaard lures me through Victor Eremita (editor of *Either/Or*), Constantin Constantius (author of *Repetition*), and Hilarious Bookbinder (publisher of *Stages on Life's Way*) so that I keep coming back to myself in the constancy of author and reader, binding self-identity by the humorous distancing of double reflection: prior to saying yes–no to a claim, I am prompted to know myself as an existing thinker. As this existing thinker, I am invited to exercise self-choice, lest I decide to ignore the evidence of my subjectivity and slip away from my self-reading. Either I slip away or I resolve to find myself as a temporal exister with limits. Existing cannot be determined from within Habermas's generalized other; reflection could go on forever, and reaching consensus could enjoy an interminable recess, since the ideal of a communication community does not require me to heed temporal limits.

Habermas places this cognitive uncertainty and motivational weakness of moral discourse under the time and place constraints of the law. Temporal limits, however, can never be offset by any such constraints. Whereas Habermas's solution abandons the radicalized individual, I describe communicative ethics in an existential mode. Hence, back to the limit: choosing myself, I learn the truth of subjectivity in a "nonmasculinist" way. Radical self-choice is a task of becoming subjective. Yet this is just as hilarious a task as writing a book; it binds me to myself in a way that also decenters me. Self-choice binds me in that it opens me to another who facilitates the possibility of my actual decentering. In this intersubjective cleavage, I begin to anticipate the direction in which the question that nags me can be raised!

Another pseudonym, Vigilius Haufniensis, helps me to grasp how language links up with possibility and actuality. He explains how one can assume a yes–no position to temporal existing, thereby facilitating my rendition of self-choice in communicative terms. In the doubling of human existing is expressed the synthesis of the psychical and the bodily; self is spirit, namely, one's self-relation to this synthesis. Spirit is "this third." By placing spirit's self-relation within the performance of communication, Vigilius, in his *Concept of Anxiety*, wins an advantage over Anti-Climacus, who lays out the anthropological categories of the spirit in the beginning of his *Sickness unto Death,* and then tries to justify them from the structure of existence. Vigilius argues that spirit relates "itself to itself . . . as anxiety," and that this self-relation "can indeed speak, inasmuch as in language . . . [an innocence of spirit] possesses the expression for everything spiritual." He affirms that one is not a private inventor of language. If anxiety is "freedom's actuality as the possibility of possibility," then one's self- and other relation is anchored in the linguistified possibility of taking a yes–no position to temporal existing.[12]

How is anxiety communicated in language? A yes–no attitude to temporal existing takes up in language the being and the nothing of human striving. There occurs a certain linguistification of that anxiety which is communicated in the possibility of one's existing. If spirit is freedom's possibility of possibility, then one's ambivalent love–hatred of the unknown presupposes that there exists an anxiety that can be communicated, ritualized, or linguistified. Habermas tells us that the core of the performative mode lies in the ritualized repetition of an ambivalent love–anxiety of the sacred, but does not explain how any individual or group can take up such an ambivalent posture. His developmental argument and linguistification thesis put the cart before the horse; they fail to address "how" one is an honest individual whom communicative ethics hopes to integrate socially. Habermas precociously celebrates the linguistification of the sacred as that reduction of sacred authorities, hierarchies, and traditions into the profane public sphere that frees culture from its ideology function. Today's sacralization of the family, flag, market, and fundamentalist religiosity colonizes identities on the level where anxious communication of freedom's possibility is not attended to.

By showing what sort of precarious identity and will formation pertains to the spirit, Vigilius emerges as a more sober resister than Habermas. "The actuality of the spirit constantly shows itself as a form that tempts its possibility but disappears as soon as it seeks to grasp for it, and it is a nothing that can only bring anxiety." To be anxious is to be qualified by freedom's possibility. This qualification cannot be eliminated from communication by a linguistification. Radical self-choice assumes the linguistification of traditions: the "existential" is neither a pathological anxiety nor an authoritarian domain; it is freedom's possibility.[13]

Whereas Vigilius contemplates how one dreaming freedom becomes dizzy with power, as in "the anxious possibility of *being able*," Climacus intensifies his communication of existence in the difficulty of death. The futurity of death qualifies every actuality. Being towards death transforms my birth in that it occasions me to choose without reservation and yet without absolutization. Such a self-choice communicates the difficulty of beginnings in my dying away from immediacy. Yet this is a good dying, since goodness exists for freedom. Dying teaches me the "how" of my yes's and no's; it opens my claimed time and existence to critique. The possibility of critique means that the immediacy of my claims is put in question along with the claims of other mortals in the community.[14]

Habermas's pragmatist expansion of Marx's material basis is granted but qualified by this existential sense of material concretion. I do not generate language and problems; they come to me. But problems and language are those contexts that place self-transformative requirements upon me. The ethical and the moral "indeed can be expressed in language but nevertheless . . . [*are*] only for freedom. . . ." Dying away from communitarian and individual immediacy delivers me into earthiness and humility, which teaches me to die in the manner of a Native American, without *ressentiment*, not in the anxious self-forgetfulness of Forest Lawn. This dying becomes the permanent task of birthing, mothering, dramatic authoring, self-reading, and generativity. In this difficulty I may meet home in my exile; my chosen ice bird nesting upon the sea becomes my dwelling on earth.[15]

In his entire authorship, Kierkegaard insists on preserving this language of inwardness or verticality. He affirms in the distinction between ordinary and transferred language my proposed expansion of Climacus's claim, "truth is subjectivity," into an intersubjective identity claim. In what is effectively a corrective to Habermas's translation of the language of either/or into the procedures of public debate, Kierkegaard distinguishes "ordinary speech" from "transferred or metaphorical language." He describes that two persons may say the same thing, "and yet there remains an infinite difference between what they say, since . . . [one of them] does not suspect the secret of transferred language, even though he uses the same words, but not metaphorically." My ordinary language, received in individualization via socialization, becomes transferred by my choice to become an individual capable of acting responsibly. There is "a world of difference between the two" persons, and still, there is "something binding which they have in common." Translation between the two cannot occur on the level of ordinary language alone, but across the difference between the content ("what") and a mode ("how") of their communication. The two individuals, while separated by a gap bridgeable only in shifting perspective, "use the same language." Here there is no incommensurability between them in the domains of ordinary speech, though the mode of their shared language differs: "Transferred language is, then, not a brand new language; it is rather the language already at hand." While this distinction cannot be redeemed atemporally, it admits translation in a mode of communication: "we rightly regard emphasis upon a directly apparent distinction as a sign of false spirituality . . . ; whereas the presence of spirit is the quiet, whispering secret of transferred language—audible to [one] who has an ear to hear." In this corrective to Habermas, Kierkegaard shows that to concretize the anonymous structures of communicative ethics we need to incorporate this qualitative back into the generically moral usage of language.[16]

Climacus's Existential Communication

Climacus does not secure communicative interaction by recourse to the Platonic metaphysics of the ideas. He maintains conversation that is Socratically open-ended. For Climacus, unlike Plato, to learn from Socrates presents a task of repetition, not a metaphysic of recollection. In Climacus the Socratic and the posttraditionally modern come together in existential communication:

> Socrates remained true to himself and artistically exemplified what he had understood. He was and continued to be a midwife, not because he "did not have the positive," but because he perceived that this relation is the highest relation a human being can have to another.[17]

All these features make Climacus more than a good Habermasian. I am not permitted to stand around Socrates. Indeed, I am drawn from a hypothetical–metaphysical slumber into an existential drama. I find myself not yet in that modern theater where I may harness possibility by virtue of the absurd. But the spirit of the Socratic *daimon* intimates that in Climacus's communication I stand on a fiduciary ground. I should exercise some caution: this is not a religiously transcendent ground, but an open mode of communication. The Socratic–Kierkegaardian task is not to learn a doctrine but rather to become an emancipated recipient of a way of life.

From Climacus I learn that sharing in another's temporality requires my becoming her con/temporary. This con/temporaneity stands for an intersubjective mode of temporality, or inter-temporality. I cannot become intertemporal with Socrates by not caring for my temporality. I cannot communicate existence and access time speculatively. Learning Socratically, I interestedly draw closer to the other through my own temporal existing. Self-choice effects my other-relations, since I harness my temporal existing directly before the other's temporal existence.

In Climacus's experimental prose, open communication functions somewhat as a concretely operative ideal requirement: student and teacher or author and reader are viewed as equals. The communicator cannot give birth to the student; she can emancipate him by providing an occasion for self-appropriation. A true teacher or author cannot make herself into more than a temporal exister. She must have both the courage and humility to maintain dialogic reciprocity. If she suspends these conditions, her language lapses into babble and she begins to prate at the learner. This equality has to be sustained by all parties involved. For each it is an uphill climb to confront one's tendency to elitism. One learns to view the alter and one-self "with equal humility and with equal pride." Every temporal exister remains a primary text, while the teacher is directly a secondary commentary, a footnote to stir up the alter's "disposition to passion." That "single individual" to whom Kierkegaard dedicates his edifications is the learner and teacher, reader and author, in existential communication.[18]

This Socratic–Kierkegaardian education and reading experience occasions a silent revolution in academia and media, which are shot through with everything from patriarchal and monocultural hierarchies, to authoritative obstacles in learning, to the rote method of instruction, to disinterest in the recipient's passion, to spiritless educators and authors. The administrator who thinks of his role as the key to educational or publication enterprise might find Climacus's experiment a slap in the face: "no human being has ever truly been an authority or has benefited anyone else by being that or has ever really managed successfully to carry his dependent along. . . . " Climacus's communication experiment, albeit carried on within the petty, Eurocentric concerns of Copenhagen, presents us with a beautiful, pluralistic, and open way of living.

Prefiguring a post-Husserlian phenomenology of embodied intersubjectivity, Climacus shows that happy love, like dialogue, must satisfy existential communication: "only in love is the different made equal, and only in equality or in unity is there understanding." Though embodied, loving cannot be identified strictly with the sexual; it is also qualified by time. Lovers' embodied time is experienced as ecstatic self-disclosure. Loving occasions recovering a nonspeculative ground for another in oneself. Without inward grounding for another, one draws to the other in idolatry and infatuation. In a moving text, Climacus shows how erotic loving intimates its ground in an ever more radical equality of self-decentering:

> Self-love lies at the basis of love, but at its peak its paradoxical passion wills its own downfall. Erotic love also wills this, and therefore these two forces are in mutual understanding in the moment of passion, and this passion is precisely erotic love.[19]

Each lover is self-related through the other, since one never inhabits an absolute self-transparency. The symmetrical reciprocity of Habermas's atemporal communications model is supplanted by Climacus's asymmetrical reciprocity among temporal individuals. This intertemporality calls on each one to become a decentered ground for the other. The invitation is not communicated directly through validity claims: fidelity cannot be communicated through spoken vows, for example, but in the lover's becoming con/temporary with loving. Grounding in fidelity remains an objective risk and a conceptual uncertainty in the relationship, rather than a complete reduction of love's ground to a direct, let me reiterate "masculinist," clarity and distinctness in speech acts. To demand that one communicate directly the certainty of love is already to fall into infidelity and, projected into marriage, into a socially sanctioned debauchery. One can fulfill vows in truth without declared speech acts; conversely, one can be married by the Church, ratified by canon lawyers, honored by the public, but live out a well-socialized infidelity.[20]

Coming to an understanding with Climacus on the truth that "truth is subjectivity" poses problems of intersubjective verification because it is often treated as an irrational leap from one stage of existence to another. Yet Habermas discusses one kind of legitimate leap when he shows that one can methodologically take either the perspective of the observer or of the participant; nevertheless, one can never verify communicative claims from the perspective of the observer. Intensifying Habermas's train of thought, I read the often misused language of the leap in terms of a perspectival shift from aesthetic curiosity to earnest identity formation. I cannot verify Climacus's claim while being an aesthetical, laterally leaping self-reader. I am invited by Climacus to become con/temporary with his claim by leaping in an inward or vertical sense. This honest communication, by occasioning my becoming subjective in radical self-choice, opens me to another. Thus, there can be nothing either monological or decisionistic in shifting perspectives. If my reading is sound, then self-choice (leaping from aesthetical management into the self-critical attitude) is necessary to cure the monologic and decisionist attitudes prematurely ascribed by Habermas to Kierkegaard's own posture. In my performative retrieval of Climacus's claim, I transform Habermas's maieutic argument with the skeptic into a concrete task of "how" to become self-responsible: I cannot use my self-activity to throw a tantrum and deny myself as temporally existing without at the same time becoming embarassingly comic. As a reader of Climacus, I win this self-discovery for myself; yet it is this same language of open communication that can make Climacus's postempiricist, "nonmasculinist" claim to truth as subjectivity acceptable to another.

B. Communication as a Way of Living

The culminating task of existence brings me, paradoxically, always to the initial difficulty of beginnings, because I originate in a temporal life form and live as an actual self- and other-relation. Therefore, it is not enough to know and affirm myself as an exister who chooses to communicate with another. Self-transformative thinking is a thought actuality, but not actuality itself; lived pathos calls for ideality to be rooted in actual temporality.[21]

I labor, then, under an invitation to live in harmony with my radical self-choice. I am to sustain my open identity more concretely than in a thought actuality alone. Unless I affirm my thought in a way of life, no repetition of a profanized ritual reciprocity can socially integrate my actuality. Without passing through passion, without becoming primitive in the Socratic sense of courage and second naïveté, and, thus, posttraditional and postnational in the mode of living, I cannot redeem and sustain my claim to temporal existing.[22]

Let me then ask about communicating actual, and not just thought existence:

> Ordinary communication between one human being and another is entirely immediate, because people ordinarily exist in immediacy. When one person states something and another acknowledges the same thing verbatim, they are assumed to be in agreement and to have understood each other. Yet because the one making the statement is unaware of the duplexity of thought-existence, he is also unable to be aware of the double reflection of communication. Therefore, he has no intimation that this kind of agreement can be the greatest misunderstanding and naturally has no intimation that, just as the subjective existing thinker has set himself free by the duplexity, so the secret of communication specifically hinges on setting the other free, and for that very reason, he must not communicate himself directly. . . .[23]

Imagine this text as Climacus's reply to Habermas! For Habermas, to understand a meaning I must know what makes it acceptable. To know this, I take the position of second-person (hearer) vis-à-vis first-person (speaker) to come to an understanding about something (this is the third-person observer or the "what" that is understood by the first and second person). In his first two sentences above, Climacus pictures the ordinary reciprocity and symmetry conditions that allow for an agreement. He gives us a dynamic account of coming to an understanding with another and is quite enamored by the ideal of communicative equality. In ordinary communication it might suffice to reach an agreement by knowing the univocal and direct grounds for accepting or rejecting claims. Habermas's view of consensus operates with this idea of nondeceptive univocity between meaning use and the grasped grounds of validity claims. When he speaks about the problematization of claims, he commences with the scenario that it is the claimed grounds, not the origins of existers, that is criticizable. He questions neither the hearer nor the speaker; they are not invited to take up the task of self-transformation. Yet if this were the whole story, then one could integrate open identity directly via linguistified traditions, rather than in one's total claim to existence.

My existential claim to a way of living becomes total when it transpires in a mode, not through the totalities of validity domains. As this exister, I inevitably can raise only a total claim. Existence, too, does not let me off the hook: if I am to live and not just remain hypothetically engaged with another about something in the world, then I am prompted to respond to life's total claim upon me. This claim, which is communicated by me in response to existing, comprises the task of reduplication (i.e., the call to embody my thought in life). Both earnest thinking and the task of existing deliver me, at the end of the day, into the difficulty of beginnings.

As I read the rest of the above text I muse about the paradoxical inversion of orders in which I find myself and my attempt to communicate existence and thought. There is a given hermeneutical dimension of my being in the world, which I inhabit in tradition, yet within which, through existential thinking, self-choice, and living, I am delivered into my beginnings. This inversion, or better, difficulty of beginnings, communicates my lived condition. I wonder: how can I raise and redeem a total, not totalitarian, claim to existing? Can an ideal communication community help me to raise, redeem, and socially integrate this claim?

6.3. RESTORING THE COMMUNITY TO THE DIFFICULTY OF BEGINNINGS

We meet Climacus's pathos most intensely when it becomes thrice removed from a communitarian perspective through radically honest thinking and self-choice, through open communication, and through the difficulty of beginnings. And yet he neither adopts the posture of the possessive individualist nor proclaims the death of the subject. Rather, he makes a stronger case for open identity than communicative ethics can. In this fashion, pathos becomes an antidote to both unexamined traditionalism and to a merely hypothetical distancing from tradition.

I have justified my present way of proceeding in performance. How I resolve to think and live will concretely inform not only how I can communicate, but likewise how I can project the ideal of a communication community. When I am prompted to embody my self-understanding in existence, I discover that an existential mode has primacy over self-relation in epistemic, ethical, and moral validity domains alike. It exercises a certain primacy in the entire process of coming to an understanding of oneself with another about something in the world. In this intensification of Climacus's pathos, I discover that I have not begun to begin! Because beginnings do not come to me immediately (I cannot be their private owner), I need to delimit my methodology of how I can become con/temporary with their difficulty. Let me performatively intensify Climacus's pathos (A), and then critically evaluate his challenge to Habermas's transcript of Kierkegaard (B). I will argue that if profane models are of philosophical value and social relevance, then Habermas's procedural translation and linguistification of Kierkegaard's theory and practice of communication fails to derive genuine equivalents to pathos.

A. Intensifying Existential Pathos

The primacy of an earnest mode is already the consequence of the invitation to self-choice and open communication. If I began in existence rather than in self-choice—even though I find myself thrown into existence—I would be applying to action something I have not experienced, understood, or affirmed in the second reflection. That beginning would involve me in the uncritical ways of naïve immediacy, not in the difficulty of beginnings. In order to ward off any methodologically communitarian access to existence, Climacus qualifies all human beginnings by pathos.

Pathos teaches me, first, that in my temporal existing I arrive on the scene, paradoxically, out of breath and late. Second, it teaches me how to choose myself as a suffering existence, from the first person perspective but under a decentered claim to home. Third, it teaches me that I cannot postpone the difficulty of beginnings into infinity, to the atemporal ideal of a communication community, without becoming compromised or deceived by an infinite regress away from temporality.[24]

Temporal Existing in the World

If I am to breath and nest in time, I need to resolve how I want to exist. I cannot, however, leap from my contingent existence in the world somewhere beyond my concrete possibility. In leaping sideways, I would flee my predicament. I cannot redeem my existential condition by projecting my possibility unto a totem, nation, church, progeny, materially utopian project, or authorship. My condition cannot be defined simply by a tradition, doctrine, or body subject; it is not identical with a material validity domain; and finally, it cannot be read off textuality. And yet, my condition is a materially concrete text of temporal existing.

This attention to the temporal limits of the human condition is omitted in Habermas's project of posttraditional and postnational identity. Though his nonconcretistic and fallibilist model prevents me from worshiping any one social form of life, it does not teach me pathos. In Habermas's deliberative procedures, I do not necessarily begin to say yes–no to temporal existing because his horizontal appropriation of Kierkegaard does not derive an invitation to self-transformation. In fact, I may redeem validity claims and yet know not how to redeem them in radically honest way. Climacus corrects this oversight when he shows that in self-transformative pathos the individual is altered, in and through her mode of existence. Metaphysics shipwrecks on interest—get all participants in Habermas's communicative ethics interested in their own pathos for ideality, and they too will suffer the difficulty of nourishing the beginnings with a finite diet of the collective will formation! In interested existing, this communicative ideality undergoes the active transformation of the individual's entire mode of existence.[25]

Affections can either have pathos or be flat like beer. But time transformed by the pathos of existing is a river which I cannot enter even once, and yet whose flow I unreservedly cross. My harnessing the movement of time neither employs a communitarian boat of eudaemonism, nor evades the moment by drifting down the stream. Pathos seems more akin to a refugee boat existence. Eudaemonistic metaphysical imaginary evades decisiveness because, just as drifting, it dreads to find its ethical *telos* exiled from immediate and absolute certainties. Communitarians want the group safety; Climacus communicates individual risk. Contemplation of happiness without venturing remains abstract, its prudence only play-acts the ethical. What separates Climacus from Aristotle and Aquinas is that "eternal happiness, as the absolute good, has the remarkable quality that *it can be defined only by the mode in which it is acquired*" (emphasis in original). What separates Climacus from traditionalism is the "chasmic abyss," which is "a suitable setting for the passion of the infinite, a chasm that the understanding cannot cross over, neither forth nor back." This setting mocks any metaphysically driven ethic. What separates Climacus from communitarians and drifters alike is an objective uncertainty of self-choice and communication.[26]

The Existential Condition of Homelessness

Coming to an understanding with another means to apprehend her concretely in suffering and as a sufferer. Intimate lovers suffer in that they open up to one another. Suffering for another, the attraction and terror of love's self-disclosure, houses the temporal exister in her permanent, exilic homecoming.

The humorist "touches the secret of existence in the pain, but then he goes home again." The true exister's mode is homelessness. A courage to care for the materially poor, homeless, and refugees begins in facing the difficulty of my beginnings and by adopting my permanent earthly exile. The latter is neither the road to nowhere nor a communitarian shelter. Pathos implores me to care for another by fostering in me a nonauthoritative and open identity. As a sufferer I come home in this exilic mode, since I cannot explain the suffering of temporal limits away. Climacus finds this suffering intimacy or disclosure of inwardness to be the highest mode of action. If Habermas tried to translate this mode into one of the validity domains, he would become like the impostor clergyman ridiculed by Climacus—afraid to admit suffering as our human condition.[27]

But let us not confuse suffering with passivity: as a sufferer I need not be a masochist. Indeed, I must relinquish the illusions of self-flagellation. Through suffering I learn that action is undergoing, *passio*. As a sufferer I need not be a quietist, just as an exister need not be a solipsist or an earnest individual need not become a decisionist. The pathos of suffering resists condemning the individual to the present age death row—injecting lethal poison into every text, evading one's own subtext. Suffering signifies "dying to immediacy" away from the cultural self; yet as a sufferer I cannot proclaim the death of myself while never having learned to die to myself. If I am not a self I cannot, ahead of myself, proclaim the death of its immediacy.[28]

Raising and Redeeming Existential Claims

By having faced my willingness to exist (as already and always late in coming to itself), I take up the most intensified beginning of my identity formation. I become "the dialectical reader." "In existence, the individual is a concretion, time is concrete, and even while the individual deliberates he is ethically responsible for the use of time." I am pinned to concretion not because I am simply a fallible being: "Existence is not an abstract rush job but a striving." I experience this condition as a qualitative breach of my culturally constructed identity. And the fallible consensual ideal cannot help me here redeem my total claim to earnest living. Because of this identity breach, the consensual ideal and procedure alone cannot block a possibly deceptive outcome. Climacus's attention to the identity breach fills the missing element in Habermas's desire to help Kierkegaard: Climacus grasps what one's identity crisis, which Habermas wants to resolve in social terms, really means. Identity breach on account of late beginnings occasions sustained motivation and legitimation crises. To be sure, this breach delivers the individual to something distinct from the cognitive uncertainty and motivational weakness of fallible consciousness; hence it cannot be offset by Habermas's legal safeguards on the time and space of our collective will formation. If I am in the right in speaking about inwardness or verticality breaking immanently within the horizontal, then it is of no avail to integrate the crisis individual with the constraints of the law. The law as something pertaining to temporal existing is qualified by the breach in this very identity and will formation.[29]

In qualifying the Habermasian recourse to morality and the law by a breach of time, Climacus assaults neither friendship nor justice. Justice does not poke its fingers into texts and other existers. Climacus is not a Gorgias. Climacus's passion holds no residue of innocence about itself, no morbid guilt channeled into a *ressentiment* against tradition. Yet justice and mercy begin in a responsibility for one's own total claim to temporal existing. Justice edifies the other by taking up its claim in a permanently decentered plea. In addressing the criminal, pathos teaches me to lay hold of that temporal mode that could make me an accomplice. In visiting the prisoner, I come home within my own prison. In pleading innocence, I encounter my will decentered by its failure to guarantee beginnings. In coming home to myself, I am chained to time, and in time I labor under the task to sustain my freedom. In this difficulty I may gain a second, not an absolute innocence. This difficulty lies along the way to my plea of innocence when I discover the breach—myself as both a criminal and a prisoner.

Now, homecoming to what Climacus calls existential guilt does not mean dishing out punishment designed by some sado-masochistic pseudo-religiosity. Climacus's pathos plays no S & M games, does not gamble with indulgences, and has no future shares to redeem at the close of commerce with humans. The "good" Catholic or "morbid" Protestant guilt is exposed by Climacus as an embarrassingly comic failure. It is just as comic as the economy driven by unconscious guilt to produce for one's own, national, or party salvation, or the patriotic gore prompted by Dow Jones omens averaging off the divine favors.[30]

The identity breach allows me to raise a claim to "spherical totalities": in this term is anchored a key distinction between validity claims in modern cultural value spheres and lived total claims. Kierkegaard's sphere inhabits neither Hegel's phenomenological totality, nor Marx's social totality, nor Habermas's ethical totalities. Therefore, the claim to an existence sphere is neither monological nor decisionist nor dogmatic, but rather earnestly communicative. Redeeming the total claims of existers, whereby one is delivered into the difficulty of beginnings, may serve as a permanent and lived corrective to any nationalist or fundamentalist zeal to bypass the breach.[31]

B. Transforming Habermas's Reading of Kierkegaard

As indicated in Chapter 1, any difficulty of beginnings drops out from Habermas's description of modernity dirempted into cultural value spheres. This difficulty vanishes from the structure of validity claims, which correspond to the value spheres of science, morality and law, and art. His model no longer appears troubled by any temporal difficulty. Communicative ethics problematizes the whole world of claims—even infallible claims to totality—except its own total claim to a starting point. Climacus makes life difficult for both Habermas's theory and the present age establishment. Let me draw out some implications of Climacus's invitation to communicative self-transformation.[32]

Pathos offends that horizontal consensus which heroically sacralizes its positive claim to existence. As if our human condition could be something other than an intimate greenhouse effect running out of ozone and time! First, my beginnings are marked by temporal existing: learning to breath, becoming timely. Second, this human condition teaches me alternative sources of energy other than my own grasping for life or my ego ecology of willing. Third, responding to existence, bound to my untimely late beginnings, I learn to communicate my eco-ethic responsibly. If I am late in going, if my coming is interminably exiled, or if beginnings always suspend my willing, how can I resolve to say yes–no to my human condition? How can I raise, problematize, affirm, or reject any claim whatsoever —validity or identity? Climacus's pathos shows that I resolve my freedom's possibility not by projecting the individual condition on the generic human condition, but by intensifying my temporality, receptivity, and decentered beginnings. This triple sign of inwardness inhabiting the lived condition qualifies every individual and collective identity and will formation.[33]

Identity

Pathos qualifies Habermas's communicative translation of self-choice. Even if we could speak of the collective identity and will formation (e.g., the forming of German postwar identity) in terms of self-choice, Habermas's structural expansion of the either/or into public debate would have to be intensified within rather than apart from Climacus's communication of temporal existing. With regard to the relationship between qualitative and generic senses of identity, Habermas rightly argues for a descriptive primacy of social–generic over individual–qualitative identity. Yet Kierkegaard correctly shows that critical self-relation to tradition grounds the possibility of universal impartiality in the moral point of view. Habermas and Kierkegaard agree that ethical communication requires a high degree of deliberative capacity. But for Kierkegaard this capacity is neither delivered by generic possibility nor guaranteed by structural discourse conditions.

Climacus invites each participant in communication to self-choice. If such an invitation is severed from communicative ethics, then needs, judgement, and responsibility are determined by an anonymous consensual ideal, not by the communicating persons themselves. Habermas's model is unfit to raise the suspicion that there might be an individual who would fulfill all the structural conditions of moral self-determination, but fail to meet the task of becoming a self. With such a critical deficit, one could not unmask the power or herd mentality that employs deceptively the generic structure of discourse. Without adverting to the difficulty of self-choice, Habermas's critique of nationalism and fundamentalism, while formally cogent, is an insufficient condition of its own sobriety.

Communication

When fallible communicative ethics comfortably relies on its own will formation, it then forgets to die away from its immediacy. Speaking of com munication, Habermas demonstrates that raising validity claims calls for dialogic equality and reciprocity. Yet Kierkegaard reveals that without suffering temporality, communicative ethics cannot occasion the invitation, placed individually on everyone, to communicate openly. Kierkegaard's authoring not only respects the other, but it articulates the temporality of communication that Habermas's atemporal model overlooks. Habermas correctly argues that self-relation is possible because of other-relations. But Kierkegaard rightly shows that communication remains abstract unless we inscribe its reciprocity structure with time, the "how" of communication. And time can never be apprehended under the perspective of the generalized other. Along with the capacity to take a yes–no position to validity claims, Kierkegaard articulates a capacity to take a yes–no position to temporality.

I am con/temporary with the alter's existence by relating directly to my own time and indirectly to another's. I can relate directly to an alter's communicated proposition; yet for me in my self-relation, this proposition is only indirectly the alter's proposition. There is a temporal gap between my and the alter's self-relation and relation to the communicated propositional content. My actual self-relation is communicated to another as a possibility; self-appropriation of the alter's possibility for me is not a mediation of the alter's actuality qua actuality in my actuality. I can understand the alter only within my own actuality, not ahead of myself; I can understand the alter only qua alter. Thus, communicated time and communicated possibility can be only occasions, invitations for self-transformation.

Kierkegaard teaches me that without attending to the temporal nature of intersubjectivity, I achieve merely bogus reciprocity: I may fulfill the structural conditions of dialogue and fail to heed the temporal requirement of communicative self-transformation. In my critique, I do not jettison Habermas's communicative structure of moral reciprocity and its symmetrical access to validity claims. I introduce into his model those asymmetrical, because individually placed, temporal requirements of communication whose "how" question unmasks the semblance of reciprocity in any mere fulfillment of anonymous and atemporal form.[34]

The Ideal of Communication Community

Habermas's community ideal is to safeguard the possibility of reaching genuine consensus. But without some qualitative constraint upon this ideal, consensual aim, which guides the consensual procedure, might fail to resist a possibly herd or totalitarian outcome. There is a danger that we could forget Kierkegaard's, Adorno's, and Horkheimer's lessons on the mass deception exercised in the public sphere by economy, state, and the culture industry alike. (We might critique Iraqi expansionist nationalism, celebrate the *ratio* of the 1991 U.N. consensus sanctioning the legitimacy of the American led mission in the Persian Gulf War, and yet remain blind to our imperial and business motives).[35]

The pathos of beginnings offers the most intense transformation of the community ideal. When we immanently qualify Habermas's horizontal axis, the vertical difficulties of self-choice and time are far removed from the communitarian, clinical question of the good. Rather, Climacus's pathos matches the operative ideal for the community of Alcoholics Anonymous. Here one lives in concretion, yet is aware that identity and will-formation are maintained and stabilized by other than its own or our concerted powers. Habermas's translation of Kierkegaard's verticality into horizontal structures leaves out Climacus's account of experience shot through with pathos. In Habermas's mind such a translation aims at getting rid of Kierkegaard's purportedly untranslatable, theistic language. Yet this aim reveals an old-fashioned view of nineteenth-century piety, while it misses the performative mode of Kierkegaard's experiment with Christendom. Because Habermas restricts himself to conceiving inwardness or verticality in no other form than this quietist piety, his translation complements Kierkegaard's individual with a life form that bypasses pathos itself.[36]

I reiterate that neither Climacus's condition nor my introduction of pathos into communicative ethics depends on theistic or atheistic contents. I commenced with descriptive accounts of identity in communication projected under certain normative ideality. I described how the horizontal domains are qualified by time, suffering, and the difficulty of both consensual procedures and the ideal aim to safeguard a total claim to beginnings. I can now argue that Kierkegaard's description of open identity and communication falsifies Habermas's claim that the language of inwardness or verticality is acommunicative, dogmatic, and untranslatable. The propositional content of this language is not directly verifiable. Yet Kierkegaard shows how inwardness or verticality operates in the temporal requirement of communicative self-transformation. Habermas's ideal of a communication community ought to undergo this Kierkegaardian corrective. Just as in actual life, so also within the very regulative ideal, the language of inwardness or verticality signifies the temporal impossibility of closure or of the total self-transparency. The requirement to communicate without the guarantee of closure or self-transparency promotes an openness in the individual and the community; it provides a qualitative, critical constraint upon the ideal and on the procedure. I substantiate my thesis with two arguments.

First, while Habermas proposes to translate Kierkegaard's vertical language of inwardness into horizontal debate, I want to argue that this verticality is nonproblematic and thus in no need of further translation. Kierkegaard's passion for the wholly other can be neither equated with substantive appeals to the sacred (e.g. the cultural Christianity of Christendom), nor transcribed into Habermas's generalized other of the community ideal. Between self-reflective inwardness and traditional forms of religiosity stands the Socratic distancing from tradition and Kierkegaard's attack on the ideological character of Christendom. Habermas omits this possibility of nonauthoritarian and ideology-critical inwardness. Yet the radicalized individual cannot appeal to the substantive contents of tradition—be it Christendom or the nation–state—to generate his categories. Rather, the category of the individual is that corrective through which all contents of the present age must pass. Kierkegaard's category of the individual, if projected within Habermas's community ideal, gives us a communicative and social meaning of this passage through inwardness.

Second, while Habermas secularizes both Hegel's deified horizontal–social axis and Kierkegaard's vertical–existential one, I need not bring theology into Habermas's profane model when I appeal to inwardness or verticality. Since my proposed corrective brackets using Christian religiosity "B," I do not hurry beyond Climacus's pathos, which marks the difficulty of individual and communal beginnings. In this difficulty, open forms of communication do not propagate theistic or atheistic contents, but rather provide equal delimitations to profane and theistic domains of totality. It is not my interest to engage the debate between Habermas and the theologians. (And I do not think that Habermas's use of Kierkegaard in a rebuttal to the theologians scores significant points against my Kierkegaardian objections.) Rather, one must ask whether or not Habermas's communications model can fulfill what it promises, whether or not his horizontal transcript offers a genuine equivalent to Kierkegaard's individuals communicating in community, and whether or not the attention to inwardness or verticality need not be preserved in the very regulative ideal.[37]

I do not find Habermas's translation of verticality into Peirce's secularized theological model of the ideal communication community a credible equivalent to Kierkegaard's model. I claim that a genuine philosophical equivalent to Kierkegaard is not Habermas's translation of verticality into the horizontal structure of communication, but rather a temporal, existentially communicating community. Inwardness or verticality thus defined stands for qualitative as opposed to quantitative identity, and for concrete communication under the critical ideal of the wholly other as opposed to the consensual procedure projected under the ideal of infinite consensus.[38]

We gain purchase on the distinction by asking, given each model, what happens to the individual in concrete multicultural self- and other-relations? I suggested that Habermas's model affords the structural conditions of its possibility, but fails to account, in principle, for the "how" of self-choice and the "how" of communication. Further, the consensual procedure and the ideal of infinite consensus provide necessary generic but not sufficient qualitative constraints that can resist a possible totalitarian or leveling outcome. Climacus's communication transforms not only Habermas's notion of ideology critique, but also his constitutionally patriotic cure for anomie and fragmentation in rationalized lifeworlds: pathos presupposes a form of the linguistified tradition and de-sacralized public sphere. Thus, any post-traditional and postnational life form for the crisis individual should remain permanently open to this mutually corrective, horizontal linguistification and inward or vertical desacralization of communication. The task is not to celebrate precautiously postmetaphysical thinking, but to ask how one is to communicate without being propelled by heroic "masculinist" identity, unconscious guilt, and self-idolizing consensual ends.

CONCLUSIONS

Kierkegaard's journal entry that he, like the Communists, struggles for human rights and equality, bespeaks a radical community ideal. His is a silent, edifying revolution, which nevertheless subverts the establishment—academia, the media, the public sphere, and churches. He addresses that single individual who is his desired self-reader, not a self-misreader. Thus, radically honest identity formation cannot occur through historical or communicated possibility as if it were already an actuality. By conflating possibility with actuality—in reflection, revolution, or, formally, in communicative ethics—one evades, in principle, the task to become revolutionary by communicating a way of existence.

I argued that posttraditional and postnational identity is not a structural given but rather a self-transformative requirement of communication (self-choice). Further, moral discourse cannot sustain the conditions of its sobriety apart from attending to the temporal and decentering character of existential communication. Finally, consensual procedure and aim cannot resist totality without qualifying the community ideal in the difficulty of beginnings. The point of my overall reading of Kierkegaard's pathos is to foster a stronger resistance to leveling—nationalist, fundamentalist or totalitarian—than is afforded in Habermas's model of postnational deliberative democracy. What Kierkegaard calls inwardness or verticality is already intimated in Socrates's refusal to give the positive ideal. Kierkegaard resists the totalities of the nation–state and of Christian positivism. His critique presupposes that individuals are integrated not by envisioned consensus, but rather by letting every expected agreement be decentered in the difficulty of beginnings. This refusal either to give or to expect positive closure from the other—even from the ideal communication community of all autonomous others—constrains every ideal against the danger of a totalitarian result.

My aim was to prevent an assimilation of Kierkegaard's inwardness or verticality into Habermas's restriction of self-choice to something justified by public policy choices. At the same time, I showed that this move need not be a theistic claim set against public deliberations; yet, it can always know itself, in principle, to be suspicious of any ideal of communicative closure. I concluded that inwardness or verticality, thus defined, gives us a theoretically cogent and socially relevant ideology/critical perspective which is necessary for the fulfillment of Habermas's own critique of recent nationalist strife. The modern crisis individual at extremity already projects posttraditional forms of solidarity and justice, and alternative visions of community. In confronting the establishment such a resister to totality, fanaticism, fundamentalism, and other forms of individual and communal hatred brings a corrective, critical attitude within social theory.

To resist self- and other-deception we should be mindful both of the difficulty of beginnings and of the critical function of inwardness or verticality. First, we introduce this lived corrective into the sociopolitical notion of totality; second, we qualify what Hegel and Marx want to heal; third, we qualify what Habermas critiques in Kant, Hegel, and Marx; and fourth, we follow what Habermas communicatively redeems through Mead, Peirce, and Durkheim. At that point we arrive at the triple "how" of identity, communication, and the communicative ideal. This gives us a more concrete and sober alternative to Habermas's model: the ideal, existentially communicating community.

CHAPTER 7

The Ideal
of Communicating Community

K ierkegaard is manifestly preoccupied with the individual, while the present age worries about the human race. This opposition will not help us very much. Is it possible to articulate the ideal of an existentially communicating community as a theory of a lived corrective to Habermas's regulative ideal of a communication community? Can such a corrective be justified by projecting a transformed Kierkegaardian possibility of community, even though neither he nor Habermas develop this ideal? Someone might, from impatience, advise me either to commit to theology or to translate Kierkegaard's verticality into the horizontal. Someone else might point out that while my way is nicely worked out to fit Habermas, nevertheless the communicative turn softens the offense of the existential; my expansion of it into the communicative is not really Kierkegaard, and thus either the social complaint against the existential holds or communicative and existential ethics are incommensurable terms. All this has been attempted with Kierkegaard. I claim that these tacks in fact forge misreadings of Kierkegaard.

"When time itself is the task, it is a defect to finish ahead of time." I cannot leave Kierkegaard's inwardness or verticality troubling Habermas's horizontal axis in communicative ethics. I let the mode break through within the ideal of a communication community. I do not rush to change hats. How can I tell what difference theism or atheism would make without living the gap in pathos? I could wage my private Thirty-Year War of religion to find myself bored with "religion," just as many appear to be with "socialism" after the 1989 fall of the iron curtain. My "boredom" would be no more or less aesthetical than either my religiosity or leftist postrevolutionary melancholy. In this veritable night of all black cows, I could not tell the difference. Trying to be different would make no more or less difference than if I changed hats.[1]

It would do me no good to slip away from a sociopolitical sect to some traditional congregation only to find my pathos burnt out and my existence stifled because I have not attended to temporal existing. It would be outrageous of me to run ahead of myself, to become an evangelist of *posthistoire*. I am more at home with Adam Michnik's admission to have butter on his head and Václav Havel's Kafkaesque self-irony and political humor. I keep my hat, or better, I intensify how I suffer under my hat, how I wear it. "With regard to the religious, the point is that this has passed through the ethical." I hold on to the troubling task of passing through. I need not fall back upon theistic or atheistic contents, since a teacher of substantive contents (I do not speak out on the future of this teaching) cannot bypass this passage. Habermas intimates a permanently democratic passage in the projected ideality of communicative ethics. But his model lacks the specification of the permanent task—the "how" of this passage.[2]

To make my way to this "how" of the ideal, existentially communicating community, I must attend to certain ambiguities in Kierkegaard's authorship: the journey to inwardness or verticality is narrated by all pseudonymous characters. Yet the stories exhibit an ambiguity in the language of inwardness insofar as the inner is opposed to the outer. This unfruitful ambiguity lies not so much in claiming that the inner is incommensurable with the outer but in designating "inwardness" sometimes as an opposition to the outer of the cultural value spheres and sometimes as a mode. I prepared the ground for my argument: I coined a new term, namely, the existential–performative mode. I downplayed the dualistic language of inwardness yet intensified the spirit's inwardness in an invitation to self-transformative thinking and living.

I will justify my intervention into Habermas's regulative community ideal. I will defend a strong corrective thesis (i.e., how a projected existential mode qualifies Habermas's communicative ideal), and a weak rapprochement thesis (i.e., whether or not there is the possibility of communicative and existential ethics). Even though I limit myself to a formal corrective of Habermas's communicative model, this is not a minor matter: it qualifies the very starting point for a critical social theory and any possible consideration of the standpoint of material justice. I will commence my argument textually by reading "inwardness" as a mode of the individual and community (7.1), and as a mode of justice and love (7.2). In the two chapters that follow I will reread my theses from within existential revolution by asking what would it mean to become contemporary with Havel's nonpolitical politics, and from within authoring in deliberative democracy by asking what would it mean to become contemporary with Kierkegaard's and Havel's dramatic authorship.

7.1. AN EXISTENTIAL MODE
OF THE INDIVIDUAL AND COMMUNITY

The texts that all Kierkegaard's pseudonyma take on concern first, Hegel's question of how to become ethical, and second, his logical principle that the inner is the outer and the outer the inner. I need not repeat what I said about Hegel (Part I). The issue here concerns his logical axiom and the privileged status of social ethics. I will begin with the complaint of the pseudonyma to Hegel and Kierkegaard's lived corrective (A), and then read along with them and with Kierkegaard some specific texts (B).[3]

A. Kierkegaard as a Corrective

Let me offer a representative sample of passages from Hegel (emphasis in original throughout):

> What is then *only* something *inner* is also *only* something outer, and what is *only* something outer, is first also *only* something *inner*. . . .

There is a symmetry that is harnessed to the socioethical totality:

> Human, as one is outwardly, i.e. in one's actions (really not only in one's bodily outwardness) is [also] inwardly; and if one [is so] only inwardly, i.e. has aims, convictions, virtue, morals, etc. inwardly but not identical with the outward, then the one is as much hollow and empty as the other.

There is a symmetry between inner and outer validity domains:

> Then the outer is . . . *the same content* as the inner. What is inner is also present-at-hand [vorhanden] as outer, and vice versa; the appearance shows nothing that is not in the essence, and there is nothing in the essence that is not manifested.

Again, the symmetry of form is depicted as that of validity domains:

> The *inner*, as a form of the *reflected immediacy* or [a form of] essence, is determined against the *outer* as a form of *being*, but both are only *one* identity. . . . The outer is in accord with this determination not only equal with the inner in [their] content, but both are the *one thing*.[4]

Hegel views the inner and the outer in a negative unity: one is the truth of the truth of the other, and both point to the totality of a relation. In contrast to Kierkegaard's posture, Hegel's truth is presented neither as an invitation to existential thinking and living nor raised as a total claim to existing. Further, his labor of the negative does not derive from suffering existence. Finally, his totality is not qualified by the total difficulty of beginnings, but rather is a sphere of immanence where one transcends towards validity domains (the thing, the content, the truth as the "what"). By introducing "inwardness" or verticality as a mode of the spirit, not as a validity domain of cultural spirit, the pseudonyma burst Hegel's reconciliation of the inner with the outer and qualify any later (e.g., Marx's) attempts to improve on Hegel without also offering such a corrective in radicalized honesty about the motives in one's praxis of theorizing or action.[5]

I read Kierkegaard's critique of Hegel as a strong corrective to any identification of cultural value spheres or validity domains—the inner–outer—with the invitation to inhabit the existential mode in one's thinking and way of living. The difficulty with Hegel's presentation (*Darstellung*) of the passage is that one can learn "everything" (totality) about the validity domains of spirit but never become edified in a total claim of one's spirit. The student can go through the whole phenomenology of spirit and never come home to himself; the teacher can explore for years the insights of this journey and never make a call on the mode of her teaching; the activist can place Hegel on his feet but never stand on his own. Such Odyssean, negative dialectic and revolutionary zeal are beautiful and commendable; yet, their sojourn marks an abstract, curiously distant, aesthetic engagement with a mere conceptual and not free possibility of possibility.

To preview my reading of the "inwardness" path: an existential mode is incommensurable with the outer not because of the dualistic opposition between inner–outer or individual–community. One may not quite commensurate a "what" with a "how." Kierkegaard's pseudonyma defend the "hidden inwardness" against Hegel's undifferentiated symmetry of the inner with the outer. Yet more often than not, the pathos of the pseudonyma dwells unawares, cloaked in the language of Hegel's conceptual dualism, such as inner–outer. I agree with Habermas's formal–pragmatic reformulation of the problem between the inner and the outer, yet I argue that an existential mode is a nondualistic posture, and therefore, allows for more adequate language than is sometimes utilized by Kierkegaard's nineteenth-century prose. If Hegel's "inner" cannot be identified with an existential mode, then neither his ethical totality nor Habermas's ethical totalities are happy options. They are unfit philosophical equivalents to "inward" pathos. If Kierkegaard's issue lies elsewhere than Hegel's inner–outer, then Habermas's translation misses the point.

Kierkegaard's mode operates against privileging the outer (the objectivist), the inner (the navel-gazer), or their symmetry (social herd). All three types commit an abstraction from concrete living. A nondualistic language of an existential mode pertains to both inner–outer, psyche–culture, and body–polis on the one hand, and to communication among individuals in community on the other. The mode of the individual and community cannot be a supersubject in validity domains. Nondualistic uses of language envision a reconciled inner–outer, yet not quantitatively but rather qualita-tively—by the "how" of self-choice, communication, and the community ideal.[6]

Permit me to introduce another reading of this pseudonymous "inward" journey. "Inwardness" initiates a lived corrective to a serious oversight in social and political theory and practice. First, "inwardness" offers a critique of cer-tain sociopolitical and psychological theories of human existing. Second, it is a critique of the forms of life in which these theories are rooted. The formal and theoretical target is the Hegelianism of Kierkegaard's contem-poraries. The attacked forms of life in any age are academia, the media, the public, and the churches that sanction and embody these theories.

Kierkegaard's corrective fulfills the analogical role assigned by Marx to ideology critique. While Marx issued a decision call to social action around the events of 1848, Kierkegaard at about the same time resolved to coin another manifesto, whereby one could root identity back in con-cretion. Kierkegaard's step confronts the status quo and in that projects a relevant form of critical theory. He explains the *Socratic correctio* as a therapy. A corrective, like a revolution or medicine, is necessarily one-sided. Its task is to be absorbed by the individual and embodied in the establish-ment. One evades the remedy if one applies this same corrective against the corrective itself. "Nothing is easier for the one providing the correc-tive than to add the other side; but then, right there, it ceases to be the corrective and itself becomes established order." Such a balancing act lacks the humility and the courage of distancing from the establishment to work as a corrective.[7]

Inhabiting a mode, Kierkegaard's corrective remains invisible. He portrays himself as "a little dash of cinnamon" that is offered and swal-lowed up by the whole, but which cannot be discovered without cooking and eating. Kierkegaard in the establishment acts like Joan Miró's erotic red mixed into a passionate composition. One's revolution may grow impa-tient and "make the corrective normative for others." Such normative cor-rectives, like mass-produced artifacts or indoctrinations of cadres, become kitsch. But Kierkegaard's corrective is at first resisted by the critics, then tolerated, and, in the end, its enemies claim to have authored it. One "must be sacrificed . . . added to give the rest a specific taste." Kierkegaard's authoring of a corrective tastes like a bit of spice; it strikes the eye as a patch of color and the ear as a modality of voices in a polyphony:[8]

> My task has continually been to provide the existential-corrective by poeti-cally presenting the ideals and inciting people about the established order, with which I collaborate by criticizing all the false reformers and the opposi-tion, who simply are evil—and whom only ideals can halt.[9]

Kierkegaard has no ideological favorites in Christendom: "inwardness" is not a form of Protestant liberal individualism. What began as a corrective to the Catholic communitarian *ethos* became the new status quo. Kierkegaard finds that the Reformation only gets worse in every generation. Martin Luther's is a corrective gone fundamentalist (totalitarian) in validity domains. Luther's and MacIntyre's spices, thus, offer but a banquet of bland gravy: Protestant individualism has become a worldly, guilt-driven work ethic; Catholic communitarianism is a backward-gazing reformation that imagines that one generation can better access the true, the good, and the beautiful than any con/temporary in any age. But a lived corrective becomes a total and permanent self-critical claim, an exception, and an invitation to every individual in every generation.[10]

Con/temporaneity in communication offers equal difficulty for every exister. Kierkegaard admits the one-sidedness of inhabiting a corrective pathos. He allows that there might emerge in another age the need for another life form for receiving a corrective. But he defines self-choice, communication, and pathos as the core requirements for all human disciplines and at every age. Transforming the human core sounds the basic educational prerequisite. Edifying this core qualifies every enrollment in a life form, thereby allowing it to receive this corrective in reforms of school curricula, the media, social justice, and the churches.

Kierkegaard offers a therapy for the spiritlessness of the present age. In contrast to the celebrated death of subject and the end of history— entrenched in humanities, new literary avant-gardes, the New World Order, and fundamentalist revivals—he attributes the discontents of modernity to the demise of a receptive identity. His corrective invents self-authoring characters. These fictively actual personages "seduce" the reader to hearing again communication in the first person. This corrective affirms a nuanced revocation of its authority: authors do not push their own identity but dramatically prompt readers to engage in self-reading. The self-reader in pathos has no direct authority even over her own autonomous beginnings. Passion does not author an identity of immediate emotion and immediate pleasure–pain. Thus, any author's direct communication of beginnings would indirectly implicate itself as an impostor–teaching, failed authoring, unjust friendship, pushy therapy, and a mis/reading of the ideal. The received view of Kierkegaard implicates itself as self-mis/reading by its very attempt to critique Kierkegaard's corrective directly.[11]

B. A Pseudonymous Journey in "Inwardness"

Victor Eremita

The editor of *Either/Or*, Victor Eremita, presents his corrective by opening his preface to the "dear reader" with a suspicion of Hegel's maxim "that the outer is the inner, and the inner is the outer."

[H]earing became my most cherished sense; for just as the voice is the disclosure of inwardness incommensurable with the exterior, so the ear is the instrument that apprehends this inwardness, hearing the sense by which it is appropriated.[12]

Victor Eremita brings on stage two author–characters: (A) exhibits a mode of life that contradicts his interiority; (B) conceals interiority beneath ordinary communication. The editor displays the failure of Hegel's maxim by showing how communication changes within the distinct authorships by (A) and (B).

The readership of *Either/Or* figures here as a theater audience, where each viewer is to author herself in responsible self-reading. To get at the editor's dramatic presentation, one must transgress that "realistic" aesthetics which divides performance (acting, authoring) from observation (reception, reading). Unless one is a communitarian or a passive consumer of art who complains when a drama ends in irresolution, one is lured to verify and reduplicate the scene of either/or in one's passion. From this angle, all of the arguments against the monological and decisionist, or even irrational and antisocial, Kierkegaard introduce their originators as author–impostors who fail to enter the authorship dramatically and only appear to be engaged by the drama of reading "Kierkegaard." By extension of this theater inscenation of Kierkegaard and of the failure to read it through one's life form, one could speak of the student who is registered for a course but daydreaming, of the professor who is resentful of students when they ask him to become what he teaches, of the public whose enthusiasm is a curious pretense of action, or of congregations that are one-dimensional ritual productions.

From the viewpoint of modern drama, any prescribed resolution to the either/or that marks self-choice becomes what art critics or authors like Kundera call kitsch. Failed kitsch art takes away the risk of repeating one's authoring in the acts of a viewer or a self-reader. The characters, because they embody complex positions, cannot be sketched out in clichés. The problem with Hegel's maxim—that the inner is the outer, and so on—is similar to MacIntyre's more traditional fear of Kierkegaard's irresolution: one can learn a great deal about the psyche and the *polis* from Hegel's historical journey and appreciate MacIntyre's anguish about lost tradition, but theirs are not convincing dramas about modernity's discontents.[13]

For this reason, the editor draws the reader away from the speculative and objectifying angle of Hegel's presentation into a performative and self-critical attitude. Even as he admonishes the reader at the end of the Preface to follow the advice of the ethical and not the aesthetical author–character, there is a revocation found in the last paragraph of the book which disclaims that any authority can enforce his requirement. This revocation, too, is a corrective to Hegel's maxim: do not try to get to inwardness by speculatively mediating the inner with the outer! Become a self-reader of your own authoring! MacIntyre implicates himself first by being offended at the dramatic irresolution described by him as Kierkegaard's emotivism, and then by rushing with an *imprimatur* into Kierkegaard's religious passion. From within Eremita's view, MacIntyre's side-stepping of the Kierkegaardian passage through nonauthoritarian authoring signifies a failure to engage in existential drama.[14]

The "listener" is asked what he or she really wants. *Either/or* teaches the way of inwardness via self-choice. It is not a text about moral problems or a general applied ethics cookbook for college students. A lived book prompts the reader to become a primary text, a questioner, a dialogical exister. Only then can I become con/temporary with *Either/Or*. The book's questioning incites the reader into self-choice and action. There should never be a legitimate requirement under which the text and I must become directly con/temporary. One ought not to read such an unethical, censoring encyclical; one should read such a text deconstructively! Yet, this is not so with the text of *Either/Or*, which lures me: "only the truth that builds up is truth for you." I am not confined in unhappy subjectivist consciousness or condemned to a uselessly free passion. The editor of this text can be my con/temporary in self-reading. To think that I know how to read by parroting the aestheticizing either–or, either in a critique of Kierkegaard's decisionism or in an enthusiasm for some cultural choices in validity domains, renders me a hermeneutical anecdote, never an earnest reader. The editor's complaint shows that Hegel's maxim allows for death from every historical immediacy and yet does not invite one to die away from conventionalism, to become a self in dramatic self-presentation and self-authoring.[15]

Frater Taciturn

This author's "Letter to the Reader" communicates that there are at least two ways to read: for results and to inhabit a path. Texts and aesthetic events can be approached from these two angles. Let us take August Rodin's sculpture "The Thinker." It can show in Washington, D.C. "a visible result," where the inner is commensurable with the outer. "The result is plain and easy to grasp." "The aesthetic result is in the external and can be shown." But what does it mean to become con/temporary with "The Thinker" as one's way of existing in America? Commensurating the inner–outer in an aesthetic study of the sculpture does not necessarily allow me to become con/temporary with thinking. Communicating honestly cannot mean looking up results. Even if I take "a night telescope" or "opera glasses," I will not learn to interpret "The Thinker" by way of self-reading. To become con/temporary with "The Thinker," I should first become one—a little difficulty for every viewer of Rodin's piece. This difficulty is present to every generation that might want to institutionalize "The Thinker" or the motto under the "Statue of Liberty" in New York. If one could simply look up thinking and liberty, then one need not bother to become con/temporary with them! One could present a great political campaign: what is read in the motto must be true of the country. The inner is the outer, and so on. One might marvel sentimentally about thinking and freedom in these sculptures, but never dare to embody anything thoughtful or free.[16]

When Taciturn defends the "internal" against the "external," his dualistic language misleads. I propose to remove this ambiguity. Reading as a way does not signify looking out or introspecting, since self-reading does not transcend towards the cultural spheres of the inner–outer, but rather within a mode of relating to validity domains. To become con/temporary with art, with a text, or with another person does not guarantee a canonical ideal. In my active receptivity to the other I am qualified in my mode. I am affected in my temporal existing by the communicated possibility of the other. I bind myself as a primary text (every other lived or written signifier is to me a secondary text, a commentary), lest I should be embarrassingly "hilarious" like the student who daydreams in the hallway while pretending to sit in on a course, or like the teacher who spits out formulas and test results as if the purpose of academia were to produce nothing but robocops.[17]

Johannes de silentio

This pseudonym targets Hegel's social theory, its culmination in ethical totality, and the form of life which both justifies and is confirmed by such a theory. De silentio qualifies the ethical totality of Hegel's *Philosophy of Right* by the total lived claim recorded in the Biblical narrative of Abraham. While Abraham's inwardness is opposed to the social theory that privileges the ethical whole, it should not be read antisocially. De silentio's *Fear and Trembling* takes a well-socialized, family-oriented, civic-minded individual and asks what is it to become con/temporary with Abraham's predicament of transgressing social ethics—sacrificing his son Isaac—while remaining a morally responsible member of the human race.

De silentio does not implore us to follow Abraham's path. He sets up an experimental situation whereby the reader would be weaned from conventional life. The experiment occasions one's edification for liberation. Going through the different beginnings of Abraham's story shows the difficulty of redeeming one's total lived claim. Hegel's social totality ignores the difficulty; Marx's and Habermas's correctives to Hegel problematize Hegel's ending point, yet they do not find any difficulty in heeding the beginnings.

The difficulty, which lies in repeating the beginning, delivers us to de silentio's experimental mood. Now to integrate socially the crisis individual—but first, the difficulty of beginnings does not deliver this individual from crisis to a stabilizing, social life form. The difficulty sustains this very social form of life! De silentio begins with the difficulty only to intensify it. Second, my deliverance into this difficulty means that I never integrate but rather end up with a motivation crisis! De silentio suspends the social whole to show that this whole is not that earth on which one stands, but that its form of life is supported by what in validity domains remains groundless and yet in a mode provides a way of walking or swimming. The mode projects one's fiduciary ground, which is not to be imitated by looking at Abraham, but rather is permanently repeated in one's own difficulty. Third, Abraham, and not some rugged individualist, embodies that mode of being an individual which projects another human race. Abraham's individuality fathers this race. Fourth, if only one were to read de silentio's Abraham pragmatically through Mead, instead of through a communitarian or possessively liberal expansion of identity! What would it mean, now to become con/temporary with Abraham's identity? Fifth, if only the ideal of a communication community had begun in the mode of this difficulty, then it would have been begotten in Abraham's human race. Abraham occasions a requirement for the entire race.

But de silentio's Abraham is nowhere to be heard in Jerusalem's bloodshed or in Middle Eastern wars for macho identities, oil, and orthodoxies. The folly of communitarian security and of modern self-transparent agency fails Abraham's projected human race: reading Abraham, I need to maintain a distance from both. I find no socioethical beginning that grounds this beginning. I learn to begin how to begin. To be a good member of the human race, it seems insufficient to begin where the race or the nation and church begin. This is not Kierkegaard's Eurocentrism to let traditional primitivity pass through a Socratic courage of primitivity. There might be a way of being modern and multicultural, and yet embrace the particularly primitive with the distancing passion of primitivity and second naïveté. Therefore, to be a good Jew or Czech or American I cannot keep getting high on flag-waving and land conquest. To cure my patriotic addiction to the worship of family, flag, market, and culture, this Abraham prompts me to become postnational. The self-reader of Abraham is, thus, weaned from songs like "my land, the beautiful," from longing for patriotic and communitarian breasts, from the narcissistic food of national semen, and from marches and hymns of mother- and fatherland. Nor is Abraham a father through self-serving dissemination. Reading Abraham does not yield a polysemic death of authoring; it occasions dying away from authoritarian authorship. With Abraham, I am fathered and mothered into the human race through passion.

That "the single individual is higher than the universal" is not an antisocial and decisionist suggestion, but rather a total lived claim that projects for the human whole a ground other than Habermas's fallible formal–pragmatic whole. For the same reason that Aristotelian and Hegelian "social morality" cannot be deemed as the highest ideal, the consensual procedure and aim of the moral point of view also cannot be so regarded. Such wholes are juxtaposed with the "residual incommensurability" of that "single individual." This individual emerges as higher than both the communitarian and the formally universal, not because private inwardness is an opposing voice to public outwardness, but rather because there must be "some way such that this incommensurability is not evil." This way is a "how" whereby one inhabits the whole and qualifies the entire structure of communication and its ideal.[18]

Abraham dwells in pathos by suffering the slipping away of time. He is not justified by what Ernest Becker calls the heroics of culture and the immortality ideologies that console for death. He fathers the race by suspending every drive to heroic self-idolization of the whole. Even a linguistified approach, such as Habermas's formally concrete, communicative ethics, when it remains stoically heroic precisely by *not* wishing to bother about time, must be teleologically suspended. The sobriety of linguistified rationality, unlike Abraham, still holds for itself the sacral privilege of reaching a performative whole within the polyphony of rational voices. Abraham takes away from Habermas this executive privilege. De silentio's Abraham shows that Habermas cannot effect a handy Kantian veto, and cannot disclaim that the difficulty of beginnings neither affects nor fits the ideal of communicative ethics. The distinction between mode and validity domains exhausted that razor of Kant's with which Habermas could have overridden the difficulty and effected a veto. Communicative rationality claims its ground fallibly, but not "by virtue of the absurd."[19]

The theater of the absurd dramatizes the groundlessness of the cultural value spheres of choosing; yet, there is a passionate and understanding ground in the mode of one's self-choice. Viewing de silentio's Abraham lures one to a self-transformation into an existential drama with no resolution given on the stage. The audience is transported into a theater without exit and ground. In this scenario the stage irrupts through the curtain of inwardness: another exit breaks through, dancing on the tightrope. *De silentio*. Formal–pragmatic claims of the community ideal are sobered up on a fiduciary and suffering sea.

Johannes Climacus

Climacus mounts de silentio's drama humorously. He ventures on the tightrope earnestly and persistently; his balancing act on the ladder of ascent (*Climacus*) intensifies in inwardness. He insists on a virtue of the "hidden inwardness," but this overstates his case. First, it is difficult to verify his claim that the less outwardness one exhibits, the more inwardly one exists.

Does the inner increase as the outer decreases? Is unexpressed inwardness an ideal mode of communication? Second, while I can verify the claim that truth is subjectivity, it does not follow that subjectivity is opposed to objectivity. Does objectivity vanish with self-appropriation? Is it true that the more passionate student or activist I am, the less objectivity I bring to the academic community or to the poor? Third, I can verify the temporal difficulty of beginnings. But does it follow that inwardness occurs merely in the individual's relation to God, or that inwardness has no integral role in intersubjectivity? Is my proposal to articulate the mode of existential communication an erroneous expansion of fiduciary grounds to the human other? Why should it be impossible to leap passionately towards the human other? Cannot the other be present in a nonidolized communication? Does not intimacy open a ground in another's self-relation beyond which there is no speculative mediation of the ego and the alter in validity domains possible?[20]

Faithful to Climacus's requirement that even his book must be thought and lived by the reader, I have downplayed these three aspects of Climacus's overstated case. I argued, first, that an existential mode qualifies the validity domains of the inner and the outer. Second, I argued a fruitful complementarity between a "what" and a triple "how": between discursive validity claims and an existential–performative mode of identity, communication, and the community ideal. Third, I argued the expansion of an existential mode of communication into Habermas's communicative theory. Before considering further how Anti-Climacus and Kierkegaard both contradict Climacus's insistence on the virtue of hidden inwardness, I pick up some clues to reading Climacus's corrective nondualistically in his own text. He tells us unequivocally that "the task is not to move from the individual to the race, but from the individual through the race (the universal) to reach the individual." An existential mode pertains to both the individual and the human race insofar as we are involved with one another communicatively.[21]

Climacus's point confirms the maxim that one is both the individual and the race (*unum noris omnes*, if you know one, yourself, you will have known all). But what gives rise to the dualistic readings of inwardness is Climacus's language of secrecy. The "knight of secret inwardness" emerges in the portraits of the ironist and humorist, the earnest religious, and the silent bearer of spiritual trial. These pose as correctives to "the desperate attempt of the miscarried Hegelian ethics to make the state into the court of last resort of ethics." The invisible corrective is to subvert the nation–state and the most "unethical attempt to finitize individuals, an unethical flight from the category of individuality to the category of the race." The corrective against that totality which colonizes the lifeworld not only systemically, but also by sacralizing the social, ethical, and moral whole, cannot but be an indirect if not underground dissent. This century's resistance to the communitarian forms of totalitarianism draws rightly on Kierkegaard.[22]

The stress on hidden inwardness targets the Hegelian maxim:

> Mediation releases a person from immersing himself in the totality-category and makes him busy externally, makes his guilt external, his suffering of punishment external, because the watchword of mediation and its indulgence are that the outer is the inner and the inner is the outer, whereby the individual's absolute relationship to the absolute is abolished.

I read this text as follows: there are two forms of mediation. The one marks Hegel's dualistic mediation, which reconciles the inner and the outer in a totality of the cultural value spheres of modernity; the other signifies a nondualist mediation of earnest thinking and living. It becomes unnecessary to defend inwardness through Climacus's dualistic language, and thus to give a false excuse to critics who act as if the honest individual were an astronaut in a social and hermeneutical vacuum. We must not handicap temporal claims by shackling them into a binary opposition over and against validity domains. It is obvious from reading the above text that the problem with Hegel's mediation lies in that, by leaving out the claims to one's total existence, it does not mediate enough! Climacus's text justifies a nondualistic reading of "inwardness": existential communication begins with the individual, goes through the race, and ends with the individual.[23]

The above maxim, *unum noris omnes*, assigned by Kierkegaard to Socrates's "know yourself," is opposed to the Hegelian principle that the inner and the outer are one and the same. It is the latter that prompts Climacus's contemporaries to cling to mass culture industries, to a collective idea of being human, and to mere differences among individuals. Thus, becoming subjective while in society occasions an offense to our age with its contempt for the existential individual. Climacus attacks the gossip mood of academia, the flight to conformism of various groupings, and the fear of existence found in the media and in churches. The collective idea of the race gives us only numerical, not even generic and certainly not qualitative, identity.

> To will to be an individual human being (which one unquestionably is) . . . in the same sense as everyone else is capable of being—that is the ethical victory over life and over every mirage, the victory that is perhaps the most difficult of all in the theocentric nineteenth century.[24]

Climacus complains that our age has forgotten "what it means to *exist* and what *inwardness* signifies" (original emphasis). He offers a critical self-reading as a differentiating criterion for various readings: "All interpretations of existence take their rank in relation to the qualification of the individual's dialectical inward deepening." For Climacus, *"unum"* in the Socratic maxim stands for the exister who carries on Kierkegaard's corrective task: to accustom the age to hearing the first person "I" in an existential–performative mode. The Socratic maieutic, intensified through pathos, can communicate only inwardly. In a dramaturgical aside, Climacus discloses that his task is to manifest in him as an author that human core which pertains to authoring, teaching, and the works of justice and love.[25]

A significant clue that allows for a nondualistic reading of "inwardness" is found in Climacus's critique of monasticism and in his attack on the nineteenth century as a passionless age. He finds the monastic movement to have been "an enormous abstraction, and monastic life cloister a continued abstraction." He thinks that one would have a better time of it searching for inwardness by "playing cards at the club" than by imagining that one is transposed to pathos via the monastic *ordo*. After Kierkegaard's disclaimer that Luther provides a sought for corrective, it is hard to brush off Climacus's critique of monasticism as a Protestant sectarian complaint against Catholicism. The problem is that religious insignia signify presumed inwardness in recognized outwardness, and that religious vows, like those of marriage, can become an obstacle to living at risk. The problem is, further, that a cleric who lives in our linguistified sacred culture might be vowing by virtue of the heroic, and yet lack pathos. The religious in central-eastern Europe who has emerged from the underground after the 1989 revolutions might be parading his religious garb only to imitate the deposed communist or some general who displays authority on his chest with a military salad bar of medals. Neither hero inspires passion. Here, Climacus is by all secular and profane standards rather unorthodox. Why go, then, to Habermas's linguistification of Kierkegaard when we can get the word from the horse's mouth? For Climacus, it is not the high ideal one is committed to that has primacy; what is important lies in the character of one's passion. One misconstrues Climacus if one substitutes for self-reading some image of what this outrageous claim provokes. His inciting pose unmasks our consensual procedures in cultural value spheres as at best highly insecure against a totalitarian outcome and at worst dangerous. If a young religious, a social activist, or a married couple should raise a total claim to existing, the claim would need to be redeemed in the shipwreck of such cultural totalities. One learns, thus, that inward vowing or leave-taking transpires only when one undergoes the difficulty of temporal beginnings.

> The dubious character of the monastic movement, (apart from the error of presumed meritoriousness) was that the absolute interiority, probably in order to demonstrate very energetically that it existed, acquired its obvious expression in a distinctive separate outwardness, whereby it nevertheless, however one twists and turns, became only relatively different from all other outwardness.[26]

Climacus admits that the religious call might inhabit more passion than can be said of Hegelian mediation. He is not fundamentally opposed to any vocation, be it a call to religious life or to social activism. He is, however, single-hearted in one concern: if the form of life cannot admit an intensification of inward journey, subvert or leave it. His claim that truth is inwardness disrupts all passionless yet dogmatic life forms in academia, the media, the public, and the churches. His lived repetition makes him a friend of neither secular nor canon lawyers.

We ought to read nondualistically why inwardness remains hidden, and why cloister, as well as both the liberal and communitarian fusion of inner–outer, abstract from the difficulty of beginnings: "The monastic movement wants to express interiority by an outwardness that is supposed to be interiority. Herein lies that contradiction, because to be a monk is just as much something outward as being a councilor of justice." A dualist reading says that inwardness is to outwardness as a monk is to a councilor of justice. The nondualist corrective distinguishes that the domains of both the monk and the councilor stand under an invitation to adopt an existential mode of thinking and acting. The dualist reading is wrong because one may not express in the language of inner–outer the mode of inwardness. One gains nothing by either religious zeal or a political path if one does not journey "inwardly."[27]

One need not believe the charge that Kierkegaard's inwardness stands for Hegel's stage of unhappy consciousness. Climacus points out that the medieval communitarian spirit harbors a form of despair that is incapable of grasping that "existing is like walking." But one cannot cure a preadolescent vision of community by supplementing an "inward" bond through some outward signs of togetherness. "[A]n unhappy inwardness . . . resemble[s] a love affair in which the lovers are jealous for the outward expression of erotic love." These lovers, no less than some monks and councilors of justice, experience unhappy homecomings when they, like some parrots, rattle off and demand from one another the pledges of allegiance and the words about love, faith, or justice.[28]

Climacus's scorn of clericalism implicates likewise any hermeneutically naïve social thinker or dogmatic activist who adopts a reductionist methodology when linking unjust human relations to the outer economic base alone: "Shame on the pastor for wanting to make us think that the fault is in the world and not in us." Does not Climacus indicate the origin of leftist melancholy and terror in those revolutionary projects that have not passed through the paths of inwardness? Unless revolution journeys through social domains inwardly, its activist wakes up in an unhappy, despairing, and sado-masochistic hangover. The insistence on non-self-flagellating, nonquietist, actively receptive interiority marks perhaps Climacus's most devastating and sobering critique of one-dimensionality in modern sociopolitical revolutions. He unmasks those life forms that give rise to such a zealotry and in which a leveled revolutionary theory and practice are justified. This critique is not reaction but self-action. Climacus's social angle is not a turnabout to tradition but an active shaping of the social domain in the difficulty of beginnings.[29]

There is another outrageous provocation by Climacus. If the cloister were a psychiatric asylum, the "inwardness of an absolute relationship" could be protected from being confused with some cultural value sphere. It would make sense, then, to become religious if this act were regarded not as sacred but as mad. "[M]aking the monastery into an insane asylum comes closest to an externality that is just like everybody else's." With the line between divine and demonic madness culturally unverifiable, one cannot run ahead of oneself. "Then the outwardness does not correspond directly to the interiority." One lacks assurances that either joining a religious community or burning with revolutionary zeal for justice is either divine or demonic. Climacus dramatizes that by the loss of outward indicators about the difference between the madhouse on the stage and that in audience or in the world; every revolution bereft of inwardness might be just as much a farce as a holiness gained by putting on a conventionally religious role/identity. Revolutionary art can be just as kitsch as the religious trinkets one buys at the "holy places." Homecoming to justice and a holy land begin in exile from all such signs.[30]

One is mis/reading Climacus's stress on the hidden inwardness if one overlooks its intersubjective significance. "The ethical is and remains the highest task assigned to every human being . . . because the ethical is . . . in the midst of solitude the reconciling fellowship with every human being." The problem is, then, "how and to what extent does the race result from individuals, and what is the relation of the individuals to the human race." Climacus complains that Hegel completed the system without resolving this issue. I proposed to explain this approach by differentiating a critical social theory that operates with a one-dimensional relation to cultural value spheres (inner–outer) from the one that pays attention also to the mode.[31]

There is a rare note that throws a helpfully dissonant tone on the whole mood of Climacus's defense of the hidden inwardness, which probably characterizes more directly Kierkegaard's own mature position:

> Only in the final qualification of the religious, the paradoxical–religious, does the race become higher, but then only by virtue of the paradox, and in order to become aware of the paradox one must have the qualification of the religious in between, that the individual is higher than the species, lest the differences of the spheres coalesce and one speak aesthetically about the paradoxical–religious.[32]

Is there a Kierkegaardian community which is "higher" than the individual?! As I stated before, I do not try to become con/temporary with Kierkegaard's substantive Christianity. I read this text for a nuanced defense of Climacus's view of inwardness as his corrective with sociopolitical intent: that the individual is higher than the race offsets the Hegelian identification of the generic identity of the inner–outer with qualitative self-choice. Yet, a community communicating in an existential mode could be regarded as on an equal footing with the sole radically honest individual. We do not have many examples of such Kierkegaardian communities, but then Marx's or Habermas's revolutionary ideals do not presuppose ready-to-hand examples either. A Kierkegaardian ideal operates with the triple "how" that qualifies the basic structure of communicative ethics: it qualifies identity by responsible self-choice, communication by an existential mode, and the horizontal community ideal by the difficulty of individual and consensual beginnings.

Climacus objects that Hegel conflates an aesthetic metaphysics of development with embodying one's development as a way. This problem remains in Habermas's reading of the "existential" under eudaemonistic self-realization. But neither Hegel's ethical life nor Marx's material justice nor Habermas's concretely operative, regulative ideal alone would or could nourish an open community since they all appeal to a socialization of individuals into a generic life form, rather than to an integration of individual pathos into a social life form. The "existential" in Kierkegaard is, however, neither the communitarian whole nor Kant's autonomy nor Habermas's qualitative identity maintained on the formal–pragmatic diet of the ideal community. The "existential" stands for a mode concerning how the individuals inhabit their cultural value spheres.

Anti-Climacus and Kierkegaard

A nondualistic reading of "inwardness" may be gained in dramatic con/ temporaneity with all Kierkegaard's texts. What does it mean to become con/temporary with another? Pathos projected into a community life discloses an impossibility of self-maintaining and self-stabilizing heroics. I argued that a journey in inwardness, while a task for every age, emerges as a structural possibility with the demise of sacred traditions and with the experience of crisis identity in the present age. This possibility, when made one's own in critical openness, confronts any new sacralization of modern cultural value spheres.

Anti-Climacus's *The Sickness unto Death* (1849) intensifies the hidden inwardness by undergoing the anxiety intimated by Vigilius Haufniensis in *The Concept of Anxiety* (1844) and the communication related by Johannes Climacus in *Philosophical Fragments* (1844) and *Concluding Unscientific Postscript* (1846). But the decisive critique of hidden inwardness is delivered in the second of the two texts by Anti-Climacus, *Practice in Christianity* (1850). This critique is found in Kierkegaard's journals as well as in his public attack on the religious and political establishment.

The doctrine of hiddenness was dear to the bishop Mynster. Out of respect for him, Kierkegaard communicated his critique indirectly and assumed responsibility for Anti-Climacus's position only after the bishop's death, when a new edition of the book was printed. Now Kierkegaard's maieutically hidden spice becomes a digestive:

> Now . . . I am clear within myself about two things: that the Establishment is, Christianly, indefensible and every day that it endures is a crime; and that one is not permitted to draw upon grace in that way. Therefore take away my pseudonymity, take away the thrice-repeated Preface and the Moral; then . . . [Practice] in Christianity is, Christianly, an attack upon the Establishment; but for a consideration of piety towards the old bishop, and because of prudential slowness, this remained hidden under the form of . . . the last defense for the Establishment.[33]

In his *Sickness* Anti-Climacus argues that "[t]he criterion for the self is always: that *directly before* which it is a self, but this in turn is the definition of 'criterion'" (emphasis added). One can constitute one's identity on an animal farm by existing merely "directly before [one's] cattle," in apartheid as "a master who is a self directly before his slaves [and] is actually no self," in social totality "directly before" the nation–state, in the United States by vegetating "directly before" TV's Persian Gulf War coverage— everywhere mirroring rather than shaping the public, academia, the media, and churches. In all these cases of identity formation, "a criterion is lacking." A temporal and communicative setting for inwardness is an expansion of existential communication in intersubjectivity "directly before" the other who becomes for me an invitation to earnest thinking and living. This criterion qualifies neither the self nor the alter but rather con/temporaneity with another. The criterion defines qualitatively not entities but freedom's possibility of possibility.[34]

Whereas Climacus claims that he is trying to become a Christian, then disclaims his book with humorous jest, Anti-Climacus posits a becoming one. Kierkegaard opts for standing between these two character claims: he does not repel Christianity by experimentally poetizing it, but neither does he demonically confuse himself with Christian ideality. He meets divine communication as an occasion for himself and every generation, and only thus considers the question of con/temporaneity with the god–man in human history. Kierkegaard knows that he would be as foolish as a college sophomore if he thought that one did not need to ready oneself to greet love's communication, or that one already knew how to love before love addresses one. If one is ever to become ready, one should receive practice in con/temporaneity with the other: Anti-Climacus subtitles his *Practice* "for awakening and inward deepening," yet insists that inwardness is to be communicated in the form of one's life.[35]

From the standpoint of cultural value spheres, the ground of inwardness appears groundless because in the "how" I learn to walk as if through a cultural void. Yet, one does not have a legitimate standpoint from which to call this "how" irrational: while critical modernity may not draw on resources other than communicative rationality, existential communication is not exhausted by modern spheres of culture. This asymmetry between the ground of cultural value spheres and the groundlessness of inwardness defines the fiduciary, indirect, leaping character of existential communication. I hold this distinction between the grounds for validity claims and a modal, groundless ground performatively true for all discursive validity domains where human existence plays a role.[36]

"The past is not actuality—for me: only the contemporary is actuality for me." Tradition cannot become con/temporary for me in virtue of its being a tradition, a sacred canon, or an authority, but the reader can become con/temporary with the past. If I affirm that tradition addresses me in my actuality through its being linguistified, I mean that I need to enter into conversation with it intertemporally. This task presents the difficulty of every beginning for every generation. One can converse with another only as con/temporary: persons, texts, art, and one's present age. This hermeneutical lesson teaches that reading invites self-reading and self-activity in communication.[37]

Self-reading activates a dangerous memory of beginnings. Becoming con/temporary with one's age subverts that establishment which mis/reads its origins. Inwardness does not affirm the *bourgeois* philistine, but it commits treason against deifying any existing socialist, capitalist, and new world orders. The demonology of Kierkegaard, the antisocial irrationalist, implicates itself in self-mis/reading:[38]

> Why has Hegel made . . . conscience . . . in the single individual "a form of evil"? . . . Why? Because he deified the established order. But the more one deifies the established order, the more natural is the conclusion: ergo, the one who disapproves of or rebels against this divinity, the established order— ergo he must be rather close imagining that he is God.

The social activists and theorists exhibit in their critiques of inwardness distinct types of monologism, decisionism, and dogmatism when they get involved in an acoustic illusion and adore the Party or some other *Führer*, revolutionary ethics or even the sobered up ideal of a communicative community. They exhibit

> [A] projection from the impiety with which one venerates the established order as divine, an acoustic illusion occasioned by the established order's tacitly saying to itself that it is the divine, and now through the witness to the truth comes to hear this, but hears it as if it were he who said he was more than human.

Theory and practice may not afford a forgetting of its beginnings: "that the established order has become something divine, is regarded as the divine, is a falsehood brought about by ignoring its own origins." This forgetfulness calls for a permanent Kierkegaardian corrective in the projection of the community ideal, lest its own critical discourse becomes unawares an ideological projection of an acoustic illusion. A Kierkegaardian, dangerous memory of temporal origins tries anything to avoid renting some nice *bourgeois intérieur*: "When a commoner [bourgeois] has become a nobleman, he usually makes every possible effort to have his *vita ante acta* [earlier life] forgotten."[39]

Kierkegaard envisions himself as a gadfly to the establishment in order to wake it up from its self-deified intoxication. Not only individuals but nations, too, would do well if they learned to unite, like the nesting icebirds upon the turbulent sea. Such postnational but rooted individuals bind their leagues not by consensus alone, but by a mutually shared acknowledgment of the difficulty of beginnings. Neither the individual nor a community can do without the humility that remembers the earth. Both "live in fear and trembling." Their shared, dangerous memories, which subvert the imperial world order and the nationalist status quo, "signify that we are in the process of becoming; and every single individual, likewise the generation, is and should be aware of being in process of becoming."[40]

Inhabitants of such a permanent corrective in an existential mode of both the individual and the community experience something analogical to a sobering memory of Alcoholics Anonymous. I have already indicated that Kierkegaard's perpetual reminder of temporal beginnings projects pathos similar to the first step of the AA model as the first entry invitation for any social and political healing of individuals in a community. To be sure, neither AA nor my reading of this inwardness or verticality requires one's allegiance to theistic or atheistic, substantive contents. That is why this AA ideal, which is operative not only for hard cases of substance and behavior addiction but also for the types of co-dependencies that seem to cover most of us in the human race, approximates what I mean by a horizontal community in an inward or vertical mode. Hence, even that which might emerge as our mutual consensus about the diagnosis and cure of addictive living becomes necessarily decentered by the vertical axis—the wholly other of cure. The shipwreck of individual and group total self-reliance on consensual procedure and consensual aim ratifies the very condition of the possibility of an addict's self and other-critical posture. My use of this model does not jettison communicative ethics and legitimate consensus as the valid regulative ideal. It shows how this ideal becomes qualified when the structural basis for its performative maintenance lies not in validity domains but rather in the "how" of self-choice and in the "how" of communication with others before the wholly other.[41]

An "addict anonymous" to drugs, nationalism, fundamentalism, or various forms of violence begins a cure not by a pledge of allegiance to a sacred tradition but posttraditionally: one begins by actively withdrawing from the claim to one's own total hold on origins and yielding to a wholly other mode of living. This first step cannot result from procedural consensus under an ideal consensus. An addict's experiential gain of inward or vertical identity within a community of equals becomes a modal condition of the possibility of receiving cure. This identity of an addict is not something one may do in privacy; it is certainly not something to be postponed after one has engaged in social and political critique or has gotten high on revolution or imperial war; yet, it is not something that can be shoved aside as sociopolitically irrelevant. Inward or vertical identity is to be sustained permanently and within a community of others who know themselves as addicts or co-dependents. (And with the opiates of fundamentalism and nationalism we suffer from addictive behavior in league with many other nations.) This repeated setting of mutually shared crisis offers a Kierke-gaardian rejoinder to Habermas's social integration of the honest individual.

Sacralization of cultural spheres occurs when the inner–outer is made commensurable with inwardness. Kierkegaard subverts this view:

> [W]ith the same bravura a brand-new nobleman can forget that yesterday he was a commoner [bourgeois], with the same bravura the established order can forget its origins. And just as the individual human being can aspire to become something, so this is the something to which the generation aspires; it wants to form the established order, to abolish God, and in fear of men to browbeat the single individual into a mousehole. . . .

Kierkegaard envisions one's becoming con/temporary with another through suffering inwardness: "the distinctive mark of the true piety" is not hiddenness but rather the fact "that it has a hard time in the world." When the individual provokes "the established order out of self-complacency," the inward signifier becomes incommensurable with the status quo, thereby making one suffer by virtue of living in the truth. Uncourted suffering, which results from such a dissent, offers an indirect sign that one is living in critical inwardness.[42]

In what, then, do the paraded monologism and the irrationality of the existential attitude lie? A dissident who repeatedly confronts a totalitarian regime embodies a form of life con/temporary with Kierkegaard's claim: "The established order wants to be a totality that recognizes nothing above itself but has every individual under it and judges every individual who subordinates himself to the established order." This individual can verify how the established totality judges one's total claim to living in truth as an arrogant, individualistic, and irrational posture. Be it at the university, in the media, within the homogenized public sphere, or from the fundamentalist pulpit, this dissenting individual might be "regarded as one who makes himself more than human." This person might be forced into a psychiatric asylum only to prove the commensurability of inwardness with some manifest social totality. One's resistance, when situated in a cultural totality whose life form has become an objective untruth, whose universities and media are domestications, and whose rituals embody self-idolatry, cannot but proceed in inwardness. Yet by being an earnest form of resistance, inwardness is public and political in an eminent sense even if this activism appears to be nonpolitical. Wherein do the charges of dogmatism and ideology of the self-critical attitude lie? The prosecuted dissident against totality can verify that the "single individual who teaches the most humble and yet the most humane doctrine about what it means to be a human being, the established order will intimidate by charging him with being guilty of blasphemy."[43]

We need not seek out extreme examples of "the possibility of offense that is . . . related to . . . an individual human being who comes into collision with an established order." How hard it is to be promoted in academic communities if one heeds inwardness rather than the publish or perish mentality. How easily offended are human groupings when one does not woo them by taking part in their gossip and self-importance. "The offense under discussion here is one of which anyone . . . can be the object if . . . the single individual seems to be unwilling to subject or subordinate himself to the established order." How offended advertisers and the public are that one is neither interested in becoming number one, nor runs with the latest intellectual fashions, nor is moved to increase profit! How offended are the churches when one does not leap sideways by pledging allegiance to the flags hanging at the altar! Kierkegaard calls these offenses of wanting to be an individual. "[P]eople are offended at . . . him [or her], even though he [or she] really is only making God God and himself [or herself] a human being."[44]

Kierkegaard's corrective to the establishment, and to the sociopolitical theory that it justifies, occasions for him an intense suffering collision. When he goes through a trial over his practice of indirect communication, he begins to doubt whether deliberate communication through pseudonyma is a form of strategic action or not. In his *Practice* he does not resolve this, but he shows how inward suffering relates to existential communication, and how it opera' ʾs as a sociopolitical ferment in the given life form:

> It is always painful to have to conceal an inwardness and to have to seem to be other than one is. . . . The collision is this, out of love for another person to have to conceal an inwardness and seem to be other than one is.

Kierkegaard distinguishes three aspects of this inward suffering in existential communication. The first lies in the hidden character of suffering. Indirection and hiddenness are sacrifices of love for love's sake. Second, one suffers because of what is occasioned in the other. Indirect, hidden communication of existence, though in love and out of love's sacrifice for the other, is experienced by the other as cruelty. The maieutic teacher, a friend, a lover, all suffer in different ways the pains of growth in another. Third, there is "the suffering of responsibility." I call this the Lévinasian dimension in Kierkegaard's existential communication. Lest we let Lévinas interpret for the reader what inwardness is, one can discover that one's decentering through responsibility for the other is rooted in the very invitation to existential communication: "Thus it is [1] out of love to annihilate, immediately and directly, one's own love, yet preserving it, [2] out of love to be cruel to the beloved, [3] out of love to take upon oneself this enormous responsibility."[45]

7.2. AN EXISTENTIAL MODE OF JUSTICE AND LOVE

I want to further highlight the shift from the pseudonymously hidden to manifest inwardness (A) and read through Kierkegaard's critique of the herd mentality my proposal of the ideal, existentially communicating community (B).

A. From Hidden to Manifest "Inwardness"

My Kierkegaard reading contradicts Climacus. First, Climacus relies on a false subject–object dualism. Yet, objectivity in all human and social disciplines is the fruit of passionate subjectivity. Second, he reacts to the overdrawn, if not positivist, notion of objectivity that nobody today except a few die-hard empiricists or analysts holds. Third, his insistence on a hidden inwardness reflects a preoccupation with the nineteenth-century demise of Christendom. Yet, he brushes off the implications that indirect communication has for human intersubjectivity. My question all along has been: how does inwardness or verticality affect human disciplines, collaboration, and communication among humans?[46]

Practice in Trust

While I affirm, leaning on Kierkegaard, that in the first two points Climacus is simply wrong, I offer my own reformulation of the last point. Climacus's third claim is a historically determined conclusion. If his religious concern really experiments within the mode of "faith," then we are not precluded to expand it to the area where Lévinas and Buber articulate ethical life. Buber is wrong to critique Kierkegaard for the position held by Climacus. We need not rob the individual of her passion when we ask how the community ideal becomes qualified in existential communication.[47]

"*That to deny direct communication is to require faith can be simply pointed out in purely human situations. . . ."* (emphasis added). Kierkegaard uses here this fiduciary mode analogically, since no human being ought to be worshipped. It would be comic to adore someone who is just as out of breath and late in coming as I am. It is then comic to project and labor under a regulative ideal of the human communication community that would be, in principle, breathing on its own and in possession of its beginnings. With these disclaimers, it is legitimate to speak about communication as transpiring in a fiduciary mode analogical to "faith."[48]

To make his point, Kierkegaard carries on a thought experiment with lovers. In the first situation we find direct communication: lovers express their passion to one another in what almost seems to be mutual adoration. They address one another with a belief claim: "Do you *believe* that I love you? . . . Yes, I *do believe* it" (original emphasis). In another situation there occurs an indirect communication of love. There are no manifest signs of love between the lovers. One lover becomes to the other "a riddle." Becoming a riddle means to embody a question about one's total claim to living. Such a claim presents a faith invitation. This indirect claim embodies possibility, which can be verified in one's actuality alone. Con/temporaneity with another lures one to a fiduciary leap towards the other.[49]

Works of Love

An open mode of loving remains both the hidden life source and a recognizable fruit. Thus, loving resembles what in Chapter 6 I identified as the transferred uses of language and the second order of receptivity. "There is a place in a human being's most inward depths; from this place proceeds the life of love. . . . But this place you cannot see, no matter how far you thrust in; the source withdraws itself into remoteness and hiding; even if you have thrust in as far as possible. . . ." A subtext of loving, of inwardness, is authored in a "nonmasculinist" way. Direct assault mis/reads love. "From this place love proceeds in manifold ways, but by none of these ways you can thrust your way in to its hidden beginning." One meets love and truth in the fiduciary mode: "as faith . . . offers to be . . . [one's] companion on life's way but turns to stone the impudent who turn about . . . to grasp it: so also it is the desire and prayer of love that . . . no one . . . will disturbingly thrust his way in to see what . . . he forfeits by his curiosity." Loving, just as the truth of subjectivity, remains veiled "to observation or investigative introspection." Neither claims nor deeds can directly abide in love. "As love itself is not to be seen (for that reason one believes in it), neither is it unconditionally and directly to be known by any one expression." A direct "masculinist" possessiveness mistakes love's veiling as monological, decisionistic, and dogmatic! Love communicates to another in the mode of speaking and acting, even if no one can be a best judge of its fruits. One is protected from an impostor–hypocrite by living in fear and trembling before love's hidden ground, afraid of one's own failure to heed it. "The best defense against hypocrisy is love; yes, it is . . . a yawning abyss." Neither the sweet fruits nor one's want of them sustain love. "[W]hen one has learned to know . . . [love] by its fruits, one . . . returns to the beginning—to believe in love—and returns to it as the highest."[50]

Loving builds up by providing a ground for its dwelling. Edifying builds "from the ground up." The paradox of love as the groundless ground of abiding, the place of the repeated building up of the other, lies in its "nonmasculinist" mode of receptivity. "*To build up* is a transferred expression": speech acts cannot edify directly, but "there is no word in the language which cannot become edifying and which in being said cannot build up if love is present." Any language game can edify if qualified by loving: "Therefore to speak of what can build up would be the most interminable discourse of all discourses. . . ." This "most inexhaustible discourse" has a limited task of making whole: "the discourse does not spread into particulars and multiplicities; it does not confusedly begin with something which must arbitrarily be cut off in order to be concluded." The holism of loving provides "the ground," "the building," and the upbuilding. This "up-building game" does not signify a play of surfaces without depth; loving lives in both height and depth. Inwardly one does not gain metaphysical depths but rather encounters oneself "in earnest and play[s] 'stranger' with the old and familiar." Kierkegaard's discourse on love follows Climacus's postmetaphysical transcript of *anamnesis* as existential communication: in human relations one edifies by drawing towards love's ground in oneself and thus indirectly, heeding love's ground in the alter. There are many discursive validity domains, "but there is only one up-building subject: how love builds up." Receptivity, "by presupposing that love is present" as the ground, by upbuilding allows the alter "to speak." An edifying mode transforms the ordinary language of communicative ethics. "Love means to presuppose love; to have love means to presuppose love in others; to be loving means to presuppose that others are loving." While love is both signifying and the signified, one becomes its actively receptive, upbuilding signifier of love by reading love in others. It is impossible that one "could be truly loving without . . . presupposing of love in others." In a mode of "faith" one "has shown itself to signify: to presuppose love in others"; one becomes "the lover, who presupposes love." Since one may not implant grounds in the alter, an upbuilding mode of discourse appeals to the presuppositions of communication. Inwardness provides this receptive ground for both direct validity claims and for the upbuilding modes of discourse.[51]

The Riddle of Justice

Climacus provides philosophies of liberation, and, at the same time, of education, and from Anti-Climacus's complementary view we come to know the links between love and justice. Let me return to Climacus's communication and supplement it with Anti-Climacus's fiduciary ground. In Socrates's maieutics, intensified through passion, the teacher becomes a riddle which cannot be solved (unlike the young Marx's claim that communism solves a history riddle), but rather is sustained. One begins as a riddle only in order to present oneself and to reach the other in the riddle. The communicator's existence remains veiled from the other and, in that, lets the recipient be herself. Against the admiring gaze of discipleship, the communicator's riddle "poses the dialectical duplexity" that can be crossed only through a mode, never within the value spheres of culture.[52]

While the movements of erotic love and of justice in the maieutic teacher appear to proceed in opposite directions, in both the motion occurs by virtue of the fiduciary ground. Neither owns the other and neither stands on a firm cultural ground. They sustain radical egalitarianism not by virtue of solving the riddle but rather in becoming riddles for each other. If love is not to become a dizzy freedom, its possibility of possibility must be sustained on a ground. The character of this ground protects this mutuality from becoming either idol worship or a sado-masochistic perversion of reciprocity. Objecting that there is dogmatism in this groundless walking implicates one in having no ground in love and justice.

In works of love and of justice the task is that of emancipating the recipient. "In the relation between individuals, one person must and shall be content with the other's assurance that he believes him; no one has the right to make himself into an object of faith for the other person." This stipulation qualifies dialogic reciprocity: the immediacy of the relationship poses the danger of idolizing, but a fiduciary mode can sustain dialogical reciprocity through indirect recognition. The task is to prevent each partner in communication from "becoming an object of faith or an approximation thereof for another." We must not tire of differentiating one's inhabiting a mode of "faith" from someone's becoming an object of faith for another. In culture, the former exercises a permanent resistance to the possibility of the latter. This mode resists the sacralizations of modern identity and will formation within those life forms in which culture has lost its traditional, ideological role. It occasions a corrective to idolized modern identities.[53]

The mode explains how in the question of justice self-relation involves other-relation: Habermas analyzes the value spheres of self-realization and self-determination; Kierkegaard is preoccupied with the mode of justice. Hence, it does Habermas no good to tilt the inward or vertical mode onto the generic or horizontal forum of justice. Just as in democracy today, the majority appears free, loving, and just; so also in Kierkegaard's time, "in hidden inwardness all are Christians." But "established Christendom, where all are Christians but in hidden inwardness, in turn resembles the Church militant as little as the silence of death resembles the loudness of passion."

Analogically, if in a democracy all seem free, loving, and just in their hidden inwardness, we cannot tell if they are so by choice. It could be that all of us are free, loving, and just. We cannot find out directly whether "all these thousands upon thousands" really are as they appear or claim to be.[54]

We can, however, get an indirect sign. The crusader for democracy and the social activist reveal themselves in their works of justice. Identity is a performative category and choice is an action category: neither a membership card in a democracy nor in a revolutionary cell can offer the sought for sign. Kierkegaard intimates how I draw towards another by drawing towards myself; and drawing towards myself, I become decentered in my cultural grounds. Yet I do not come to dwell in a bourgeois renter's privatist inwardness. "[A] self is a redoubling, is freedom; therefore in this relation truly to draw to itself means to posit a choice. . . . [S]elf can truly draw another self to itself only through a choice." Therefore, the hidden inwardness that anonymously feeds on the junk foods of herd religiosity occasions no more freedom, love, and justice than identity and choice shaped by the mass culture and revolutionary terror.[55]

B. Kierkegaard's Critical Community Ideal

Let me further pursue this analogy between Kierkegaard's critique of the churches and his critique of academia, media, and the democratic public:

> [E]stablished Christendom became a collection of what could be called honorary Christians, *in the same sense as* as we speak of honorary doctors, who receive their degree without having written and defended a doctoral dissertation. In hidden inwardness, we all took the degree, or we all received it, the one from the other, as a compliment, and thus were honorary Christians in the same sense . . . as one speaks of fireside students [matriculated without an examination on the basis of age–maturity alone].[56] (emphasis added)

Kierkegaard's "in the same sense as" may be read in reverse order closer to home. It is a convex mirror of the life form, in which the theory that the inner is the outer, and the outer is the inner, becomes rooted and justified. This life form comprises, then, besides Kierkegaard's critique of the churches, also the university, media, and the debating public. In the hiddenness of anonymity every one can proudly parade the identity of the democrat living in or a revolutionary aspiring for a just republic. Is not such anonymity prematurely matriculated in freedom and justice? Having taken no core requirements, one's patriotism or activism gapes like an unread book, a degree by correspondence, or justice in quantitative stages. Kierkegaard suggests that maybe in the present age we have been awarding one another honorary identities and voting for those leaders who best confirm these individual and national delusions of grandeur. Perhaps such identities only reflect the latest fad. Especially if one manages not to become a self, one might then receive public honors for books on the death of the self, and even get oneself tenured and invited to give speeches. At the cocktail hour this one can forget every difficulty of beginnings. Getting dizzy on freedom, one is, then, complimented for being like the rest and at rest.

Kierkegaard's critique of the congregation carries implications for a broader community ideal:

> "[T]he congregation" is at rest what "this single individual" is in unrest. But this life is indeed a time of testing, of unrest, and therefore "the congregation" does not belong in time but belongs first in eternity, where it is at rest, the gathering of all the single individuals who . . . passed the test.[57]

Yet how can we explain that Kierkegaard critiques the congregation and also sets it critically against the mass public sphere? Is not there a contradiction? Must not he presuppose some criterion for such a two-pronged critique? I want to justify textually the following thesis: the ideal of a communicating community presents that way of life which is appealed to in both of Kierkegaard's critiques. This ideal offers a permanent lived corrective both to the secular and the religious value spheres of culture. One appeals to this ideal in raising the total claim to existing; and yet the community ideal itself is defined not metaphysically but by praxis of communication.

Habermas's formal–pragmatic ideality, albeit concretely operative, seems to be a comfortable rest home which does not take temporal existing to be its urgency. While under his ideal one "transcends from within and on this side" of communicative practice, one is not prompted to transcend towards the other in venture and risk. Habermas's *"von innen"* (from within) remains like Hegel's inner–outer. Habermas's *"diesseits"* (on this side) takes place *"jenseits"* (on the other side) of temporal existing. Against the backdrop of Habermas's secularization of Peirce's quasi-theological ideal of the communication community, let me read how Kierkegaard's individual communicates in the medium of time and in an idealized eternity of congregation.[58]

In fact, two readings are possible. First, Kierkegaard might not be saying anything new beyond the Augustinian distinction between the inner–outer city (psyche–polis) of humans and their life in the City of God. The individual exists in the medium of becoming, and so "here there is no congregation." Congregation, like Augustine's ideal justice in the *ordo* of God, offers a criterion of eternity that becomes available through recollection and by one's participation in the salvation history. In this earthly city there are only shadows of justice, but no actually just city for an inward life of the psyche. This Augustinian distinction between the two cities can be read along the lines of the anecdote about Alexander the Great and the pirate: the pirate says to Alexander that the only difference between them is that one has many ships and is called an emperor and the other has a small fleet and is called a pirate. What are human life forms and politics, says Augustine, but bands of robbers, rapists, hangmen, and spiritless administrators?[59]

Second, Kierkegaard is really offering a postmetaphysical view, while Augustine abstracts from existing: one has no direct line to the political recollection of ideal justice. Not even the christened Ciceronian view of the common weal combined with the corrective, pre-Machiavellian political sobriety of Augustine can provide the temporal blueprint for a just republic. Augustine's political pessimism is concrete merely hypothetically: he views the political in the outward direction of the dominions but does not project in inwardness the concretely existing just form of life. He turns pessimism into political quietism and a wrongly accentuated inquisitorial activism. His remains an uncritical reading of one's mode of existing in the actual polis.

Given Climacus's postmetaphysical rendition of Platonic recollection in existential communication, Kierkegaard insists that ideality is an invitation and a requirement. Justice, whether a vestige or ideality itself, requires one's self-choice and pathos. The ideality of justice, whether in a human or a divine city, occasions a temporal task. Augustine's justification of violent force to suppress the donatist heresy cannot be sustained without metaphysical appeals and strategic uses of power. Such approximating action, reaching out for the ideality of the congregation of God through the historical domains rather than through an existential mode, falls into decisionist politics and fails to become con/temporary with justice. The communitarian criterion, whether it be Augustine's hypothetical pessimism or, later, Aquinas's high medieval real-politics, does not present justice as a call to contemporaneity. But justice begins on the ground of pathos, and there with regard to one's late beginnings one is already a heretic. Even legitimate consensus suffers a lag in the mode of justice. Augustine journeys to religious faith as if through the predestined cultural value spheres of justice in the two cities, but Kierkegaard walks, even Christianly speaking, on a groundless ground of a mode of "faith" where nothing—politically, ethically, morally, religiously—is predestined and all is risk.

Kierkegaard's is then a non-Augustinian stress on repetition, on making one's own the criterion of justice and action. He does not rely on an ideally projected congregation at eternal rest. Insofar as Habermas's communicative ethics is postmetaphysical, his ideal of justice does not fall under Kierkegaard's critique of concretistic privileging of, for example, Augustinian communitarian *ethos*. Yet insofar as the community ideal does not occasion an invitation and a task, Habermas, too, remains abstract.

Thus, Kierkegaard attacks "congregation" when its ideality is taken as an excuse for abdicating one's own task to embody the ideal:

> I am no Christian—but is it not true that a sum of such Christians gives a
> Christian congregation. . . . [A]ll, each one, will say: Well, in the strictest sense
> I do not dare call myself a Christian, but nevertheless there certainly is a
> Christian congregation. Always this statistical cheating. . . . [T]he congrega-
> tion . . . is cosmeticized as "the objective," "the utmost earnestness". . . .

This abstract ideality bespeaks the numerical, mass identity which in modern life forms seeks new sacral ideologies. Yet, the numerical strikes any
exister as embarrassingly comic: one calls oneself one of the "faithful" just
because the congregation for the "propagation of faith" stands already out
there to guarantee reality and one happens to be a card-carrying member
led by its infallible party. One considers oneself free since from kindergar-
ten onwards one parrots the pledge of allegiance to the signifier of freedom and to all for which it stands. One thinks of oneself as undeceptively
just by professing a revolutionary or work ethic; one redeems a total claim
to existence by terrorist or productive acts. Here one walks a tragically
comic, not a just path. Only with this critique can Kierkegaard set the
congregation against the crowd. "The public is the most idea-less of all. In
fact, it is the very opposite of the idea. For the public is numbers." After
1848, he resolves that revolution—politically, ethically, and religiously
speaking—today passes through the individual. He means by "congregation" a community of individuals.[60]

Note that this community can be identified neither with the eternal
retirement home, nor with a possibility that abstracts from the groundless
ground on which the project stands, nor with some communitarian life
form. And it makes, at this point and as a performative distinction between
numerical and qualitative identity, no difference whether we "decide" to
seat this community in a church, or in the public assembly, or in a square
where Nietzsche's madman declares God dead. The question of Christianity or of the death of God should be addressed first to one's difficulty of
beginnings.

I claim that unless one makes the distinction between identity in communicative ethics and in an existential mode, it is impossible to grasp
Kierkegaard's criterion for a critique of both the secular public and the
congregation. It gets us nowhere simply to parrot that he critiques the social
in the name of the individual. The monological, decisionist, and metaphysical readings of Kierkegaard provide no help in understanding the link
between critiques of secular and sacral ideologies. Only when we expand
the radically honest individual so as to envision a mode of community can
we comprehend Climacus's paradoxical insistence that the individual is
higher than the race and at the same time his admission that community
can become equal to the individual. I argued that an existential mode
qualifies how one exists in communicative ethics at the same time that in
this "how" one projects the criterion of the ideal, existentially communicating community.[61]

The criterion for this ideal lies in the other before whom I raise my identity claim. A mass has no individuals, it cannot be a criterion:[62]

> In the "public" and the like the single individual is nothing; there is no individual; the numerical is the constituting form and the law for the coming into existence; . . . detached from the "public" the single individual is nothing, and in the public he is, more basically understood really nothing at all.

A community of earnest individuals differs from mass groupings:

> In community the single individual *is*; the single individual is dialectically decisive as the presupposition for forming *community*, and in *community* the individual is qualitatively something essential and can at any moment become higher than "community," specifically, as soon as "the others" fall away from the idea. (original emphasis)

Note above that two senses of community or congregation are used, the latter being distinguished from the former by quotation marks. The individual is higher than "community" or "congregation" but functions integrally in the idea of *community* or *congregation*. To "fall away from the idea" means to cease inhabiting an existential mode of the individual in community. *The individual who is higher than the group is so, then, by virtue of the higher idea of community*, along Mead's critique of a conventional "me" via the individual "I":

> The cohesiveness of community comes from each one's being a single individual, and then the idea; the connectedness of a public or rather its disconnectedness consists of the numerical character of everything.

Kierkegaard would agree with Habermas that community is not a subject writ large, but would add that an individual mode of existing projects an ideal mode of community. It is, then, insufficient to define qualitative identity on the basis of autonomous action in cultural value spheres. Modally, the community of concrete others has a priority over the community of the generalized other:

> Every single individual in community guarantees the community; the public is a chimera. In community the single individual is a microcosm who qualitatively reproduces the cosmos; here in a good sense, it holds true that [who knows one, knows all] *unum noris omnes*. In a public there is no single individual and the whole is nothing; here it is impossible to say [who knows one, knows all] *unum noris omnes*, for here there is no *one*. (original emphasis)

The primacy of the mode over the generalized other does not implicate my argument in a dualistic defense of the inner against the outer. The individual is higher than community insofar as the former projects a community mode by which it qualifies the value spheres of the generalized other. One knows "all" by facing the difficulty of the "one":

> "Community" is certainly more than a sum; but yet it is truly a sum of ones; the public is nonsense—a sum of negative ones, of ones who are not ones, who become ones through the sum instead of the sum becoming a sum of the ones.

Now, the self-critical attitude need not be set against the social one since it projects an ideal already from a modal ground of the social. Therefore, the difficulty of beginnings provides a qualified basis for a critical social theory:

> [T]he human race in contrast to animal species is characterized by the fact that the single individual is higher than the race. Whereas the overlapping factor in regard to particular animal . . . specimens is the race . . . the single individual . . . when in truth [one] is the single individual, is the overlapping factor. *The race is binding on a lower level.* . . . *[T]he single individual is more than the species . . . for [one] is the whole race and also the individuation.*[63] (emphasis added)

The mode transforms the priority of value spheres over the single individual: freedom's possibility qualifies both the conventional priority of ethical self-realization and the normative priority of moral self-determination.

When one's freedom becomes dizzy, then one falls away from the self-critical ideal into the numerical; but in critiquing both the secular public and religious herd, the individual appeals to the ideal, existentially communicating community. The critical criterion is neither the individual of possessive individualism nor the community of communitarianism. Community can take precedence over the individual only when the mode sustains the walkers, and when honest communication provides the medium of the identity and will formation.

CONCLUSIONS

An indication that the ideal, existentially communicating community is a modal ground presupposed in the critique equally of secular and religious imaginary occurs in the text that Buber uses against Kierkegaard:

> [T]he only medium, through which God communicates with [humans], the only thing [God] will talk about with [humans] is: the ethical. But to speak ethically about the ethical . . . means unconditionally to render everything else infinitely unimportant. . . . [T]he watchword is stick to the point—that is, stick to the ethical.[64]

As I interpret it, this passage confirms Kierkegaard as the most unread modern sociopolitical thinker. One finds here exemplified how his concern with inwardness or verticality is centrally set in the heart of communication. I note a support for my previous claim that one may not move into any level of the religious apart from going through the existential–performative mode. Because my argument has been developed from within existential communication, I was able to critique Habermas immanently (i.e., within the modal conditions of the possibility of communicative ethics).

A fascinating journal entry that supports these conclusions is "the dialectic of community [congregation] or of society." There are three qualifications of the self- and other-relation recorded here:

(1) individuals who relate to each other in the relation are individually inferior to the relation.
(2) individuals who relate to each other in the relation are individually equal in relation to the relation.
(3) individuals who relate to each other in the relation are individually superior to the relation.

The text explains how critical theory is to begin with the individual, pass through the social whole, and end up defending the individual in community. The first qualification shows what it means to be a specimen of the race. The single member of an organic body seems less important than the whole, from the viewpoint of an organism or a cosmic system. A naturalistic model cannot ground a social theory. The second scenario applies to works of love and justice. In erotic love one both embodies something and exists temporally ecstatic for another. Even though shared love may not be owned by either lover, natural erotica and erotic reason remain insufficiently egalitarian and revolutionary. The self-critical attitude requires a downfall of natural self-love. The natural is transformed into one's task. The spirit cannot be given, but rather it emerges as a self-critical journey. The way of the spirit includes one's self-analysis of the natural, the unconscious, and the demonic—all of which can distort both communication and the ideal requirement of equality in love and justice. Just as in love, so also in education, friendship, or communal justice; by virtue of earnest communication there is embodied a call for radical equality in rank. Lastly, pathos teaches one to relate totally in the mode and relatively in cultural value spheres. The total claim of temporality qualifies one's every beginning. The total claim of inward or vertical identity exercises a permanent resistance to the totality formed in culture and society. The following theorem sums up these interrelations: the exister is higher than both the ethical and religious cultural value spheres, and yet in a mode of the total claim to living remains equal to other individuals projected in the temporal ideal of existentially communicating community.[65]

The ideal of an existentially communicating community maintains experimentally a communicative–pragmatic expansion of radically honest crisis identity. This expansion satisfies Habermas's regulative ideal of maintaining the attitude of the other. Moreover, it undermines the critiques brought against Kierkegaard's presumed monologism, decisionism, and dogmatism. Therefore, Kierkegaard's communicative ethic corrects and integrates Habermas's communicative ethics by the triple "how" of identity, communication, and the community ideal.

PART III

IDENTITY, TRADITION, AND REVOLUTION

CHAPTER 8

Identity
and Existential Revolution

W hen in his 1987 Copenhagen lecture Habermas translates Kierkegaard's either/or characteristic of self-choice into a public choice of postnational identity, he could not have anticipated that two years later many Germans would choose themselves not posttraditionally but rather in a renewed nation–state. Habermas's description of November 1989 as the "catching-up revolution" (*die nachholende* or *rückspulende Revolution*) does not pick up Havel's projected possibility of existential revolution. Habermas's stylization of the central-eastern European revolutions of 1989 as regressions to "old national symbols" and to traditions of the era between the two world wars—as well as to a desire to catch up with western bourgeois revolutions—expresses the sentiments of many people in the east, especially the former East Germany. But it is misleading as an explanation of Havel's reflections on revolution and identity. The explanation might partially clarify why East Germans have sold out for the West German mark, but it fails to account for the radically honest resistance to totality. Why would Havel call November 1989 in Czechoslovakia not only the "velvet revolution" but also the "existential revolution"? Habermas makes it too easy for himself when he neglects to place the "existential" among his interpretative portraits of 1989, and when he interpolates his solution from this narrow horizontal account.[1]

I do not turn to Havel as a heroic ideal, since both he and the "velvet revolution" might fail, but rather to the counterfactual ideal of 1989. This projection of the earnest community ideal, with its solidarity of the shaken, corrects and complements Habermas's formal rendition of the revolutionary ideas of 1789 which leaves out Havel's confrontation of totality in the very identity formation. Habermas's instructive oversight expresses the general bias against existential thought that prevails even among sophisticated noncommunist leftists and critical theorists. Havel's reading of this concrete situation of the present age exemplifies Kierkegaard's dissenting praxis.

Havel doubts that radical self-choice can be replaced by the group choice, or that the modern crises of identity can be settled through social revolution alone. In his view of "existential revolution" he picks up Lévinas's motif of responsibility to the other: since individuals maintain and stabilize any social revolution through the retrieval of honest identity, radical self-choice cannot rest in some private *intérieur*. It demands social responsibility. We could imagine that, perhaps, Havel might ask Habermas if democratic revolution—apart from the existential one—could heal that melancholy which results from the paradox of every revolutionary project.[2]

To contrast Habermas's and Havel's beginnings: there is the experience of the noncommunist left of fighting the western drive to systemic totality. There is also Habermas's communicative reinterpretation of socialism that explains this experience. A permanent democratic revolution stands for a confrontation of the systemic colonization of the lifeworld by the economy and state. It seems that eastern and central Europeans have produced scarcely anything fresh in this regard, both because they lacked western experience of real existing capitalism and because their own struggles carry a particular bias against socialist revolutions.

There is the experience of dissent against real, existing socialism and of resistance to totalitarian systems of power. There is also Havel's reinterpretation of inwardness or verticality in terms of sociopolitical dissent that explains this experience. Existential revolution stands for a historically specific question not raised by Habermas: how can one expose the totalitarian colonization of modern crisis identity at the level of its very formation? It seems that the noncommunist left has had little to say on the possibility that identity formed in inwardness or verticality resists ideology and fragmentation alike. This left lacked the communitarian experience of communist totality. The leftist confrontation of fundamentalist religiosity and traditionalism carries a particular bias against the theme of inwardness or verticality.

Given the asymmetry of these experiences and the need to bring them together in the situation of the present age, what would an unbiased dialogic reciprocity between critical theory and existential philosophy mean here? Some critics depict Havel's position as politically conservative, elitist, antidemocratic, and dogmatically religious. But Havel replies to the motivational and legitimation crises of identity neither by returning to premodern communitarian models nor by finding refuge in the present age oversight of the problem of identity. Further, existential revolution can be identified neither with a myth eliciting conservative revolution nor with a liberal possessive individualism or political decisionism. The "existential" in Havel is not opposed to the "social" and the "political." Finally, mindful of Horkheimer's view that both theism and atheism have their tyrants and martyrs, we should seek an insight into Havel's concern with inwardness or verticality in its function as a critical "existential praxis." Hope lies neither in theism nor in atheism but in the dangerous memory of the victims of history, in an opposition to totalitarian power and to empty words.[3]

Because identity in crisis represents a key theme that enters Havel's literary and political writings as well as his public life, I approach his ideal of November 1989 from the angle that relates identity and revolution. There are two movements of revolution: we have seen how Habermas aims to integrate socially posttraditional and postnational identity against its modern pathologies in a radical democratic republic. Havel moves from earnest self- and other-relation to the sociopolitical aspects of self-choice (8.1). Further, nonpolitical politics, by fostering nonauthoritarian and open identity formation, can provide a lived modal corrective to Habermas's structural model of a radical democratic revolution (8.2).

8.1. HAVEL ON IDENTITY CRISES AND THE PRESENT AGE

In his second Sunday radio reflection after becoming the Czechoslovak president, Havel asks what happens when after a long time one moves from prison to freedom. His question is a repetition of his own journey, but it now focused on the national exodus from totality. In the prison everything is clear, because here meaning and the hope of freedom are delimited by the daily routine. After leaving the prison, one lacks this context. The paradox of the world "without the prison walls" is the seeming loss of identity.[4]

Havel voices the absurd, Kafkaesque anxiety of freedom; he self-ironizes that power into which he was brought on the wings of revolution:

> It is the greatest paradox, but I must confess it: if I am a better president than some other would be in my place, it is so because somewhere in my relation to my work I discover ongoing doubts about myself and the right to exercise my function. I am a person who would not be at all surprised, if someone, in the middle of my activities as a president, would bring me before an obscure tribunal. . . . if I would now hear the word, "wake up!" and I would find myself in my prison cell. . . .[5]

He develops this theme face to face with Kurt Waldheim, the former president of Austria, at the opening of the Salzburg Music Festival: different fanaticisms and nationalisms in central Europe originate from the renewed crisis of individual and group identities. "Anxiety of small souls about themselves and the world has led many times to violence, brutality, and fanatical hatred." But a fresh lie about our past and future cannot save us from a repressed lie. One cannot make an exception for oneself and somehow drift through history, even though this is the most common temptation of central and south-eastern European anxieties. "We are like the prisoners who got used to the prison and, released under the sky and into desired freedom, do not know how they should deal with this freedom, and are in doubt because they alone must decide." This "social–existential situation" is the anxiety of the victorious Sisyphus who has succeeded in rolling the stone onto the mountaintop and leaving it there.[6]

In the paradox of exile in totality and the exodus to freedom, Havel raises his key political question: if the modern totality differs from the classical dictatorship by permeating every identity from within and without, and so makes us at the same time responsible and without responsibility, how can one escape from its prison? Havel's how question, just as in Kierkegaard, implies that inwardly transformed critical theory and practice must find that mode of human identity formation which provides a check on power in one's self-relation and in one's relation to the other alike. Havel does not ask merely about the type of prison or about the structures to be built upon our deliverance. He searches for an enabling confrontation with anxiety, for the manner of resisting totality by living in truth with our past and future no matter where we are. He is inspired by the philosophy and civic courage of the phenomenologist and co-founder of the pluralist dissident solidarity in *Charta 77*, Jan Patočka. Further, in prison Havel reads and interprets Lévinas's thought of responsibility: he agrees with Lévinas and Kierkegaard alike insofar as the impetus to found "an alternative polis" and a "parallel culture" in a dissent community was to carry on the works of justice and love. Next, I focus on this less obvious influence of Lévinas.[7]

In prison Havel records three stages on a journey to freedom. In the first, he agrees with Lévinas about the primordial responsibility that one has towards the other who shapes one's own identity. In the second, he argues that one must take responsibility for that primordial responsibility into which one is thrown, but he interprets this self-choice at once socially, politically, and dramatically. In the third, he finds out that the horizontally conceived responsibility that takes itself too seriously shipwrecks. The journey through these stages is a repetition of ever more intensified pathos marked by an identity formed with fluid and nonauthoritarian ego boundaries—an identity in crisis, which becomes an unrepressed and open way.[8]

Let me sum up some those features of Lévinas's position that are found in Havel. In place of an exclusive entry into Kierkegaardian inwardness, Lévinas begins in a vertical transformation of the horizontally conceived sociality. Verticality means, for Lévinas, that identity is shaped ethically, not egologically. Lévinas's is a posttraditional and postnational ethics: it is the naked openness of the face to the nakedness of the other. Lévinas critiques the horizontal moral point of view—Buber's dialogic or Habermas's communicative ethics—based on the notion of symmetry: my existence is subjected to the other, hence the essential asymmetry; the other calls me to responsibility and, in that, is above me, not reciprocally next to me, hence verticality. "I" is where the face of the other is met. I am thrown into the world asymmetrically because responsibility to the other always severs me from my private ownership of myself. Asymmetry and verticality ground this noncommunitarian ethic of the other.[9]

Responsible freedom is permanently uneasy because its identity carries the demand of the other, not my personal will to exist. Identity permanently lives in exile; freedom reminds one of a permanently dangerous memory of exodus. In my desire to exist I am always a refugee from my ego; I am vertically robbed of my horizontally projected possession of identity. Every horizontal project of an ideal community necessarily experiences exile and exodus. This might explain the leftist melancholy that Habermas hopes to heal with his permanent democratic revolution, and those modern identity crises that he wants to resolve by socially integrating the vulnerable individual in postnational forms of life. Lévinas's ethics of the concrete other is ever suspicious towards totalitarian ambitions of liberal egological freedom; towards historical projection of the ego on revolutionary identity; towards conservative nostalgia for the ego of a nation, party, totem, or church; and towards the present age ethos celebrating the end of history and the ubiquity of power.

Lévinas comes from the Judaic, socially ethical inspiration. He does not reject Athens, but situates his phenomenology between Jerusalem and Auschwitz. Like Habermas's horizontal communicative ethics and Kierkegaard's resistance to totality, Lévinas's vertical ethics shows that the question about being in the world does not have any meaning apart from the ethical and temporal priority of the other. Undecentered identity forgets its permanent exile, its difficulty of beginnings, and so also its ethical mandate of exodus from totality thinking. This twice forgetful identity in the end divinizes the totality of itself or projects its own unrealized possibility—its philosophical and activist melancholy—on the intentionality of some nationalist, political, or fundamentalist *Führer*. In his critique, Lévinas does not leave philosophy. Rather, and this is the sense retrieved in Havel, he translates into the language of ethics in exile/exodus the question of the meaning of being.

For Lévinas, notions such as "God" and "religion" do not entertain dogmatic theology but remain a philosophical hermeneutic of ethics in exile and exodus. The wholly other, the not yet, that calls me from myself is not that face with which I am ever directly confronted. Face to face, I am sobered up with the question of responsibility. I do not have a reply to this question; I do not know who asks. In this question—neither decisively theistic nor atheistic—there is a relation, which precedes the beginning of my relation, is a possibility of my relation, but does not allow me to own this beginning or this relation. Holding my identity open to this question exercises a form of ideology critique: the relation between identity and an other that does not create totality Lévinas calls "religion." The ethics of the other destroys the natural political, national, and religious positions that we have taken on in the world and prepares us for that meaning, which is otherwise than being.[10]

Lévinas offers that nonauthoritarian and receptive model of identity which fulfills the conditions raised in Havel's key political question: responsible decentering of the subject does not lead to the end of history and identity, but rather to an open identity as a critique of totality and anomie. Existing oriented to the wholly other prevents one's will from gravitating to itself repressively or to the other oppressively.

Havel interprets Lévinas's primordial responsibility existentially: not every will to exist needs to be egological and totalitarian. Only horizontally delimited ethics and consensual aims or procedures are vulnerable in this sense. The problem is the lack of responsibility, not towards the other but towards oneself, and towards one's relation to the other. Without an identity that is neither melancholy nor terroristic, it is of little help that I am primordially thrown into the world as a responsibility to the other.

Havel's approach problematizes Habermas's beginnings: how am I to participate in discourse? How can the moral appeal to the symmetrical conditions of discourse and its force of the better argument be sustained against an entanglement of even the rational democratic will formation in the disabling forms of power? Would every posttraditional and postnational identity allow for actual moral discourses? What type of ideally concrete identity is presupposed by the idealized participant in the moral discourse?

Havel not only rejects the concept of the national and collective guilt, but also depicts with a nuance the difference between the mode of existential revolution and the necessity of creating democratic structures. (Remember that Habermas, while also rejecting the notion of collective guilt, translates the Kierkegaardian either/or self-choice into the public choice based on postnational identity in constitutional patriotism.) In his radio address Havel explains the concept of the "second revolution": he means neither the French Revolution that moved from the storming of the Bastille to the execution of the king to the universal terror, nor the Bolshevik revolution that gave birth to Trotsky's notion of permanent revolution. He means a need to complement ongoing democratic structures through the elimination of the new economic mafia made up from the deposed communist nomenclature. The "second revolution" should remove through local elections the hidden Communist Party monopoly in business enterprises, and determine to whom, in the state where all own all and nobody nothing, which property is to belong. Still, he confronts the present postrevolutionary melancholy and anxiety in Czechoslovakia by appealing not to the collective but to individual self-choice. That Czechoslovakia can remember the Soviet invasion of August 1968 for the first time in truth is important not nostalgically but decisively: he concludes that because the Soviet tanks did not come in November 1989, the outcome of November

1989 events depends on democratically harnessed individual self-choice rather than outside force.[11]

Havel undergoes such a decisive moment of self-choice earlier when he assumes responsibility for his responsibility: in the passivity of prison, he confronts the passivity of some of his activist friends: "Whether all is lost or not depends on that, if I am lost or not. . . ." Responsibility for responsibility is a chosen, not an ascribed role. "I agree with Lévinas, one cannot preach responsibility, one can only bear it. Thus, one cannot begin anywhere else but with oneself. It sounds comical, but it is so: I must begin."[12]

This self-appropriation of Lévinas explains why Havel differs from Milan Kundera. He objects to Kundera's "a priori skeptical attitude towards the civic acts which are without hope for an immediate success" and which appear to be arrogant gestures. In his *Unbearable Lightness of Being*, through the main character Tomáš, Kundera voices his own position from the years after 1968 when Tomáš explains why it does not help the political prisoners if he signs the petition for their release. Kundera ironizes the self-importance of the authors of such petitions: they believe that "the defeat of the just thing will shine lightning on the whole misery of the world and the whole glory of the author's character." Havel places different accents on solidarity with victims than Kundera's emphatic celebration of the death of the subject and the author. Havel's self-irony does not replace responsibility to the concrete other. In an early support of the imprisoned, Havel fostered a civic process towards that honest praxis which gave rise to *Charta 77* and to the "velvet revolution" of 1989. He agrees today that moral acts, even in diplomacy, might offend because they seem "exhibitionistic . . . gestures of the shipwrecked." Such risky acts offer some ground for Kundera's laughter. But Kundera "programmatically refuses to see . . . the hopeful" side of the absurd: "It seems to me as if he were a bit the prisoner of his own skepticism which does not allow him to admit that sometime it makes sense to behave courageously as a citizen. That it makes sense even though one can look comic." Havel's pathos offends equally a fanatic activist and a skeptic.[13]

Havel always interprets the "existential" as coterminous with the social, political, and dramatic: he joins the social in Lévinas with individual self-choice in a Kierkegaardian sense. This double reflection rejects the decisionism and monologism often ascribed either to the political existentialism espoused by Heidegger's Nazi contemporaries, or to the mainly French left existentialists. One ought to differentiate both of these variants of political decisionism from what Havel calls existential revolution. The shorthand for Havel's model might read as follows: while living in truth is the fruit of earnest subjectivity, self-choice calls for ethico-moral intersubjectivity.

Havel's dramatic work makes this point when it communicates to the viewer that she carries the resolution to her crisis of identity. His plays invariably remind us of our dilemma: "The only resolve [and] the only hope which have sense are those which we find ourselves, in us, and on our own." Drama communicates socially the "untransferable act of one's own existential awakening." There is a continuity between Havel's dramas and his civic posture: "Even the most difficult truth, if pronounced publicly and before all becomes something emancipatory...."[14]

This continuity links the political legitimation and the sociocultural motivation crises with the complementarity between absurdity and hope. An experience of the absurd or anomie awakens one's search for meaning. This desire for meaning that shapes one's identity is the very source of hope. Hope does not have an object; hope is a mode of one's identity. Hope provides a capacity to take responsibility for one's responsibility. Havel finds hope in an attitude between irony and self-irony on the one hand, and a sense for the absurd and humor on the other. These dimensions allow for both concretion and distance from oneself. They empower one to take on tasks that seem unbearable. The capacity for the absurd and laughter in the midst of revolutionary zeal or serious diplomatic effort testifies to the finitude of human acts, of every revolution: "If one . . . is not to melt in one's own seriousness, and so become comic to all, one must have, even though one were engaged in the most important thing . . . healthy consciousness of one's human laughability and smallness." A social revolution inhabits honesty when it grows from a realization of its own temporal limit. "[O]nly this consciousness can breath possible greatness. The contours of real meaning can be grasped only from the bottom of the absurd." One can understand here how the earnest, nonutopian utopia of a moral act can be engaged together with the sense of the absurd without the temptation of traditionalism, lyrical–romantic revolutionary melancholy, or the present day skepsis.[15]

Havel's intense prison experiences of the absurd and of hope do not mark a conversion to a religion. "I did not become 'participating Catholic': I do not attend regularly the Church, I have not 'institutionally' confessed since my childhood, I do not pray, and when I am in the Church, I do not cross myself." When Havel speaks of inwardness or verticality, he refers to the nonutopian utopia—the radical other "something" that gives meaning to one's acts in the world. "[T]he event called the world has a deeper meaning." When he speaks of "faith," this does not carry a confessional pledge of allegiance:

> I believe that . . . the universe and life [are] not "accidental." I believe, that nothing disappears without a trace, and still less our actions, by which I explain my conviction that it makes sense to strive for something in life, to strive for more than what comes visibly back or what pays off. In thus defined faith can be placed many people, and it would not be responsible to call them all, automatically, believing Christians.[16]

Havel dramatizes the conflict between words about responsibility and irresponsible action. He does so indirectly through a disclosure of self-deception and through a critique of ideology within himself. For this reason his dramas and political performances are equally autobiographical and universal, even though none of the dramatic characters or political dramatizations preaches Havel's direct position, and none of them offers a universal manual for authentic living or a successful revolution. Lévinas's thesis that one is responsible for the world becomes critical towards totality in the self-critical and dramatic senses given to it by Havel. Havel agrees with Lévinas's sympathy for Alyosha Karamazov's saying that we are not only responsible for the other but are more responsible than anyone else. Havel interprets this thought of greater responsibility as taking responsibility for one's own responsibility.[17]

For Havel, human life demands social–political and dramatic–existential responsibility. Open identity maintains a revolutionary mode that confronts totality within identity formation itself. Havel articulates a complementary mode of life that exercises a lived corrective to a social revolution based on horizontal identity alone. This corrective can be specified in the following legitimation and motivation theorem: open identity without ongoing democratic structures lacks a public sphere for drama and communication by words; democracy without an existential mode is blind and impotent to form those identities that can be a counterweight to totality. The condition of the possibility of the ideal community lies in its "inter-existentiality"—a life form shaped by a mode of revolution against lie and self-deception.[18]

In the third stage of his journey Havel meets limits of his horizontal moral will. Individual autonomy can become an imperceptibly self-deceptive and intimate prison. The will to freedom can either prevent one from leaving this prison within or become the terror of moralizing universalism. This discovery is Havel's main reason for self-irony towards himself as a president and a leader of the revolution. He hesitates to pledge allegiance to this church or that national or political movement, and clings to living at risk. He raises no sacred symbols—family, flag, market, and belief—in place of the disenchanted promise of communism. He communicates, paradoxically, open identity without fanaticism and terror. Havel defines the fanatic as the person

who, without having a clue, exchanged the love of God for the love of some one religion; the love of truth for the love of an ideology, doctrine or sect which promised him to guarantee their validity; and the love of people for the love of a project which he considers . . . to be a real service to the people. Fanaticism thus covers up the existential nakedness. . . . Fanaticism makes life easier for the price of its hopeless destruction. The fanatic's tragedy is that the beautiful and highly authentic longing . . . to take on the pains of the whole world imperceptibly changed into the creator of this suffering: into an organizer of the concentration camps, into inquisition, into genocides and executions.

Inwardness or vericality is neither resignation (it would not be a possibility) nor fanaticism (it would not be a paradox of identity as an activity and a way). Without self-responsibility one cannot claim to be receptive to the other. Fanaticism disregards the permanent nakedness of its own traditions, and thus cannot prevent its will from violating the other. Fanaticism, not existential revolution, creates from its given responsibility in the world a fetish. The fanatic escapes identity in fear of living in exile and exodus. The "real responsibility, and so real identity," lies in one's "dramatic self-confrontation" of oneself as a possibility.[19]

8.2. HAVEL'S NONPOLITICAL POLITICS

Havel speaks of existential revolution and nonpolitical politics as one's self-transforming relation to the democratic structures of society. He refers to the events of November 1989 and to the ongoing need for one's "general awakening of human conscience, human spirit, human responsibility, and human reason" as aspects of an existential revolution. We find this notion in his works, which call at once for dramatic, ethico–moral, and socio-political self-transformation.[20]

First, Havel's plays are marked by a certain dramatic irresolution. This means that the resolve to act ought to be found within the self-authoring audience/reader, not through Havel's works. His dramas do not certify the nowadays celebrated deaths of the author and the recipient, but rather call for their mutual edification. Self-transformation can be only occasioned in another, not coerced: neither authorship nor moral universals nor deliberative democracy can provide the guarantee of such a qualitative change. To be sure, drama, the moral point of view, and democratic procedures comprise the main stage, since for Havel one's self-transformation is always linked with other individuals via intersubjective, moral, and sociopolitical settings. Yet, this link between self-transformative and intersubjective relations is not causal. The stage of the authorship signifies only that possibility which individuals in community must learn to embody on the stage of self-transformative authoring.

Second, not only existential drama but also the struggle for human rights invites one to become a self-responsible author. Havel envisions this moral and sociopolitical authoring formed in resistance to totalitarian power, to mass society, and to words emptied into slogans. Moreover, such an authoring requires an ongoing dissent to totality within the very identity born of one's zeal for moral and political universals. Havel warns that the point of existential revolution cannot be some mastery over one's ego or over the collective, but rather it is a permanent revolution within identity formation. In Havel's dramas and in his prison letters one learns about that which can resist totality: neither mere drifting self- and other-relations, nor one's will to truth, nor moral universals, nor freedom, but a solidarity of responsible authors who embody open identity.[21]

Third, the nether side of both earnest identity formation and moral and political dissent cannot, then, point to "The End of History and the Last Man"; the move is instead toward nonpolitical politics. Neither the Cold War nor the New World Order deserve the victory palms for the defeat of totalitarianism in 1989. Havel claims that it was defeated by those counterinstitutions of nonpolitical politics that are anchored in self-responsibility to the other, not in the functionalist imperatives of technocratic power and business administration. Here we have a model of the pluralist politics emerging from that lifeworld that was shaped by the human rights movement *Charta 77*, and which is ushered into the nonviolent November of 1989. This politics—both during the dissident years and in Havel's present affirmation of it parallel to his presidency—is "nonpolitical" insofar as it raises the moral imperatives of solidarity and human rights over and against the systemic imperatives of markets and professional politics. Yet it is still "politics" since it gathers responsible individuals in the multiple public spheres. There is an analogy between authorship and honest authoring on the one hand, and between professional and nonpolitical politics on the other: in drama and in the public spheres alike, Havel greets an open-ended character of identity formation, rooted in the call for an ongoing existential revolution, as a check-and-balance on the resurgence of totalitarian, nationalist, and authoritarian power in individuals and communities alike.[22]

Now just as the honest individual may not be a fanatic, so also existential revolution may not espouse traditionalist religiosity and ethnocentric nationalism. To be sure, the ideal of the nonviolent, solidary, "velvet revolution" projected in the week of 17 November 1989 is just as demanding as is that of radical democracy. The centrifugal forces of Balkanization, Lebanonization, and fundamentalism problematize both Habermas's Kantian–Hegelian projection of rational community into our not so rational world, and Havel's call for sober communication within democratic institutions, procedures, and professional politics.

Yet I submit that this two-fold problematization of the community ideal by the nationalist strife with which the present age errupted after 1989 does not invalidate the need for posttraditional and postnational forms of life. These very conflicts call for the emergence of communicative and existential ethics as a critical theory and a way of living. Habermas's earlier defense of postnational deliberative democracy, echoed verbatim in his Copenhagen question to Kierkegaard, justifies likewise the projection of Havel's ideal:

> If world-views have foundered on the separation from socially integrative components, if world-maintaining interpretive systems today belong irretrievably to the past, then what fulfills the moral–practical task of constituting ego- and group-identity? ... We can no longer avert recognizable contingencies by producing a rationalizing illusion.[23]

Havel's critique of the present age neither aims at mere utopianism or skepticism nor espouses another ideology. Thus, the interest in the future that guides Havel's ideal of 1989 should be viewed as a qualifying complement to Habermas's communicative translation of the ideas of 1789:

> Does not the perspective of the better future of this world lie in some international community of the shaken which, disregarding the boundaries of the states, of political systems, and of power blocks, outside of the high game of traditional politics, without aspiring to the political functions and portfolios, will attempt to turn into a real political force that phenomenon, today laughed at by the technocrats of power, that is human conscience?[24]

Havel's adoption of a postnational solidarity among the shaken envisions a way to an earnest democratic community. That a type of equality can be opposed by Havel to the failed experiment in totalizing equality on the one hand, and to Western mass culture on the other, defines his "nonpolitical politics": the politics of human beings, not of the apparatus; the politics "from below ... growing from the heart not from a thesis"; the concrete politics from the lifeworld not a systemic politics by "the professional technologists of power." The responsibly reconstituted lifeworld rather than an anonymous administration of subsystems becomes the "appropriate ground of politics." Havel finds in such lived solidarity the corrective to both totalitarian and technocratic politics. He admits that this is rather "impractical." Yet, given his experience of "life at the very extreme of modern dehumanized power," he seems to communicate to his own people and abroad no other alternative. This explains why he invited those who are qualified but uninterested in power politics to join him in the present service, and why he called such work in the midst of leveled post-Communism the rule of sacrifice.[25]

It is a mistake to read Havel's opposition to "real existing socialism" either as a conservative or a liberal move: some take Havel's term "nonpolitical politics" (now also bringing moral concerns into diplomacy) as a return to premodern life forms; others want to co-opt him for a liberal individualist agenda or line him up with postmodernism; leftists are offended by his concern for vertical transcendence and find in it a dogmatic religious ploy; and still others legitimate by Havel's concern their own authoritarian religiosity. All of these interpretations substitute concretism for a lived concretion. Yet I argue that Havel's self-critical praxis and Habermas's concrete communicative transcendence meet one another. Both, though differently, depict the concretely operative formal properties of that life form which allows for a formation of nonauthoritarian and open identities.[26]

Havel does not long for a system-free lifeworld. One may apply the sociological distinction between system and lifeworld to the events of 1989 and find in them both the material and symbolic struggles of the autonomous public sphere: parallel polis against being colonized by a totally administered, one-dimensional society. Further, one can depict these societies as laboratories that anticipate some of the conflicts with anonymous functionalist reason in Western democracies. Finally, one finds in the events of 1989 a falsification of the present age thesis about the ubiquity of power asymmetries in politics.

Havel does not exchange the Stalinist utopia of paradise on earth for another utopia. Rather than designing either a positive or negative material utopia or longing to transform the poetry of those revolutionary days into a drifting carnival, Havel is concerned with the concrete other. The solidarity of the shaken forms a critical polis that can motivate resistances to totality as well as promote new pluralist civic forums in democracy.[27]

When Havel writes about "postdemocracy," he has in mind the moral vacuum in both the totalitarian and the mass democratic societies. He finds in dissident groups like *Charta 77* the futurological experience of "interexistential" communication that has been freed up from the "weight of emptied traditions." Havel's dissident experience suggests that responsibility to the other is the necessary condition of the possibility of a critically reconstituted democracy. There does not seem to be, in principle, any contradiction between the position of powerless dissent and Havel's presidential power in a parliamentary democracy that draws on this earlier experience.[28]

Nonpolitical politics embodies Havel's lived corrective to the Marxist–Leninist revolutionary ethic. Both Havel and Habermas are aware of the fallible character of revolutionary projects, but Havel attends also to a vulnerability of revolution to deception by the totality within. Havel articulates in open identity the necessary check on the colonization of the lifeworld in the very identity formation. Thus, he would judge Habermas's democratic revolution insufficiently concrete. Havel might ask Habermas: how does this formal–pragmatic reformulation of socialist revolution as a permanent and projected possibility console the melancholy revolutionary leftist, since she has no self-critical axis that functions as a corrective to the shipwrecking utopia? Permanence and the fallible projection of possibilities do not form that temporal mode of existence which can maintain and stabilize modern crisis identity in complex societies. Havel might object: Habermas's communication turn is a necessary structural but insufficient modal condition of the possibility of the democratic community. Yet Havel might find the critical impulse in Habermas's radical and permanent democratic revolution a kin of posttotalitarian society. While Havel might prefer not to use the word "socialism," since in the east it has lost all semantic meaning, he would not be necessarily opposed to what Habermas means by the "S" word.[29]

There are some misunderstandings about why Havel does not wish to use the "S" word. Today "this word which [once] led to the zeal of the masses is nothing more than a thoroughly deceptive cipher." The word has become an ideological symbol standing for the good as opposed to the evil empire: "To criticize this or another cow is not difficult, but to criticize that cow which proclaims itself for decades as holy is more difficult: one is imputed a feeling that one does not critique only the cow but the very divine principle which has made it sacred." Havel proposes to avoid such ideologically sacred words, but not the questions of solidarity and justice. He thinks that it would be better to speak concretely about economy, decision-making processes, ownership of enterprises, power structures, and dogmatism, and leave the "S" word out of it. If someone wants to use this word, "let him first clearly say what he means and with what economic and political system he links this word."[30]

Havel speaks of existential revolution not because he harkens back to either myth or a necessarily bourgeois life form. He designates himself twice as "left-leaning." To exilic anticommunist pamphlets that call dissidents "bolshevik-green gangs," Havel replies: "I do not know if I am left or right, but I admit that face to face with this branch of right-wing spirituality, I am rapidly becoming left-leaning." In his radio address he says that face to face with the millionaire estates on the island of Bahamas and the slums in Nicaragua, he tends to the left. Both remarks show that though he is from a millionaire family, after suffering in the regime that made him pay for his class origins and activism, he has not shielded himself from experience.[31]

Yet, Havel refuses to answer the interviewer's questions that try to box him in: one should say exactly what one means and not hide behind such words as "socialism," "capitalism," "people," "religion," and "peace." Havel finds this labeling to be an ideological concern. Insofar as Habermas restores a more concrete meaning to the revolutionary project, Havel might share his attitude. When Havel argues that "socialism" became an empty phrase, he appeals to his definite experience of the disenchantment of communism:

> I was always for democracy and I have considered myself for a long time a
> socialist. . . . I realized that this word no longer means anything and that it

can only confuse, not disclose my views. . . . My divorce from this word arose from my traditional disgust with too inflexible (and therefore semantically rather empty) categories, ideological phrases and oracles, by which thinking becomes a structure of static terms where one cannot breath, and the more suffocating thinking is, the more distant it is from life. . . . [E]ven though I did not change my political views, I stopped presenting myself as a socialist. Also in times when I considered myself a socialist, I did not identify with some concrete political and economic doctrine, theory or ideology, with some wholesome project of the better world order. Socialism was for me rather a human, moral, and affective category. There were times when those who called themselves socialists were on the side of the oppressed and downcast, not on the side of the masters, and resisted illegitimate advantages and inherited privileges, exploitation of the powerless, social injustice and immoral barriers which condemned humans to servitude. I was such an "affective" and "moral" socialist—and I remain so until today only with that difference that I do not use that word to designate my posture.[32]

The leftist offense at Havel misses what is here at stake.

CONCLUSIONS

In the last chapter I have attempted to justify textually my two theses: the strong one offers a theoretical corrective to Habermas's formal notions of identity, communication, and the community ideal; the weak one seeks a *rapprochement* model of communicative and existential ethics. In this chapter, in the second round of justification, I have read my theses from the point of view of existential revolution by asking what it would mean to become con/temporary with Havel's nonpolitical politics in a deliberative democracy.

Havel and Habermas represent two complementary, not exclusive, alternatives beyond the communitarian–liberal controversy. Their complementarity lies in the relation of Habermas's horizontal normativity and Havel's inward or vertical mode. Existential revolution is not a decisionist, monological, or dogmatic withdrawal into a bourgeois *intérieur*. Havel builds upon political pluralism and an intersubjective context for identity formation. He articulates the self-critical attitude nondualistically (i.e., on this side of the world and identity formation, in dissent and politics within the horizontal). The nonpolitical politics is to empower deliberative democracy and professional politics, whereby permanent risk and fallibilism are to cure both the revolutionary melancholy and terror.

A critique of Habermas's project from Havel's perspective is the following: the horizontal permanence of a revolution that does not attend to the mode of its revolutionary project cannot heal the consequent temptation of every revolution—the activist's anxiety in the face of freedom, right and left fanaticism, and the present age skepsis or abdication of responsibility. Without self-choice and communication, the public debate is too weak to resist self-deception, and thus to resist also the traps of the leveling community relations in the New World Order.

A critique of Havel's dramatic irresolution of existential revolution from Habermas's perspective of fallible but concrete democratic structures raises a question that cuts across the asymmetrical experiences of the east and the west: how can honest thinking and ways of living along with nonpolitical politics foster open, nonauthoritarian, yet responsible forms of life?[33]

In the next chapter, in the third round of justifying my two theses, I will read this last problem by asking what would it mean to become con/temporary with Kierkegaard's and Havel's dramatic authoring projected within Habermas's project of deliberative democracy? In the last chapter I will seek to root the categories of communicative and existential ethics in Habermas's, Kierkegaard's, and Havel's critiques of the present age.

CHAPTER 9

Self-Reading and Authoring

The prevailing myth that Kierkegaard's view is antisocial and apolitical prevents us from appreciating the existential attitude in sociopolitical terms. In order to further challenge this received view, I will reread Kierkegaard against the backdrop of Havel who, as we have encountered him in the last chapter, speaks of existential revolution and nonpolitical politics as one's self-transforming relation to the democratic structures of society. I will argue that the myth about Kierkegaard prevails because of the confusion between authoring and authorship: Kierkegaard's works allow us to grasp the ramifications of his authorship only from the perspective of the self-transformative activity of a reader/author (i.e., self-authoring) (9.1). Dispelling the Kierkegaard myth still leaves us with the question of whether or not a self-transforming activity of authoring, as read from Havel's perspective of existential revolution and nonpolitical politics, can provide a contribution to deliberative democracy (9.2).

9.1. KIERKEGAARD: AUTHORSHIP AND AUTHORING

Imagine a dramaturge staging Pirandello's *Six Characters in Search of an Author*, but abdicating any search for identity and responsible authoring. Imagine a critic concluding that Havel's *Largo Desolato* ends in dramatic irresolution because of either emotivism or the author's fear of the establishment. Imagine a scholar inaugurating a series "Kierkegaard and Postmodernism," describing Kierkegaard's *Prefaces* as precursors to revocations of authoring and to reading/writing under erasure.[1]

Imagine, then, ignoring Kierkegaard's *Point of View*: here one is like a freshman trying to interpret and direct a play while disregarding the author's staging instructions. When Kierkegaard's dramatic mask ceases to be an occasion for the individual dramaturge or viewer to communicate her identity with a pathos of self-reading/authoring, the production becomes kitsch.

This round of justifying my strong, corrective thesis (the "how" of self-choice, communication, and the community ideal) and my weak, *rapprochment* thesis (the possibility of communicative and existential ethics) takes place within a way of living as a decentered author. I wish to propose a reading of Kierkegaard from the point of view of drama: his polemical view, like modern theater, communicates by virtue of the absurd; and his sociopolitical critique occurs through dramatic irresolutions as a way of nonpolitical rather than professional politics.[2]

I want to argue that the received view of Kierkegaard takes offense at the qualifying "how" (i.e., at that mode of identity, communication, and the ideal which, in Kierkegaard's writing, marks the vocation of an author). One becomes con/temporary with such an offense, for Kierkegaard, most importantly in a paradox–religious view of Christianity. I argue that already an intensified pathos communicates authoring in an ideology-critical action of decentering, revoking, and upbuilding the self-authoring ego for the sake of the alter. Kierkegaard's authoring, as a way of life, dramatizes how inwardness or verticality can become an offense; he, thus, makes academia, the media, the public, and the churches take notice of the excluded voices of alterity.

Kierkegaard initiates a critique of reason and society that antedates many of the concerns of our age: his authoring ironizes the "masculinist" vocation of the author (A); his practice of indirect communication repels any tendency towards the homogeneity with the other (B); and his non-partisan activism unmasks the authoritarian trends in tradition and politics (C). I want to explain how the dramatic, ethico–moral, and sociopolitical character of Kierkegaard's authoring can be better grasped from the foregoing portrait of Havel's existential revolution and nonpolitical politics. In the concluding section I will show how this reading of Kierkegaard sheds light on the role of sober authoring in deliberative democracy.

A. Kierkegaard's Critique of the "Masculinist" Author

Kierkegaard, despite of his despair about the possibility of sustaining both his writing and the love of Regine Olsen—a despair which marks perhaps his inability to transcend the male-dominated nineteenth-century institution of marriage—is that author who self-ironizes the subject-centered, "masculinist" view of authorship. The evidence for this thesis lies within Kierkegaard's authorship and in his retrospective glance at it in the *Point of View*. I suggest that Kierkegaard stages each of the pseudonyma as a dramatic mask: these characters show forth the nonauthoritative portrayals of different walks of life. The task of the reader resembles that of the dramaturge who is about to present the pseudonyma in an existential drama.

The temptation of producing (becoming) kitsch lies in two extreme stage directions: one can either try to gain mastery over the author's intentions, and perhaps get a hold of some "conclusion" that can be taken home; or one can emphatically declare the death of the author/reader and disregard the play instructions (i.e., Kierkegaard's "point of view" for existential drama), thereby suffocating the tension of the dramatic whole. Kierkegaard blocks both moves: he critiques the "masculinist" certainty of the mastering and the self-evading author/reader alike.

Prefaces in Search of a Book

I unfold my case from Kierkegaard's Preface to *Prefaces*. Here he conceals his existential drama behind the satirical mask of "masculinist" vocation. Nicolaus Notabene is not an anonymous word-processing program for academicians, but rather a paradigm of anonymity (NN) signifying both the reading public and the "publish or perish" mentality of higher education. NN is an author who is perpetually frustrated by his wife who confiscates at the outset all that he composes. His "production is constantly stifled at birth." He never gets beyond "an introductory paragraph." Upon his reading to her, she burns his manuscript. "The fire prevailed; there was nothing to save; my introductory paragraph went up in flames—under general rejoicing, for my wife rejoiced for both of us." Yet she is neither a censorious nor aggressive midwife of his birthing; she acts with the authority of irony. She ridicules his self-repressive asceticism. She unmasks his ostensive fidelity to writing a book as a cover-up for an impatience with the receptive process of giving birth. His writing is nothing but an escapade of a self-evading author on the one end, and a pretext for constructing a public facade of authorship on the other. She claims that "to be an author when one is a husband . . . is open infidelity." An author–husband is more unfaithful than a husband who daily visits the men's club, since as author he remains absent from her even while at home. NN now writes Prefaces, footnotes to the primary texts of existers: his identity, while not certified in a systematic and formal book, nevertheless offers a task. She symbolizes NN's insurmountable difficulty of the "masculinist" authorship.[3]

To be sure, this obstacle does not mean that one (a man or a woman) should never write a book. Rather, one cannot give birth from a "masculinist" view of the task to become an author by thinking that the power to create lies in one's effort and will. The ironic laughter brings NN to a greater awareness of the difficulty of beginnings. It leads NN, in the end, to transform the attitude of self-control into a pathos of openness vis-à-vis the possibility of completing the book not at the author's own whim. NN does not evade his want to become an author, but now he writes *Prefaces* to unwritten books. He becomes a mask of an author of Prefaces in search of a book and of himself as an author. Having shed the anxiety to "publish or perish," he can now afford to caricature systematizing and narcissistic authors, pedantic printers and binders, conformist critics and arrogant reviewers, pompous editors of books and of scholarly journals, and readers who either misread or gossip about unread books. His *samizdat* posture of a dissident against the reading public of the media and academia does not bespeak the end of the author or of readers: "Prefaces," which play the role of footnotes to uncompleted texts, remind the self-assured author about the primary difficulty of authoring one's own existing. To be exact, *Prefaces* are written over and against Hegel's speculative and quite "masculinist" master and slave struggle for recognition, a fight that links Hegel's Preface to the male's absolute self-possession. NN safeguards his journey through fidelity to authoring without an assurance of completing either the authorship of the book or the pathway. The task of authoring, in a "nonmasculinist" fashion, does not erase the author but lays her bare to the risks of existing and loving.[4]

NN's Prefaces remind some of our contemporaries of the postcards written under the erasure of the responsible author and reader. Yet they are revocations of the book for the sake of a decentered self-reading/authoring. Kierkegaard's authoring occasions an offense in another by the sustained difficulty of beginnings. Thus, NN's "feminine" difficulty can be neither renounced nor pronounced as a fiction.[5]

B. Kierkegaard's Critique of the Homogenizing Communicator

Kierkegaard is that communicator who translates dramatic authoring into a moral imperative: one ought to act in such a way as to always meet as an individual the other as an individual. Both in his signed works and in his pseudonyma Kierkegaard respects another's authoring by addressesing that single individual who is his beloved self-reader. A direct communication of authorship levels individuality in that it can become self- and other-deceptive and lead to homogeneity or to an imposition of one's authored existence on the other. Kierkegaard repels this followership or homogeneity, thereby contributing to our contemporary search for a radically democratic multiculturalism.

Reviewing Either/Or by Staging the Offense of Self-Choice

That the identity and communication of the author are born under an invitation to self-choice becomes quite apparent when we turn to Climacus's critical review of (Kierkegaard's) pseudonyma. His review of the *Either/Or* shows that one's taking offense at the irresolution of this text indirectly signifies the "truth as inwardness." One is invited to understand that (e.g., in the *Either/Or*), "[t]he absence of an author is a means of distancing" from the reader. Climacus reviews this book as a modern dramaturge would; he interprets the text as a script and judges its success from the viewpoint of drama rather than of formal–logical categories. How can one meet the call to author oneself in an either/or choice, either A or B? One could read oneself either as an author–character A, who acts "an existence-possibility that cannot attain existence" or B, who alone enters the scene by becoming an individual. Paradoxically, in a possibility of scene A, there are masks that represent something like the death of the author and the end of the book. This is a precocious celebration, since only in scene B, for the first time, one has an occasion to become an author whose individuality allows one to raise NN's and Climacus's question of pathos about the difficulty of authoring text or one's own beginnings. Climacus defends the drama by mocking the unrefined reader or audience: "If it [the book] has any [merit], it must essentially be that it does not provide conclusion but in inwardness transforms everything. . . ."[6]

One's latter difficulty with self-mastery (B) differs from scene (A) which marks the premature death of the author who never faced the task to become a self. This task not only calls for a revocation of the "masculinist" certainty of both the self-evading and self-mastering author, but for a permanent resistance to homogenization, a resistance via sober authoring.

From Climacus we learn that existential drama communicates by sustaining the independence of the other. Notice that this revoked, decentered, and upbuilding authoring, typified in Climacus but true of all pseudonyma and of Kierkegaard's own posture, occasions taking offense at both the transferred, indirect language and at the "nonmasculinist" mode of receptivity to the other. We can witness how NN's difficulty delivers the author into a self-actively receptive mode of beginnings. Climacus incorporates this posture into his dramatic view of dialogic reciprocity in open communication. "The most resigned a human being can be is to acknowledge the given independence in every human being, and to the best of one's ability do everything in order truly to help someone retain it."[7]

From my foregoing account, it is still unclear how one is edified by this offense, and, yet, how one can center on self-choice in authoring. Climacus praises "a doubly reflected communication form" of repetition, which moves not dogmatically but by virtue of the absurd. The author's absurd and her ordeal lie in an immediate vocation that ends up consumed by flames; taking offense at this author's difficulty throws the reader back on his own beginnings. The double form of communication posits "a chasmic gap between reader and author" in order to edify both in repetition. "The imaginary construction is the conscious . . . revocation of the communication, which is always of importance to an existing person who writes for existing persons, lest the relation is changed to that of a rote reciter who writes for rote reciters." An authoring author does not write for "paragraph-eaters" but for passionate self-readers. Author and reader edify one another in motion "away from each other in inwardness." The pseudonyma offend by irony or edify by humor; their staging of authoring resists the dogmatizing of authorship. "The pseudonymous books are generally ascribed to one writer, and now everyone who had hoped for a didactic author suddenly gives up hope upon seeing light literature from the same hand."[8]

Thus, Climacus refuses to review his own dramatic experiment in either/or: "my dissenting conception of what it is to communicate," "my idea of communication through books is very different from what I generally see presented on the topic. . . ." The essential experiment is "that the receiver is an existing person" not to be persuaded "to go the same way" but emancipated "to go his own way." Climacus stylizes himself as "only a reader" of pseudonyma. While the age and its "professors" are offended by his risky posture, "the true interpretation of the confusion of our age is that there must not be didactic instruction, since the confusion arises simply because of the excess of the didactic." Climacus works as a dramatic author who erects in himself the repelling form of communication against dogmatic writers or readers and against doctrinaire canonical interpretations of authorship alike: "I ask for nothing more than to be singled out as the only person who is *unable* to instruct didactically, and thereby also as the only person who does not understand the demands of the times" (original emphasis). Thus, the charge that one's leaping through the stages on life's way is dogmatic implicates the accuser in a doctrinaire standpoint: "the different stages are not like cities on a [direct] journey. . . . [Rather] to change place is to be changed oneself." In authoring and self-reading, the mode of dramatic staging itself "demonstrates that one has reached that far place in the world of spirit."[9]

Revoking Authorship for the Sake of Authoring

Climacus self-ironizes his own book, which seems to have perfected the intent of other pseudonymous characters. In his feature book review on the recent efforts in Danish literature, itself inserted in a larger book-length text, he ironically revokes this very text and yet stylizes his revoking gesture into a "tragic-comic interested witness" of other Kierkegaard's books. To grasp his mask is tricky, since "Climacus" represents an author–character who plays a double stage role of a chorus or dramatic commentator on other characters, and a self-authoring "reader." Thus, Climacus

> [unlike Hegel, has not] *misused a preface to take an official position on the production,* as if in a purely legal sense an author were the best interpreter of his own words, as if it could help a reader that an author "intended this and that" when it was not carried out; or as if it were certain that it had been carried out, since the author himself says so in the preface; or as if *an existence-deviation* were amended by being brought to a final decision, such as insanity, suicide . . . or as if an author were served by a reader who, precisely

because of the author's bungling, knew with certainty all about the book. (emphasis added)

This kind of existential double bind is missed by recent efforts in Continental thought because some thinkers review the Kierkegaardian revocation of the authorship as signifying the end of the book and the death of the author. But Climacus self-ironizes his own authorship in order to upbuild and decenter the reader into a sober mode of authoring. The revocation of the book is a corrective to confusing authoring with authorship (i.e., a corrective to the "masculinist" certainty of both the self-evading and mastering author.) Is it not, then, hubristic if one claims to know more than Climacus, or pontificates about the end of the author and the book? Climacus can vouchsafe canonical authority neither for reviewing other author masks better than they or other readers do, nor for a revocation of responsibility for his own book. Since he is an author–character, he can with certainty proclaim neither the death of the author nor the end of the book in which he is himself dramatized. If "Climacus" does not have the certainty of an author, he cannot safeguard the authority of revoking the book that bears his name, and this is so in spite of the fact that he might be more aware than other author masks about what is going on in the text.[10]

The instructive thing about this existential double bind is that the very writing of book reviews, when undertaken from the posture of a stage observer, bypasses the task to resist the homogenization of individuality. By focusing on the "what" of Climacus's revocation of authorship and of the book one misses the "how" of his authoring. One gains the latter insight not by attending the peep show between the inside–outside of Kierkegaard's authors and masks, but by entering his drama face to face—as a reader and an author at once. Here one would learn to read and review Kierkegaard's books as a dramaturge of a modern drama does—as a self-transformative task. In modern drama, while the public "gallery" has interest in the "costumes," inwardness or verticality is communicated by virtue of dramatic irresolution, by polemical, suffering authoring. "A book without an ending has no doubt been written before; the author may have died or chose not to complete it etc. [But here, that] there is no end, no conclusion . . . [signifies] suffering. . . ."[11]

Whereas NN persists in prefacing the difficulty of his authoring, Climacus authors himself by revoking the book for the sake of decentering and upbuilding the reader. He desires "an understanding with the reader" on the mode of authoring/reading required for earnest thinking and living of texts:

[H]e can very well be an author, if only he sees to it that it is for his own enjoyment, that he remains in isolation, that he does not take up with the crowd, does not become lost in the importance of the age, as an inquisitive spectator. . . .

This is how I understand Climacus's revocation of authorship: he claims that writing need not be superfluous if it is done in pathos rather than for a dissertation committee, publishers, or renown: one's text becomes useless as an authority to which one might appeal. Note that he revokes the book not against all authoring of identity but against an authoritarian *imprimatur*: "what I write contains the notice that everything is to be understood in such a way that it is revoked, that the book has not only an end but has a revocation to boot." Revoking the author upbuilds by decentering the reader: Climacus is loving an "imagined reader" whom he is not obliged to satisfy in order to reap profit or praise from the "tyranny" of mass pseudodemocracy. "The negative" imaginary of possible readership "is the courtesy" to an actual reader, not to the herd in which all anxiously "want to rule." This individual reader can be addressed: just as author yields to the revocation of authority through receptive laughter, so also a reader who refuses to be a misreader becomes decentered from the focus on this authority of the author. Edifying discourse bonds in an inward mode of authoring and reading: love draws the self-reading author and reader in autonomy away from the authority of the authoring author. An imagined sober author and self-reader "can stick it out as long as the author. [She] can understand that the understanding is a revocation. . . . [She] can understand that to write a book and to revoke it is not the same as refraining from writing it. . . ." Revocation of the author and decentering of the reader cannot simply erase identity, but rather embody—and this offense is incurred by the present age—"nonmasculinist" and polemically suffering modes of temporal existing: "to write a book which does not demand to be important for anyone is still not the same as letting it be unwritten. . . ."[12]

C. Kierkegaard's Critique of the Authoritarian and the Traditionalist

Kierkegaard as a drama may be read from the view of Havel's existential revolution and nonpolitical politics. Kierkegaard as an individual emerges as a nonpartisan activist without authority who unmasks authoritarian traditionalism.

Kierkegaard's Proper Name

Kierkegaard's name signs with a "pseudonymity or polyonymity" of names. His signature, recorded in the stage instructions as the author's "Point of View," is legible only in a dramatic whole. He retrospectively takes off the mask by disclosing the character of his autograph as "religious." Let us not misread this face to face with "Kierkegaard as a religious author" as if he had disclosed something important concerning his authorship rather than about authoring![13]

The "religious" signifies that the individual is distinct from official production and from professional politics, and yet that one must positively resist any deification of the author and of social ethics. The "religious" signifies that the individual cannot appeal to canonical certitudes and metaphysical grounds, and yet that one must positively resist any self-assured, nonethical, fundamentalist confounding of religion with politics. Kierkegaard's "religious" view is political in the nonpolitical sense described by Havel: it claims the individual indirectly via the existential revolution of self-transformation, but it is directly embodied in a nonpolitically political resistance to any absolutization of the public sphere.[14]

The corrective void of a Kierkegaardian activism—his nonpolitical politics—protects professional politics from idolizing tradition, authority, or their imperial ambitions for a world order. Further, on the side of religious integrations, this corrective protects any politics of identity and difference from falling prey to the fundamentalist political correctness of the Grand Inquisitor. The void that separates professional and nonpolitical politics, just as that between authorship and authoring, is not religious fundamentalism, authoritarianism, or nationalism, but rather a permanent openness of one's identity. This open mode of authoring transpires without authority and appeal. Kierkegaard's dramatic whole brings us permanently face to face not with uttering his name, but with this void. The void signifies that one should learn to author by becoming "an absent one." This revolutionary permanence, whose sober politics resists the "masculinist" impatience of getting to the victorious point, creatively restrains the satisfaction of a desire for mastering the proper name by Kierkegaard, by another, or by the ideal communication community of all others. "Religious" activism, that is oriented to the wholly other than our rush to the point of agreement, marks not the end of history and politics but the good death of any self-certain authoring of historical and sociopolitical consensus. "Kierkegaard"—the name of the self-transforming activist and of the dramatic whole—does not bypass deliberative democracy. The name signifies existential revolution and nonpolitical politics as two mutually permanent correctives to any cocksure authorship of authoritarian tradition or politics.[15]

Kierkegaard as a Drama

Kierkegaard, firstly and lastly, takes responsibility for the entire pseudonymous authorship. Yet he declares that the character–authors do not utter his words: he poses as a self-reader who cannot authoritatively interpret his or their productions. He writes less personally than a poet (he is "a *souffleur* [prompter] who has poetically produced" the dramatic masks) and more so than the present age: the poetical identities are characters in a drama in which Kierkegaard is personal in the second person vis-à-vis "the *authors*, whose *prefaces* in turn are their production, as their *names* are also"[16] (original emphasis).

Identifying the author with the staged characters misreads the dramatic duplicity of the mask. In the theater of the absurd "what and how I [SK] am are matters of indifference." The sayings of the pseudonymous books should be cited as dramatic not authoritative lines. "My role is the joint role of being the secretary and, quite ironically, the dialectically reduplicated author of the author or the authors." The dramatic mask, like ritual, seeks out the single participant. The pseudonymous name emancipates the viewer by occasioning her reexamination of the given tradition, "to read through solo, if possible in a more inward way, the original text of individual human existence–relationship, the old familiar text handed down from the fathers." The posttraditional mask cannot be authoritarian; it signifies an invitation to participate in an existential drama. One cannot grasp this signified by remaining a traditionalist couch potato in the gallery or a joker without any embodiment. Kierkegaard's signed works contain dramatic notes for this type of nontraditionalist staging. They woo the audience into edifying conversation with the author—in a "nonmasculinist" voice and polemically.[17]

In the prefaces to his signed works, the reader is constantly wooed and loved by Kierkegaard. Although the author has no authority to preach or teach, he edifies by being a lover. The author waits on love, on "that single individual, whom he with joy and gratitude calls his reader." This reader does not seek out fundamentals or canonical certitudes, does not parrot slogans. This individual loves the author by becoming an emancipated self-reader. The book goes into the world but its signified may not be directly legible to academic, media, public, and church reviewers. The book by its mask enables the reader's authoring. Kierkegaard's nonpseudonymous, signed text cannot but communicate through dramatic authoring as well.[18]

Kierkegaard as a Polemical Activist

This lover, Kierkegaard, who at the end of his activity as an author openly attacks the establishment, speaks to his reader in one of the last written pamphlets. Here he does not defend himself against the latest discreditations of his character, but rather addresses a question to his "dear reader": if in public action one had only horizontal public consensus in view, would not that lead one to publicly conducted self-defence? (The point is that Kierkegaard operates within the horizontal domain from an inward or vertical perspective and so public debates, while useful and necessary, remain insufficient to carry through his sociopolitical ostracism.) He does not justify himself, but rather in the midst of "lies and slander . . . prate and twaddle" incites the individual to action. The suffering *polemos* indirectly signifies to this individual a sobered up mode of authoring. Thus, Kierkegaard is "not . . . in a hurry to get rid of [suffering], unless . . . [he] wishes as soon as possible to get on the wrong road." If one is offended by this author's incurring many public attacks, if one shuns this author as "a lackey," then one has been all along a self-misreader. A faithful, dear reader becomes receptive to this author's being "in service of something true." This reader overcomes any offense at this seeming passivity in Kierkegaard's attack and ceases to judge it by male standards as presumed womanly inaction. One learns to welcome the "nonmasculinist" openness to the other as an intense but nonviolent form of sociopolitical critique and resisting action.[19]

That between "politics" and "the religious view" there yawns a "heaven-wide" gap marks Kierkegaard's own descriptive and critical invective against his present-age, authoritarian traditionalism and politics. Against the received view of Kierkegaard's individualism as apolitical, I claim that his corrective basis for sociopolitical critique requires a radically honest communicative action. "An impatient politician who hurriedly peeps into these pages will find little to edify him; so be it." From Kierkegaard's open mode one may learn to read without hurrying to get on with it, be it loving or revolution. Kierkegaard woos activists to grasp "that the religious is the transfigured rendering of that which the politician has thought of in his happiest moment." Action must grow from loving the other, not from an impatience which disregards suffering sobriety as "impractical" idealism. The Socratic lover of the individual is "head over heels in love with *this* unpracticality." "But 'unpractical' as he is, the religious is nevertheless the transfigured rendering of the politician's fairest dream." Kierkegaard argues that unless politics inhabits an earnest mode of action, it cannot but fail to "think through or realize to its last consequences the thought of human equality." I identified this failure as a confusion between validity domains and a mode of equality, between authorship and authoring.[20]

I can become con/temporary with Kierkegaard's dramatic writing and activism by inhabiting this radical, indirectly symmetrical or asymmetrical egalitarianism and by adopting this corrective mode of sociopolitical critique in the point of view of decentered authoring. I need not be offended at Kierkegaard's claim that the crowd is "the untruth," "an abstraction . . . [which] has no hands," since this critique of "the numerical, a number of noblemen, millionaires, high dignitaries, etc." projects another mode of the social whole. I need not suffer offense at inwardness: Kierkegaard does not have a private love affair with himself; his drama and activism render authoring naked and responsible to the neighbor, thereby unmasking the perverted courage and passivity of the crowd.[21]

Kierkegaard's address to his dear reader is just as "impolitic" as Lévinas's face to face encounter with the other or Havel's "nonpolitical politics" would seem to be: "I could weep . . . at thinking of the misery of our age . . . owing to the fact that the daily press with its anonymity makes the situation madder still with the help of the public, this abstraction which claims to be the judge in matters of 'truth.'" One who desires to live existentially, be it as poet–politician Havel or polemical writer Kierkegaard, addresses equally all common humans and yet disentangles them from the herd as individuals. The public qua "nobody" and "anonymity" speaks untruthfully: it lacks responsibility. Since one cannot fall in love with the crowd, the call to radical equality invites one to love the concrete other. "[T]he 'neighbor' is the absolutely true expression for human equality."[22]

Kierkegaard as an Individual

To answer my last question from the preceding chapter (how can existential identity foster open, nonauthoritarian, and responsible forms of life?), Kierkegaard maintains and stabilizes the individual by subverting that social integration that absorbs each single one. By sustaining in works of justice and love an abysmal distance among individuals, each as a unique species, Kierkegaard projects a mode of social integration other than the infinite consensual whole of the human race. He critiques both empirical communities (the crowd) and the generic notion of community (consensual ideal), by decentering, inwardly or vertically, a possible authoritarian outcome.

The category of "that individual" signifies a "duplex movement": the individual stands both for the unique one and for everyone. "The starting-point of the pseudonyms is the difference between [human] and [human] with respect to intellect, culture, etc.; the starting-point of the edifying works is the edifying thought of the universal human." That single individual has both qualitative and generic character.[23]

We witness Kierkegaard critique the "demoralization" of the individual "by means . . . of a fantastical notion of society." One is not born or socially integrated with qualitative identity; rather one must become edified into it. "Edification, even more expressly than love, is related to the individual." Identity formation presents an unfinished task: Kierkegaard claims to have become an individual no more than a Christian. He strives "as one who does not forget that 'the individual' in its highest measure is beyond . . . [human] power." The ideal individual escapes one's private self-ownership for the same reason that the ideal community would: neither can redeem the claim to self-transparent beginnings under a fully authored ideal projection without incurring that offending laughter experienced by NN, the author of *Prefaces*. An ideal of authoring is to become an individual. Is it not precisely because Kierkegaard admits that he only tries to become an individual, and in that anything else, that his authoring radicalizes that flame under NN's authored yet hardly originated manuscript?[24]

The corrective flame applies, then, both to the individual and communal aspects of Habermas's horizontal–consensual ideal. Kierkegaard authored himself as a prophet in extremity and as a provocation and an enticement for his age: "'The individual' is the category through which, in a religious respect, this age, all history, the human race as a whole, must pass." What lies outside social consensus is "the individual, ethically and religiously conceived and existentially accentuated." When Kierkegaard engraved this offense of becoming the individual into his necrology, he not only confronted his own postrevolutionary age but our present age as well: "if I were to desire an inscription for my tombstone, I should desire none other than 'That Individual'. . . ." He called ours "an age of dissolution." This prognosis, too, must pass through the decisive category of the individual: "Without this category, and without the use that has been made of it, reduplication would be lacking in my whole activity as an author."[25]

Is this proposed passage socially conservative? Like Hegel in Germany, he does not join the political opposition against the Danish monarchy. "I have managed to fall out with the opposition and the public, and have encountered . . . the disapprobation of one and another . . . official of the bureaucracy." But unlike Hegel's communitarian vision of the ethical whole in the actual social form of his age, Kierkegaard dissents against *any* political rule which disregards the individual. The political corrective to the establishment is designed by Kierkegaard in Havel's "nonpolitical" manner: his seeming "idealistic support for the establishment" also "makes contrary interpretation equally possible, and the judge will be made manifest by his judgment."[26]

Kierkegaard as a Dissident in Permanent Opposition

It is apparent that Kierkegaard not only dissents against all herd and fundamentalist religiosity and its technocratic cousin in political and economic administration, but subverts the nation–state by abiding in a permanent opposition to it. At the time when the revolutionary 1848 promoted a new government, Kierkegaard enlisted his perpetual dissent in "an inward transformation which would consolidate the state in the fear of God." I read this text without substantive commitments about Kierkegaard's Christianity. I rely on the open-ended last paragraph of Camus's *Rebel*, which suggests that we admit to one another as individuals and nations that none of us is God or an imperial number one. We need not interpret either Camus or Kierkegaard through theistic or atheistic glasses.[27]

I claim that sober authoring occasions this lived corrective of a permanent revolution. To be sure, Kierkegaard's concrete form of life does not communicate some doctrine. The need for the corrective, and yet, the possibility of *rapprochement* between Habermas's communicative turn and Kierkegaard's self-critical attitude are justified by the posture which takes offense at the failure to author truthfully the fallible self and the general consensus. Paradoxically, the *Point of View* does not offer a canon or a consensual procedure for reading Kierkegaard; it presents an author and a reader acting receptively through the reciprocal asymmetry of negating signs. True, such signs admit Habermas's fallible immanence of discourse. Yet the negative lies inevitably in resisting motivated self- and other-deception. It blocks that consensual ideal which cannot, in principle, protect itself against a possible homogenizing outcome. Habermas's fallibilism of discourse does not offend; Kierkegaard's attention to the radical loss of immunity to deception does.

Climacus shows how this corrective delivers one to a permanent emergency room where both patients and doctors are afflicted by "the autopathic collision." This surgical situation confronts one with an offense at the "how": the "offence comes at the beginning, and the possibility of it is the continual fear and trembling in his [or her] existence."[28]

Evans parallels this self-critique not only with "the position of the left Hegelians with respect to society," but with Marx's constructive perpetual revolution in tradition:

> Climacus' attitude towards the self could be described as a sort of "perpetual revolution." The individual can never fully realize the ideal in existence; hence [s/]he must continually "negate the status quo." Existentially, *positive* development and growth are recognizable by the negative.[29] (original emphasis)

I adopt from Kierkegaard an attitude of perpetual opposition, his readiness to nonviolent resistance, which entrenches neither theocracy nor one-sided left-Hegelian or Adornoesque negative critique, but checks all theistic or atheistic sacralizations of tradition, culture, and authority.

When in its desire for "Liberty, Equality, and Fraternity" the human race elevates the nation–state into the unconditional, then the offense that one takes at self-choosing, open identity acts as a permanent corrective: underneath any such counterfeit domain of the unconditional lies the "whirlpool"—the "tyranny . . . of the numerical"—as its subtext. Kierkegaard is suspicious towards any totalizing unconditional precisely to the extent that he does not shove under the unconscious carpet how "the race itself and the individual within it needs and craves to have something which unconditionally stands fast." He raises the hermeneutically suspicious question that Habermas does not ask: how is one to relate postmetaphysically to the need and desire of the unconditional? Since Kierkegaard argues that one can neither breath the unconditional in its immediacy nor exist wholly unrelated to it, he questions the third, modal aspect of the "how," rather than Habermas's horizontal "what" of postmetaphysical thinking. We can view this third as a philosophical equivalent to Kierkegaard's religiosity, since he depicts the unconditional postmetaphysically: "To stick to my subject, the religious, I say that the race, or a considerable number of the individuals within the race, have outgrown the childish notion that another person can represent the unconditional for them and in their stead." Kierkegaard's postmetaphysical thinking and his methodological atheism exercised vis-à-vis the sacralized traditions of Christendom do not contradict his claim that in one's existing "the unconditional does not cease to be necessary." The more linguistified traditions are, the more crucial such a corrective unconditionality becomes in order to resist the future of any illusion, of any new sacral culture: "it is the more necessary the more the individual outgrows childish dependence upon other . . . [humans]." Kierkegaard's authoring, which is a far cry from privatism, functions as a permanent ideology critique on the one hand, and a check on the supplementation of modern anomie and fragmentation by nationalistic, fundamentalist, and other authoritarian social forms of life on the other. "Hence 'the individual' . . . [herself] must relate . . . [herself] to the unconditional." This viewpoint of authoring marks the passage through which Kierkegaard appropriates Christianity, writes his pseudonymous texts, and acts directly in works of justice and love.[30]

Kierkegaard as a Hermeneut of Suspicion

One could describe Kierkegaard's religiousness from the perspective of methodological atheism, just as one could study Foucault's critique of power asymmetries from the perspective of methodological theism. To become con/temporary with Kierkegaard's view and to admit it into conversation, I need not be preoccupied with the doctrines of redemption, atonement, or the death of God. For Kierkegaard, the human individual Jesus offends because in him unconditional love is communicated within the decisive moment of the temporal and the historical: just as through motivated deception the individual in one temporal act loses that unconditional ground in oneself which no ideally communicated consensus could retrieve, so also in con/temporaneity with love's existence communication, one receives this grounding back. Yet, Kierkegaard neither catechizes nor elevates breach as breach into a *sine qua non* condition of all reading and authoring in the present age. "Sin . . . is no teaching or doctrine for thinkers . . . it is an existence-category and simply cannot be thought." One could not be an edifying author if all discourse were marked by a "Protestant" subtext of total human depravity; but one would be unable to sustain oneself as a responsible author if a Catholic *imprimatur* replaced all requirements of self-transformation. Kierkegaard can be Habermas's ally against contemporary liberal, dogmatic, and demythologizing theologies, just as much as against any heroic nationalist–fundamentalist *Führer* principle, since he holds on to pathos, not to the authority of texts or traditions.[31]

Kierkegaard limits his observations on the spiritual situation of his age: one author (viz., Hegel) cannot evaluate the entire epoch. The honest individual is to strive to become a witness for the truth. This one who lives in tension between the poetic and the self-critical attitude "is between the two as a border line, which, however, is related with categorial precision to history in its future stage." The individual stands "opposite to politics" just as Havel's past dissent confronted a totalitarian regime. The individual either sacrifices for the common good or occasions a catastrophe: in both cases, action bespeaks "the category of the spirit" (i.e., a way and not certitudes). The authoring individual is to religious authorships what nonpolitical dissent is to professionally and strategically managed politics.[32]

A margin for my argument lies in this qualification: one need not convert to Christianity to become that individual, but one cannot claim to be a Christian and commune with a worshipping crowd. (Again, I am not relying here on a thesis of Christianity but on the passage through the category of the individual.) Kierkegaard's authoring introduces the individual as a subversion of Christendom's security in its deposit of religious authorship. Insofar as any revolutionary appeal to the entire race profanized merely the sacred crowd, it would inevitably receive Kierkegaard's subversive, nonpolitical, and, at the same time, political blow. If this race adopted "the *wrong and unchristian form* one gives the *Christian* message" (original emphasis), then any revolution that would linguistify such a form would merely secure injustice in its overt promise of equality. Therefore, Kierkegaard's "alone before God" does not signify an egocentric soliloquy of apolitical religiousness but rather an exile from oneself and an openness to the other.[33]

The category of Kierkegaard's authoring as a way of life "is an originator who, as author . . . [called] attention to the religious, more specifically to Christianity—but *without authority*" (original emphasis). His authoring as a whole strives from the beginning "in one breath" at reaching a certain "simplicity" of expression and mode. He begins at the level of the crowd in order to win the individual over. Directly, he begins with the "dear reader"; indirectly, his aesthetic carnival mask seduces the public. "[T]he movement was, maieutically, to stir up the 'crowd' in order to get hold of 'the individual.'"[34]

When religious characters enter the scene, the public, previously seduced by aesthetic masks, becomes "repelled" by the production. Offended at the religious mood, the public is really offended at what honesty reveals. The gallery stands confronted with Kierkegaard's polemically suffering act of unmasking. The edifying author, a lover from the beginning, unmasks and at the same time woos this public by the decisive category of "that individual" who becomes his "dear reader." The duplicity of the dual movement—the masquerade/stripping of the mask—aims at naked simplicity "from the public to the individual." Note that the individual does not oppose the ideal of community, as was broadly outlined in Chapter 7:

> And in so far as there is, in a religious sense, such a thing as a "congregation" [community], this is a concept which does not conflict with "the individual,"

and which is by no means to be confounded with what may have *political* importance: the public, the crowd, the numerical, etc.[35] (original emphasis)

The secular reader should not be bothered by the "religious sense" of this community, since, as I noted, Habermas's ideal of a communication community itself secularizes Peirce's religious paradigm. The problem, for Kierkegaard as a hermeneut of suspicion, is that in Habermas's horizontal ideal a religiously deficient model becomes profanized. If such models are to be of value, then the equivalents to Kierkegaard's individual in a community must describe the passage from the individual through the human race to the individual, and the requirement of openness by each to the wholly other in existential communication.[36]

If we take up Kierkegaard's point of view of authoring as our critical angle, then even fallibilism claims too much authorship and authority for its consensual procedure and its ideal of consensus. Put in simple terms: Habermas's model communicatively broadens the narrow "masculine" rationality yet does not overcome the "masculinist" bias against the difficulty of beginnings. Among such reformed models of rationality, his is probably the most flexible and comprehensive that we have at our disposal in the West. But the rational criteria of overcoming one-sidedness and achieving greater comprehensiveness pertains to validity claims. They are the criteria about what counts as a formally sound "masculinist" model of communicative rationality. These criteria are not much help in getting a handle on the "how" question (this, however, does not exclude the cooperation with the domains of validity claims). Habermas's communicative ethics, albeit fallible, authors an ideality which suffers an offense at the possibility of its consensus hiding behind a self-deceptive mask. Kierkegaard's suspicion of authorships necessarily qualifies any model that secularizes a religious authorship but fails to embody sober authoring.

"I regarded myself preferably as a *reader* of the books, not as the *author*" (original emphasis). Kierkegaard, a hermeneutically suspicious self-reader, declares himself to be a responsibly polemical author rather than no author at all. His point of view towards his work only complicates every hermeneutical task of reading him. Further, it implicates any commentator who either parrots this little testament to history as if it were a voice in the wilderness announcing the death of the book and the dawn of *posthistoire* or who sidesteps the text as the last straw of Kierkegaard's arrogance. Kierkegaard remains a reader of his own authorship: he can read himself as a primary, lived text. Yet this primacy is not something between the covers of the book: his actual writings stand as secondary commentaries, footnotes to a preface, pamphlets to be edited not by bookish librarians but by polemically ironic and suffering bookbinders. Kierkegaard can become con/temporary with himself as an author not in a plenitude of self-presence but in a transferred language, by revoking any canonical authorship or Kierkegaard's seal of approval.[37]

Kierkegaard as a Riddle

Kierkegaard cannot conduct a dissertation defense of his authorship: "the
religious totality in my whole work as an author" does not admit of truthful apologetic. The reader becomes con/temporary with this Kierkegaard
through sacrificial love: "Only the . . . [one] who know . . . in [one's] own
experience what true self-denial is can solve my riddle and perceive that it
is self-denial." The author's riddle delivers the reader into her own riddle.
The religious is not, however, another dramatic mask but a disclosure of
inwardness. A manifest face of inwardness veils; an unmasked and nude
otherness reveals the vertically wholly other.[38]

Kierkegaard insists that there is no *Kehre* (change) in his authoring,
though there might be one in his authorship: he is a writer of aesthetic,
ethical, and religious names from beginning to end; yet, the entire composition carries the polemically suffering signature as a trace across the various stage appearances. This point of view acts as a corrective against possible translations of his texts into some intentionality of a secular or sacralized
Führer principle. *The Point of View* cannot be regarded as Kierkegaard's
self-exorcism upon rereading. Rather, he views here anew —just as young
and old readers in all generations would have to—author and reader becoming con/temporary with one another directly before that which is wholly
other.[39]

One cannot become con/temporary with this authoring Kierkegaard
unless one woos him and oneself—upbuilds the vocation, authors in a
revocation of the author, reads by decentering the reader—in a "nonmasculinist" mode. The proper name, "Kierkegaard," veils the riddle of
existence and the truth of texts; at last, not behind dramatic masks in search
of an author but in a naked face to face encounter:

> For as a woman's coyness has a reference to the true lover and yields when
> he appears, but only then, so, too, dialectical reduplication has a reference to
> true seriousness. To one less serious the explanation cannot be imparted, for
> the elasticity of the dialectical reduplication is too great for him to grasp: it
> takes the explanation away from him again and makes it doubtful to him
> whether it really is the explanation.[40]

The duplicity of the incognito costume and of hidden veiling are both
deceptions to ward off the intruder and to lure the true lover. Like
Nietzsche and the author of *Prefaces*, Kierkegaard laughs at ego's march
towards a system. The self-involved drive to comprehensiveness, albeit today
fallible in its rational claims, bespeaks a male illusion of grandeur.

Kierkegaard's mode veils in the service of disclosure: "One must not let oneself be deceived by the word 'deception.' One can deceive a person for the truth's sake . . . one can deceive a person into the truth." Distorted communication cannot be restored directly: "the receiver's ability to receive is [not] undisturbed." The author's riddle works as a "caustic fluid" which indicates the illusory subtext, "a text which is hidden under another text." The riddle signifies by perpetual negativity, indirection, and metaphoricity. It deceives first by receiving "the other man's illusion as good money," and then by transferring the counterfeit into a new communicated possibility.[41]

Kierkegaard as a Way of Life for a Dramatic Author

"[A]uthorship is and ought to be a serious calling implying an appropriate mode of existence." If asked how one is to be an author in today's demoralized and anonymous age, Kierkegaard envisions authoring as "a wholesome corrective." It implies a fallacy of misplaced concreteness to set Kierkegaard's revoking play against his earnest vocation. To tease out the essentialist fervor of a systematizer, it will not help if an author gets lost in textuality and becomes "merely an x . . . something quite impersonal, which addresses itself abstractly, by the aid of printing, to thousands and thousands, while remaining itself unseen and unknown. . . ." Our age does not need to end the book, kill the author, and arrest the reader, but rather to unmask dramatically that communication which does not correspond to a mode of existing. To write under the erasure of the abyss between reader and author is to block any communication of emancipatory possibilities. Kierkegaard begins in pseudonymity and draws an anonymous public into self-critical communication. His critique of technocratic "politics" projects another politics which need not exclude the concrete other. His corrective to textuality—"furnished for the abstractness of printed communication"— is the individual way of living.[42]

Kierkegaard distinguishes two periods in the link between his authorship and his authoring existence. Both are set against the public. The first dramatic costume is his aesthetic incognito of a seducer. Kierkegaard seduces one from the gossiping groupings of "mutual admiration," from anonymous tyranny by the many, into a breakdown of all illusions. Behind the signatures of aesthetic works, he writes against himself in order to induce academia, the media, the public, and the churches into believing the mask of unseriousness: "by my personal mode of existence I endeavoured to support the pseudonyms. . . ."[43]

Kierkegaard's second stage appearance is prefaced by a "concluding postscript" that unmasks the ridiculousness of herd irony and humor. "Irony is absolutely unsocial; an irony which is in the majority is *eo ipso* not irony. . . . [but] sheer vulgarity." A change in mode cannot occur behind the curtain or during the intermission, but rather must suddenly overcome the next scene in which the master of irony becomes the target. The stripping bare of an ego appears from within the space and time of the audience and among the critics when the staged character is delivered into a moment of "shudder." The seducing carnival stares into the public sphere with a grimace: "now, instead of the incognito of the aesthetical, I had erected the danger of laughter and grins, by which most people are scared away." The inward or vertical mask veils one as *polemos*; its mode signifies suffering. "A victorious religious author who is *in the world* is *eo ipso* not a religious author. The essentially religious author is always polemical, and hence [s]he suffers . . ." (original emphasis). For a "grinning age" of nation–states (1848/1989), Kierkegaard's "costume was correct." His drama mirrors to the crowd an offense, indeed a catastrophe, of the individual:

> If it be kings and emperors, popes and bishops . . . [sic] and powers that constitute the Evil, the religious author must be recognizable by the fact that [s/]he is the object of their attack . . . Every religious writer, or speaker, or teacher, who absents [her or] himself from danger and is not present where it is, and where the Evil has its stronghold, is a deceiver, and that will eventually become apparent.[44]

Yet along with this angularity, Kierkegaard seeks an individual reader as if he were a lover who woos a loved one: "When some day my lover comes, [s/]he will easily perceive that at the time I was regarded as ironical the irony was by no means to be found where 'the highly esteemed public' thought." The lover knows that she cannot fall in love *en masse*. She understands irony—hidden, first, behind Kierkegaard's aesthetical mask and, second, squelched by the choking cocktail party irony of the public. In both, she is not drawn into the subtext, but rather loves that same veiled polemical and suffering author. An "ironical generation" is not yet a community of ironical individuals but a "great aggregation of fools."[45]

For Kierkegaard, authoring posttraditionally signifies that "the author *qua* author has been absolutely weak. . . ." Paradoxically, the weakness for Kierkegaard lies in the overwhelmingness of his talent. This realization yields a decentering of this author's self-involvement: out of a strength that threatens to break him, he desists from becoming a religious genius and adopts the posture of an obedient clerk. In a moment of shudder in his drama, this author rests in wonder, face to face with the full meaning of his way and form of life. Yet, the polemical and suffering author does not die to authoring. He addresses the alter in revocation, from decentered strength. That he cannot systematize the totality of his authorship delivers his poetic and philosophical moods to polemical suffering. This genius also becomes edified by something wholly other. The book is authored and read not under erasure, but rather under a signature of inward or vertical identity.[46]

A decentered name, a pseudonym, signs like "a policeman, a member of the detective force," who works undercover and "without 'authority.'" Yet all authored authors in Kierkegaard's authorship as a whole sign-up the name which addresses the reader. This responsibility indicates a policing action quite opposite to the one attacked by that present age *ethos* which revokes authoring because it is offended by its requirements. Kierkegaard disclaims to be an apostle, a teacher, or an educator, but he takes responsibility for his action as "a fellow student" educated into an earnest way of life.[47]

Kierkegaard acts as a dissident, a hermeneut of suspicion, a riddler, working for some wholly unknown intelligence agency:

> I have nothing new to proclaim; I am without authority, being myself hidden in a deceit; I do not go to work straightforwardly but with indirect cunning; I am not a holy man; in short, I am a spy who in his spying, in learning to know all about questionable conduct and illusions and suspicious characters, all the while he is making inspection is himself under the closest inspection.

Before confounding this negative way of communication with alienating gazes or disciplinary power, note that this secret service is not the CIA or the KGB but rather merciful love, which subverts by presupposing love, by edifying.[48]

Kierkegaard does not wish to preserve an enigma and draw profits on yuppie campuses from an interesting play on textuality and masks. From within *The Point of View* his name should cease to be the interesting or boring item. This book marks how "Kierkegaard" "was" as an author. Its text is relegated to history, not the end of history. In the final call of his drama, itself part of the act, when actors present themselves without masks, Kierkegaard makes his exit, but this is not his death as an author. The courage of authoring is not marked by the false modesty of revoking responsibility, and yet the humility of authoring decenters by not expecting to bear fruits for oneself. An irresolution of *"Kierkegaard"* qua drama defines the name of the "author" as that individual. This posthumous point of view concludes "the whole authorship" and itself prefaces authoring as another difficulty of beginnings. The author of occasions—of all author masks and of the entire "authorship"—turns his face "to meet the future." A decisive entry into eternity need not be with the dramatic aid of some *deus ex machina* or of some publisher's *imprimatur* seal. Drama can be mocked or rehabilitated by posterity, yet one leaves the stage without exit and with the curtain up. The author "takes care" to be absent. The epigram in the program reads that the author–genius, martyred in a petty, Eurocentric Danish town, became "that individual" who died historically of mortality and poetically of passion.[49]

When earlier, in 1846, Kierkegaard thinks that he can write only *A*

Literary Review rather than another book, it is neither NN's difficulty of becoming an author nor Kierkegaard's presumed vocation to the priesthood that disturbs his quiet hours. Rather, it is the burning situation of his present age. The envisioned end of Kierkegaard's dramatic authoring marks the beginning of his main sociopolitical, polemical, and public act.[50]

9.2. HAVEL AND AUTHORING IN DELIBERATIVE DEMOCRACY

One pending query lies in our articulating of the relation between existential revolution or nonpolitical politics and professional politics. This burning question emerges for those who want to integrate the experience of dissent with institutional structures. My remarks about the present feasibility of linking the imperatives of the opposition movements with the demands of political procedures necessarily remain programmatic: I will define what problem one faces if existential revolution and nonpolitical politics are to embody a Kierkegaardian authoring, communication, and activism in deliberative democracy.

Contrary to the victory parades for markets and the New World Order, I stressed Havel's view that totalitarianism was defeated by existential revolution and nonpolitical politics—by the solidarity emerging from lifeworld imperatives against the anonymous system imperatives of state economy and power. Habermas, in his reflections on the future tasks of a critical social theory, calls attention to such solidary associations (i.e., "counterinstitutions that develop from within the lifeworld in order to set limits to the inner dynamics of the economic and political–administrative action systems"). These counterinstitutions preserve within civil society "liberated areas" which are neither primarily oriented to profit nor to professional party politics, and yet, which develop "new forms of a 'politics in the first person.'" Habermas's definition of "a politics that is expressive and [which] at the same time has a democratic base," theoretically clarifies the place of Havel's existential revolution and nonpolitical politics in relation to state socialism and to present market-oriented constitutional democracy. Both in dissent and in the context of Havel's presidency, nonpolitical politics continues to carry "the polemical significance of the new resistance and withdrawal movements reacting to the colonization of the lifeworld" by markets and technocratic power.[51]

But Habermas in his recent thematization of constitutional patriotism and postnational identity nowhere explains the related problem: how can expressive (nonpolitical) politics interact with the procedural structures of deliberative democracy? The problem centers on the character of these counterinstitutions: their polemical creation of the pockets of civil society liberated from systems of profit and technocratic power cannot be directly legislated or institutionalized. Yet if their resistance is to bear upon deliberations in the public spheres, then nonpolitical politics may be neither relegated to one's privacy, for example, caricatured by Adorno as Kierkegaard's bourgeois *intérieur*, nor simply given over to the public policy choices alone, as in Habermas's translation of Kierkegaard's either/or self-choice into procedural justice. Havel's existential revolution and nonpolitical politics need an embodiment in a democratic form of life.

I limit myself to two negative examples of this problem where the dimension of sober politics is missing, where it can be supplied neither by system imperatives of money and power nor by procedural justice alone, but where it itself seems necessary for any survival of deliberative democracy.

First, many in Yugoslavia believed that civil war would have been prevented via the integrative roles of the markets and democratic institutions. (The same sort of trust in the markets and in the rationality of procedural justice is often cited today in the Czech Republic, Slovakia, and in the rest of the postcommunist world.) But the theory that the factional war, which appeared as utter economic suicide, would be blocked by its very irrationality and by the global interests of the markets in the Yugoslavian case proved to be wrong. (Thus, some offer Yugoslavia as the paradigm likely to be followed in other postcommunist countries.) The motives of the nationalist politics of identity and difference seem to override the existing democratic consensus against the economic and political dead ends of ethnic strife.

Ivan Vejvoda recently explained the situation in Yugoslavia by suggesting that nationalism colonizes that void which occurs upon the breakdown of totalitarian structures. To be sure, this is that void of the authorship in which Kierkegaard's authoring rubs our face. Yet, nationalism becomes authored thanks to the anxiety of life in such a power void. To posttotalitarian regimes, democracy appears too risky without some sort of motivational backing. Hence, this void is filled with arbitrarily constructed national frontiers and with ethnically purified zones for an exercise of herd mentality—both cover up anxiety and block the avenue to developing mature democratic culture.[52]

Since nationalism is not that colonization which Habermas critiques under the rubric of communication distorted by systems of money and power, we cannot protect against it simply by calling upon the help of deliberative democracy. The missing link is, therefore, some ongoing critique of the nihilistic side of nationalist constructions. For this task we need but do not have a democratically structured yet counterinstitutional solidarity against posttotalitarian traditionalism and authoritarianism.

Second, Havel unwittingly brought upon himself his previous political quagmire when early in his first presidency he proposed a new name for the republic and later called for a "second revolution" which would prevent the communist nomenclature from becoming a new economic and power mafia. The first proposal was to remove the disenchanted word "Socialist" from the name of the state, yet it got bogged down in the struggle of the Slovak nationalists against Czechs about the dual-national name Czechoslovakia. In the beginning the nationalists wanted to insert a "-" into the name Czecho-Slovakia; they then became dissatisfied with the new name, "the Czech and Slovak Federal Republic" and created two separate states, the Czech Republic and Slovakia. The struggle about the proper name of the state thus blocked authoring of a new democratic Constitution. Havel's second call emerged in one of his weekly radio addresses in response to a new postrevolutionary depression and apathy in the country. Yet his personal appeal for an ongoing revolution later gave rise to new "purgation" Parliamentary legislation. This is the infamous "lustrace law," which uses the notion of collective guilt (membership in some groups or an evidence of cooperation with the secret service) to eliminate from high public posts for five years anyone who in the past collaborated with the Czechoslovak secret service, the Communist Party, or the national militia.[53]

To be sure, these events need not be attributed to Havel's will: the fact is that nationalist ideology would have emerged even if Havel had practiced cabinet politics rather than nonpolitical acts in politics, which reminds people too much of their void. The purgation law with its hunt for scapegoats would have been passed by the Federal Parliament even if he dissented and did not sign it into law. He says this much in the most recent addendum to his last book. But is Havel's meekness just a poor apology?

In the book on his presidency he defends nonpolitical politics not as a function of his dissident past, but as the only kind of politics that he wants to author. He argues for an integration of morality with everyday politics: the work in the polis need not be dirty, he says, but can become practical morality. He argues for sustaining existential revolution (now a self-transformation effecting our global responsibility for the planet) within political professionalism.[54]

But in the aftermath of the new legislation he discloses a shipwreck of his project of moral politics. "Again fate played a joke on me: it punished me for my self-confident words by presenting me with an immensely difficult dilemma: what was I to do when a democratically elected Parliament passed a bill which I did not consider morally proper, yet which our Constitution required me to sign?" Simply signing would bring Havel in contradiction with his opposition to the concept of collective guilt. Not signing would be a "dissident-like, morally pure yet immensely risky act of civil disobedience." The latter would have aggravated the instability in the country and the Parliamentary crisis, Havel reflected. So he signed it with a proposed amendment on the basis of the Human Rights Charter, but the Parliament put the law into effect without even debating any possible amendments. In reply, Havel, who does not want to give up the notion that politics can be moral, admits now "that the way of truly moral politics is not simple, or easy." Yet this nonpolitical posture, when compromised by concerns of expediency, appears to be more risky than the option of a "dissent-like act" by Havel who, as a president, lacked the constitutional right to a Parliamentary veto, but who, as a decentered author, still aims to integrate an earnest way of thinking and living with professional politics.[55]

The missing link with which I am concerned here is not necessarily greater presidential powers, even though these might have given Havel the constitutional right to outright veto the dubious legislation. Nor does it seem that the purgation fever is only a reply to economic insecurities. Havel is perhaps one of the few among the public figures today who identifies the origins of these fevers in the disappointed longing for something to fill the totalitarian vacuum. He locates this longing in the anxiety of individual and collective identities in crisis. But in spite of his diagnosis and in spite of his active role in the democratic shaping of professional politics, Havel—just as Habermas does on the opposite side of this same issue—faces a problem of linking sober politics with deliberative democracy.[56]

One could be happy if Fukuyama were correct in his celebrations of a posthistoric age and of the last man, and if nationalism and hatred were transitional phenomena which pass away with the rationality of the markets and the state. Today's examples do not give us any indication that this is so, however, and we should not rely on the New World Order to legitimate as rational what are more sophisticated forms of imperial identity.[57]

CONCLUSIONS

Though I offer only a negative delimitation of the problem, I argued that we need a transcript of a Kierkegaardian authoring, communication, and activism into democratically based solidary groups, and perhaps into nontraditionalist and nonauthoritarian critical forms of culture. If Havel's existential revolution and nonpolitical politics are not to be mistaken by others as an offer of an enlightened but ineffective executive, one must refrain from facile populism and elitism and foster counterinstitutional yet democratic forms of resistance and solidarity. Such life forms, when expanded from the individual way of thinking and living to the community perspective, can offer a supporting link between professional politics and developing civil societies.

Yet filling the missing link is not to resolve the riddle of the lived void or eliminate the difficulty of authoring one's own and communal beginnings. The question is not to resolve some problem; the question is how to translate radically honest authoring into a democratically counterinstitutional corrective that, at the level of identity formation in civil society, can stimulate the development of mature political culture.

CHAPTER 10

Critical Theory
and Existential Philosophy

I began my narrative with Habermas's 1987 paper delivered in Copenhagen, where he argues that while Hegel rooted the universal point of view in a communitarian principle of the nation–state, Kierkegaard raised a postnational identity claim. Habermas agrees that Hegel's modern state exhibits a critical appropriation of culture. Yet this is a nation–state which expects a strong conformity of the individual to the group and which allows for a heroic–patriotic war. Habermas rejects a normative privileging of the descriptive–communitarian "We" over the deliberative–procedural we: one ought to be self-determined not by the nation–state, but rather in the common weal of citizenship. Constitutional patriotism admits only that love of nation which, in place of imperial warfare among the nation–states, promotes a more rational postnational league.

In Part II I examined Kierkegaard's texts that admitted the possibility of communicative ethics in an existential mode. In Chapter 8 I read this innovation through Havel's existential revolution and nonpolitical politics as a way of life. In Chapter 9 I introduced Kierkegaard's and Havel's existential authoring into tradition, culture, and deliberative democracy. Returning now to my opening problematic, I aim to derive from Habermas's, Kierkegaard's, and Havel's views of the present age a programmatic proposal for a new composite figure of critical theory of identity, culture, and politics.

Let me recall the two problems stated at the end of Chapter 1: I argued, first, that the principle of constitutional patriotism, without an existential critique of the regional appeal of nationalism, cannot secure the conditions of the possibility of enacting deliberative democracy; and, second, that consensual procedure, without a distinction between leveling and radically honest modes of identity, communication, and the community ideal accords only weak means by which to safeguard that enactment from reproducing homogeneity and deception. Habermas's translation of Kierkegaard's critique of the nation–state into consensual aim invites me to propose my next line of inquiry.

First, should not an earnest critique of nationalism provide the concrete mode whereby citizens who are, in principle, to embody postnational identity and enliven political culture learn to communicate soberly on the level of regional cultures? Second, do not these openly communicating citizens, in principle, render consensual aim and procedures both possible and self-critical? In sum, does not deliberative democracy require a more thorough critique of nationalism—namely, a middle term that inhabits postnational identity as a lived corrective to both regional and political cultures? If in communicative ethics undistorted life forms are anticipated by critical social theory, then an existential mode of communication and action should be viewed as both a corrective and a complement to this imaginary. We can expect an encounter between critical social theory and existential critique in those forms and ways of life which call for their emergence. I begin with Jaspers's rejoinder to Habermas's observations on our age (10.1), then contrast Habermas's critique of nationalism with Kierkegaard's (10.2) and Havel's respective critiques (10.3). I then conclude with a programmatic invitation to resume the early Marcuse's abandoned project of a critical social theory in an existential mode (10.4).

10.1. HABERMAS AND JASPERS: READING THE SITUATIONS OF THE PRESENT AGE

In 1979, Habermas gave impetus to a two-volume collection by thirty-two contemporary leftist German intellectuals. He conceived of the project as volume 1,000 of the *Edition Suhrkamp*, to be published in the year that commemorated the thirtieth anniversary of the Federal Republic of Germany. He explains that in soliciting these essays, he provided Karl Jaspers's cultural critique of Weimar Germany as a model for the type of diagnosis of the "present age" needed to confront the new neoconservative trends in Germany.[1]

Habermas clarifies the quotation marks in *Observations on "The Spiritual Situation of the Age."* While Jaspers adopted "the absolute perspective of the great philosopher," Habermas abandons Hegel's and Marx's grand fusion of reason and history. Instead, he frames social critique with fallible empirical and hermeneutical parameters. A critique of the present age cannot be accomplished by one individual; it requires the collaborative effort of disciplines and inquirers who adopt the standpoint of communicative reason. Given the shift in focus from the philosophy of history and its *Zeitgeist* to communication, social critique must differentiate between the pathologies of the present age and those emancipatory potentials of modernity which have not been leveled along with the diagnosed disease.[2]

Habermas's communicative model underlines the composition of this book: the text presents no grand metanarrative on the present age; the editor of the book cannot be its sole author; and the emancipatory possibilities lie in the ideal of a communication community concretely operative among the participating contributors who present their *Observations*. The book marks neither a closure nor an exclusion but an open-ended permanence of the projected radically democratic republic. In place of arguing for a theory, the book exemplifies an unmasking of the colonization of the lifeworld by systemic rationality.

The "observations" are a corrective to the perceived reactionary spirit of the age, and therefore exhibit a certain one-sidedness: all contributors come from the undogmatic left. They defend the project of modernity, the values of reason, democratic institutions, and in some cases secular humanism, while others, like Metz, defend posttraditional religious noncontemporaneity. The purpose of this edition was to offset contemporary German thought and politics, with its recent shift to the New Right in the aftermath of the terrorist action in the German Autumn of 1977. The one-sidedness is to be a pedagogic reversal of the totalizing, leveling discourse of the present age. Just as in 1931 Jaspers engaged in cultural critique, so today Habermas finds "the duty of the intellectuals to react with partiality and objectivity, with sensitivity and incorruptibility, to movements, developmental tendencies, dangers, and critical moments. It is the task of intellectuals to make conscious a murky reality."[3]

Yet neither Habermas nor the reviewers of his *Observations* lets us know that Jaspers's cultural critique used another paradigm as the prototype —namely, Kierkegaard's *Two Ages* (1846). Habermas objects to Jaspers's monological culture critique, but overlooks that Kierkegaard communicates his spiritual observations as one common single individual to another, and that he carries on both an upbuilding and a critically repelling conversation.[4]

Habermas does not note how Jaspers's model agrees with Kierkegaard and differs from Hegel's, where "an image of universal history was the mode in which the present became aware of itself," and from Fichte's analysis of the present, which is methodically tied to "the abstract construction of a universal history." It is unclear in what sense Jaspers is supposed to carry on a narrative of the great philosopher, and whether Habermas wants to differ not only from Hegel's grand narrative but also from Jaspers's explicit adoption of Kierkegaard. Jaspers states his position with less ambiguity than Habermas makes us believe: "Kierkegaard was the first to undertake a comprehensive critique of his time, one distinguished from all previous attempts by its earnestness. This critique of his was the first to be applicable to the age in which we are now living, and reads as if it were written but yesterday."[5]

Habermas settles for a fallible prognosis, but his observations hold a Hegelian notion of "spirit" and a Marxist notion of the "situation" whereby he subsumes the concrete situation of the individual under the generic spirit of the age. Jaspers argues with Kierkegaard that "situation" pertains only to the individual; the situations of groups and life forms are mere analogies. "When the will of the individual espouses the cause of one of these things or institutions, his will and the cause he has espoused are in a situation."[6]

A poignant example of this difference between generic and qualitative senses of the "spiritual situation of the age" is the issue of nationalism. Both Jaspers and Habermas expose the nationalist politics of identity. But while allowing space for a recovery of national and cultural traditions, they nevertheless envision different cures for the "fathomless abyss" that is the present loss of immediate tribal and religious cultures. True, Habermas might agree with Jaspers's rather Kierkegaardian claim: "Nationalist movements throughout the world are more intolerant than ever, and yet in them 'nation' is nothing more than the existence of a common speech in conjunction with a levelling type." Habermas aims at a postnational identity integrated into a radically democratic republic; Jaspers finds the alternative to both "the nationalized people and the vague mass" of those who lost their tradition in "the selfhood which was originally connected with the obscure foundations of the people." Jaspers resists the nation–state through the individual who provides for the reversal of an oppressive situation of the age.

> It is true that the life-order existent through the power of a state can never be surrendered or sacrificed, for therewith everything would go to ruin; but a life in radical opposition to the state may arise, under stress of the fundamental question how the conquest of the life-order is once more to be achieved.[7]

Resting satisfied with these differences will not get us too far. We will not find much support in Löwith, even though he links the revolutionary decisiveness of Marx's *Communist Manifesto* (1847) with Kierkegaard's *Two Ages* (1846): Marx attacks possessive individualism and calls upon workers to unite; Kierkegaard deplores herd Christianity and turns to the individual. Löwith's conclusion sounds crude: "Kierkegaard's particular concern was not human equality. . . ." and "[h]is criticism of the present age . . . is therefore directed both against emancipated 'mankind' elevated by Marx to the status of a fundamental principle and against 'Christendom' emancipated from the imitation of Christ." A more nuanced complement lies between the equality sought by Marx's social praxis and that projected in Kierkegaard's praxis. With this sensitive reading we can profit from Löwith's vague note that Kierkegaard's "basic concept of the individual is a corrective to the 'mankind' of Social Democracy and to the 'Christendom' of the liberal intelligentsia."[8]

Several commentaries on Kierkegaard's *Two Ages* go beyond these deficits. Robert L. Perkins passionately demands an end to the myth of an asocial and apolitical Kierkegaard. He attacks Marc C. Taylor's Hegelian and Martin Buber's illegitimate *ad hominem* caricatures of Kierkegaard. He argues that in unmasking personal and institutional envy, Kierkegaard's inwardness dialogically confronts the sociopolitical situation of his age.[9]

Anton Hügli, while accepting Adorno's critique of Kierkegaard's presumed conservatism, argues for a corrective to Marx's historical materialism. He admits that bringing Marx's view of history together with the self-critical attitude in history forms a "square circle." He finds, however, in Marx's communist idea of society a structural possibility of full and free individual development. The end of social alienation meets the individual half-way: "Marxism arrives . . . there, where Kierkegaard . . . has begun."[10]

Merold Westphal and James L. Marsh draw a parallel between Kierkegaard's critique of the passionless age and Habermas's ideology critique. Westphal attends to Kierkegaard's religious hermeneutics of suspicion, which unmask envy behind the professed interest in equality, and cowardice behind prudence. Marsh argues that "interiority and revolution require one another and imply one another." Against conservative inwardness and terrorist revolution, he moves beyond Hegel's uncritical reconciliation and Marx's eclipse of interiority by revolution: "interiority, in order to be fully itself, must externalize itself in radical critique and action." But "revolution is not God."[11]

Bruce H. Kirmmse presents a decisively political and "fiercely egalitarian" portrait of Kierkegaard and situates him against three other prevalent positions in "Golden Age Denmark": the conservative "mainstream" (which holds a romantic view of history and a mandarin view of culture), liberalism (which remains agnostic on the ultimate significance of history and also holds a mandarin attitude towards culture), and Grundtvig's movement (which shares the romantic view of history with the conservatives and adopts a populist notion of culture). Kirmmse argues that Kierkegaard had no truck with the mandarin, romantic, and conservative positions; he shares neither an elitist notion of culture nor a romantic faith in history: "Kierkegaard was thoroughly his own person, an original—an agnostic on the significance of History, a populist on the locus of Culture, and a genuinely modern, post-1848 alternative to the *ancien regime* worldview of the Golden Age."[12]

Habermas jettisons the romantic philosophy of history, the mandarin view of the intellectual, and the liberal notion of a disencumbered individual as unfit for critical theory. His normative position envisions radically egalitarian and solidary human relations. Let me develop a Kierkegaardian complement to Habermas's reading of the present age and argue its relevance for a critical social theory of and a resistance to nationalism and fundamentalism.

10.2. KIERKEGAARD'S CRITICAL THEORY OF THE PRESENT AGE

A Kierkegaardian critique of the present age exercises that middle term between regional cultures and the deliberative procedures of political culture which, in principle, aid in resisting nationalism, fundamentalism, and totalitarianism both locally and politically (A). This critique is a corrective and complement to any future interest in postnational culture and politics (B).

A. Leveling in Culture and Politics

After distinguishing between two forms of reciprocal relations, I will show how both operate in regional and in political cultures.

Existential and Leveling Reciprocity

Kierkegaard distinguishes the passionate revolutionary age from a formless, wobbling, and crude one:[13]

> However externally oriented [one's] ambitions, the person who is essentially turned inward because [s/]he is essentially impassioned for an idea is never crude. . . . If the essential passion is taken away, the one motivation, and everything becomes meaningless externality, devoid of character, then the spring of ideality stops flowing and life together becomes stagnant water. . . .

His critique of the present assumes a normative basis of relations:

> When individuals (each one individually) are essentially and passionately related to an idea and together are essentially related to the same idea, the relation is optimal and normative. Individually the relation separates them (each one has [oneself] for [oneself]), and ideally it unites them.

This is a concrete, not communitarian, projection of the ideal.

> Purely dialectically the relations are as follows, and let us think them through dialectically without considering any specific age.

And yet this critical angle has social relevance:

> Where there is essential inwardness, there is decent modesty between [human] and [human] that prevents crude aggressiveness; in the relation of unanimity

to the idea there is the elevation that again in consideration of the whole forgets the accidentality of details.

This relevance is to block a possible totalitarian outcome:

> Thus the individuals never come too close to each other in the herd sense, simply because they are united on the basis of an *ideal distance*. The *unanimity of separation is indeed fully orchestrated music*.[14] (emphasis added)

That which blocks a herd or totality lies, then, not on the horizontal axis of their relations but rather within their ideal con/temporaneity in difference. Thus, this ideal qualifies their intersubjectivity, and yet none of the individuals nor Habermas's horizontal ideal of a communication community provides this temporal distance in principle. This ideal distance among individuals can never be approximated by the infinite consensus.[15]

Kierkegaard offers a criterion by which his model is falsified:

> [I]f individuals relate to an idea merely *en masse* (consequently without the individual separation of inwardness), we get violence, anarchy, riotousness; but if there is no idea for the individuals *en masse* and no individually separating essential inwardness, either, then we have crudeness.[16] (original emphasis)

This is a three-pronged criterion: first, there is the "how" of self-relation; second, there is the "how" of communication; and third, there is the "how" of the very idea to which we relate as individuals in community. If any of them is missing, then we get different forms of individual, social, and political pathologies. I claim that Habermas's model operates with a simple reciprocity of relations but fails to explain "how" individuals relate to themselves as individuals, to one another, and to that which binds and separates them in the idea. The consensual ideal quantifies ad infinitum a structural, generic reciprocity; it does not add a qualitative middle term whereby procedures could block a herd outcome and sustain "the unanimity of separation."

Kierkegaard's model provides such a critical and relevant angle:[17]

> The harmony of the spheres is the unity of each planet relating to itself and to the whole. Take away the relations, and there will be chaos. *But in the world of individuals the relation is not the only constituting factor and therefore there are two forms.* Remove the relation to oneself, and we have the tumultuous self-relating of the mass to an idea; but remove this as well, and we have crudeness. . . . No one has anything for himself, and united they possess nothing, either: so they become troublesome and wrangle. . . . [T]hen gossip and rumor and specious importance and apathetic envy become a surrogate for each and all. (emphasis added)

His criterion distinguishes existential from leveling reciprocity:

> Individuals do not in inwardness turn away from each other, do not turn outward in unanimity for an idea, but mutually turn to each other in a frustrating and suspicious, aggressive, *leveling reciprocity*. (emphasis added)

Kierkegaard explains how there can be that consensual sociality which, in principle, *cannot* block a totalitarian outcome:

> The avenue of the idea is blocked off; individuals mutually thwart and contravene each other; then selfish and mutual reflexive opposition is like a swamp—and now they are sitting in it.

Kierkegaard objects that the age "has invented the swiftest means of transportation and communication," but it engages in chatter. He might ask Habermas what the point is in learning about communicative action and the collective identity and will formation if one cannot communicate and act.

What does the criterion of genuine reciprocity imply for local cultures and modern politics? Kierkegaard's invitation to become an individual in an open way of life unmasks and checks the integrating appeal of nationalist cultures (their herd mentality). Authentic reciprocity grounds, thus, a possibility of the sober politics of identity and difference.

Leveling in Regional Cultures

The category of the individual facilitates Kierkegaard's critique of both the liberal and the conservative establishment: academia, the media, the public, and the churches. He defines their leveling associations by an absence of earnest reciprocity:[18]

> "[T]he public" [is] made up of unsubstantial individuals who are never united or never can be united in the simultaneity of any situation or organization and yet are claimed to be a whole.

The media creates such an illusory whole in order to justify to the public its polls on a national heroic:

> Only in a passionless but reflective age can this phantom develop with the aid of the press, when the press itself becomes a phantom. . . . But just as sedentary professionals are particularly prone to fabricating fantastic illusions, so a sedentary . . . age . . . will produce this phantom if the press is supposed to be the only thing which, though weak itself, maintains a kind of life in this somnolence.

When the *public* permeates academia, then education becomes domesticated:

[T]he aggregate is not the concretion that reinforces and educates the individual, yet without shaping him [or her] entirely to become wholly educated— if [s/]he does not perish.

A church *public* is just as "nobody" as any other leveling reciprocity.

The public is not a people, not a generation, not one's age, not a congregation, not an association, not some particular persons, for all these are what they are only by being concretions.

Kierkegaard's critique of the Catholic *public* does not provide an alibi for Protestant Reformers or secular social activists:

[A]nyone can presume to have a public, and just as the Roman Catholic Church chimerically extends itself by appointing bishops . . . in non-Catholic countries, so too a public is something anyone can pick up, even a drunken sailor exhibiting a peep show . . . [since] he has the same right to a public as the most distinguished of men, the absolute right to place . . . many zeros *in front of* his figure one. (original emphasis)

Note that Kierkegaard's modal criterion of reciprocity projects that integrating and stabilizing form of life which Habermas seeks in vain within mere structural reciprocity of communicative ethics:

Contemporaneity with actual persons, each of whom is someone, in the actuality of the moment and the actual situation gives support to the single individual.

Kierkegaard critiques society for failing to maintain the radically honest individual. His criterion is derived from the category of the individual by which he critiques pathological forms of life: the public/crowd projects an equality of nobodies; con/temporaneity with actual persons projects an equality of human existers. Habermas's communicative symmetry could be, in principle, inhabited by either projection, though its ethical communication is sustainable only by the latter.

Kierkegaard's attention to the "how" of communication allows for this nuanced critique of systematically distorted communication:[19]

Nowadays it is possible actually to speak with people, and what they say is admittedly very sensible, and yet the conversation leaves the impression that one has been speaking with an anonymity.

He compares an alienating work place with anonymous discourse:

And eventually human speech will become just like the public: pure abstraction—there will no longer be someone who speaks, but an objective reflection will gradually deposit a kind of atmosphere, an abstract noise that will render human speech superfluous, just as machines make workers superfluous.

With Kierkegaard, this comparison extends to lovers who rely on the anonymous joy of sex "handbooks," to academics who measure the suitability of individual students for doctoral work by their GRE test scores alone, to a glut of information from an industry devoid of passion.

Leveling in the Politics of Identity and Difference

Kierkegaard's critique of leveling is addressed also to the political; to that type of togetherness which turns activists and citizens into spectators and a mass. He depicts the present age as a passionless, flag-waving, indolent swamp with sparks of sentimentally nationalist or pseudoreligious enthusiasm. It makes no difference that Walter Kaufmann ridicules Kierkegaard's 1846 diagnosis as an error vis-à-vis the revolutionary year 1848. In the journal entries after 1848 Kierkegaard employs the same critical criteria in order to differentiate between a leveling reciprocity and a reciprocity which allows for the unanimity of separation. Politicians and activists often pretend to know what is to be done, but cover up behind their abstract understanding when they are unable to translate it into action.[20]

Kirmmse depicts Kierkegaard's reflection on the present age as a political critique of "bourgeois liberalism and aristocratic Hegelian conservatism" of the 1840's from the standpoint of the revolutionary age of the 1790's. Kirmmse points out that Kierkegaard attacks his present-age "shallow and reflexive" liberals and conservatives on the basis of his affirmation of the passionate revolutionaries of the eighteenth century. Kierkegaard does not reject the individual roots of constitutional and popular forms of government, but rather the Philistine bourgeois, sentimental patriotic, and snobbish mandarin "ways of being political" that characterize not only his age but much of our democracy. The revolutionary "knew how to combine the integral and autonomous individual self with the group associations that political endeavour requires." The present liberal *ethos* speaks for a passionless crowd while the conservative moral majority of the Copenhagen Hegelians cultivates the elitist good taste. Thus, Kierkegaard's standpoint is revolutionary rather than "just another Golden Age endorsement of antiliberalism, authoritarianism, and absolutism."[21]

A Kierkegaardian sociopolitical action would bring "inwardness in politics"; it would bring sobering dissent and nonpolitical movement into professional government and consensual procedures. In place of "transactions in *paper money*," one would foster a level of honesty. Kierkegaard parallels passionless politics to circulation economy:

> Certain phrases and observations circulate among the people, partly true and sensible, yet devoid of vitality, but there is no hero, no lover, no thinker, no

knight of faith, no great humanitarian, no person in despair to vouch for their validity by having primitively experienced them. Just as in our business transactions we long to hear the ring of real coins after the whisper of paper money, so we today long for a little primitivity.

Just as passionless indolence creates from human relations a swamp, so in the market economy an object is no real mode of exchange but "token money, an abstraction," and in mass democracy, the object is no longer individual participation.[22]

Kaufmann's insipid introduction to the *The Present Age* is instructive in one more regard: he caricatures both Kierkegaard and Jaspers as poor prophets of their own times, since the former failed to envision how the so-called passionless age of the 1840's would occasion the revolutionary year 1848, and the latter, unawares, published his observations a short while before Hitler's rise to power. Yet Kierkegaard clearly jokes about the act of "forecasting the future" as a recreational sport, since "every person has to work out his [or her] own salvation." He insists that the key question is not about which age we should prefer as the better one. "The question is only about the 'how' of the age, and this 'how' is reached through a more universal view. . . ." If one in any sense mis/reads one's epoch, then it is due to an oversight of the "how" rather than to a failure to forecast progress in validity domains.[23]

Kierkegaard's critical social anchor lies in the "how" of the age rather than in the linear and frontal view of history. He privileges the revolutionary 1790's to his "present" 1840's, but he does so because of the passion held by the revolutionaries for constitutional human rights. He opposes the Danish progressivist view that simply parrots the emancipatory ideas of 1789. Kirmmse notes that Kierkegaard critiques Danish middle class liberalism for its failure to integrate individuals who would relate to one another through a passionately held common idea. The liberal ideas of 1789 became diluted in associations of mutual admiration. From this vantage point, Kierkegaard neither defends nor rejects the principle of representative government. He is concerned with "the way in which the principle is appropriated." He is neither against liberalism nor for conservatism, since this is that either-or which will not get one far beyond the aesthetical method of rotating the crops. He unmasks those Danish liberals who spin off ideas of equality but fail to think and embody their politics in the equality of passion and action, and those snobbish conservatives who esteem high culture but ignore the common human lot. Kirmmse admits that Kierkegaard's "how" criterion ("any honestly and passionately held idea which respects the individual as an integral unit and as a starting point for all other association") allows equally for "conservative, liberal, democratic, etc." politics.[24]

Kirmmse is quick to point out that the openness of Kierkegaard's political criterion does not mean that any government would be acceptable. As noted, Kierkegaard is a radical egalitarian rather than a cultural mandarin. He espouses "pragmatic" agnosticism in politics rather than a romantic faith in historical and political developments. And he presupposes a modern view of the individual freedom to choose oneself rather than a communitarian pledge of allegiance to some historical form of life which must first permit this choosing. Yet all these aspects take a unique shape in Kierkegaard:

> Very much a hybrid and his own person, SK, in his most political work, *A Literary Review*, cannot be called a liberal, a democrat, or a conservative in the usual senses of the terms, although it can be seen how dependent upon liberalism in its origins and how egalitarian and antielitist in its expression his "conservatism" was. "Radical," in the deepest, original, sense seems to fit him best. *A Literary Review* stands as programmatic statement of SK's politics. . . .[25]

If we could transcribe Habermas's model of deliberative democracy into this sobering criterion of politics, then this transformed model could be adopted by a Kierkegaard in the present age. There is a vision of individuals in community that fits our situation: we cannot return to the classical nor the revolutionary age; we cannot seek criteria from any positive age; therefore, the reflective quality of the present age calls for a highly developed individuality. Habermas's democratic model requires this corrective on an individual basis, thereby inviting an encounter between critical theory and existential philosophy.

When in 1848 Kierkegaard attacks the revolutionaries for wanting to solve the question of equality through the fourth estate (the people), he is not driven by an anti-egalitarian or conservative view. He attacks in their solution the same problems that he unmasks in his present-day liberals and conservatives: if the age is marked by leveling, then wanting to forge equality by making the crowd the sovereign entrenches this same process. Such an equality promotes what later Adorno and Horkheimer name mass culture, and Foucault calls disciplinary power relations. Against leveling, Kierkegaard affirms the possibility of a deliberative union of individuals in their difference.[26]

A Kierkegaardian problem in critical theory is not an institutionalization of the regulative ideal of communicative ethics, but a prior question: how to critique the impact of leveling relations on the process of individualization through socialization. Mass culture and all of the economic and sociopolitical theorizing which originates therein are subject to leveling. Leveling begins when a "negatively unifying principle" stifles passion and establishes apathy and "deathly stillness" over the age as "the vast penitentiary."[27]

This portrait of the age of leveling has an air of Foucault's Panopticon where, Kierkegaard says, "reflection is holding the individual and the age in a prison." Panopticon stands for a modern, Benthamite invention of functional control over multiple individuals through a centrally adminis-

tered space with one-way windows open to an observation tower. Kierkegaard's account of leveling has the character of this impersonal power of
which all our efforts are functional effects. In this omnipresent but imper-
ceptible prison of apathy, individuals can join a democratic committee, and
while "the whole generation becomes a representation," no one is being
represented. We may relate to one another, but "the relation itself has
become a problem." The age cuts off the king's head, then institutionalizes disciplinary power relations in the law and representative government.
It is no longer the sovereign, "the tyrants and secret police," or "the clergy
and the aristocracy," but reflection and envy that use life to stifle living,
thinking to impede "critical sense," and the moral point of view to produce "characterlessness."[28]

Read carefully the following addendum to Habermas's Mead thesis:

> The people is the force which has demolished kings and emperors; kings and
> emperors again have sometimes used the people to demolish nobility or the
> clergy. The people has demolished the clergy, and the clergy has used the
> people to demolish the nobility, and the nobility has used the people to
> demolish the clergy. But always "the people." . . . The process of bringing up
> a human race is a process of individualization. This is why the race first of all
> has to be cut up into three estates—but then finally the chopping of this enor-
> mous abstraction, the people, into pieces begins with the help of the "single
> individual."[29]

The stress on the category of the individual as the proposed cure to leveling differentiates Kierkegaard from both Habermas and his present day
interlocutors.

Let me define these differences in negative terms. First, leveling is "a
quiet, mathematical, abstract enterprise." Kierkegaard admits that leveling
could employ the very structures of reciprocity and equality assumed in
the hypothetical distance of argumentative discourse. "The dialectic of the
present age is oriented to equality, and its most logical implementation,
albeit abortive, is leveling, the negative unity of the negative mutual reciprocity of individuals." He complains that leveling elevates generic identity over the concrete one: "about so and so many human beings *uniformly*
makes one individual" (original emphasis). The generalized other gives us
"mathematical equality" but not qualitative relations.[30]

Second, one can lead a rebellion but cannot choose to level at will.
Kierkegaard shows how the possessive individualist, too, is leveled in the
process, whereby "particular individuals may contribute to leveling." He
shows how our age contributes to leveling while remaining unaware of its
own abstract posture:

> Leveling is not the action of one individual but a reflection-game in the name
> of abstract power . . . [A]lthough the individual selfishly enjoys the abstrac-

tion during the brief moment of pleasure in the leveling, he is also underwriting his own downfall. The forward thrust of the enthusiast *may* end with his downfall, but the leveller's success is *eo ipso* his downfall. No period, no age, and therefore not the present one, either, can halt the scepticism of leveling, for the moment it wants to halt leveling, it will once again exemplify the law.[31] (original emphasis)

Third, Kierkegaard spares no strong words to expose "the idolized positive principle of sociality"—be that Hegelian and revolutionary *Sittlichkeit* or "national individuality"—as "the demoralizing principle." Nationalism cannot cure the social fall from the unity in an ideal distance to the "spontaneous combustion of the human race." Regionally reified sociality congregates "people who only have town-gossip for a national consciousness," but who lack a genuine mode of togetherness. The "market-town mentality" marks such a collectivist identity. Politically speaking, Kierkegaard attacks the Grundtvigian conservatives who justified Christianity on the basis of cultural nationalism on the one hand, and the Danish liberals who rallied behind the hysteria against German nationalists in the 1848–1850 war over the German-oriented Danish dukedoms Schleswig and Holstein on the other. He diagnoses regional and political forms of nationalism as a "hallucination" that covers up the envy which establishes itself in the process of leveling. His radically egalitarian, anti-imperial imperative follows the category of the individual which, by resisting the movement of leveling in principle, disintegrates the local herd mentality and the homogenized public sphere: "the nation–states have to be broken up into smaller pieces. The more development, the less [nation–]state. If everybody is to share in governing, the state must be very small."[32]

While this concrete critique of hatred need not appeal to Kierkegaard's Christianity, can we not learn from his horror at the linking of cultural orthodoxy or fundamentalism with nationalism, which nowadays provides a justification for the New World Order?[33]

> It is obvious that one of the factors in Christ's death was that he repudiated nationalism, wanted to have nothing to do with it. . . . But how convenient—precisely when nationality is the order of the day—it fits in neatly to posit the religious: and then orthodoxy becomes recognizable precisely by being genuinely supernationalistic.

Thus, is not Kierkegaard's abhorrence at the nationalist justification of warfare critical of imperial political motives?

> The tragedy at this moment is that the new ministry needs war to survive, needs all the agitation of national feeling possible. Even though we could easily enough have peace—if the ministry is not completely stupid, it must see that *it* needs war.

Let me sum up the regional and procedural implications of Kierkegaard's distinction between authentic and leveling reciprocity: the present age has done away with the monarchy and hierarchies, and it embraces the idea of universal equality. Yet, after the breakdown of classical tyrannies, modernity developed totalitarian, nationalist, and fundamentalist identities. This situation presents an inescapable choice between an academically domesticated, media-induced, politically manipulated, and church-blessed patriotic yes-saying and flag-waving mass or postnational culture in which each person learns to communicate as a single individual. Habermas's political culture requires, but does not have ready at hand, a critical theory of earnest self-choice, communication, and the community ideal. His procedural justice begs the question insofar as it does not require a resistance to leveling mentality. This resistance applies to both the regional and global view: the genuinely communicating individual is the middle critical term that operates a living corrective to formal procedures and to local cultures from which the consensual idea of politics abstracts. To get purchase on equality and reciprocity, the present age needs to critique crowd envy and herd mentality. Yet, this new age is not a regression to classical communities, to the nationalist activism of 1848, to the lonely individual of the existentialism of the 1960s, or to the post-1989 spring of new nations which again tried to justify nationalism with various versions of conservative mandarin pietism, now mixed with the New World Order. Kierkegaard's critique of herd mentality from the standpoint of authentic reciprocity does not raise an empirical objection that unduly burdens critical theory with issues of authenticity. Rather, he warns that one must address the possibility that when the communicators reach consensus through the process of leveling, the procedure and the outcome can translate into nationalist, authoritarian, fundamentalist or totalitarian identities. Thus, true reciprocity is necessary both for regional openness and for deliberative procedures in any social or communicative union.[34]

B. Toward Postnational Culture and Politics

How do we get these radically honest individuals and the type of community they project if the politics of identity and difference in the present age embody a leveling fury signifying nothing? When Kierkegaard expresses his interest in the future, he generates a polemic with the communist faith in the idea of a proletarian unity. "It is very doubtful, then, that the age will be saved by the idea of sociality, of association." I argue that he assumes a critical social angle insofar as he shows that quantitative revolution alone cannot bring about any qualitative change. If "the principle of association" "strengthens by numbers" alone, then "from the ethical point of view this is weakening." Kierkegaard's critique diagnoses a root of the leftist revolutionary failure in lands of real existing socialism, yet it likewise makes it difficult to legitimate the capital–public in existing democracies. "Not until the single individual has established an ethical stance despite the whole world, not until then can there be any question of genuinely uniting. . . ."[35]

Leveling by the culture industry cannot be stopped through Habermas's performative arguments and formally structured reciprocity. But one can be edified by the *examen rigorosum* of this age. The very undergoing of an identity crisis opens the opportunity for a constructive breakthrough insofar as nothing in cultural value spheres seems capable of healing such a total identity upheaval. Kirmmse indicates that Kierkegaard's present age "is a sort of holocaust" of options whereby we gain self-knowledge of our limits. This tragic awareness, which is sometimes gained only upon the ruins brought by nationalist and sectarian wars, can alone empower a dissent. Kierkegaard envisions that in the radical breakdown of our epoch individuals are thrown upon themselves. He hopes that in the absence of alternatives they choose to walk on a groundless ground; that they discover how each, in the multiplicity of an ideal distance, is "an essentially human being in the full sense of equality."[36]

On Kierkegaard's outlook, normative structures cannot function without individuals educated in an attitude of honesty. Habermas presupposes such individuals, but he neither disposes of them nor thematizes how he wants to develop them in local cultures or through public debates. Equality and reciprocity in deliberative democracy, however, seem possible only with such edified, individuated, and decentered communicators.

Kierkegaard argues that modernity began with religious Reformation, which provided a hero for all to follow at a bargain price. Now our leveling age appears to be only permeated with political action. Kierkegaard unmasks romantic activism and cultural heroism as new, sacralized, ideological forms of understanding. "No hero, then, suffers for others or helps others; leveling itself becomes the severe taskmaster who takes on the task of educating." Let one graduate from the autodidactic schooling of leveling and one becomes decentered in one's willingness to commit heroic deeds for the mother- and father-land. Let one meet one's shipwrecked will, which wanted to level at will. Let one experience that envious *ressentiment* of tradition that loses its momentum of gravity. This one may one day learn to rule oneself instead of others, to be an audience to one's own pastoral care in place of a ministering eminence, and "as an author . . . [to] be [one's] own reader" and not a public star. "[T]he tension but also the forward step will necessarily be that everyone must . . . learn in earnest to be master . . . without the supportive indulgence of having leaders and rulers."[37]

Kierkegaard indulges in an antiprophetic imaginary when he describes future leaders, who will be capable of giving support to individuals against leveling not as monarchs, popes, generals or chief executives but as those who remain *"unrecognizable"* (original emphasis) and "without authority."

This is an antiprophecy, since these nonauthoritarian and nonpolitical agents act as undercover spies and not party bosses; they exercise influence "by repulsion" rather than by positive teachings. These unrecognizables are not to rule as philosopher–kings nor should expect to receive respect on account of a title. Socrates was not a failed Platonic hero. For Kierkegaard, he prefigures an unrecognizable leader by virtue of his martyrdom as a hero–king. Unrecognizables are to govern precisely by being such Socratic witnesses to the untruth of the herd. They do not express the times and are not subjects of revolutionary change. This antiutopia throws ironic sand against those who scrutinize Kierkegaard's account of historical events: when those of the leveling age become scattered like the ice-birds upon the turbulent sea, "that is the time when the work begins—then the individuals have to help themselves, each one individually."[38]

This kind of help transpires not primarily through social but through existential revolution, not in professional but in nonpolitical politics. And yet, Kierkegaard invites dissidents into professional politics, oppositional movements into institutions: the former in each pair does not, in principle, preclude the latter; but the latter cannot deliver us, legislatively, into the former. All are invited to "leap over the blade [of totally abysmal leveling]," but all "must make the leap by themselves." The unrecognizables can neither directly help another to leap nor stop the leveler by force: the law is "not to rule, to guide, to lead, but in suffering to serve, to help indirectly." We would mis/read Kierkegaard if we depicted such curing leaps as monological, decisionistic, and dogmatic. First, the unrecognizable operates on the principle of radical self-choice, which sustains an identity of oneself and another identity in communication. In the school of leveling, one learns "to love men infinitely by constraining . . . [oneself] rather than faithlessly constraining them by dominating them, even if they asked for it."[39]

Second, indeed even if we asked for totalitarian rule and reached a consensus to accept the help of a tyrant, a Kierkegaardian lived corrective of genuine con/temporaneity, in principle, precludes such a deceptive outcome. His dissent calls for that form of consensual procedure and institutionalization which can "split up 'the crowd' and turn it into individuals."[40]

Third, the argument that Kierkegaard mis/reads history implicates the standpoint of the interlocutor in an oversight of honest self-reading. "[T]hat everyone is to be a single individual and that as a single individual . . . [one] relates . . . [oneself] to the ideal, means equality before the ideal, means human equality and humanity." Kierkegaard neither "evaluates the ages" nor normatively forecasts the future on the basis of a substantive ideal. Yet, in addition to Habermas's ascetical denial of substantive yardsticks, Kierkegaard gives such a descriptive account of the ages that, just as in *Either/ Or*, the critic is invited to self-choice and sober living.[41]

Both Habermas and Kierkegaard articulate a theory of communication within which they defend rights to self-realization and self-determination. While they derive a communicative ethic from solidarities in a concrete form of life and safeguard it performatively (maieutically) they refrain from justifying social critique by a philosophy of history or by appeals to substantive validity domains. True, both hold substantive commitments—be it Habermas's leftist desire to harness the project of critical modernity or Kierkegaard's desire to become a Christian. Yet, these commitments are not their criteria; they, too, must pass through their respective communicative models. Both project an ideal which does not dwell in a metaphysical heaven, but which possesses a critical role vis-à-vis concrete interaction. The regulative ideal envisions relations of dialogic reciprocity and equality. Even though this is a formal ideal, its imaginary clearly has sociopolitical implications insofar as it calls attention to excluded voices and invites the rectification of material injustices in concrete social forms of life.

Kierkegaard provides a corrective to Habermas's model. He problematizes autonomy by the "how" question, which lays out the requirement of self-choice for the possibility of ethical self-realization and moral self-determination. Genuine communication qualifies structural symmetry by an invitation to inhabit a con/temporaneity with another. The "how" of communication sets off the leveling type of togetherness from authentic reciprocity. The ideal of an existentially communicating community attends to the difficulty that an infinite consensus might not, in principle, be able to block the possibility that a leveling age might agree to the Kierkegaardian "public" as its ideal in the public sphere. The "how" of the ideal provides an inward or vertical resistance to the leveling in every politics of identity and difference.

The unrecognizable sufferer is no sissy. In his last public scene Kierkegaard exits with a bang: his attack on the Danish church shows as much vigour as Frederick Douglass's on North American slave-holding Christendom in 1845. The figures who come even closer to Kierkegaard's anti-prophecy are the witnesses who "rule" without authority by their resistance to racial or gender apartheid or to totalitarian regimes. It is these dissidents, rather than the class or the historical agents of *perestroika* (restructuring), who seem to grasp the age of leveling in its real socialist and real democratic varieties.[42]

10.3. HAVEL'S EXISTENTIAL POLITICS IN THE PRESENT AGE

Havel shares with Habermas concerns about the same set of problems emerging in multicultural Europe and the need for postnational democratic institutions. Moreover, analogically to Kierkegaard's distinction between the herd and authentic types of reciprocity, Havel's leitmotif that runs through all his works before and after 1989 is a resistance to the leveling of words and, more concretely, to the deceptive appeal of the nationalist and racist cultures of hatred, and to motivated insincerity in politics. I identified this posture of resistance as existential revolution.[43]

Because any individual may meet the invitation to oppose distorted communication, thereby embodying a self-critical posture within local cultures and in deliberative democracy, we need not and ought not to idolize Havel or cover up the problematic aspects of his present politics. The danger of elitism (e.g. in Havel's presidency) and the opposite danger of homogenizing consensual procedures (e.g. in applying Habermas's proposal) both give impetus to my call for an encounter between critical theory and existential philosophy. These dangers emerge in the concrete situations of our age, which manifests a need for this two-pronged critical–existential corrective. As before, I begin with the distinction between authentic and leveling types of communication (A). I will then return with Havel and Habermas to Copenhagen in order to argue how the leveling of words operates in regional cultures, to which Havel directs his phenomenology of hatred, and in political cultures, to which he addresses his self-critique of exercising power in deliberative democracy (B).

A. The Leveling of Words

Havel, both before and after 1989, critiques the leveling of words and strives to recover "inter-existential" communication. We have seen how and why he gives up using the word "socialism." Yet in his dramas and essays, besides the "S" word, he exposes the hollowness of other ordinary words found in the mainstream culture: capitalism, liberalism, market, people, peace, religion, and so on. He argues that one should communicate what one means, not use slogans. By refusing to pledge allegiance to labels, Havel today makes "a little mad" not only some post-1989 melancholy leftists, but anyone who communicates by using phrases good only for parades.[44]

Accordingly, Havel does not think it very smart to exchange the idolization of "socialism" for the worship of "capitalism." Most recently, he calls the latter trend in the east the "ideologization of the economic reform." "The right-wing dogmatism with its intolerance and fanatical belief in the general rules [of the 'systemic purity' of the market] irritates me in the same manner as the leftist prejudices, delusions, and utopias." Havel's call for an active role for morality vis-à-vis markets and administrative power is often criticized by the right wing as a sign of his "crypto-socialism." Yet here again he refuses to be identified with labels like socialism and capitalism: "yesterday's feared communists are today's unscrupulous capitalists, who are laughing directly and without shame at that same worker whose interests they before supposedly defended." Havel opposes the centralized economy and power of state socialism, but argues for bringing the existential and the moral points of view to bear vis-à-vis the systemic imperatives of markets and administrative politics. "Systems are here for people, not people for systems."[45]

While one can get offended at "what" Havel drops from his vocabulary, nevertheless both his dramatic–satirical invention of the perfectly cybernetic yet depersonalized language called "ptydepe," and his essay *Word about Word* show that his real concern is with the "how" of communication. The words always deceive unless they are rooted in one's thinking and acting. Havel counsels sobriety about how we speak words, but not because he has given up the validity of truth, rightness, and sincerity. Rather, he criticizes the ordinary language usage of words that have become empty ciphers. Thus, both the leftist and rightist offense at Havel miss the point since from his critique it does not follow that some words must be forever lost. If one could infuse a new life into disenchanted words, then, given Havel's Kierkegaardian critique of leveling, there would have to be the possibility of an honest repetition of such words. (A word of caution against idealistic reading: not every "what" can be justly retrieved through an earnest "how" because the material careers of some racist, sexist, and classist words are irretrievably bankrupt. Here, the changes in the "what" affect the possibilities of a "how".) This repetition, because it must close the gap between one's words and communicative action, cannot be safeguarded dogmatically by revolutionary catechisms. Individual and social transformation, the "how," cannot be accomplished by the path to the "what" alone, or vicariously through Havel as the author of a drama or a leader of the "velvet revolution." "What" the author and the politician communicate may become an occasion for the "how" of individual and social transformation. The very same words that stand for authenticity and justice—ironically often Havel's own philosophical reflections parroted by his stage masks who lack any lived relation to what they say—can sound as mere clichés, pretense, or a Faustian path.[46]

Through unmasking this absurdity of slogans, existential drama occasions in the individual the recovery of a capacity for addressing another as an individual. Therein lies Havel's egalitarian and anti-elitist project of existential revolution, both within local cultures and in the structures of deliberative democracy: empty speech gives birth to leveling culture; this in turn admits the possibility of a leveling politics of identity and difference; thus, one's recovery of genuine communication inevitably resists totality.

B. Havel and Habermas in Copenhagen

Havel and Habermas meet indirectly with Kierkegaard and one another in Copenhagen: Havel's critique of power occurred in 1991 when he received the Sonning's prize. We have seen that when Habermas obtained this same award in 1987, he transposed Kierkegaard's resistance to the nation–state into the procedures of deliberative democracy. Analyzing the politics of identity and difference in the service of deception, Havel argues that a self-critical politician ought to be sober about the leveling of words. He voices a strong opposition to political nationalism and to all forms of hatred. His writing and action help us to place an existential critique of nationalism, fundamentalism, and political insincerity within deliberative democracy (without idolizing Havel as someone who exemplifies the fullness of this resistance).

Hatred in Regional Cultures

Havel, in an earlier Oslo paper, "The Anatomy of Hatred," prefigures the themes developed in Copenhagen: he performs an autopsy on the pathology of nationalist, fundamentalist, racist, and one-dimensional identities. Hatred originates from a disappointed longing for the absolute, and it "is the condition of the person who wants to be God." Such a person desires total recognition, total power, total ownership of truth, and total identification between the personal and world orders. Imperial egocentrism is neither "capable of self-irony" nor of accepting the absurd side of human finitude. Havel does not draw essential differences between individual hatred and "religious, ideological–doctrinaire, social, nationalist, or other group hatred." Yet he finds the resources for group hatred not in collectives per se but rather in "collectives of individuals who are capable of hating other individuals." To be sure, group hatred exercises great appeal to any drifting individual: the collective designation of injustice can be projected onto any hated object, whereby the powerless individual gains a vicarious sense of just struggle. "One can always find plenty of . . . Germans, Arabs, Blacks, Vietnamese, Hungarians, Czechs, Gypsies or Jews in whose behavior one can wonderfully prove that they are all guilty!" Further, belonging to a privileged hating elite can be blessed by "a cult of symbol and ritual." Group uniforms and marches with flags and songs can confirm the value of individual identity. Moreover, by its promise of universal order, the community of hatred gives an air of legitimacy to an otherwise risky individual act of aggression. Group hate takes on an illusion of righteousness. Finally, for someone who is frustrated but unimaginative, group mediocrity offers a common denominator of hatred or guilt—the skin color, the name, the sound of speech, or the religion.[47]

Havel claims that collective hatred takes root the quickest in places where people have experienced longtime neglect and suffering. Further, the "evil of racism" originates from our otherwise positive rational capacity to generalize from individual cases to something universal. Individuals can become targets of hatred because of some such generalization of the regional identity. Finally, the herd communication of "collective otherness" can give rise to intolerance towards everything that is foreign to the collectivity to which I belong. Without some radical distancing from the individual and group identity formed by one's region, culture, and personality, neglect, myopic universalization, and negatively differentiated identities can become the local seedbeds of the oppressive forms of the politics of identity and difference.[48]

Hatred and Deception in Politics

In Copenhagen, Havel critiques himself as a politician in power, but he likewise defends nonpolitical politics. He distinguishes three motivational sources behind political power which are, however, often mixed together. First, there are motives that make us believe in a better, new world order and that justify political power as a way to realize this ideal. Second, there are those who are motivated by the need to fulfill a desire for self-confirmation. A politician can form the world into his or her own image and can gain respect because of the very essence of political power. Third, political power offers numerous elite privileges. Havel understands his political role as a form of service to the community; nevertheless he asks whether or not he is not more interested in making the world into his own image, in self-confirmation, and in special treatment. The want of self-realization is not something to be condemned, but by observing abuses of political power, Havel grows suspicious of the sincerity of his own motives. He finds himself with all the privileges that he used to criticize about the communist nomenclature.[49]

Havel's "power unto death" paraphrases Kierkegaard's "sickness unto death," namely, one's living a lie. Not unlike Foucault, Havel is aware that political power can produce identity by offering an ambiguous self-confirmation. This ambiguity lies in the illusory character of political power, which can distort even the Habermasian just deliberative procedures by motivated self- and other-deception. Political power—just as fanaticism, nationalism, and totalitarianism—can fictitiously confirm one's unique identity and differentiate one's place in the world in opposition to others. These configurations of the power politics of identity and difference colonize the lifeworld, thereby distorting Habermas's sincerity claim to be maintained in consensual procedures: one becomes a prisoner of one's world order, of an identity mirrored by the leveling public, or of one's executive privilege.

Yet Havel's Kierkegaardian critique of hatred and deception does not bespeak a panoptical politics unto death. He is neither suspicious of politics nor of the public sphere as such. Rather, he argues for a necessary complement to the procedures of deliberative democracy: to resist either a nationalistic or political lie, participants in discourse need a high degree of self-critical distance. Havel does not claim to have such a sobriety. But he reminds himself that one should remain sober about the possibility of motivated deception if one is involved with political power. Sobriety is to give one that hope by which one will be able to recognize the moment when the nationalist politics of identity and difference, on the one hand, and Habermasian procedural universalism, on the other hand, turn into just two forms of intoxication with one's world of power.[50]

Now, we have witnessed how Havel transmuted an invitation to open the Salzburg Music Festival into an opportunity for an indirect hermeneutics of suspicion. He could not have known when still a dissident that later as the president of Czechoslovakia he would be standing next to Kurt Waldheim, the president of Austria, who was shunned by most diplomats for his unrepented Nazi past. In Salzburg, as in Oslo and Copenhagen, Havel argues that the recent wave of nationalism and fanaticism emerges from the breakdown of communitarian identities and from an inability to face one's newly won freedom. Nationalist separatists often suffer from an illusion that they have ceased to drift through history. They fail to integrate individuals in groups on the groundless ground of open identities. Havel names this sincere openness living in truth—an unrepressed and communally nonoppressive receptivity to otherness. He argues that a political lie that rewrites history or redraws and purifies the present ethnic or racial boundaries cannot sustain regional cultures on the basis of nationalist strife. This argument is reminiscent of Habermas's disclaimers, made in Brussels, that nationalism cannot mount the tasks of multicultural Europe. Havel complements this postnational proposal: deliberative democracy cannot be sustained apart from facing, in a mode of one's thinking and living as well as in politics, that xenophobic anxiety which would meet every postnational, nonfundamentalist, or posttotalitarian society.[51]

At the Hebrew University in Jerusalem, Havel communicates this same complement to a Habermasian model of deliberative politics, here using Kafkaesque self-distancing from his own political power. He views himself as an ex-prisoner from totality who would not be surprised if one day he woke up from his presidential office in his prison cell. He exhibits a sobering awareness of that anxiety of finitude which drives one to hatred and domination. He argues that unless one stands guard against insincerity in one's own house—within individual and group identity formation—it is naïve to expect checks and balances from democratic procedures alone. To be sure, this posture itself is neither antidemocratic nor elitist. Rather, we have here an attempt at a mutually corrective *rapprochement* between Habermas's model of deliberative democracy and Havel's Kierkegaardian sobriety about power. Just as before in prison so also now as president, Havel wants to begin with his own situation. Yet this highly personal self-critique of possibly insincere motives carries sociopolitical repercussions: Havel's point of making this hermeneutics of suspicion a theme of public speeches and actions provides a dramatic invitation to individuals within multicultural audiences to do likewise both in regional and in political cultures.[52]

Coming back to my discussions in the last two chapters, Havel thematizes this sobriety in an activist appeal to existential revolution and nonpolitical politics. We have seen that the meaning of his invitation is often misunderstood, especially since he took the post of professional politician and became entagled with separatist desires for the Slovak and Czech nation–states and with the quagmires of the present political witch hunt. In spite of his failure to refrain from signing the purgation legislation, which gave rise to new scapegoating, Havel's nonpolitical politics embodies a form of resistance to a leveling type of politics. This resistance is also political insofar as radically honest dissent permanently inhabits and transforms institutionalized procedures rather than needing to tear them down from outside. Havel requires a "counterinstitutional" politics which, as Habermas says, emerges from the lifeworld, not from the impersonal imperatives of economy and technocratic administration. Herein lies the rationale for an encounter between critical theory and existential philosophy: raising the imperatives of the lifeworld against the systems of money and power is the task presupposed—though in a different mode—by Habermas's project of deliberative democracy and by Kierkegaard's and Havel's nonpolitical politics alike.[53]

Toward a Sober Politics of Identity and Difference

From this encounter emerges a vision of multiculturalism without ethnocentric and nationalist hatred, postnational identity without an internationalist homogenization of regional cultures, and deliberative democracy undistorted by an imperial world order or by fragmentation and anomie. The dramatic ironization of empty speech, the unmasking of nationalism, and the invitation to existential revolution and nonpolitical politics resist leveling in various forms of dogmatism and in the backlash of identity politics and xenophobia alike.

Havel argues that without radical sobriety deliberative democracy lacks that self-distancing from one's regional culture and from political power which is required to sustain consensual procedures against destructive nationalist and homogenizing outcomes. This sobriety delivers us to postnational identity: "We are at the beginning of the global era, the era of open society, the era in which ideologies give way to ideas." To those who want to keep nonpolitical politics inwardly pure, and thus apart from the ambiguous field of professional politics, he replies that without democratically restructured civil society one's self-critical attitude lacks any public sphere for manifesting inwardness and thus tends to elitism. Genuine communication, while it cannot be directly institutionalized or legislated, is to be embodied in professional politics, not in external movements of dissent alone. "Politics as practical morality" is not only possible but necessary to sustain the "lawful and democratic state."[54]

Regarding my rejoinder to Habermas from Kierkegaard and Havel: one cannot but confirm Habermas's urgency, voiced in Brussels, about maintaining multicultural rather than homogeneous society. Yet given Havel's Kierkegaardian dissection of hatred, political motives, and leveling communication, critical theory must address the regional neglect and suffering of marginalized peoples. These often result when, in the procedures governed by universal reason, one abstracts from but does not return to local cultures.

Taking up Habermas's procedural resistance to nationalism and fundamentalism, I offered a programmatic proposal to complement political culture with a sobering transformation of the politics of identity and difference. This special case in the overall critique of leveling communication would operate as the middle term between deliberative democratic consensus and the lifeworld identities of local cultures. Such a posture, in principle, can sustain national–communitarian identities, yet it fosters political culture by resisting nationalism. This combined approach is receptive to otherness, respectful of human rights, and critical of trends which fuel hate. The principle of deliberative democracy and constitutional patriotism, if it is' not to beg the question, requires a sustained existential critique of leveling communication and deception. In this fashion we may oppose the possible indifference of the universal point of view without at the same time becoming communitarian in a problematic way.

10.4. A PERMANENT DEMOCRATIC AND EXISTENTIAL REVOLUTION?

The young Herbert Marcuse argues that philosophy becomes practical and radical when it takes a public stance on the concrete material conditions of existence. He finds the capitalist form of life responsible for the major crises of the present age. But in contrast to the orthodox Marxist privileging of productive labor, the young Marcuse grants the revolutionary role to concrete philosophy and action. He aims at integrating the self-critical attitude with a critical social theory: in order to actualize possibilities, concrete philosophers must take a public stance. Marcuse exemplifies here this concrete and public action with Kierkegaard.[55]

Douglas Kellner notes how Marcuse's appeal to Kierkegaard's activism "represents a critique of the German existentialist tendency to withdraw from history and society in order to cultivate subjectivity far from social issues and struggles of the day." Marcuse's targets come readily to mind—the German conservative ideologues who developed political existentialism in order to justify National Socialism. I agree here with Marcuse, and therefore have argued against the received view of Kierkegaard and against the confusion of the existential attitude with rightist or leftist decisionist politics.[56]

Thus, one cannot equate Carl Schmitt's political existentialism—characterized here by Richard Wolin—with Kierkegaard's texts, with Havel's nonpolitical politics and existential revolution, or with their reading/authoring in the present age:

> It is the state alone that retains ultimate power of decision to suspend conditions of political normalcy and declaring a state of exception. In this way, Schmitt transposes Kierkegaard's teleological suspension of the ethical from the moral to the political sphere.

In his critique of Schmitt, Wolin fails to differentiate the "decisionistic theory of sovereignty" from a Kierkegaardian attitude of radical openness. Without this distinction, Wolin, like Lukács, parrots the received view which makes Kierkegaard guilty by association with positions like Schmitt's anticonstitutional political theology of dictatorship or the *Führer* principle.[57]

It is inconceivable that Kierkegaard would translate existential identity into "heroic realism." "Political existentialism," as attacked by Marcuse, moved from conventionalism to a totalitarian, acommunicative politicization of existence, thereby appealing to the heroic destiny of the nation or to the warfare duty for the fatherland. Marcuse points out that "political existentialism," just as liberalism, in the very opposition to the normative standpoint, inevitably leads to a totalitarian outcome: both positions abandon the individual to the irrational void of fascism. He defines this failure by a faulty substitution of the national destiny of the people for "material facticity." We have seen that Kierkegaard critiqued both the Danish liberal and Grundtvigian "Christian" nationalists. While Marcuse praises Kierkegaard as an intellectual becoming concrete, radical, and public, he does not explain how Kierkegaard, in principle, disallows this nationalist substitution even if he does not develop a substantive analysis of the concrete material conditions of historical existence. The missing explanation is that a Kierkegaardian critic joins the critical theorist's concern for material and social conditions with the concretion of radical honesty about our motives.[58]

Marcuse's affirmation of a critical theory becoming concrete, and at the same time, his lack of explanation, give me that nuanced setting in which I can lay my claim to the theoretical significance and social relevance of this new encounter between critical theory and existential philosophy. Habermas would agree with Marcuse's material basis for critical theory: the cognitive relation of existence to history and the concrete critique of the forces of history. I have shown how Habermas retrieves cognitive criteria formally, not by appealing to a grand philosophy of history. Now Kierkegaard does not require us to abandon the cognitive structure and material context (the "what") of validity claims, yet he qualifies the equal-ity of communicative ethics by an openness about the "how" of self-choice, communication, and community ideal.[59]

When I programatically invite critical theory to adopt the corrective and complementary modes of a permanent democratic and existential revo-lution, I aim to demarcate my position from decisionist "political existen-tialism" or its convex mirror image in totalitarian identity. Yet, I aim to follow the path of the young Marcuse, which he later abandoned. Two openings allow for my innovation: first, my presentation of Kierkegaard lies within an egalitarian, reciprocal model of communication, and therefore can be admitted into the formal–pragmatic domain of validity claims. Sec-ond, both the requirements of con/temporaneity in conversation and of the noncontemporary language of inwardness or verticality block, in principle and in the temporal mode of a revolutionary permanence, any possibility of a totalitarian outcome. We have found how Kierkegaard distinguishes the leveling nationalist reciprocity of the heroic "public" from the reciprocity of "well-orchestrated music." Inwardness or verticality does not project a material utopia but a materially concrete difficulty of noncontemporaneity—that which is wholly other than my beginnings in the present age. When we derive philosophical equivalents to Kierkegaard, we cannot be secur-ing historical domains but only the concrete mode they can take.[60]

To be sure, there are many specific issues, such as the shifts from a Eurocentric, Kierkegaardian Christian, and male perspective to a less nine-teenth-century, more multicultural, nonsectarian, and gendered perspec-tive, that my reading of Kierkegaard did not directly develop. But, through Habermas, Kierkegaard, and Havel I present a model of communicative ethics in a way that invites an introduction of these issues: postnational identity allows for a receptivity to many cultural and gender contexts even though no formal model alone can replace, for instance, in the USA the need for an African-American or feminist core curriculum.

The solidarities among the victimized in history, and the AA-type com-munities of perpetually recovering sobered-up individuals, come close to the corrective ideal of concrete, democratic, and existential revolution in permanence. At times Kierkegaard compares these new communities of dissent to "the world of crime" that forms "a little society which ordinarily also has an intimate solidarity not altogether common in the world." These are the outcasts, the marginalized who are "expelled from human society." Kierkegaard seeks a genuine Christian congregation, something nowhere to be found in his Christendom; nevertheless, I took the liberty of har-nessing this search in order to project a radically honest way of inhabiting democratic multiculturalism or Havel's alternative cultures of resistance to fanaticism. This critical ideal envisions "[t]he society of those who have voluntarily placed themselves outside society in the usual sense of the word. . . ." This ideal lures those individuals of the world to unite "whose mark is that . . . [they] are polemical to the utmost towards society in the usual sense." Such individuals in community can learn to resist heroic identity by sharing "the intimacy of the society . . . conditioned by the polemical stance against the great human society." The lessons of racism and totalitarianism teach how oppression can give rise not just to hatred but to the nonviolent acts of a civilly disobedient solidarity, which in the end represent more serious threats to the status quo than the momentary rage of an urban riot: "the nausea at common human bestiality make the association more intimate." These groups form a Havelian parallel polis "on the other side of 'society.'" Here communicative critical theory and praxis join in resisting oppression by defending the individual: "the basis of the association is, among other things, a common consciousness of the way each of the individuals is in a certain sense deprived of ordinary human rights. . . ."[61]

While I have much sympathy for Habermas's own sociopolitical stance, I think that the same lived gap ascribed by Marcuse to the German politicized mis/readings of the existential attitude reappears formally in his failure to integrate, in principle, existential philosophy and critical theory. Unlike Habermas's procedural formalism that aims at justice through a generic projection of a social form of life, Kierkegaard presents justice as a concrete revolutionary demand to embody a just way of life. While both Habermas's structural and Kierkegaard's temporal communicative models are to some degree still formal, the latter prescribes honest concretion as the condition of the sober embodiment of the former's material concretion.

That Kierkegaard did not elaborate a democratic theory makes his position incomplete but in no way politically dogmatic. That he neither advocated a conservative, nationalist revolution of blood and soil, nor a positively Marxian or negatively Adornian material utopia, allows for his complementarity with Habermas's democratic project. I took the path abandoned by the early Marcuse and ventured with Kierkegaard: I expanded his category of the individual through Habermas's community ideal into an invitation to inhabit a permanent democratic and existential revolution.

From my study there emerged a manifesto of what the young Marcuse had envisioned—a concretely radical philosophy. We all read and mis/read our social, political, and economic environments. There is no shame and no blame in being fallible. Habermas shows well that fallibilism ought to enter formally into one's theory-construction and practical discourse. But there remains an unproblematized surd in this fallibilism: how not to self-mis/read a mode of communication! A mis/reading of the other and the situation of one's present age (those misreadings make all the difference) indicate indirectly that there occurred a self-mis/reading. The critical social theorist and activist who mis/reads the individual will inevitably mis/read the mode of other texts and concrete situations. We cannot postpone the difficulty of beginnings, which marks every reading/authoring, until some later moment in history. One cannot evade this task by relegating it to something to be determined by public policy choices alone. If we are to admit the nonabsoluteness of our reading/authoring—as we need to, if we are to live soberly—then we may have to share in common our difficulty of beginnings. We may have to remind ourselves of this difficulty in the very ideal of socially integrating the modern crisis individual into a post-national identity of the present age.

CONCLUSIONS

By returning to the early Marcuse's view of Kierkegaard's revolutionary concretion, this study took the path left untravelled by a critical social theory. There remain burning questions concerning the present Yugoslav tragedy, the rise of the new hate groups in Germany and the USA, and the diremptions of Czechoslovakia or of the former Soviet Union, to name a few. How can existential revolution be exercised in a democracy? Can the nonpolitical politics of dissident movements contribute to the transitional civil societies of central-eastern Europe? Can it resist that "Grand Inquisitor" who behind the mask of the New World Order hides the deceptive motives of homogenizing political correctness? We need to ponder what, if anything, in that solidary experience of resistance to totality, so well documented and dramatized by Havel, can inhabit from within the very deliberative ideal of democratic multiculturalism. Can dissent and professionalized politics live together in order to meet this task?

The fact is that the dissidents did not remain sitting around debating the possibilities; they took part in the epochal change. For better or worse, almost overnight, the protesting individuals were brought on the wings of revolutions within the political and economic institutions. When the powerless became powerful, their appeals to radical honesty raised a new problem. On the one hand, professional politics requires compromise. On the other hand, calls to sincerity and authenticity cannot be directly institutionalized lest the ruling voice become that of a moralizing authority. Did not Havel's model of nonpartisan, nonpolitical politics fail morally when, in spite of his opposition to collective guilt, he signed the purgation law against former collaborators? Did it not fail politically when in his meekness he could not stop the nationalist breakdown of Czechoslovakia? The importance of my contribution is other than prognosticating on these matters. Let history be the judge.[62]

Yet it is the present events which lead me to conclude that unless we find some way of integrating dissent against oppression with democratic politics, our critiques of the present age will remain abstract. The objection that Havel's call to honesty is just as weak a remedy as is Habermas's appeal to the moral core of modern institutions seems besides the point. Habermas is correct; the theory can neither deliver us to justice nor console for death. Kierkegaard and Havel are right; genuineness and receptivity to otherness cannot be legislated. My argument is not about how theory fairs in practice. Rather, this is a theoretical point about the praxis of theorizing: unless we join a radical critique of our motives with sociopolitical and economic critiques, our manifest destinies, velvet revolutions, and shining paths to justice turn into nightmares.

The Yugoslav civil war is the case in point: what possible material critique could unmask the roots of this senseless violence? In a situation where there are no political or economic victors, but where people nevertheless do not stop killing because they do not want to stop, socioeconomic critique alone is too abstract to make a dent. The politics of identity and difference, built on the binaries of hate, colonize symbolic life not via the material imperatives of profit and power but through the void of identity in crisis. There was and is no guarantee that a critique of totalitarian identity, such as that by Havel, could resist the former totalitarians, now converted into unenlightened capitalists or nationalists, from colonizing this new post-1989 void. I do not seek this kind of guaranteed security zone. Yet there emerges a sense of urgency that we have no other option in facing the identity crises of the present age but a reaching out for a new level of radical honesty about the groundlessness of all identity constructions.[63]

Dissent, which remains "outside" of official politics, might be necessary within a totally administered epoch, but it stages only a destructive rebellion on the urban outskirts of complex modern societies. Without domesticating the voices of transgression, we need to invite the movements of resistance into our daily affairs. Critical theory and practice that want to remain sober must discuss motives. Such a theory and action needs to integrate dissent against dishonesty and deception into the very emancipatory praxis.

First, the invitation to radical self-choice requires an ongoing self-critical posture which would resist any heroic institutionalizations of autonomy and authorship. Second, the call for con/temporaneity in communication renders both the motivation and the legitimation of the nationalist or fundamentalist politics of identity and difference defunct. Third, the need to bring inwardness or verticality into politics acts as a lived corrective to totalitarian trends in power relations, but does so without any authoritarian gesture: by way of multicultural openness to otherness, it occasions an emergence of the solidarities among the excluded, shaken, and oppressed. In cooperation with a permanent democratic revolution, whereby communicative action nurtures material needs and cultural solidarities against the domination by money and state power, an existential revolution stands permanent guard against the absolutization of the symbolic structures—family, flag, market, and cultural value spheres—of the lifeworld.

Habermas's Reading
of Kierkegaard:
Notes from a Conversation

I asked Habermas to answer questions concerning his not widely documented rereading of Kierkegaard's texts. In the following notes I paraphrase Habermas's replies and comment on our conversation.[1]

1. *In* The Theory of Communicative Action, *Vol. 2, in reply to Dieter Henrich and Ernst Tugendhat, you distinguish, along with George Herbert Mead, two aspects of posttraditional ego identity. These are self-determination (the generic identification of an autonomously acting person) and self-realization (the qualitative identification of radical self-choice; i.e., the Kierkegaardian choice of who I am and want to be). The generic and qualitative aspects of ego identity are then differentiated from the numeric sense of identity. How do the following two theses, which you develop, relate to one another: (a) only autonomous action first provides the ground for one's self-realization, and (b) the qualitative self-identification is a presupposition for the possibility that others can identify one generically and numerically?*[2]

Habermas noted that this question about interpreting Kierkegaard within the communications paradigm presents a solvable problem. The difficulty either for the discourse model of identity formation or for existential self-appropriation occurs only when we try to pit self-determination (generic identity, autonomy) and self-realization (qualitative identity) against one another, rather than considering them as replies to distinct moral and ethical–existential questions. He explained that one should not interpret the relation of self-determination and self-realization in a linear fashion. The generic and qualitative components of the "I" are complementary, not

---

This chapter was originally published in *Philosophy and Social Criticism* 17/4 (August 1991) 313–323. Copyright 1991 by *Philosophy and Social Criticism*. Reprinted by permission.

contradictory, aspects of ego identity. Habermas did not disagree when I noted that this attempt at the *rapprochement* between a Kierkegaardian existential individual and the communicative, performative notion of an identity claim marks not only the uniqueness of Habermas's approach among the thinkers in the field of critical theory, but also contradicts the mainstream existentialist, social, and political receptions of Kierkegaard.[3]

2. *When in the "Excursus on Identity and Individuation"[4] you discuss self-realization, you admit to adopting an "existential mode of expression."[5] Had your interest in Kierkegaard emerged already in that 1981–1985 context? Did it come back only later in your 14 May 1987 Copenhagen lecture—where you seek out that type of rational, posttraditional group identity that could sustain and integrate socially the existential crisis individual[6]—and during 1988 in your Mead paper?[7]*

Habermas acknowledged the biographical nature of this question. He made a three-fold reminiscence. First, he returned to his student years in Bonn because it was here that he first read Kierkegaard. Like many others (e.g., Karl-Otto Apel, who was also in Bonn at that time) Habermas was interested in the reception of Kierkegaard through Heidegger's *Sein und Zeit*. He encountered Kierkegaard along with St. Augustine through the Protestant education of his family. Second, the reference to "the existential mode of expression" is not so much to Kierkegaard as to Ernst Tugendhat. Tugendhat attempted to reread Heidegger and Kierkegaard through Wittgenstein's linguistic analysis and Mead's pragmatism. Third, Habermas comes back to Kierkegaard's texts directly first in his 1987 Copenhagen lecture. In this paper he addresses Kierkegaard's either/or to Germans evaluating their collective history. Habermas confronts the recent conservative reinterpretations of the Nazi past with the angularity of Kierkegaard's self-choice.[8]

3. *On the one hand, in your Copenhagen lecture on German identity, to which you return most recently in your reflections on the events of November 1989, you want to translate Kierkegaard's existential mode of the either/or characteristic of self-choice into the procedural ethics of communicative, collective will formation. You depict constitutional patriotism (Verfassungspatriotismus) as the main cure for the melancholy spirit of the leftist revolutionary striving. Moreover, you suggest that this sober patriotism alone can socially integrate the extreme and endangered type of identity that is embodied by Kierkegaard's existential individual. On the other hand, you affirm that "existential decision is a necessary condition for a moral attitude towards one's life history, but [this existential decision] is not the result of a moral deliberation."[9] What is the mode of constitutional patriotism about which you write in* Die Nachholende Revolution? *Didn't you sustain and translate Kierkegaard's existential individual into communicative ethics so well that you have meanwhile lost his or her existential mode?[10]*

Habermas took care to answer this question at length. He distinguished the levels where it is fruitful to relate a Kierkegaardian analysis to *Verfassungspatriotismus* from those where the levels must be kept apart. First, in general sociological categories, Kierkegaard refers to the personal aspect of the lifeworld, whereas the term constitutional patriotism includes the collective rationalization and the symbolic reproduction of the lifeworld.

Second, within this collective component one must distinguish between the cultural and institutional aspects of the lifeworld. The closest relation between Kierkegaard's existential individual and collective identity formation lies in the link between culture and personality. In this relation the "ethical–existential" self-understanding of the individual must be sustained and integrated by the social history of one's community. Therefore, modern culture and existential personality constitute the two aspects of posttraditional identity.

Third, the theme of constitutional patriotism falls between the categories of cultural and personal self-understanding. To be sure, in modern societies this patriotism is to supervene nationalist identity formation. Habermas agreed when I noted that Kierkegaard offers a strong argument against nationalism and both religious and secular fundamentalism, since all these trends represent those life forms that prevent one's existential self-appropriation. I added that Kierkegaard's existential critique of the aesthete and of nineteenth-century nationalism complements Habermas's procedural critique of nationalism. Moreover, without this existential mode, it seems questionable whether either communicative ethics or permanent democratic revolution and constitutional patriotism alone could counter, on the level of posttraditional identity formation, the tendencies towards the Balkanization of central-eastern Europe, towards renewed German nationalism, towards violent nationalist upheavals in the [now former] Soviet Union, or towards sentimental patriotic glory in the United States.[11]

Fourth, Habermas, however, distinguished the institutional question of constitutional patriotism from the cultural and personal questions of posttraditional identity. This patriotism has an interpretation of the constitutional norms of citizenship which supervenes national destinies while allowing them to enter along with their national differences under this interpretation. Democratic constitutions represent universal norms; nevertheless, these norms, in turn, interpret the historically concrete experience of personal and cultural identities.

4. *In your reply to the theological reception of communicative ethics, you argue with Kierkegaard against theological criticisms of you. You portray three options of how one can discourse about the wholly other after Kierkegaard. Either one is a Protestant theologian, appealing to his or her private faith, and then, while in a privatized context, one cannot enter discourse ethics; or one translates faith into scientific terminology and social action and becomes a modernist Catholic theologian, and then one has lost the contents of faith as anything distinct from validity claims and their secular value spheres; or one resorts to demythologization and becomes a methodological atheist, and then religious discourses are not distinguishable from the nontheistic contexts of communicative ethics. Either religious claims are untranslatable, so that they cannot be redeemed in discourse, or they are wholly translatable, so that they are not distinctly religious claims. Is there not a formal*

equivalent to the Kierkegaardian existential mode of communication that represents an alternative to these three possibilities that you offer?[12]

First, Habermas thought for a moment that perhaps I was asking as a theologian, and so he suggested that I should answer my own question, which he as a philosopher and social critic could not tackle. I explained that my question had little theological interest. Rather, I picked up on Habermas's own argument and followed its immanent implications. I sought out the formal equivalents to Kierkegaard's vertically oriented existential pathos of communication. Such equivalents do not need to rely on the substantive contents of Kierkegaard's Christian religiosity "B." A Kierkegaardian formal corrective lies in a parallel to the formalism of Habermas's communicative egalitarianism. Both thinkers bracket substantive frameworks: Kierkegaard's "how" of communication does not rely on Christian doctrines; Habermas's communications theory does not depend on the substantive (e.g., Marxist) notions of material justice.[13]

It seemed to me that Habermas, leaning on Kierkegaard's irony, quite effectively disarmed both the negative theological objections to and the positive theistic uses of communicative ethics. Yet I was not convinced that Habermas's argument affected Kierkegaard's own posture, which itself does not rely on a theology. Habermas did not have an answer to my question about the ramifications of his use of Kierkegaard to critique dogmatic or demythologizing atheologies.

5. *T. Hviid Nielsen, in his question to you, seems to imply that the neo-Kantian morality you have worked out in intersubjective and procedural terms comprises if not presupposes Kierkegaard's radical self-choice. In your attempt to outline a collective life form that would socially integrate the existential individual, you appear to suggest that this can be accomplished in a "mode of public, discursive struggle" such as constitutional patriotism. Do you recognize anything that Kierkegaard's existential mode and the procedural form of communicative ethics have in common? Are there existential, Kierkegaardian elements in the project of communicative ethics?[14]*

Habermas replied in terms reminiscent of his handling of the first question. He affirmed the complementarity between collective identity formation and existential self-choice. He clarified this point by drawing a contrast: we often have today the asymmetrical situation where the postconventional procedural rationality of moral discourses corresponds to a conventional ethic on the level of individual and collective identities. Now such an asymmetry must always limit the effective realization of the ideal presuppositions of communicative ethics. It follows that the regulative ideal of autonomy and reciprocity requires a postconventional existential ethic.

By Habermas's affirmation, I argued that an existential mode, on the level of identity formation, embodies the concrete personal and cultural condition of the possibility for carrying out the ideality of moral discourses: not only is Kierkegaard's existential individual sustained and integrated socially through reciprocal recognition by the public forum of the universal communication community; the reverse must be also true. Without Kierkegaard's corrective to herd religiosity and to aestheticizing and nationalist identity formation, the regulative ideal of communicative ethics remains existentially ineffective.

6. *Do you agree with postmodern receptions of Kierkegaard? Could not one develop a strong Kierkegaardian argument against a postmodern thesis of the ubiquity of power (Foucault) or the aestheticizing view of human relations, friendship, or the postmodern asymmetry of noncommunication (Derrida)?*

To the first question Habermas answered no; to the second, yes.

7. *Do you have plans or suggestions about how to work out these implicit Kierkegaardian themes more explicitly?*

Habermas indicated that he has this project on his agenda. Through the communicative paradigm, he wants to work out a secular reading of Kierkegaard's existential ethic. I asked him whether he would be sympathetic to the moves that the later Horkheimer made when he defined critical theory by its relation to the wholly other. Habermas does not share two premises in the later Horkheimer's formally vertical approach: his rejection of the rational basis for morality, and, connected with it, the adoption of noncognitivist recourse to dialectical atheism. We did not discuss further a Kierkegaardian possibility—whether one could keep the rational and cognitivist basis of communicative ethics, and yet be in need of an existential corrective to its critical theory.[15]

8. *What do you think of Václav Havel's term "permanent existential revolution" as applied to the events of November 1989 in Czechoslovakia? How would you relate this "inter-existentiality" of Havel to your term* Nachholende Revolution, *or to "permanent democratic revolution," which you describe under constitutional patriotism?*[16]

Habermas responded with sympathy to Havel, but he was disturbed by Havel's mixing the personal relation with Pope John Paul II during a pastoral visit to Czechoslovakia and Havel's Presidency. I explained that Havel's vertically oriented community ideal, which he does not hide away from the horizontal public sphere, should not be understood in substantive terms of a church or religious affiliation, but rather within a broader, formal, philosophical frame of the specific central-eastern European experience of resisting Communist totality.

One could relate better to Havel's existential posture if one recalled that for the later Horkheimer dialectical atheism is based on the experience that both theism and atheism have their martyrs and tyrants. In authoritarian states, atheism is the sign of courage; in totalitarian systems, theism plays the same role since here atheism is fanatically intolerant. Hope lies neither in the validity domains of theism nor in those of atheism but rather in the mode of existing among those who became the victims of history. They share a community ideal projected by their resistance to totalitarian power and ideology. In today's central-eastern European context, Havel's vertical orientation—by qualifying immanently the notions of autonomy, ordinary communication, and the projected ideal—provides an existential critique of nationalism, authoritarianism, fundamentalism, and totalitarianism.[17]

More generally, Habermas worries that even noncommunist leftism, to which he appeals, might not have at this time a receptive audience in central-eastern Europe. I noted that today in these lands one became tired of the categories like "socialism" and "leftism" as much as one was once tired of "Christianity" and "religion" after Europeans ended the Thirty-Year War of religion. Habermas added that this tiredness need not be a cause for melancholy despair among the leftists, but rather can occasion a transformation of the classical meaning of the words like "socialism."[18]

I suggested that another comparison in reading our situation in the present age lies at hand: with Kierkegaard one had to appropriate one's existence apart from the substantive structures of Christendom and of its religious or national mass cultures. All these contents were required to pass through the existential category of the individual. Analogically, social activists today can sustain their action only posttraditionally. They must learn to act as those capable of deliberation in democratic procedures and not be co-opted by the mass orthodoxies, the violent revolutionary ethics, and the propagandist catechisms.

From Habermas's explanation,[19] it seems obvious that on the grounds of constitutional patriotism, one could incite only with difficulty a violent revolution or patriotic gore. One should find it problematic to promote a heroic–nationalist frenzy or lay down one's life for such a postnational patriotism. Being patriotic in a sobered up sense should not invite any new repetition of the religiously, nationally, and revolutionary motivated wars. Posttraditional identity should call for another New World Order than that based on imperial peace.

Yet, can both this deliberative "should" and this procedural expectation of nonviolent consensus be safeguarded without integrating permanent democratic revolution with permanent existential revolution? Are not these the two necessary modes of permanent resistance to nationalism, fundamentalism, authoritarianism, and totalitarianism—the two mutually corrective forms of critique? Does not such resistance to self- and other-deceptive uses of legitimate power to further imperial consensus require that communicative ethics be, in principle, complemented by a materially concrete existential ethics as the condition of its very sobriety?[20]

Abbreviations and Bibliography for the Primary Works Cited in Notes

I n the Notes, numbers directly following an abbreviation refer to the page numbers of the English translation. If a volume number is necessary, it is followed by a colon and the page numbers. Numbers (with an abbreviation, if appropriate) following a slash refer to the volume (where necessary) and pages of the German, Czech, or Danish original. Abbreviations of the original title indicate that the original German or Czech text was used, even when the pages of the published translation are first noted.

JÜRGEN HABERMAS

For other bibliographies about Habermas, consult Thomas McCarthy's *The Critical Theory of Jürgen Habermas* (q.v.), René Görtzen's bibliography in David M. Rasmussen's *Reading Habermas* (q.v.), and Michael Zilles's bibliography in Rasmussen, Ed., *Universalism vs. Communitarianism* (q.v.).

AG "Das Absolute und die Geschichte: Von der Zwiespältigkeit in Schellings Denken." Ph.D. dissertation, Universität Bonn, 24 February 1954.

AI "Arbeit und Interaktion: Bemerkungen zu Hegels Jenenser Philosophie des Geistes." In H. Braun and M. Riedel, Eds., *Festschrift: Natur und Geschichte: Karl Löwith zum 70. Geburtstag*. Stuttgart: W. Kohlhammer, 1967, 132–155.

CD "Civil Disobedience: Litmus Test for the Democratic Constitutional State." *Berkeley Journal of Sociology* 30 (1985) 95–116. ["Ziviler Ungehorsam—Testfall für den demokratischen Rechtsstaat." In NU (q.v.), 77–99.]

CES *Communication and the Evolution of Society*. Trans. Thomas McCarthy. Boston: Beacon Press, 1979. [An incomplete trans. of ZRHM (q.v.).]

E "A Reply." In Axel Honneth and Hans Joas, Eds., *Communicative Action: Essays on Jürgen Habermas's "The Theory of Communicative Action."* Trans. Jerry Gaines and Doris L. Jones. Cambridge, Mass: MIT Press, 1990, 214–264. ["Entgegnung." In Honneth and Joas, Eds., *Kommunikatives Handeln* (q.v.) 327–405.]

EAS *Eine Art Schadensabwicklung: Kleine Politische Schriften VI.* Frankfurt a/M: Suhrkamp, 1987. [A partial trans. is NC (q.v.).]

EzD *Erläuterungen zur Diskursethik.* Frankfurt a/M: Suhrkamp, 1991.

FuG *Faktizität und Geltung: Beiträge zur Diskurstheorie des Rechts und des demokratischen Rechtsstaats.* Frankfurt a/M: Suhrkamp, 1992.

GS "Justice and Solidarity: On the Discussion Concerning 'Stage 6'." In Michael Kelly, Ed., *Hermeneutics and Critical Theory* (q.v.), 32–52. ["Gerechtigkeit und Solidarität: Eine Stellungnahme zur Diskussion über 'Stufe 6'." In Wolfgang Edelstein and Gertrud Nunner-Winkler, Eds., *Zur Bestimmung der Moral* (q.v.), 291–318.]

HRPS "Human Rights and Popular Sovereignty." Public lecture at Northwestern University (23 September 1992). Manuscript. [This lecture began with a new systematic reference to Kierkegaard with which Habermas goes beyond the Exkursus in FuG (q.v.) 124–135.]

ICI "An Intersubjectivist Concept of Individuality." Paper presented at the World Congress of Philosophy, Brighton, England (24 August 1988). Manuscript. [This is a partial English version of the Mead essay in ND (q.v.), 149–204/187–241. The presented paper does not include Habermas's Kierkegaard discussion.]

KFnT "Kommunikative Freiheit und Negative Theologie." In Emil Angehrn, Hinrich Fink-Eitel, Christian Iber, and Georg Lohmann, Eds., *Dialektischer Negativismus: Michael Theunissen zum 60. Geburtstag.* Frankfurt a/M: Suhrkamp, 1992, 15–34.

KHI *Knowledge and Human Interests.* Trans. Jeremy J. Shapiro. Boston: Beacon Press, 1971. [*Erkenntnis und Interesse.* Frankfurt a/M: Suhrkamp, 1968.]

KK *Kultur und Kritik: Verstreute Aufsätze.* Frankfurt a/M: Suhrkamp, 1973.

LC *Legitimation Crisis.* Trans. Thomas McCarthy. Boston: Beacon Press, 1975. [*Legitimationsprobleme im Spätkapitalismus.* Frankfurt a/M: Suhrkamp, 1973.]

LM "Law and Morality." In Sterling M. McMurrin, Ed., *The Tanner Lectures On Human Values.* Vol. 8. Cambridge: Cambridge University Press, 1988, 219–279.

MkH *Moral Consciousness and Communicative Action.* Trans. Christian Lenhardt and Shierry Weber Nicholsen. Cambridge, Mass.: MIT Press, 1990. [*Moralbewußtsein und kommunikatives Handeln.* Frankfurt a/M: Suhrkamp, 1983.]

MS "Morality and Ethical Life: Does Hegel's Critique of Kant Apply to Discourse Ethics?" Added in the English trans. of MkH (q.v.), 195–215. ["Moralität und Sittlichkeit: Treffen Hegels Einwände gegen Kant auch die Diskursethik zu?" In Wolfgang Kuhlmann, Ed., *Moralität und Sittlichkeit* (q.v.), 16-37.]

NC *The New Conservatism: Cultural Criticism and the Historians' Debate.* Ed. and Trans. Shierry Weber Nicholsen. Intro. Richard Wolin. Cambridge, Mass.: MIT Press, 1989. [An incomplete ed. of NU and EAS (q.v.), with the 1987 Copenhagen lecture, additional essays, and intro. to Viktor Farias's *Heidegger und der Nationalsozialismus* (q.v.).]

ND *Postmetaphysical Thinking: Philosophical Essays.* Trans. William Mark Hohengarten. Cambridge, Mass.: MIT Press, 1992. [*Nachmetaphysisches Denken: Philosophische Aufsätze.* Frankfurt a/M: Suhrkamp, 1988.]

NR *Die nachholende Revolution: Kleine politische Schriften VII.* Frankfurt a/M: Suhrkamp, 1990.

NU *Die Neue Unübersichtlichkeit.* Frankfurt a/M: Suhrkamp, 1985.

OSSA *Observation on "The Spiritual Situation of the Age."* Ed. and Intro. Jürgen Habermas. Trans. Andrew Buchwalter. Cambridge, Mass.: MIT Press, 1984. [*Stichworte zur "Geistige Situation der Zeit."* Frankfurt a/M: Suhrkamp, 1979.]

PDM *The Philosophical Discourse of Modernity: Twelve Lectures.* Trans. Frederick Lawrence. Cambridge, Mass.: MIT Press, 1987. [*Der philosophische Diskurs der Moderne: Zwölf Vorlesungen.* Frankfurt a/M: Suhrkamp, 1985, 1988.]

PPP *Philosophical–Political Profiles.* Trans. Frederick Lawrence. Cambridge, Mass: MIT Press, 1983. [*Philosophisch–politische Profile.* Frankfurt a/M: Suhrkamp, 1971, 1981].

PwR "Der Philosopher als wahrer Rechtslehrer: Rudolf Wiethölter." *Kritische Justiz* 22 (1989) 138–156.

RC "A Reply to My Critics." In John B. Thompson and David Held, Eds., *Habermas: Critical Debates.* Cambridge, Mass.: MIT Press, 1982, 219-283. ["Replik auf Einwände" (1980). In VTKH (q.v.), 475–569.]

SnI "Citizenship and National Identity: Some Reflections on the Future of Europe." *Praxis International* 12/1 (April 1992) 1–19. ["Staatsburgerschaft und nationale Identität: Überlegungen zur Europäischen Zukunft." Paper presented at the conference on "Identity and Difference in Democratic Europe," European Commission, Brussels (23–25 May 1991). In FuG (q.v.), 632–660.]

TAHP "Taking Aim at the Heart of the Present." In David Couzins Hoy, Ed., *Foucault: A Critical Reader.* Oxford: Blackwell, 1986, 103–108.

TCA *The Theory of Communicative Action.* Trans. Thomas McCarthy. Boston: Beacon Press. Vol. 1. *Reason and the Rationalization of Society,* 1984. Vol. 2. *Lifeworld and System: A Critique of Functionalist Reason,* 1987. [*Theorie des kommunikativen Handelns.* Frankfurt a/M: Suhrkamp. Band 1. *Handlungsrationalität und gesellschaftliche Rationalisierung,* 1981. Band 2. *Zur Kritik der funktionalistichen Vernunft,* 1985.]

TCRW "Towards a Communication-Concept of Rational Collective Will-Formation: A Thought Experiment." *Ratio Juris* 2/2 (July 1989) 144–154.

TGS *Theorie der Gesellschaft oder Sozialtechnologie—Was leistet die Systemforschung?* Written by Habermas and Niklas Luhmann. Frankfurt a/M: Suhrkamp, 1971, 1985.

TP *Theory and Practice*. Trans. John Viertel. Boston: Beacon Press, 1974. [This trans. is an abridged ed. of *Theorie und Praxis*. Frankfurt a/M: Suhrkamp, 1971. The English trans. of TP includes in addition AI (q.v.).]

TuK *Texte und Kontexte*. Frankfurt a/M: Suhrkamp, 1991.

ÜMS "Über Moralität und Sittlichkeit—Was macht eine Lebensform rational?" In Herbert Schnädelbach, Ed., *Rationalität: Philosophische Beiträge*. Frankfurt a/M: Suhrkamp, 1984, 218–235.

V "Vorwort zur Neuaflage." In *Strukturwandel der Öffentlichkeit*. Frankfurt a/M: Suhrkamp, 1990, 11–50.

VaZ *Vergangenheit als Zukunft*. Zürich: Pendo, 1990.

VTKH *Vorstudien und Ergänzungen zur Theorie des kommunikativen Handelns*. Frankfurt a/M: Suhrkamp, 1984, 1989.

VV "Volkssouverentität als Verfahren: Ein normativer Begriff von Öffentlichkeit." In FuG (q.v.), 600–631. [Also in *Merkur* 6 (1989) 465–477 and in *Forum für Philosophie Bad Homburg*, Eds., *Die Idee von 1789*. Frankfurt a/M: Suhrkamp, 1989, 7–36.]

ZE "Zur Einführung." In Rainer Döbert, Jürgen Habermas, and Gertrud Nunner-Winkler, Eds., *Entwicklung des Ichs*. Königstein/Is: Athenäum, 1980, 9–30. [This introduction is authored by all three editors.]

zLB "Die zweite Lebenslüge der Bundesrepublik: Wir sind wieder 'normal' geworden," *Die Zeit*, No. 51 (11 December 1992) 48.

ZLS *Zur Logik der Sozialwissenschaften: Erweiterte Ausgabe*. Frankfurt a/M: Suhrkamp, 1982, 1985. [The German text is preferred to a shorter English ed.]

ZRHM *Zur Rekonstruktion des Historischen Materialismus*. Frankfurt a/M: Suhrkamp, 1976, 1982.

VÁCLAV HAVEL

For other bibliographies about Havel, consult Havel's Drs, H, LT, and Oli (q.v.).

AF *Angst vor der Freiheit: Reden des Staatspräsidenten*. Trans. Joachim Bruss and Hudrun Heissig. Ed. Ingke Brodersen. Reinbek bei Hamburg, 1991.

AH "Anatomie des Hasses." Paper presented at a conference sponsored by the Elie Wiesel Foundation (29 August 1990). In AF (q.v.), 118–130. [Reprinted in Vo (q.v.), 19–26.]

Cs The Copenhagen speech on the occasion of receiving Sonning's prize (Copenhagen University, 28 May 1991). "Politika není špinavá" [Politics is not dirty.] *Lidové noviny* (29 May 1991) 11. [Reprinted in Vo (q.v.), 81–85.]

Dv *Dálkový výslech: rozhovor s Karlem Hvížďálou*. Praha: Melantrich, 1989. [*Disturbing the Peace*. Trans. and Intro. Paul Wilson. New York: Random House, 1990.]

DO *Dopisy Olze*. (1983). Praha: Atlantis, 1990. [*Letters to Olga*. Intro. Paul Wilson. New York: Owl Books, Henry Holt, 1989.]

Drs *Do různých stran* [To Different Sides]. Praha: Lidové noviny, 1990. [Includes essays from 1983–1989 and the Bio-bibliography.]

EME "The End of the Modern Era." Paper presented at the World Economic Forum in Davos, Switzerland (4 February 1992). *New York Times* [Op-Ed], 1 March 1992, p. E-15. [Reprinted in Vo (q.v.), 147–151.]

H *Hry: Soubor her z let 1963–1988* [Collected Plays from 1963–1988]. Praha: Lidové noviny, 1991. [Includes the Bio-Bibliography.]

HL "Hovory z Lán" [Conversations from Lány]. Czechoslovak Radio. Sundays beginning in 1990 through 19 July 1992, and again from 31 January 1993 to the present.

IHW "In His Words: The Effort to Exercise Power in Accord with a Vision of Civility." *New York Times*, The Week in Review, 26 July 1992, p. E-7. [Edited excerpts from various recent speeches and essays.]

Jk "Jsou křivdy, které nelze napravit." [There Are Wrongs That Can't be Corrected]. *Respekt*, 2–8 March 1992, pp. 7–8. [An interview about the Czechoslovak–German relationship.]

LD *Largo Desolato*. Trans. and Adapt. Tom Stoppard. London: Grove-Weidenfeld, 1987.

Lp *Letní přemítání*. Praha: Odeon, 1991. [*Summer Meditations*. Trans. Paul Wilson. New York: Knopf, 1992.]

LT *Living in Truth: Twenty-Two Essays Published on the Occasion of the Award of the Erasmus Prize to Václav Havel.* Ed. Jan Ladislav. London: Faber & Faber, 1986, 1990. [Includes the Bio-bibliography.]

Mb "Moc bezmocných" (1978). In Oli (q.v.), 55–133. ["The Power of the Powerless." In LT (q.v.), 36–122.]

Np "Nejistota posiluje" [Uncertainty Gives Strength]. *Mladý svět* 33/19 (1991) 16–17, 26. [Interview.]

Oli *O lidskou identitu* [For Human Identity]. Praha: Rozmluvy, 1990. [Includes essays from 1969–1979 and the Bio-bibliography.]

P *Projevy* [Speeches]. Praha: Vyšehrad, 1990. [Includes his Jerusalem speech, "Kafka and My Presidency," upon receiving an honorary doctorate from the Hebrew University (26 April 1990), 100–103, in AF (q.v.), 52–55, and the welcoming speech for Richard von Weizsäcker, the President of Germany, on the anniversary of Hitler's invasion of Czechoslovakia (Praha, 15 March 1990), 79–86 in AF (q.v.), 41–50.]

PCN "The Post-Communist Nightmare." A commencement speech at George Washington University, Washington D.C., April 22, 1993. Trans. Paul Wilson. *The New York Review of Books*, 27 May 1993, 8, 10.

PH "The Paradoxes of Help." *New York Times* [Op-Ed], 14 July 1991, p. E-19.

PL "Paradise Lost." Trans. Paul Wilson. *New York Review of Books*, 9 April, 1992, 6–8.

Ps "Politika a svědomí" (1984). In Drs (q.v.), 41–59. ["Politics and conscience." In LT (q.v.), 136–157.]

RNM "Rio and the New Millenium." *New York Times* [Op-Ed], 3 June 1992, p. A-15.

SI Speech on the anniversary of the Soviet invasion. Praha, Wenceslas Square (21 August 1990). *Lidové noviny* [Praha], 22 August 1990, pp. 1, 4. [Reprinted in Vo (q.v.), 16–18.]

Sos *Slovo o slovu* [Word about Word]. In *Friedenspreis des Deutschen Buchhandels 1989*. Frankfurt a/M: Buchhändler-Vereinigung, 1989.

Ss Salzburg speech, given at the opening of the Salzburg Music Festival. *Lidová demokracie* [Praha], 27 July 1990, pp. 1–2. [Reprinted in Vo (q.v.), 9–13. "Angst vor der Freiheit," in AF (q.v.), 99–108.]

uR "Die unvollendete Revolution: Václav Havel im Gespräch mit Adam Michnik." *Transit: Europäische Revue* 4 (Summer 1992) 7–26.

Vo *Vážení občané: Projevy červenec 1990–červenec 1992*. [Dear Citizens: Speeches July 1990–July 1992]. Praha: Lidové noviny, 1992. [Contains among others the following speeches: AH, Cs, EME, SI, and Ss (q.v.).]

SØREN KIERKEGAARD

References to Kierkegaard's JP are by year and section numbers; references to Kierkegaard's P are by volume numbers (roman numerals), year, and section numbers. For other bibliographies about Kierkegaard, consult Vol. 1 and distinct entries in JP (q.v.) and Bruce Kirmmse's *Kierkegaard in Golden Age Denmark* (q.v.).

AUCH (By Kierkegaard, 1854–1855). *Attack upon "Christendom."* Trans. Walter Lowrie. Princeton, N.J.: Princeton University Press, 1944.

CA (By Vigilius Haufniensis. Ed. Kierkegaard, 1844). *The Concept of Anxiety*. In KW (q.v.), Vol. 8 (1980).

COR *The Corsair Affair*. Trans. Howard V. Hong and Edna H. Hong. Princeton, N.J.: Princeton University Press, 1982.

CUP (By Johannes Climacus. Ed. Kierkegaard, 1846). *Concluding Unscientific Postscript to "Philosophical Fragments."* In KW (q.v.), Vols. 12.1 and 12.2 (1992).

DDE (By Johannes Climacus, 1842–1843). *De Omnibus Dubitandum Est*. In KW (q.v.), Vol. 7 (1985).

E/O (By Victor Eremita, 1843). *Either/Or*. Vols. 1 and 2. In KW (q.v.), Vols. 3 and 4 (1987).

EUD (By Kierkegaard, 1843–1845). *Eighteen Upbuilding Discourses*. In KW (q.v.), Vol. 5 (1990).

FT (By Johannes de silentio, 1843). *Fear and Trembling*. In KW (q.v.), Vol. 6 (1983).

GW *Søren Kierkegaard: Gesammelte Werke*. Vols. 1–36. Trans. Emanuel Hirsch. Köln: Eugen Diederichs, 1952–1969.

JP *Journals and Papers*. 7 Vols. Trans. Howard V. Hong and Edna H. Hong, assisted by Gregor Malantschuk, and with Index, 7, by Nathaniel Hong and Charles Baker. Bloomington: Indiana University Press, 1967–1978.

KW *Kierkegaard's Writings*. Ed. and Trans. with Intro. and Notes Howard V. Hong and Edna H. Hong, Henrik Rosenmeier, Reidar Thomte, Albert Anderson, et al. 26 Vols. (projected). Princeton, N.J.: Princeton University Press, 1978– .

P *Søren Kierkegaard's Papirer*, Vols. I–XI³, Ed. P. A. Heiberg, V. Kuhr, and E. Tortsing, 1st edition. Copenhagen: Gylendal, 1909–1948. Vols. XI–XIII, Ed. Niels Thulstrup, 2nd edition with two supplemental Vols. Copenhagen: Gylendal, 1968–1970, with Index. Vols. XIV–XVI, Ed. N. J. Cappelørn. Copenhagen: Gylendal, 1975–1978.

PF (By Johannes Climacus. Ed. Kierkegaard, 1844). *Philosophical Fragments*. In KW (q.v.), Vol. 7 (1985).

PC (By Anti-Climacus. Ed. Kierkegaard, 1850). *Practice in Christianity*. In KW (q.v.), Vol. 20 (1991).

Pr (By Nicolaus Notabene, 1844). *Prefaces: Light Reading for Certain Classes as the Occasion May Require*. Foreword Marc C. Taylor. Trans. and Intro. William McDonald. Tallahassee: Florida State University Press, 1989.

PVA (By Kierkegaard, posthum. publ. 1859). *The Point of View for My Work as an Author*. [Includes (by Kierkegaard, 1855), "'The Individual': Two 'Notes' Concerning My Work as an Author," and (by Kierkegaard, 1851) *My Activity as a Writer*.] Trans. Walter Lowrie. New York: Harper, 1939, 1962.

R (By Constantin Constantius, 1843). *Repetition*. In KW (q.v.), Vol. 6 (1983).

SD (By Anti-Climacus. Ed. Kierkegaard, 1849). *The Sickness unto Death*. In KW (q.v.), Vol. 19 (1980).

SLW (Ed. Hilarious Bookbinder, 1845). *Stages on Life's Way: Studies by Various Persons*. In KW (q.v.), Vol. 11 (1988).

SV *Søren Kierkegaard's Samlede Voerker*. Vols. I–XIV. Eds. A. B. Drachman, J. L. Heiberg, and H. O. Lange. Copenhagen: Gylendal, 1901–1906.

TA (By Kierkegaard, 1846). *Two Ages: The Age of Revolution and the Present Age. A Literary Review*. In KW (q.v.), Vol. 14 (1978).

WOL (By Kierkegaard, 1847). *Works of Love: Some Christian Reflections in the Form of Discourses*. Trans. Howard V. Hong and Edna H. Hong. New York: Harper & Row, 1962.

Notes

CHAPTER 1

1. Habermas, SnI; the shorter version of this paper was presented in English. The original, longer German text was discussed in Habermas's Frankfurt project, *Rechtstheorie*, one week after the Brussels conference. Among the participants at the conference were Ronald Dworkin, Jean-Marc Ferry, Jan Kis, Charles Taylor, and others. Among those who took part in the Frankfurt discussion were Kenneth Baynes, James Bohman, Helmut Dubiel, Peter Frankenberg, Klaus Günther, and others. Francis Fukuyama, *The End of History and the Last Man* (New York: Free Press, 1992). Max Horkheimer and Theodor W. Adorno, *Dialectic of Enlightenment* (1944), trans. John Cumming (New York: Continuum, 1987) xi. Cf. the debate that followed Rüdiger Bubner's presentation, "Brauchen wir einen Begriff der Nation?", in the Philosophy Department of J. W. Goethe-Universität, Frankfurt a/M (June 1991, manuscript). Cf. also the lectures, "Nationen in schlechter Verfassung: Nationalismen nach der Perestrojka," at Palais Jalta (Frankfurt, a/M, 21 April–30 June 1991).

2. For constructions of the phobia of political correctness, see Arthur M. Schlesinger, Jr., *The Disuniting of America* (New York: Norton, 1992); Paul Bergman, ed., *Debating P.C.: The Controversy over Political Correctness on College Campuses* (New York: Laurel Books, 1992).

3. See Timothy Garton Ash, *The Uses of Adversity: Essays on the Fate of Central Europe* (Cambridge: Granta Books, 1991). Cf. Habermas's urgency with that of Jacques Derrida in the paper given at the conference on "The Cultural Identity of Europe," 20 May 1990, published in *L'autre cap* (Paris: Gallimard, 1991), trans. by Pascale-Anne Brault and Michael B. Naas as *The Other Heading: Reflections on Today's Europe* (Bloomington: Indiana University Press, 1992) 5f., 61ff.

4. Habermas, SnI 3/FuG 634f. Cf. Derrida's defense of the Enlightenment ideas of 1789—universal human and civil rights—along with a defense of the universal inscribed with the singular. Derrida argues for "the double duty" of going beyond Eurocentrism and anti-Eurocentrism, nationalism and homogenization of cultures, and the oppositional politics of identity and difference (*The Other Heading* 9, 29, 39, 44, 47f., 73ff., 76–80, and trans. Intro. *xxi, xlvi, lvii*); he critiques both Fukuyama (32) and Habermas (54f., 96ff.) for overlooking one aspect of this duty.

Abbreviations used in the notes and bibliography for the works of Habermas, Havel, and Kierkegaard are spelled out in full in Appendix B, pp. 265–271.

5. Habermas, NC 260f./EAS 172f. In the Preface above, I define the *crisis individual* as the one who experiences the breakdown of the traditional ways in which his or her identity-formation can be justified. The existential individual mounts this crisis of identity with radical honesty.

6. Habermas, VV in FuG 609, 626–630.

7. Habermas, NR 177–204; Havel, Drs 51, 67, 202ff. See Seyla Benhabib's editor's reply, *Praxis International* 11/1 (April 1991) 1–6, to Helmut Dubiel, "Beyond Mourning and Melancholia on the Left," *Praxis International* 10/3–4 (October 1990– January 1991) 241–249; my "Havel and Habermas on Identity and Revolution" (261– 277); and other essays from volume 10/3–4. See also Claus Offe, "Bindung, Fessel, Bremse," in Axel Honneth, Thomas McCarthy, Claus Offe, and Albrecht Wellmer, eds., *Zwischenbetrachtungen: Im Prozeß der Aufklärung* (Frankfurt a/M: Suhrkamp, 1989). The term *non-communist leftist* comes from Maurice Merleau-Ponty, last chap. of *Adventures of the Dialectic*, trans. Joseph Bien (Evanston, Ill.: Northwestern University Press, 1973). (See Chap. 10, n. 44, below.)

8. Cf. Erikson's study of adolescent crises with Habermas's LC on the legitimation and motivation crises of late capitalism. Erik H. Erikson, *Identity and the Life Cycle: Selected Papers* (New York: International Universities Press, 1959) and *Insight and Responsibility: Lectures on the Ethical Implications of Psychoanalytic Insight* (New York: Norton, 1964). See also Jerald Wallulis, *The Hermeneutics of Life History: Personal Achievement and History in Gadamer, Habermas, and Erikson* (Evanston, Ill.: Northwestern University Press, 1990).

9. Habermas, ZRHM 92ff., TCA 2: chap. 5. See Chap. 4, section 4.1.B, and Chap. 5, section 5.1, of the present volume.

10. Habermas, ZRHM 106; TCA 2:109f./167f.; ND 165–170/203–209.

11. On the first two points, see Habermas on Kierkegaard, NC/EAS; on Wittgenstein, TCA 2: chap. 5, section 5.1.C; and on identity and individuation, TCA 2: chap. 5, section 5.3.D. On the third point, see "Transzendenz von innen, Transzendenz ins Diesseits" in TuK 138f., where he addresses the theologians. I disagree with the readings of Kierkegaard by Alasdair MacIntyre, *After Virtue: A Study in Moral Theory* (London: Duckworth, 1985–1987) and Charles Taylor, *Sources of the Self: The Making of the Modern Identity* (Cambridge: Cambridge University Press, 1989).

12. Habermas, NC 261/EAS 172; AG, Part I.

13. Habermas, MkH 45, 98ff./55, 108ff. These corollaries are crucial if we want to differentiate Habermas's position from those critiqued by the communitarians such as A. MacIntyre and C. Taylor. Cf. C. B. Macpherson, *The Political Theory of Possessive Individualism: Hobbes to Locke* (Oxford: Clarendon Press, 1962) and Michael Sandel, *Liberalism and Its Critics* (New York: New York University Press, 1984) and *Liberalism and the Limits of Justice* (Cambridge: Cambridge University Press, 1982).

14. Merold Westphal, *Kierkegaard's Critique of Reason and Society* (Macon, Ga.: Mercer University Press, 1987) 32; on Habermas, 41, 43, 57 n. 53, 117–120.

15. Habermas, ND 164/203, cites Kierkegaard (SD/SV 11, Part 1, sections A, a), where Kierkegaard's definition of the self occurs.

16. See Westphal, *Kierkegaard's Critique* 30ff.

17. Kierkegaard, FT 54ff./SV 3:104ff.; PC 85–94/SV 12:81–89; Habermas, AG, Part I. Bruce H. Kirmmse depicts a portrait of Kierkegaard as a radical egalitarian

critical of both liberals and conservatives of his day in *Kierkegaard in Golden Age Denmark* (Indiana Series in the Philosophy of Religion, ed. Merold Westphal) (Bloomington: Indiana University Press, 1990). (See Chap. 10 below.)

18. Habermas, MS; MkH 98ff./108ff.; ÜMS; PDM, lectures I–III; AI.

19. Habermas, ZRHM 94 n. 4; cf. TP, chap. 4, 297 n. 11/AI 154 n. 10; TCA 2: chap. 5; MkH 65f./75 and n. 40; PDM, lecture XI; GS 38ff., 44/299ff., 307. (I shall return to Habermas's reading of Kant and Hegel in Chap. 2 and to his appropriation of Mead in Chap. 4 below.)

20. Habermas, ND 164, 22–26/203, 31–34 (my translation); TCA 1:I, sec. 3.

21. Habermas, NC 261f./EAS 173f.

22. Habermas, NC 260/EAS 171f.

23. Habermas, ND 164/203 (my translation); NC 263/EAS 174f.

24. Habermas, ND 165/204 (my translation). For Karl-Otto Apel's unhappy complementary scheme of objectivist scientism and subjectivist existentialism, under which he lumps Kierkegaard with Weber, see his books (from Frankfurt a/M: Suhrkamp): *Transformation der Philosophie*, Vol. 2 (1973) 177, 369f., 376; *Der Denkweg von Ch. S. Peirce* (1967) 14ff., 103ff., 354; and *Diskurs und Verantwortung: Das Problem des Übergangs zur postkonventionellen Moral* (1988) 15–41, 56, 88ff.

25. Habermas, TuK 138f.; he proclaims a temporary truce between sacred and profane domains in ND 15, 25f., 51, 144f./23, 34, 60, 185; VV in FuG 630f.; and fig. 28 in TCA 2. See Edmund Arens, ed., *Habermas und die Theologie: Beiträge zur theologischen Rezeption, Diskussion und Kritik der Theorie kommunikativen Handelns* (Düsseldorf: Patmos, 1989). On alternative uses of methodological atheism, see Peter L. Berger, *The Sacred Canopy* (Garden City: Doubleday, 1967); Merold Westphal, *God, Guilt, and Death: An Existential Phenomenology of Religion* (Bloomington: Indiana University Press, 1984); Westphal, "Taking Suspicion Seriously: The Religious Uses of Modern Atheism," *Faith and Philosophy* 4/1 (January 1987) 26–42. (Cf. n. 11 above.)

26. Habermas, NC 260f./EAS 173 and my earlier citation of this question.

27. See Habermas, ND 167/206, 165/203f.; TCA 2:58f./93.

28. Habermas, ND 188/228, VV, TCRW, LC. (Cf. n. 8 above.)

29. Habermas, ÜMS 221–225, 234.

30. Habermas, TCRW; TuK 127ff.; TCA 1:287/387; TCA 2:46, 52/74, 83.

31. Kierkegaard, SD 79/SV 11:191, and Habermas, ND 166f./204f. (my translation).

32. Habermas, ND 167/206 (my translation).

33. The proposal to profanize Kierkegaard's existential discourse in itself is not original. In the framework of this study, I cannot compare Habermas's translation of Kierkegaard's either/or into social terms with the world-immanent release from metaphysics of Heidegger, the communicative model of existence in Jaspers, the nihilating action of Sartre, or the social phenomenology of Merleau-Ponty. My focus here and in Chap. 4 is on Habermas's translation of Kierkegaard under a sociological thesis of the linguistification of the sacred.

34. Habermas, ND 165/204 (my translation).

35. Habermas, ND 24f./33f.

36. Habermas, ND 25f./34; VV in FuG 608f.; Kierkegaard, SD 41f./SV 11:153f. and CUP. On *das ganz Andere*, see Max Horkheimer, *Gesammelten Schriften*, Vol. 7

(Frankfurt a/M: Fischer, 1985) 182–186, 429–434. On Horkheimer, see Habermas, TuK 91–126; Seyla Benhabib, "Feminism and Postmodernism: An Uneasy Alliance," *Praxis International* 11/2 (July 1991) 147.

37. Habermas, NC 251, 259, 261/EAS 163, 171, 173; on Havel, see Chap. 8 below.

38. Habermas, NC 252/EAS 163f.

39. Habermas, NC 253f./EAS 165 and citation from SnI 3/FuG 634.

40. Habermas, NC 255ff./EAS 167ff. Translation is just as misleading as is the Anglo-American fusion of "nation" and "state": if Habermas argued for a citizenship in a "nation" he would be a nationalist; he refers to a citizenship in a "state." See Jean-Marc Ferry's interview with Habermas in David Rasmussen, ed., *Universalism vs. Communitarianism* (Cambridge, Mass.: MIT Press, 1990) 207ff.

41. Habermas, NC 257/EAS 169. I want to stress these anti-imperial implications of Habermas's theory, rather than focus on his dubious claim that the 1991 allied intervention against Iraq was justified by the rational core of the consensus reached within the U.N. (VaZ 9–44). We need to ask whether consensual procedures alone can remain radically sober against succumbing to their own homogenizing oversights. See Derrida's *The Other Heading* 29, 47f., 75–80.

42. Habermas, NC 257ff./EAS 169ff.

43. Habermas, NC 259ff./EAS 171ff.

44. Habermas, NC 261f./EAS 173f. On the existential crisis individual, see Habermas's reply to Weber's rationalization paradox and to Horkheimer and Adorno, *Dialectic of Enlightenment*; cf. Habermas, TCA 1: chaps. 2 and 4, and PDM, lecture V.

45. Habermas, NC 263, 266/EAS 175, 178 (my translation). This conclusion takes a disjunctive, existential posture of the Kierkegaardian either/or against Hegelian mediating, rhetorical posture of both/and ("Sowohl-Als-Auch"—EAS 178).

46. He critiques the type of modern communitarianism exhibited by C. Taylor and R. Bubner. (See the references in n. 1 above.)

47. Habermas, SnI 2–7/FuG 633–643; cf. TCA 2:353ff./519–522. Not only Habermas, in his critique of nationalism as a second-generation bourgeois ideology, but also contemporary debates correct the error of conflating nationhood with nationalism. Gellner critiques the nationalist claim that citizenship must equal culture: nation and state are two separate units that coincide only with nationalist voluntarism. Hobsbawm argues that it is not nations that give rise to states and fuel nationalist aspirations, but rather it is nationalism that originates "nation" as a socially and politically constructed category: "nationalism comes before nations." Ernest Gellner, *Nations and Nationalism* (Ithaca, N.Y.: Cornell University Press, 1983) 11, 55; E. J. Hobsbawm, *Nations and Nationalism since 1780: Programme, Myth, Reality* (Cambridge: Cambridge University Press, 1990) 9f.; cf. Johann P. Arnason, "Nationalism, Globalization, and Modernity," *Theory, Culture and Society* 7/2–3 (June 1990) 207–236.

48. Habermas, SnI 1/FuG 632f., cf. zLB.

49. Habermas, SnI 7, 12, 17f./FuG 642f., 650f., 658 ff.. He comments on C. Taylor's different position, "Cross-Purposes: The Liberal–Communitarian Debate," in Nancy Rosenblum, ed., *Liberalism and the Moral Life* (Cambridge, Mass.: Harvard University Press, 1989) 178f.

50. Habermas, SnI 17f./FuG 659f.; cf. HRPS. Derrida's postmodern vision of society comes here much closer to Habermas's critical modernism than either thinker would let us believe (*The Other Heading* 47f., 54–57, 70–80).

51. On this weakness, see Habermas, LM 219–279. Derrida projects the possibility of radically open identities, too, but beyond a descriptive stance, he does not articulate the "how" of this openness (*The Other Heading* 9f., 29, 44, 72f., 75ff.)

CHAPTER 2

1. Habermas, MkH 97, 102/107, 112; Kierkegaard, PF. Cf. Wilfried Greve, *Kierkegaards maieutische Ethik* (Frankfurt a/M: Suhrkamp, 1990).

2. Habermas, GS 44f./307; MkH 128f., 142ff./139, 153ff.; MS 213 n.15/35 n.14.

3. "Hegel turns against the abstract universalism of justice, as this came to be expressed in the individualistic claims of modernity, in rational natural law, and also in Kantian ethics; he is equally decisive in rejection of the concrete particularism of general well-being, as this came to be expressed in Aristotle's *polis* ethic or in the Thomistic ethic of the good" (Habermas, MS 202/22; my translation). Cf. Ludwig Nagl, "Zeigt die Habermassche Kommunikationstheorie einen 'Ausweg aus der Subjektphilosophie'? Erwägungen zur Studie *Der Philosophische Diskurs der Moderne*," in Manfred Frank, Gérard Raulet, and Willem van Reijen, eds., *Die Frage nach dem Subjekt* (Frankfurt a/M: Suhrkamp, 1988) 346–372.

4. Habermas, MS 195f., 210/16f., 31; MkH 98ff./108ff.; PDM, lectures I–III. For Hegel's Kant critique, see Georg Wilhelm Friedrich Hegel, *Werke* (Frankfurt a/M: Suhrkamp, 1970): for the first objection, *Werke* Vol. 2 ("Über die wissenschaftliche Behandlungsarten des Naturrechts, seine Stelle in der praktischen Philosophie und sein Verhältnis zu den positiven Rechtswissenschaften") 460f.; for the second, *Werke* Vol. 3 (*Phänomenologie des Geistes*) 448, Vol. 2: 464, Vol. 7 (*Hegels Grundlinien der Philosophie des Rechts*) paragraph 135; for the third, *Werke* Vol. 2: 444; for the fourth, *Werke* Vol. 2: 289 and Vol. 3 ("Absolute Freedom and Terror"). Cf. Joachim Ritter, "Moralität und Sittlichkeit: Zu Hegels Auseinandersetzung mit der Kantischen Ethik," in M. Riedel, ed., *Materialien zu Hegels Rechtsphilosophie*, Vol. 2 (Frankfurt a/M: Suhrkamp, 1974); Dieter Henrich, ed., *Kant oder Hegel? Über Formen der Begründung in der Philosophie* (Stuttgart: Klett-Cotta, 1983); Karl-Otto Apel, "Kann der postkantische Standpunkt der Moralität noch einmal in substantielle Sittlichkeit "aufgehoben" werden?" in Wolfgang Kuhlmann, ed., *Moralität und Sittlichkeit* (Frankfurt a/M: Suhrkamp, 1986) 217–264; and Apel, *Diskurs und Verantwortung: Das problem Des Übergangs zur Postkonventionellen Moral* (Frankfurt a/M: Suhrkamp, 1988) 69–178, 306–369.

5. Habermas, MkH 43ff./53ff.; ÜMS; ZRHM 92ff.

6. See Nagl, "Zeigt die Habermassche," 351–366.

7. Hegel, "Entwürfe über Religion und Liebe" (1797–1798), in Hegel's *Werke*, Vol. 1: 244ff., 248. Cf. Paul Stern, "On the Relation between Rational Autonomy and Ethical Community: Hegel's Critique of Kantian Morality," *Praxis International* 9/3 (October 1989) 234–248.

8. Hegel's *Phänomenologie des Geistes*, paragraph 177, *Werke* Vol. 3: 140.

9. Merold Westphal, *History and Truth in Hegel's Phenomenology* (Atlantic Highlands, N.J.: Humanities Press, 1978) 81ff., 129–143.

10. Habermas, TP 144/AI 133f. See Chap. 4 below.

11. Habermas, TP 145/AI 134, translating a Kierkegaardian self-relation.

12. Habermas, TP 146f./AI 135 (my translation).

13. Jean Grondin, "Habermas und das Problem der Individualität," *Philosophische Rundschau* 36/3 (1989), notes that Habermas argues against the priority of the "We" to an "I" in order to prevent the charge of "collectivism" (202). Kierkegaard depicts "spirit" as an existential mode of both the individual and community (see Part II of this book and Kierkegaard, SD 13f./SV 11:127f.).

14. Nagl, "Zeigt die Habermassche," 347–372. Habermas, TCA 2:185/275.

15. Habermas, TP 150f./AI 138f. for all quotations below in this section.

16. Habermas, MS 207f./28f.

17. See Habermas, "Erläuterungen zur Diskursethik," in EzD 142f.

18. Habermas, PDM 29–41, 295, 337/39–55, 344f., 339.

19. Habermas, NR 126 and "Lawrence Kohlberg und der Neoaristotelianismus," in EzD 93.

20. Habermas, PDM 376, 359ff./434f., 416–419.

21. Habermas, "Kohlberg," in EzD 96–99.

22. Habermas, MkH 44/55; MS 201f./22f. (my translation).

23. Habermas, "Erläuterungen," in EzD 143ff.

24. See Habermas, "Erläuterungen," in EzD 145ff.; MS 213 n. 15/35 n. 14.

25. Habermas, "Erläuterungen," in EzD 148–152.

26. See Habermas, MS 204/25; "Erläuterungen," in EzD 136f.

27. Habermas, MS 205f./26f.; cf. "Kohlberg," in EzD 96.

28. Habermas, MS 207ff./28f.

29. Habermas, MS 209/29f. (my translation).

30. Habermas, MS 209f./31; CD/NU 79–99; LM 244f.

31. Habermas, LM 245, 224, 241–243. I cannot dwell here on M. Foucault's critique of morality and law. My recourse to Kierkegaard can be read as a reply to a Foucault-type objection that every moral symmetry is shot through with power asymmetries, that every form of modern law in its universal principles of justice institutionalizes disciplinary counterlaw. Can law sustain this circular link with morality without leaving both vulnerable to institutionalized deception?

32. Habermas, MS 205, 208f./26, 29.

33. Habermas, MkH 99f./110 (my translation) and NC 261/EAS 172.

34. Habermas, MkH 102/112.

35. There is an unresolved issue of *anamentic* reason, which was not raised by Hegel against Kant. How can communicative ethics compensate for sufferings and injustices of the past generations? Habermas admits these limits yet refuses to console philosophers: "Communicative ethics cannot reach back to an objective teleology, in particular, not to a power which could sublate the irreversibility of the results of historical events." Habermas, MS 210f./31f. (my translation). Cf. Edmund Arens, ed., *Habermas und die Theologie* (Dusseldorf: Patmos, 1989); Helmut Peukert, *Science, Action, and Fundamental Theology: Towards a Theology of Communicative Action*, trans. James Bohman (Cambridge, Mass.: MIT Press, 1984–1986); and Rudolf J. Siebert, *From Critical Theory to Communicative Political Theology: Universal Solidarity* (New York: Peter Lang, 1989).

36. Habermas, RC 261ff./VTKH 537–540; TGS 136–141.

37. Habermas, TGS 136–141. Against a concretistic reading of the regulative ideal, Habermas speaks now of pragmatic presuppositions where he before spoke about the ideal speech situation. Robert Alexy, "Eine Theorie des praktischen Diskurses," in W. Oelmüller, ed., *Normenbegründung, Normendurchsetzung* (Paderborn, 1978) 40, developed on the basis of Habermas's analysis the following *general rules of discourse*: "[1] Every subject with the competence to speak and act is allowed to take part in a discourse. [2a] Everyone is allowed to question any assertion whatever. [b] Everyone is allowed to introduce any assertion whatever into the discourse. [c] Everyone is allowed to express her attitudes, desires, and needs. [3] No speaker may, by internal or external coercion, be prevented from exercising her rights as laid down in [1] and [2]" in Habermas, MkH 89/99—(my translation). See also Karl-Otto Apel, "Das Apriori der Kommunikationsgemeinschaft und die Grundlagen der Ethik," in *Transformation der Philosophie*, Vol. 2 (Frankfurt a/M: Suhrkamp, 1973) 358–435.

38. Habermas, TGS 140f.; RC 261ff./VTKH 537–540.

39. Habermas, NU 228ff. Read Habermas's question to Kierkegaard through a pragmatist meaning of ideality: "I have understood from the beginning that American pragmatism—following Marx and Kierkegaard—represents the third productive answer to Hegel." (NU 215).

40. Habermas, MkH 126f./136f. Habermas follows Lawrence Kohlberg's six moral stages of development and corresponding six social perspectives (MkH 123ff./134ff.). Kohlberg, *Essays on Moral Development*, Vol. 1 (San Francisco: Harper and Row, 1981) 409ff.

41. Habermas, MkH 89, 133–141/99, 144–152; MS 197f./18; "Erläuterungen," in EzD 125–131; TCA 1: chaps. 1, 3; RC 263f./VTKH 540f.

42. Habermas, MkH 126f./136f. (my translation) for all quotations below; cf. NR 88, 194–203.

43. Habermas, NC 260f./EA 172f.

44. Habermas, MkH 184–187/195–199. See also John Michael Murphy and Carol Gilligan, "Moral Development in Late Adolescence and Adulthood: A Critique and Reconstruction of Kohlberg's Theory," *Human Development* 23 (1980) 77–104. Habermas notes that the transitional stage 4½ in Kohlberg's six-stage theory of moral development is difficult to classify: we have postconventional thinking mixed up either with context-sensitive ethic of the concrete other or with skeptical, relativist, and nihilist attitudes. The regression hypothesis does not explain the stabilization of this stage (in Gilligan's studies among some Harvard graduate females or in modern value skepticism). Habermas's two-alternative model, while coherent both with regard to the classification of the data and the theory explanation, does not further develop the gender-problematic and the possibility of a posttraditional ethic of the concrete other (RC 260f./VTKH 536f.).

45. Habermas, MkH 89f., 97/99f., 107 for the first two and again for both quotations below.

46. Habermas, MkH 93f., 121ff./103f., 132ff.; MS 196ff./17ff.

47. Habermas, MkH 65f., cf. 93, 121ff./75f., cf. 103, 132ff.; see also MS 197/18. Seyla Benhabib, in the Afterword to *The Communicative Ethics Controversy*, Benhabib and Fred Dallmayr, eds. (Cambridge, Mass.: MIT Press, 1990) 337, 344ff., argues that (U) adds nothing new to (D), which entails the principles of universal moral respect and of egalitarian reciprocity.

48. Habermas, MkH 66ff., 122/76ff., 132f. (my translation).

49. Habermas, MkH 125/136; to be consistent, I use a broader term "communicative ethics" instead of the translator's "discourse ethics."

50. Habermas, MS 199/20.

51. Habermas, MS 200f./21f. (my translation); GS 41ff., 46f./303ff., 310f.; "Erläuterungen," in EzD 173ff., 185–199.

52. Habermas, GS 47ff./311ff.

53. It is disappointing that Habermas did not adopt this posture against imperial solidarity and false universality in his view of the Persian Gulf War (VaZ 9–44).

54. Habermas, GS 43f./306, NR 142f. See Klaus Günther, *Der Sinn für Angemessenheit: Anwendungsdiskurse in Moral und Recht* (Frankfurt a/M: Suhrkamp, 1988) 176–197; and for the summary of this argument, Gunther, "Impartial Application or Moral and Legal Norms: A Contribution to Discourse Ethics," in David Rasmussen, ed., *Universalism vs. Communitarianism: Contemporary Debates in Ethics* (Cambridge, Mass.: MIT Press, 1990) 199–206.

55. Habermas, MkH 104/113; on "ethical–existential" see NR 118ff. and 126, 144; ÜMS; and GS. In Seyla Benhabib and Drucilla Cornell, eds., *Feminism and Critique: On the Politics of Gender* (Minneapolis: University of Minnesota Press, 1987), see Benhabib, "The Generalized and the Concrete Other: The Kohlberg–Gilligan Controversy and Feminist Theory" 77–95, and Nancy Fraser, "What's Critical about Critical Theory? The Case of Habermas and Gender" 31–55. On the ethic of care, see Virginia Held, "The Non-Contractual Society," *Canadian Journal of Philosophy*, Vol. 13 suppl. (1987), and Annette Baier, "The Need for More Than Justice," ibid.; both are cited in Will Kymlicka, "Two Theories of Justice," *Inquiry* 33/1 (March 1990) 119 n. 32. See also Sara Ruddick, "Maternal Thinking," *Feminist Studies* 6 (1980) 342–367.

CHAPTER 3

1. Habermas, NC 261/EAS 172f. See Chap. 1 above.

2. See Karl Marx, *Early Writings,* trans. Rodney Livinstone and Gregor Benton (New York: Vintage Books, 1975): "Critique of Hegel's Doctrine of the State" 57–198, and "A Contribution to the Critique of Hegel's Philosophy of Right" 243–257.

3. Habermas, ZRHM 97.

4. Axel Honneth, "Diskursethik und implizites Gerechtigkeitskonzept: Eine Diskussionsbemerkung," in Wolfgang Kuhlmann, ed., *Moralität und Sittlichkeit* (Frankfurt a/M: Suhrkamp, 1986) 192; and Honneth, *Kritik der Macht: Reflexionsstufen einer kritischen Gessellschaftstheorie* (Frankfurt a/M: Suhrkamp, 1986) 331, 334.

5. Habermas, TCA 2:374f./548f.

6. Habermas, E 223f., 245f., 253f., 292 n. 66/339, 369f., 382, 402 n. 66; TCA 2: chap. 6.

7. Habermas, E 224f./340f.; cf. TCA 2: chap. 6; E 245f./372f.

8. Habermas, TCA 2:329/486.

9. Habermas, TCA 2:329/486f. See Charles Taylor, *Sources of the Self: The Making of the Modern Identity* (Cambridge: Cambridge University Press, 1989).

10. Habermas, TCA 2:330f./487f.

11. Habermas, E 250ff./377ff.
12. Habermas, E 225f./342.
13. Habermas, E 256f./386f.
14. Habermas, E 259f./390f.
15. See Gehard Schweppenhäuser's critique of Habermas, "Die 'kommunikativ verflüssigte Moral: Zur Diskursethik bei Habermas," in Gerhard Bolte, ed., *Unkritische Theorie: Gegen Habermas* (Lüneburg: zu Klampen, 1989) 122–145, an anti-Festschrift to the 60th birthday. See also James L. Marsh, *Post-Cartesian Meditations: An Essay in Dialectical Phenomenology* (New York: Fordham University Press, 1988), chap. 8.
16. Habermas, TCA 2:339/498f.
17. Habermas, TCA 2:339f./499f.
18. Habermas, TCA 2:340/500f.
19. Cf. Marsh, *Post-Cartesian Meditations* 218ff., 233f., n. 30, and 234f., n. 33.
20. Habermas, TCA 2:340ff./501ff.
21. 'Parallel *polis*' is Václav Benda's and 'nonpolitical politics' Václav Havel's term. (See Part III below.)
22. Habermas, TCA 2:342f./504.
23. Habermas, TCA 2:374ff./548.
24. Habermas, TCA 2:378ff./553ff.
25. Habermas, TCA 2:382/561f.
26. Habermas, TCA 1:70–74/107–113.
27. Habermas, TCA 1:73/111f.
28. Habermas, TCA 1:73f./112. Cf. Theodor W. Adorno, *Negative Dialektik*, in *Gesammelte Schriften*, Vol. 6 (Frankfurt/M: Suhrkamp, 1984) 281f., 358; and Anke Thyen, *Negative Dialektik und Erfahrung: Zur Rationalität des Nichtidentischen bei Adorno* (Frankfurt a/M: Suhrkamp, 1989) 59ff., 213ff., 222–288.
29. Habermas, TCA 2:396f./583; 403/593; cf. 168/251.
30. Habermas, TCA 2:383/562.
31. Habermas, TCA 1:64ff./100ff.
32. Habermas, ZE 9ff., 20; PDM 342/396.
33. Habermas, TCA 2:97/148; MkH 100, 126/110, 136; PDM 346/401; NC 261/EAS 172f.
34. Habermas, PDM 344/399.
35. Habermas, PDM 344–347/399ff. for all quotations below.
36. Habermas, PDM 343/397.
37. Habermas, TCA 2:196/292f.
38. Habermas, TCA 2:fig. 28 and 187/278f.
39. Habermas, TCA 2:189f., 191/282, 285.
40. See Habermas, TCA 2:fig. 28, where the two bottom areas were left blank.
41. Habermas, TCA 2:353ff./519ff.
42. Habermas, TCA 2:355f./522.
43. Habermas, TCA 2:354/520, fig. 28; see Part II below. That Habermas bypasses Kierkegaard's critique of motives and his call for radical honesty in any praxis of theorizing or in activism, and that he does so by moving to legal warrants for the moral and democratic theory, seem problematic. In his most recent work on law, Habermas for the first time systematically and descriptively accounts for a Kierkegaardian self-choice as the modern condition of the possibility that a person and groups can assume reflective distancing vis-à-vis given cultures and traditions.

Yet, in his rereading of Kant's liberalism and Rousseau's republicanism through a discursive–procedural model, he fails to reconnect this Kierkegaardian attitude normatively with the very praxis of harnessing the moral point of view and sustaining the politics of deliberative democracy. (This book was completed one month before the German publication of Habermas's new work (FuG). My critical points of reference rely on my knowledge of Habermas's developing position from his seminar on law [Frankfurt a/M, 1989–1991] and on his feature presentation of the book's argument (HRPS) at Northwestern University [Evanston, Ill., 23 September 1992].)

44. Habermas, NR 195f. Cf. Havel, uR, and Part III below.

45. In spite of Jacques Derrida's facile critique of Habermas's perceived drive to a transparency of one cultural public sphere—something that the latter's commitment to plurality of public spaces denies—Derrida's post-1989 rethinking of Marx has much in common with Habermas. See Derrida's *The Other Heading: Reflections on Today's Europe*, trans. Pascale-Anne Brault and Michael B. Naas (Bloomington: Indiana University Press, 1992) 54–57, 76–80, 96f.

46. See Habermas, NR 191–203 for all references below.

47. This section develops Habermas, LC, chaps. 3–8, and TCA 2: chap. 8, sec. 3.

48. Habermas, NR 181–187.

49. Habermas, ZRHM 96, 115–121; GS 47f./312.

CHAPTER 4

1. Habermas, TCA 2: chap. 5; cf. NC 249ff./EAS 161ff.; ND 149ff./187ff.; NR 220.

2. Charles Taylor, *Sources of the Self: The Making of the Modern Identity* (Cambridge: Cambridge University Press, 1989), views modern identity as "much richer in moral resources than its condemners allow, but . . . this richness is rendered invisible by the impoverished philosophical language of its most zealous defenders" (x–xi). See Alasdair MacIntyre, *After Virtue: A Study in Moral Theory*, 2nd ed. (London: Duckworth, 1985–1987); MacIntyre, *Whose Justice? Which Rationality?* (Notre Dame, Ind.: University of Notre Dame Press, 1988); Michael Sandel, *Liberalism and Its Critics* (New York: New York University Press, 1984); Sandel, *Liberalism and the Limits of Justice* (Cambridge: Cambridge University Press, 1982); Carol Gould, *Rethinking Democracy: Freedom and Social Cooperation in Politics, Economy, and Society* (Cambridge: Cambridge University Press, 1988). (On Honneth, see Chap. 3 above.)

3. See Seyla Benhabib, *Critique, Norm, and Utopia: A Study of the Foundation of Critical Theory* (New York: Columbia University Press, 1986) 339–351; Benhabib and Drucilla Cornell, eds., *Feminism as Critique* (Minneapolis: University of Minnesota Press, 1987). Nancy Fraser, *Unruly Practices: Power, Discourse and Gender in Contemporary Social Theory* (Minneapolis: Uniuversity of Minnesota Press, 1989).

4. Habermas, ZRHM 94 n. 4; TCA 2:97/148. On Hegel's influence on Mead, see Vorwort by Kellner to George Herbert Mead, *Philosophie der Sozialität* (Frankfurt a/M: Suhrkamp, 1969) 15, 25; and Hans Joas, *Praktische Intersubjektivität: Die Entwicklung des Werkes von G. H. Mead* (Frankfurt a/M: Suhrkamp, 1980):

"Mead went through a period of Hegelianism before he grounded his intersubjectivist pragmatism" (57).

5. George Herbert Mead, *Mind, Self, and Society* (Chicago: University of Chicago Press, 1934) 379–387.

6. Mead, *Mind* 389. On the link of existential phenomenology and Mead's pragmatism, see Werner Bergmann and Gisbert Hoffmann, "G. H. Mead und die Tradition der Phänomenologie," in Hans Joas, *Das Problem der Intersubjektivität: Neuere Beiträge zum Werk George Herbert Meads* (Frankfurt a/M: Suhrkamp, 1985) 93–130. They ask the phenomenological question "How can I know anything about the other?" and they repeat it from Mead's concern about the conditions of the possibility of human cooperation. Bernard Waldenfels, "Grenzen der Universalisierung: Zur Funktion der Rollenübernahme in Meads Sozialtheorie," in his *Der Spielraum des Verhaltens* (Frankfurt a/M: Suhrkamp, 1980), relates the difference between Mead's "I" and "me" to Freud's Id and Superego (254).

7. Mead, *Mind* 136–209.

8. See Habermas's essay on Mead in ND 149ff./187ff.

9. Mead, *Mind* 142; cf. 140.

10. Mead, *Mind* 147ff.

11. Mead, *Mind* 150–162.

12. Mead, *Mind* 174–177.

13. Mead, *Mind* 177f.

14. Cf. Mead, *Mind* 180–182; see also Chap. 7 below.

15. Mead, *Mind* 198ff.

16. Martin Luther King, Jr., "Letter from Birmingham City Jail" (1963), in James Melvin Washington, ed., *A Testament of Hope: The Essential Writings of Martin Luther King, Jr.* (New York: Harper & Row, 1986) 291 and 297f. (I follow Havel's example in Part III below.)

17. Mead, *Mind* 201f.

18. Mead, *Mind* 203f.

19. Mead, *Mind* 208f.

20. Waldenfels, "Grenzen" 255–260 for all quotations below.

21. Habermas, TCA 2:99/151. Ernst Tugendhat is the first to question Hans Joas's German translation of Mead's *Mind, Self, and Society* as *Geist, Identität, und Gesellschaft* (Frankfurt: Suhrkamp, 1968). He depicts this as an interpretative error: "identity" is an unclear term and is not used by Mead. The translation thus leads to misreadings. Ernst Tugendhat, *Selbstbewusstsein und Selbstbestimmung: Sprachanalytische Interpretationen* (Frankfurt a/M: Suhrkamp, 1979) 246.

This objection has been picked up by Richard Grathoff in a review of contemporary reception of Mead. He not only goes after Joas, but also implicates Habermas because of his dependence on the translation of "self" as "identity." Grathoff adds to Tugendhat's earlier concern that Joas projects into Mead's focus on sociality the Hegelian problem of practical intersubjectivity. Even though Hegel's influence on Mead can be traced to Mead's teachers, Grathoff argues against this being decisive. I mention the translation controversy because it elucidates Habermas's reference to it when he defines identity. [See Habermas, ND 149/187ff.; Richard Grathoff, "Zur gegenwärtigen Rezeption von Georg Herbert Mead," *Philosophische Rundschau* 34 (1987) 131, 138–142. Not only Habermas, but also Tugendhat (*Selbstbewusstsein*, lectures 12–14) and Taylor (*Sources* 34–47, 524 n. 12) develop the Hegel–Mead–Habermas linkage.]

Habermas says that he does not offer an explicit justification for rendering Mead's sociopsychological concept of self as identity. There are two disciplinary areas that utilize the term "identity." He acknowledges that the term comes from symbolic interactionism and psychoanalysis. This reason is also given by Joas in his introduction to the German edition of Mead's collected works. *Ich-Identität* is the sociological equivalent of "self," but this, according to Joas, is a terminological anachronism, since in Mead's time no such concept was available. The uncertainty of the term "identity" does not come from its application to Mead's field, where it is quite appropriate, says Joas. The uncertainty of the concept occurs, rather, when Tugendhat brings an older tradition of the word to bear on sociological and psychological terminology. In a sociopsychological context, Freud, Mead, and Durkheim analyze how individuals are constituted in relation to group identity. Identification, transference, the idealization of the generalized other, the membership in the sacred ritual, and gender construction are all different aspects of social and psychological identity formation. [See Hans Joas's Intro. to George Herbert Mead, *Gesammelte Aufsätze*, Vol. 1 (Frankfurt a/M: Suhrkamp, 1980) 17f.; Joas, *Praktische Intersubjektivität*; and Joas, ed., *Das Problem der Intersubjektivität*.]

22. TCA 2:100f./153ff. Habermas comments on Dieter Henrich, "Identität," in Odo Marquard and Karlheinz Stierle, eds., *Identität, Poetik und Hermeneutik*, Vol. 8 (München: Wilhelm Fink, 1979) 372f.

23. Derek Parfit, *Reasons and Persons* (Oxford: Oxford University Press, 1984), cited and discussed by Taylor, *Sources* 47.

24. Tugendhat, *Selbstbewusstsein* 284–291, critiques Habermas's earlier position as expressed in KK 226, 228, 230 and in ZRHM 94f., 79f.

25. Habermas, ND 154f./192f. (my translation).

26. Habermas, ND 168f./207 (my translation).

27. Habermas, ND 189/229 (my translation).

28. Habermas, TCA 2:8–12/19–25.

29. Habermas, TCA 2:13f., 17/26ff., 32.

30. Habermas, TCA 2:41, 58f., 105f., 97ff./66, 92f., 161f., 147ff.

31. Habermas, TCA 2:109/167. Yet he doubts the "existential" by placing "decision" in quotation marks.

32. Axel Honneth distinguishes three types of reciprocal recognition: affective recognition in love (this reaches back to early Hegelian motives), solidarity (ethical reciprocity and self-realization), and the right (moral reciprocity and self-determination). Inversely, he develops a moral sociology based on the recognized injury to embodied integrity, to psychological wholeness, and to the relations of justice. While this division might satisfy Benhabib's quest for the posttraditional ethic of the concrete other (Hegel's moral subject who can take distance from conventional *Sittlichkeit*), it does not yet help us to locate Kierkegaard's exister. See Seyla Benhabib, *Situating the Self: Gender, Community and Postmodernism in Contemporary Ethics* (New York: Routlege, 1992), especially on post-conventional *Sittlichkeit* 3–17 and 68–88; Axel Honneth, "Integrität und Mißachtung: Grundmotive einer anerkennungstheoretischen Moralkonzeption," inaugural lecture presented at the Habilitation proceedings, Frankfurt (28 June 1990), manuscript; and Honneth, *Kampf um Anerkennung: Zur moralischen Grammatik sozialer Konflikte* (Frankfurt a/M: Suhrkamp, 1992).

33. Habermas, TCA 2:98f., 105f./150f., 161f.

34. Habermas, TCA 2:98f.; cf. 105f./150f., 161f.

35. Habermas, TCA 2:109/167; "Lawrence Kohlberg und der Neoaristotelismus," in EzD 97.

36. Habermas, ND 186f.; cf. 145f., 192f./227f.; cf. 186, 233.

37. Habermas, "Vom pragmatischen, ethischen und moralischen Gebrauch der praktischen Vernunft," in EzD 112; ICI 6–9, 13; ND 177f./217; last citation, ND 187/227f. (my translation).

38. Habermas, ND 152/190f. (my translation).

39. Tugendhat, *Selbstbewusstsein* 149ff., 161; Habermas, ND 152f./191 (my translation).

40. Habermas, TCA 2:102/156 (my translation) and 2:105/161.

41. Habermas, TCA 2:109/167 and 2:98/150.

42. Habermas, TCA 2:100/153. I corrected a translator's error in parallelism. Cf. ÜMS 222, 225f.; ND 183/223.

43. Habermas, ÜMS 221.

44. Habermas, ÜMS 222, 225; TCA 2:109/166.

45. See Appendix A below. I am sympathetic to Alessandro Ferrara's recent attempt to articulate a posttraditional ethic of the good, thereby "sidestepping . . . the modern split" (e.g., between Habermas's procedural justice and Kierkegaard's concerns with authenticity). Yet I argue that the latter is doing something quite different from articulating the postconventional eudaimonistic ethics of the good: Kierkegaard attends to an existential mode of both posttraditional morality and ethics. Thus, this mode figures as the condition for both of their mutual possibilities. See Ferrara, "Postmodern Eudaimonia," *Praxis International* 11/4 (January 1992) 387–411, and his *Modernity and Authenticity: A Study in the Social and Ethical Thought of Jean-Jacques Rousseau* (Albany: SUNY Press, 1993). On the new hybrid category, "ethical–existential," see Habermas, EzD 100–118; NR 118, 120, 126, 141, 144; ND 164–200/203–241; KFnt 31f.

46. Maurice Merleau-Ponty, *Phenomenology of Perception*, trans. Colin Smith (London: Routledge & Kegan Paul, 1965, 1986) xiv.

47. Habermas, TCA 2:22–27/39–46, 43ff./69ff; PDM 2f., 334, 359/10f., 388, 417.

48. Habermas, PDM 325/377f.

49. Habermas, ND 166–169/204–208.

50. Habermas, TCA 2:48ff./77ff.; Kierkegaard, CA 42/SV 4:313.

51. Habermas, TCA 2:51–53/82–86.

52. Ulf Matthiesen, *Das Dickicht der Lebenswelt und die Theorie des kommunikativen Handelns* (München: Wilhelm Fink, 1983–1985) chaps. 5–6. Cf. Anke Thyen, *Negative Dialektik und Erfahrung* (Frankfurt a/M: Suhrkamp, 1989) 272–288; Kierkegaard CA 42/SV 4:313; and Habermas, PDM, lecture VIII on Bataille.

53. Matthiesen, *Dickicht* 112, 114ff.

54. Ernest Becker, *Escape from Evil* (New York: Free Press, 1975); Becker, *The Denial of Death* (New York: Free Press, 1973). He critiques the social utopias of the resurrected body: Norman O. Brown, *Life against Death: The Psychoanalytical Meaning of History* (Middletown, Conn.: Wesleyan University Press, 1959, 1985); Brown, *Love's Body* (New York: Vintage Books, 1966); Herbert Marcuse, *Eros and Civilization* (New York: Vintage Books, 1962).

55. Habermas, NC 260f./EAS 172; ND 165ff./204ff.

56. Unlike Habermas's hope recorded earlier in VaZ 9–44.

CHAPTER 5

1. For the lectures, see JP 1847:648–657/P VIII² B79–B89; n. by Malantschuk to the entry "communication," JP, Vol. 1:518; and Hirsch's Intro. to Kierkegaard, GW, Vol. 33, *ix–xv*. The two published texts are Kierkegaard's PVA.

2. Kierkegaard, JP 1847:656/P VIII² B88.

3. Kierkegaard, JP 1849:6440/P X¹ A531; JP 1854:3219/P XI¹ A51.

4. Kierkegaard, JP 1854:3219/P XI¹ A51.

5. Kierkegaard, JP 1847:656/P VIII² B88; JP 1849:6440/P X¹ A531.

6. Kierkegaard, JP 1848:4851, 4134/P VIII A605f.; JP 4132f./P VIII A599f.; JP 4139/P VIII A614.

7. Kierkegaard, JP 1848:4131/P VIII A598; on equality, see Kierkegaard, WOL, Part I, chap. 2B; PF; and CUP. See also Bruce H. Kirmmse, *Kierkegaard in Golden Age Denmark* (Bloomington: Indiana University Press, 1990); Anton Hügli, "Kierkegaard und der Kommunismus," in Michael Theunissen and Wilfred Greve, eds., *Materialien zur Philosophie Søren Kierkegaards* (Frankfurt a/M: Suhrkamp, 1979) 511–538; and Chap. 10 below.

8. Is not there a parallel between Kierkegaard's project after 1848 and Habermas's (interviews in NR) critical rejection of "left fascism" in the revolutionary Germany of 1968? Does not his move to communication win Habermas, among some leftists, epithet of a conservative thinker who justifies the status quo? But do not the symmetry and reciprocity conditions of communication raise a sober yet concrete imperative of radical revolutionary egalitarianism?

9. Kierkegaard, JP 1847:656/P VIII² B88; JP 1848:6125/P VIII A602; JP 1849: 6440/P X¹ A531.

10. Habermas, TCA 2:109/167.

11. Ernst Tugendhat, *Selbstbestimmung und Selbstbewusstsein Sprachanalytische Interpretation* (Frankfurt a/M: Suhrkamp, 1979); Tugendhat, *Vorlesungen zur Enführung in die sprachanalytische Philosophie* (Frankfurt a/M: Suhrkamp, 1976). On Tugendhat, see Manfred Frank, *Die Unhitergehbarkeit von Individualität: Reflexionen über Subjekt, Person und Individuum aus Anlaß ihrer "postmodernen" Toterklärung* (Frankfurt a/M: Suhrkamp, 1986) 70ff.; and Frank, "Subjekt, Person, Individuum," in Frank, Gérard Raulet, und Willem van Reijen, eds., *Die Frage nach dem Subjekt* (Frankfurt a/M: Suhrkamp, 1988) 17ff. (See also the Appendix A below.) Frank argues that Tugendhat builds upon Peter Strawson's *Individuals*: one is not a Kantian "I think" but an empirical entity in space and time. Self-consciousness is not an objectivating, reflexive self-relation of "I" to itself, but an attitude of the concrete individual to propositional contents. The other-relation expands the propositional structure of self-consciousness on the basis of the "semantic principle of verificatory symmetry" between ascription of conscious predicates to myself and to another. Self-consciousness exhibits an attitude towards a proposition that describes experiences—"I know, that I *p*"; the other-relation is sustained by the formally semantic convertibility of the deictic expressions under which the personal pronominal "I" falls. See Peter Strawson, *Individuals* (Garden City, N.Y.: Doubleday, 1963); and Richard Rorty, *Philosophy and the Mirror of Nature* (Princeton, N.J.: Princeton University Press, 1979).

12. Tugendhat, *Selbstbewusstsein* 149f., 158. For an opposite reading of Kierkegaard, see Michael Wyschograd, *Kierkegaard and Heidegger* (New York:

Humanities Press, 1954), chap. 4, who links both Kierkegaard and Heidegger to Aquinas's ontology of being.

13. Tugendhat, *Selbstbewusstsein* 159.

14. Tugendhat, *Selbstbewusstsein* 160.

15. Tugendhat, *Selbstbewusstsein* 176, 179f., 181f.

16. See Tugendhat, *Selbstbewusstsein* 182f. In commenting upon Heidegger's *What Is Metaphysics?*, Tugendhat translates Heidegger's ontological being/nothingness into semantically affirmative "yes" and negating "no" positions in dialogue: generic yes/no positions are rooted in specific qualitative yes/no self-relation, which one assumes towards one's own temporal existing (170f.). See Tugendhat, "Das Sein und das Nichts," in V. Klostermann, ed., *Durchblicke: Festschrift: Martin Heidegger zum 80. Geburtstag* (Frankfurt a/M: Klostermann, 1970) 132–161, and Martin Heidegger, *Was ist Metaphysik?* (1929) (Frankfurt a/M: Klostermann, 1955).

17. Tugendhat, *Selbstbewusstsein* 184; Habermas TCA 2:62ff./97ff.

18. Tugendhat, *Selbstbewusstsein* 189.

19. See Tugendhat, *Selbstbewusstsein* 190f.

20. Cf. Tugendhat, *Selbstbewusstsein* 161, 156.

21. "The criterion for the self is always: that directly before which it is a self" (Kierkegaard, SD 79/SV 11:191). Cf. Habermas, ND 22ff./31ff.

22. Habermas, TCA 1:396f./530ff.; "Handlungen, Sprechakte, sprachlich vermittelte Interaktionen und Lebenswelt," not in the English ed. of ND 76ff.; ND 57ff./105ff; Karl Bühler, *Sprachtheorie*, (Jena: Gustav Fischer, 1934) 28. Habermas's position would seem to contradict Bill Martin's claim that Habermas privileges the intentional function of speech and thus operates with an instrumental view of language. See Martin's *Matrix and Line: Derrida and the Possibilities of Postmodern Social Theory* (Albany: SUNY Press, 1992), especially Chap. 3.

23. Habermas, ND 25/33 (my translation).

24. Habermas, TCA 1:288f., 292/388f., 393f.; cf. CES, "What Is Universal Pragmatics?" figs. 15, 16/VTKH 427, 440. For a critique of Habermas's model, see David M. Rasmussen, *Reading Habermas* (Oxford: Blackwell, 1990) 37–55. See also J. C. Austin, *How to Do Things with Words* (Cambridge, Mass.: Harvard University Press, 1975).

25. Habermas, E 241f./365; ND 65, 80f., 103—not in the English ed.—and 64/113.

26. Habermas, ND 48/57; E 241f./365; cf. ND 19ff./28ff.

27. Habermas, TCA 1:330, and n. 84/441f. and n. 84.

28. Habermas, TCA 2:75f./117; cf. ND 177–193/217–233.

29. Kierkegaard, JP 1847:653/P VIII² B85:1–16 and 28–30.

30. Kierkegaard, JP 1847:649/P VIII² B81:10f., 21f.; JP 1847:650/P VIII² B82:12f.; JP 1848: 1169/P VIII A616. (See Chap. 2 above.)

31. Habermas, TCA 2:109f./167f.; ÜMS 221, 225f.; ND 183–199, 192, 199/223–228, 233, 240. Many an existentialist confuses self-choice with choosing goods or values.

32. Kierkegaard, JP 1846:1040/P VII A33 and JP 1837:1971/P II A187.

33. Kierkegaard, JP 1847:657/P VIII² B89. See Howard R. Mueller, "The Dialectic of Self-Transformation: A Study in the Structure and Development of the Historical Consciousness in the Thought of Søren Kierkegaard" (Ph.D. dissertation, University of London, Heytrop College, 1977) 16–140.

34. Habermas, "Vom pragmatischen, ethischen und moralischen Gebrauch der praktischen Vernunft," in EzD 108–110; ND 170/209; cf. NC 249ff./EAS 161ff.
35. Kierkegaard, E/O 2:188f., 204/SV2: 170f., 184.
36. Kierkegaard, E/O 2:157ff., 168f., 176f./SV2: 143ff., 152ff., 160f.
37. Kierkegaard, E/O 2:219–224/SV2: 196–201.
38. Kierkegaard, E/O 2:213ff./SV2: 191ff.
39. Habermas, ND 189f./230 (my translation).
40. Habermas, PDM 18/29. Cf. Seyla Benhabib, *Critique, Norm, and Utopia: A Study of the Foundations of Critical Theory* (New York: Columbia University Press, 1986), the systematic portions of chaps. 4, 6, and 8.
41. Habermas, PDM 260ff./306ff.
42. Habermas, PDM 256/300.

CHAPTER 6

1. Kierkegaard, JP 1837:1023/P II A612; E/O 1:324f./SV 1: 296. Merold Westphal, "Kierkegaard's Teleological Suspension of Religiousness B," in George B. Connell and C. Stephen Evans, eds., *Foundations of Kierkegaard's Vision of Community: Religion, Ethics, and Politics in Kierkegaard* (Atlantic Highlands, N.J.: Humanities Press, 1992) 123–126, introduces the topic of "religiousness C" (i.e., one's dying away from the immediacy of sacred and secular culture). Suffering of this death is not merely inward, but comprises both public resistance to ethico-moral self-sufficiency and dissent against a fundamentalist "'religious' way of being irreligious." I generate philosophical equivalents to this resistance and dissent by intensifying the sociopolitical path through existential pathos.
2. Between two communicators transpires a *doubly existential contingency*: communicative ethics provides necessary structural conditions of ethical communication, yet these are not modally sufficient conditions. Habermas's claim that practical self-relation exercises performative primacy over epistemic and expressive self-relation becomes now the primacy of an existential mode in both the individual and community. (On double contingency, see Chap. 5 above.)
3. Kierkegaard, CUP 528/SV 7:461.
4. Kierkegaard, CUP 191, 203, 242/SV 7:160, 170, 203. For the last two citations, C. Stephen Evans, *Kierkegaard's Fragments and Postscript: The Religious Philosophy of Johannes Climacus* (Atlantic Highlands, N.J.: Humanities Press, 1983) 9; cf. Evans, 57f., 96ff., 100ff., 104ff., and the last paragraph of chap. 6.
5. Kierkegaard, CUP 129f./SV 7:105. Evans, *Kierkegaard's Fragments* 282. Defending existential communication, Climacus does not object to empirical deficits but to certain theoretical views that distort practice. Empirical deficits are often argued against Habermas by those who parade the nonexisting reality of a highly idealized consensus. I am not raising this type of objection.
6. Habermas speaks about "interiority" within the process of understanding: "[t]he dimension of validity dwells in the interiority of language." This interiority of language houses one's communicative orientation to validity claims; its inner dwelling-house of the performative mode of speech acts belongs to the formal–pragmatic conditions of possible understanding as such. This "*telos* of the understanding lives in the interiority of the linguistic medium," but it cannot be grasped as means to a

goal. This *telos* is not something I can strive for unreflectively, apart from performance. Communicative action is oriented "beyond all entities," "*beyond* the world." Strategic action aims at "entities *in the world*." A "beyond" is not here the vertical unknown, but rather a cooperative, *immanently horizontal*, doubly *contingent transcendence* of actors in communication. Communicative ethics is not "objective" in the way action oriented to success is. To say that communicative action and ethics are in the basic performative mode means that they are oriented to the understanding among subjects capable of speech and action. Habermas, E 238–242/360–365.

7. Kierkegaard, CUP 189ff./SV 7:157ff. Anti-Climacus shows some such plight. "[H]is despair is: not to will to be himself. But he certainly does not entertain the ludicrous notion of wanting to be someone else; he keeps up the relation to his self. . . . His relation to the self is like the relation a person may have to his place of residence (*the comic aspect is that the self certainly does not have as contingent a relation to itself as one has to a place of residence*), which becomes an abomination because of smoke fumes or something else, whatever it might be. So he leaves it . . . but he does not set up a new residence; he continues to regard the old one as his address. . . . As long as the difficulty lasts . . . he visits himself . . . only occasionally, to see whether the change has commenced. As soon as it commences, he moves home again, 'is himself once again', as he says" (SD 55/SV 11:167f.; emphasis added).

8. Kierkegaard, CUP 72ff., 129–360/SV 7:55ff., 104–312.

9. I adopt the methodology of Tamsin E. Lorraine, *Gender, Identity, and the Production of Meaning* (Boulder, Colo.: Westview Press, 1990), who speaks of the "feminine" and "masculine" modes in the nonessentialist, tentative sense of one's positioning vis-à-vis the other. My metaphor of the two orders of receptivity and activity neither reduces one actual gender to the other, nor identifies gender with one type of rationality or even exclusively identifies the female with communicative and the male with dominant instrumental rationality. (Historically, it is the case that males dominate females and privilege "masculinist" domains of rationality to an existential mode.) Regardless of gender construction, existential self-choice qualifies emotional–expressive, moral–practical, and cognitive–objectifying validity domains. Lorraine's analysis of Kierkegaard shows the "feminine" positioning in his religious attitude, yet she omits, just as Tugendhat does, to expand this self-relation into reciprocal relations within existential communication among humans.

10. See Alasdair MacIntyre, *After Virtue: A Study in Moral Theory*, 2nd ed. (London: Duckworth, 1985–1987) 39, and on Kierkegaard, chap. 4.

11. Kierkegaard, CUP 611ff., 613f., n./SV 7:533ff., 534 n.

12. Kierkegaard, CA 41–47/SV 4:313–318; JP 1844:2321/P V B53:12.

13. Kierkegaard, CA 42f./SV 4:313f. Anxiety defines existential communication as "*a sympathetic antipathy* and *an antipathetic sympathy*" (original emphasis). One *is* ambivalently anxious about *nothing*. A "what" becomes defined by a "how": this nothing is not an object but rather existing time, which qualifies every self- and other-relation.

14. Kierkegaard, CA 44f./SV 4:315f.; CUP 165–178/SV 7:137–147.

15. Kierkegaard, CA 46/SV 4:316.

16. Kierkegaard, WOL 199f./SV 9:201f.

17. Kierkegaard, PF 10/SV 4:180.

18. Kierkegaard, PF 9–11/SV 4:179–181.

19. Kierkegaard, PF 25, 48/SV 4:194, 215; cf. WOL.

20. Kierkegaard, CUP 73f., n./SV 7:56f., n. Climacus intensifies by existential communication the ethical demand of Judge Williams from *Either/Or*: the alter can communicate love directly only as a possibility, as a requirement for the ego. The indirect character of this communication is neither deceptive nor even pseudonymous, since no matter how directly loving is declared, this may be verified in one's temporal existence, not through the manifest validity claim. Cf. an analogical claim: "The one prays in truth to God although he is worshiping an idol; the other prays in untruth to the true God and is therefore in truth worshiping an idol" (CUP 201/SV 7:168).

21. On reduplication, see Evans, *Kierkegaard's Fragments* 69f., 100ff. "[T]he second reflection is not the reduplication of existence itself, but the 'existential thinking' that precedes the action. Subjective communication must be intellectually understood (first reflection), but its concrete relevance to the individual's life must also be thought through (subjective thinking—second reflection). This latter process is permeated with passion, has an essential relationship to action, and may indeed be the first aspect of an act, but it alone is not action" (100).

22. Note the distinction between primitive traditions and posttraditional and postnational primitivity. While the latter is decisively modern, it cannot, in principle, be confined to ethno- and egocentric views.

23. Kierkegaard, CUP 74/SV 7:57. Cf. CUP 79/SV 7:60f.

24. Kierkegaard, CUP, Part II, A, "Pathos." (See n. 1 above.)

25. Kierkegaard, CUP 387ff./SV 7:335ff.: "The Initial Expression of Existential Pathos."

26. Kierkegaard, CUP 423f., 426f./SV 7:367, 370.

27. Kierkegaard, CUP 447, cf. 431–446/SV 7:389, cf. 374–388.

28. Kierkegaard, CUP 463ff./SV 7:403ff.

29. Cf. Kierkegaard, CUP 525f./SV 7:458f.

30. Ernest Becker's *Escape from Evil*, cited in n. 54 of Chap. 4 above, analyzes from the angle of unconscious guilt the modern capitalist and socialist economies and their sacralized cultures of immortality and hero ideologies. Becker appeals to psychoanalysis and critical social theory, and to a postheroic ethic from exile and a Kierkegaardian phenomenology of the existential.

31. Kierkegaard, CUP 534/SV 7:466.

32. I continue here my systematic examination from Chap. 5, section 5.2, above.

33. Existential communication presupposes the fiduciary or the tacit ground in all my knowing and acting. This ground is a qualitative self-transformation, not an absolute given in validity domains. See Michael Polanyi, *Personal Knowledge: Towards a PostCritical Philosophy* (Chicago: University of Chicago Press, 1958). Ludwig Wittgenstein in his last book, *On Certainty*, ed. G. E. M. Anscombe and G. H. von Wright, trans. Denis Paul and G. E. M. Anscombe (Oxford: Blackwell, 1969, 1974), argues against G. E. Moore that the earth on which one stands is a ground which it makes no sense to doubt. Evans implies that the post-Kuhnian philosophy of science had to rediscover Climacus's claim to the subjectivity of truth. The strong march to absolute knowing, and its inverse empiricist drive for protocol sentences and an immediate verification of truth, have been given up for the fallibilist and self-corrective methodologies in human, social, and natural sciences. Habermas

argues the shift from the *telos* of the Hegelian–Marxist philosophy of history and from the claims of the old critical theory to an experimental, provisional character of a social critique. These and similar developments change the context in which Climacus critiqued the Hegelian absolute. They bring the hermeneutical and existential dimensions into all disciplines, not just into the ethico-religious angle that Climacus takes. Evans rightly remarks that "even the approximative truth sought by objective historical science is regarded by Climacus as grounded in subjectivity [and that] . . . he would draw the same conclusions with respect to the other social sciences and the natural sciences, insofar as these provide conclusions that transcend 'the immediate conclusions of sensation'" (Evans, *Kierkegaard's Fragments* 132 with reference to Kierkegaard PF 105/SV 4:248). In the next chapter, I will explain why Climacus overstates his case for subjectivity as a case against objectivity and why this implicates him in an unhappy dualism. I will critique his limitation of the fiduciary mode in communication to the religious. In light of the postempiricist philosophy of science, Wittgenstein's later theories, and learning from recent criticisms of rationality, I argue that this mode pertains to all levels of existential communication.

34. Kierkegaard, PF 23f./SV 4:192f.; cf. TA 63/SV 8:60. In the next chapter, I will argue that the existential tension does not transpire between inner and outer validity domains but rather in an existential mode: in the individual, we can distinguish between her communicated possibility and actuality; in the community, we can distinguish projected communicative possibility and actually communicating individuals.

35. Max Horkheimer and Theodor W. Adorno, *Dialectic of Enlightenment* (1944), trans. John Cumming (New York: Continuum, 1987). Cf. the prototype of this kind of critique in Kierkegaard's TA and Chap. 10 below. Cf. also Habermas's interview on the Persian Gulf War, VaZ 9–44.

36. See Kierkegaard, CUP 553ff./SV 7:483ff.

37. Kierkegaard, JP 1850:2952/P X² A390; JP 1850:2024/P X² A489; JP 1850: 1614/P X² A426; JP 1846:4110/P VII¹ A20.

38. See Habermas, "Peirce and Community," added only to the MIT Press ed. of ND (88–112). For Charles Sanders Peirce's profanized theological principle of the ideal, indefinite, and unlimited community, see his *Collected Papers*, eds. Charles Hartshorne and Paul Weiss (Cambridge, Mass.: Harvard University Press, 1931–1958), Vol. 2: 655.

CHAPTER 7

1. Kierkegaard, CUP 164/SV 7:136. Climacus considers existential communication by Christ, the god–man, not by Judaism or Islam or Buddhism, to be a religiosity "B" (viz., the offense of God becoming human). I cannot answer here whether this is a limited nineteenth-century concern with dying away to immediate Christendom, or whether one should seek instead a differentiation between "A" and "B" in other world perspectives. My desire to remain *in situ* comes from a self-discovery that one may not *leap* to either A or B except through existential communication. Post-traditional identity emerges *structurally* under the linguistification

of the sacred and *modally* from an invitation to existential thinking, self-choice, and living with pathos. (See Chap. 6, n. 1 above.)

2. Kierkegaard, CUP 338/SV 7:336.

3. On this Hegelian logical principle, see Kierkegaard, CUP 52, 138/SV 7:41, 112.

4. For the first three citations, see Hegel, *Enzyklopädia*, paragraph 139f. and addenda, in *Werke*, ed. E. Moldenhauer and K. M. Michel (Frankfurt a/M: Suhrkamp, 1970–1971), Vol. 8: 274f.; for the last citation, see Hegel, *Wissenschaft der Logik*, Book II, section II, chap. 3 (C), in *Werke* Vol. 6: 180. All translations are mine.

5. Kierkegaard means by existence a mode; Hegel means a totality of validity domains. Hegel claims that the unity of the inner and the outer is "a unity of the whole which in itself comprises existence." *Logik für die Mittelklass*, paragraph 60, in *Werke* Vol. 4: 178f.

6. Contrast Kierkegaard's existential language of a mode with Charles Taylor's epiphanic language emerging from a neo-Hegelian communitarianism. Charles Taylor, *Sources of the Self: The Making of the Modern Identity* (Cambridge: Cambridge University Press, 1989).

7. Kierkegaard, JP 1849:3567/P X^1 A679; JP 1849:6467/P X^1 A640; JP 1849: 707/P X^1 A658.

8. Kierkegaard, JP 1852:709/P X^4 A596; JP 1849:707/P X^1 A658.

9. Kierkegaard, JP 1851:708/P X^4 A15.

10. Kierkegaard, JP 1854:711/P XI^1 A28; JP 1854:2550/P XI^1 A193; JP 1854: 2763/P XI^1 A198. (See Chap. 10, n. 35 below.)

11. Kierkegaard, JP 1847:656/P VIII B88; JP 1849:6440/P X^1 A531; and Pr.

12. Kierkegaard, E/O 1:3/SV 1:v. See the translator's n. 2, E/O 1:603.

13. Milan Kundera, *The Unbearable Lightness of Being*, trans. Michael Henry Heim (New York: Harper & Row, 1984); cf. his *Art of the Novel*, trans. Linda Asher (New York: Grove Press, 1988). For Alasdair MacIntyre's mis/reading of Kierkegaard, see *After Virtue: A Study in Moral Theory*, 2nd ed. (London: Duckworth, 1985–1987) 40ff., 49.

14. Kierkegaard, E/O 2:354/SV 2:317f. Alasdair MacIntyre pictures Kierkegaard first as an emotivist (*After Virtue* 5, 41, 73, 203, 242) and then, in a curious reversal, as an Aristotelian Thomist placed over and against the critical modernism of Rawls (*Whose Justice? Which Rationality?* [Notre Dame, Ind.: University of Notre Dame Press, 1988] 164ff.). I believe that both MacIntyre's readings are wrongheaded.

15. Kierkegaard, E/O 2:354/SV 2:318.

16. Kierkegaard, SLW 441f./SV 6:411f. SLW are "compiled, forwarded to the press, and published by Hilarious Bookbinder."

17. Kierkegaard, SLW 375, 428/SV 6:350f., 399; see translator's n. 381, p. 728.

18. Kierkegaard, FT 54ff./SV 3:104ff.

19. Kierkegaard, FT 59/SV 3:109. My reference to Becker (see end of Chap. 4 above) is to *Escape from Evil* and *The Denial of Death*. Both texts, using Kierkegaard, Otto Rank, Paul Tillich, and Max Horkheimer, offer a formal critique of heroism.

20. See Kierkegaard, CUP 382, 413, 326/SV 7:331, 358, 281.

21. Kierkegaard, CUP 428/SV 7:371f.

22. Kierkegaard, CUP 499, 503n./SV 7:434, 438n. On *unum noris omnes*, see CA 79/SV 4:348; CA 240, see editor's n. 50; P 1844:V B49:15 as cited in CA 183; JP 1846:3327/P VII¹ A70.

23. Kierkegaard, CUP 541/SV 7:472; cf. CUP 542–555/SV 7:473–484.

24. Kierkegaard, CUP 356/SV 7:309; cf. CUP 353ff./SV 7:306ff.

25. Kierkegaard, CUP 242, 249, 571/SV 7:203, 210, 498.

26. Kierkegaard, CUP 401, 405/SV 7:348, 351.

27. Kierkegaard, CUP 409/SV 7:355.

28. Kierkegaard, CUP 413f./SV 7:358f.

29. Kierkegaard, CUP 415/SV 7:360. Cf. Herbert Marcuse, *One-Dimensional Man: Studies in the Ideology of Advanced Industrial Society*, new intro. Douglas Kellner (Boston: Beacon Press, 1964, 1991). The inciting/prohibitive sacral of revolutionary projects is well dramatized by the mad chorus in Peter Weiss's play from the 1960s, rediscovered in 1989 by European theaters, about the French Revolution: *The Persecution and Assassination of Jean-Paul Marat as Performed by the Inmates of the Asylum of Charenton under the Direction of the Marquis de Sade*, trans. Geoffrey Skelton, intro. Peter Brook, verse adapt. Adrian Mitchell (New York: Atheneum, 1964).

30. Kierkegaard, CUP 416/SV 7:361. That *Marat–Sade* takes place in a psychiatric clinic and that revolutionary events are dramatized by mad actors might protect a critical margin of inwardness through which the play can become contemporary with today's audience. (See preceding n.)

31. Kierkegaard, CUP 151f., 154/SV 7:125, 127.

32. Kierkegaard, CUP 554 n./SV 7:484 n.

33. Kierkegaard, AUCH, May 16, 1855:55/SV 14:81; see PC for the internal reference.

34. Kierkegaard, SD 79/SV 11:191. Anti-Climacus calls the greatest possible projection of identity "the theological self, the self directly before God." I confine my argument to an existential corrective to Habermas's formal criterion of the ideal community.

35. Kierkegaard, JP 1849:6433/P X¹ A517.

36. Kierkegaard, PC 9/SV 12:1.

37. Kierkegaard, PC 64/SV 12:61.

38. For the quotations below, Kierkegaard, PC 87f./SV 12:83f., PC 87, ed. n. 22. Cf. Hegel, *Hegel's Philosophy of Right*, trans. T. M. Knox (London: Oxford University Press, 1967) 92, 94; Theodor W. Adorno, *Kierkegaard: Construction of the Aesthetic*, trans. Robert Hullot-Kentor (Minneapolis: University of Minnesota Press, 1989); György Lukács, "Die Zerstörung der Vernunft," in *Werke*, Vol. 9 (Neuwied: Luchterhand, 1962) 219–269.

39. Kierkegaard, PC 88/SV 12:84. Adorno's *Kierkegaard* depicts a commoner who evades material problems by living on interest income in a bourgeois home; his objectless inwardness is shown as a mirror image of this material exterior.

40. Kierkegaard, PC 88/SV 12:84.

41. While Kierkegaard calls the descriptive signification of vertical identity in existential communication a God, "And fear and trembling signify that there is *a God*—something every human being and every established order ought not to forget for a moment" (PC 88/SV 12:84; emphasis added), my argument is limited to the philosophical equivalents for his way of proceeding.

42. Kierkegaard, PC 89f./SV 12:85.
43. Kierkegaard, PC 91f./SV 12:87. (On Havel's nonpolitical politics, see Part III below.)
44. Kierkegaard, PC 85, 92/SV 12:81, 87.
45. Kierkegaard, PC 137/SV 12:127f.; cf. JP/P entries from 1848. See Emmanuel Lévinas, "Humanism and An-archy," in his *Collected Philosophical Papers*, trans. Alphonso Lingis (Hague: Martinus Nijhoff, 1987) 133. See also "No Identity" in *Collected Papers*: "The rediscoveries of self with self are missing. Inwardness seems to be not strictly inward. *I is the other*" (143).
46. See Kierkegaard, PC 139ff./SV 12:130ff.
47. See Martin Buber, *Die Frage nach den Einzelnen* and *Ich und Du*, in *Werke*, Vols. 1–3, (München: Kösel, 1962–1964), especially Vol. 1: 150ff., 217, 229, 233ff., 238, 244–265; see references to Lévinas in n. 45 above.
48. Kierkegaard, PC 141/SV 12:131.
49. Kierkegaard, PC 141f./SV 12:131f. One need not take Kierkegaard's extreme, perhaps demonic, case of becoming a duplex being—either a deceiver or the faithful lover—for Regine Olsen. One need not derive the mode of "faith" in a test of lovers upon one another. Kierkegaard always uses a disclaimer to indicate the inward suffering and self-doubt that he has undergone in this regard: "I do not decide whether . . . [the testing lover] has the right to do this, I am merely following the thought-categories" (PC 142/SV 12:132). Cf. PC 137/SV 12:127; PC 138f./SV 12:129; JP/P entries from 1848.
50. Kierkegaard, WOL 26–33/SV 9:13–20.
51. Kierkegaard, WOL 200–212./SV 9:202–215.
52. Kierkegaard, PC 142/SV 12:132. For the metaphor of the riddle, see Plato's *Republic*, in *Great Dialogues of Plato*, trans. W. H. D. Rouse (New York: New American Library, 1956) 452B–474A, on the riddle of the philosopher–king; *Hegel's Philosophy of Right* 12 and 3, on the riddle of "reason as the rose in the cross of the present"; and Karl Marx, *The Economic and Philosophic Manuscripts of 1844*, trans. Martin Milligan (New York: International Publishers, 1964) 135, on Communism as the riddle of the history solved. See also Marc C. Taylor's Hegelianized reading of Kierkegaard's riddle, *Journeys to Selfhood: Hegel and Kierkegaard* (Berkeley: University of California Press, 1980) 227f.
53. Kierkegaard, PC 143/SV 12:133.
54. Kierkegaard, PC 220f., 214/SV 12:202, 196.
55. Kierkegaard, PC 159/SV 12:149; cf. PC 123f./SV 12:116f.; WOL 343/SV 9:354.
56. Kierkegaard, PC 253/SV 12:231. (See the opening of Chap. 5 above.)
57. Kierkegaard, PC 223/SV 12:205.
58. Note the title of Habermas's "Transzendenz von innen, Transzendenz ins Diesseits," in TuK 127–156. See Charles Sanders Peirce, *Collected Papers*, ed. Charles Hartshorne and Paul Weiss (Cambridge, Mass.: Harvard University Press, 1931–1958), Vol. 2: 655. See also n. 6 and n. 38 in Chap. 6 above.
59. The citation is from Kierkegaard, JP 1848:2011/P IX A450. See Augustine, *The City of God*, ed. David Knowles, trans. Henry Bettenson (Baltimore: Penguin Books, 1981) Book IV, chap. 4.
60. Kierkegaard, JP 1854:2969/P XI^1 A64; JP 1854:2985/P XI^2 A26; cf. JP 1854:2970/P XI^1 A227.
61. Cf. Kierkegaard, CUP 554 n./SV 7:484 n.

62. Below, I am quoting Kierkegaard, JP 1850:2952/P X^2 A390; cf. SD 79/SV 11:191. The Danish *Menighed* may be rendered both as "community" and as "congregation." Hirsch's German trans. (Kierkegaard, GW) uses the second sense, Gemeinde.

63. Kierkegaard, JP 1850:2024/P X^2 A489. "[T]he error lies mainly in this, that the universal, which Hegelianism considers the truth (and the single individual to be the truth by being swallowed up in it) is an abstraction—the state, etc. . . . Hegel basically regards men . . . as an animal-race endowed with reason. In an animal-race 'the single individual' is always lower than the 'race'. . . . That this can be taken in vain and horribly misused, I concede. But . . . *here* is where the battle must really be fought" (JP 1850:1614/P X^2 A426).

64. Kierkegaard, JP 1853:2823/P XII X^5 A73. (On Buber, see n. 47 above.)

65. Kierkegaard, JP 1846:4110/P VII[1] A20. Cf. CUP 428f./SV 7:371f. and the organization of WOL.

CHAPTER 8

1. Habermas, NC 249–267/EAS 159–178; NR 179ff.; see also Chap. 1 above. On "existential revolution," which applies also to the November 1989 "velvet revolution" in Czechoslovakia, see Havel, Mb, chaps. 20-21; DO, letter 143; Dv 15; cf. Havel, uR.

2. On themes from Lévinas, see Havel, DO, letters 129–145, and later notes in this chapter. For the Bio-bibliographies, see Oli (1969–1979), Drs (until 1989), and H (until 1992).

3. See Max Horkheimer, *Gesammelten Schriften*, Vol. 7 (Frankfurt a/M: Fischer, 1985): "Theismus und Atheismus" (1963) 182–186; "Zur Zukunft der kritischen Theorie" (1971) 429–434. See also Havel, DO, letter 139. Havel (Sos) depicts the source of ideologies in the gap between words and acts, not, as Habermas does (TCA 2: fig. 28), in the rationality differential between the sacred and the profane domains.

4. Havel, HL (18 March 1990). Havel appeals to Foucault's analysis of the prison as the place that does not punish the crime but destroys human identity. He admits here that the differences between the communist totality and the destruction of identity in the western Panopticon approximate one another. The postprison nihilism approximates the character of the existential condition (Drs 15). See Michel Foucault, *Discipline and Punish: The Birth of the Prison*, trans. Alan Sheridan (New York: Random House, 1977).

5. Havel, Jerusalem speech, in P 102.

6. Havel, Ss and its trans., "Angst vor der Freiheit," in AF 99–108. See "Havel mahnt Waldheim indirekt: Rede in Salzburg—Ohne volle Wahrheit keine volle Freiheit," *Frankfurter Rundschau* (27 July 1990) 1; Henry Kamm, "Havel's Lesson for Austria: Don't Fear the Past," *International Herald Tribune* (27 July 1990) 1. Further, contrast two Jewish writers who analyze Havel's performance in Salzburg: A.M. Rosenthal, "Havel and Waldheim," *New York Times* (29 July 1990) E-19 "Havel's Message Deserves Hearing" *International Herald Tribune* (15 August 1990) 6. Rosenthal takes offense at Havel's appearance with Kurt Waldheim, who has falsified his Nazi past; Goldmann points out that politicians have made it too easy for themselves by simply making a no longer meaningful gesture of nonappear-

ance. Havel acted with an existential type of ostracism against Waldheim—that is, not by being absent but by making known the absence of truth and the presence of a lie. Havel's dramatic–moral and "nonpolitical" approach to professional politics is today criticized by his dissident peers, by market liberals, and by the noncommunist leftists at home. He seems to be that victorious Sisyphus intellectual about whose success something remains suspicious (Havel, Dv 144f.). This also explains the existential character of the above address. Cf. Havel's AH; "Havel über die Anatomie des Hasses: Eine Konferenz der Stiftung Elie Wiesel in Oslo," *Neue Zürcher Zeitung,* "Hinweise" (3 September 1990) 4; and Chap. 10 below.

7. Through Patočka, the student of Husserl and Heidegger, Havel turns to moral and political implications of phenomenology. Following the first Czechoslovak President, the philosopher Tomáš G. Masaryk, he aims to renew a west-oriented culture of democracy. Reflecting on Lévinas's vertical ethics, discovered through the prison letters received from his brother Ivan, Havel articulates social-existential concerns. For other formative influences on Havel, see Václav Bělohradský, *Krize eschatologie neosobnosti* [The Crisis of the Eschatology of Nonpersonality] (London: Rozmluvy, 1983) and "Je Masarykovo pojetí Německa ještě aktuální?" [Is Masaryk's Understanding of Germany Still Actual?], *Přítomnost* (Praha, 4 June 1990) 16–17; Václav Benda, "Paralelní Polis," and Petr Uhl, "Alternativní společenství jako revoluční avantgarda" [Alternative Community as a Revolutionary Avant-Garde], both in Vilém Přečan, ed., *Charta 77: 1977–1989. Od morální k demokratické revoluci* [From Moral to Democratic Revolution] (Bratislava: ARCHA, 1990) 43–51 and 81–88. See also Ivan Dubský's Introduction to Patočka's *Kacířské eseje o filosofii dějin* [Heretical Essays about the Philosophy of History] (Praha: Academia, 1990) 5–19; Andreas Kuhlmann, "Der Kerker als Front: Jan Patočka's existential-istischer Begriff des Politischen," *Frankfurter Allgemeine Zeitung,* "Gesteswissensel-erften"(23 May 1990) N-3; Guido Kalberer, "Ein Denker zwischen Husserl und Heidegger: Jan Patočka's Habilitaionşarbeit in deutscher Übersetzung," *Neue Zürcher Zeitung,* "Hinweise" (11 September 1990) 35; Patočka's *Ausgewählte Schriften,* ed. Klaus Nellen and Jiří Němec, trans. Eliška and Ralph Melville (Stuttgart: Klett-Cotta, 1987); and, for Lévinas's influence on liberation theology, Enrique Dussel, *Ethics and Community,* trans. Robert R. Barr (New York: Maryknoll, 1988).

8. Havel, DO, letters 122–144. The stages are marked by Havel in his letters by the numbers 1–3 (cf. letters 131–136, 138f.).

9. Emmanuel Lévinas, "Dialogue with E. Lévinas," in Richard A. Cohen, ed., *Face to Face with Lévinas* (Albany: SUNY Press, 1986) 26f., 23f., 31. Cf. Lévinas, "Humanism and Anarchy" and "No Identity," in *Collected Philosophical Papers,* trans. Alphonso Lingis (Hague: Martinus Nijhoff, 1987) 127–140 and 141–152.

10. Lévinas, *Totality and Infinity: An Essay on Exteriority,* trans. Alphonso Lingis (Pittsburgh: Duquesne University Press, 1969) 40; "Dialogue" 21; and *Otherwise Than Being or Beyond Essence,* trans. Alphonso Lingis (Hague: Martinus Nijhoff, 1981).

11. On collective guilt, see Havel, P 79–86, the welcoming speech for Richard von Weizsäcker, the President of Germany, on the anniversary of Hitler's occupation of Czechoslovakia (Praha: Hrad, March 15, 1990); see also Jk, HL (1 March 1992), and the new state agreement between Czechoslovakia and Germany (27 Feburary 1992) where Havel publicly condemns the postwar global expulsion of Germans from Czechoslovakia. On the "second revolution," see HL (19 August

1980) and uR. During a political happening on St. Wenceslas Square, an overturned Soviet tank, painted with Solidarity and peace signs, dramatized Havel's call for an ongoing responsible revolution; see SI (Praha, 21 August 1990—the 22nd anniversary of the Soviet-led Warsaw Pact invasion that crushed Dubček's attempt at democratic socialism in 1968).

12. Havel, DO, letter 142.

13. Havel, Dv 149–153 and 101ff.

14. Havel, Dv 172ff. Not all inscenations of his dramas respect this insight. One of the best-understood interpretations of his dramatic work is the performance of LD in Havel's alma mater theater Na zábradlí, directed by Jan Grossman (Praha, opening on 9 April 1990).

15. Havel, Dv 101ff.

16. Havel, Dv 163f. A Czech activist priest, Rev. Václav Malý, in his public talk (Bonn, 7 March 1990) explained Havel's prison experience: while there Havel found friendship with imprisoned priests, took part in secret liturgies, and grew tolerant of the Christian churches, he kept his autonomy from a specific church affiliation. Before becoming offended, one should dramatically interpret why Havel took part in the *Te Deum* after his first election to the Presidency (the Czechoslovak communist President who led the pro-Soviet coup in 1948, Klement Gottwald, also attended a *Te Deum* in 1948 while he began a hunt on the churches by imprisoning all religious in the concentration monasteries), and why, after hosting the Tibetan Dalai Lama, he invited Pope John Paul II. By encouraging the Pope to speak publicly about the reformer Jan Hus and the special Jewish heritage, about the communist liquidation of the churches and the new nationalist conflicts, the painful religious and national past had the first occasion to heal.

17. Havel, Sos and DO, letter 142. Cf. Lévinas, "Dialogue" 23. On the inspiration of Lévinas's ethic in the concept of *Charta 77*, see DO, letter 122.

18. Havel, DO, letters 143, 142; Mb, chaps. 20–22.

19. Havel, DO, letter 141.

20. Havel, Lp 89; see also his Mb and Ps.

21. See Havel, H and DO.

22. See Francis Fukuyama, *The End of History and the Last Man* (New York: Free Press, 1992); Havel, Lp 97–115 and EME.

23. Habermas, LC 120, 121/166, 167: Habermas speaks of "the repoliticization of the biblical inheritance . . . which goes together with a leveling of this-worldly/other-worldly dichotomy . . . [in which] "God" becomes the name for a communicative structure that forces humans, on pain of a loss of their humanity, to go beyond their accidental, empirical nature to encounter one another *indirectly*, that is, across an objective something that they themselves are not" (original emphasis).

24. Havel, Ps 59.

25. Havel, Ps 55–59, 53.

26. Cf. James de Candole, "Václav Havel jako konzervativní myslitel," *Proglas*, No. 1 (Brno, 1990) 52–57, trans. Z. ["Václav Havel as a Conservative Thinker," *Salisbury Review* (December 1988).] On "nonpolitical politics" as existential, see Havel, Mb, chaps. 19–20; as opposed to fundamentalism, Mb, chap. 18; and as opposed to fanaticism and fetishism, DO, letter 141 and Ps 58f. See also P, Jerusalem speech. Czechoslovak foreign minister Jiří Dienstbier shares with Havel the notion of "moral diplomacy without tricks"; see Dienstbier's interview on PBS Tele-

vision, 20 Feburary 1990, and his *Snění o Evropě* [Dreaming about Europe] (Praha: Lidové noviny, 1990).

27. See Havel, Ps 41–59. On November 1989 as a "carnival," see Ss.

28. On "postdemocracy" as opposed to formal democracy, see Havel, Mb, chaps. 21–22; on "inter-existential" community, see DO, letters 142–143; cf. Chaps. 9–10 below.

29. Habermas, NR 202f.; see Chaps. 1 and 3 (section 3.2.B) above, and Chap. 10 below. Cf. Havel, uR.

30. Havel, Drs 202ff., essay, "Šifra socialismus" [Cipher Socialism] (June 1988).

31. Havel, HL (19 August 1990) and Dv 147.

32. Havel, Dv 12f. Havel situates himself in the generation of the Beatles, the America of the 1960s, American music and art, and civil rights movements (Dv 23f.).

33. My critical questions to Havel and Habermas reflect a concern variously raised in connection with my topic by Klaus Günther, Axel Honneth, Seyla Benhabib, Drucilla Cornell, and others: how is the concrete other maintained within the anonymous structures of radical democracy, and how is the ideal of communicative ethics qualified by an existential ethic of the concrete other? My questions assume the possibility of answering the typical discourse-theoretical objections raised during my earlier presentation of a shorter version of this chapter (at Habermas's colloquium, Frankfurt, 22 October 1990): Habermas identified the vertical with prayer, and thus he found my reading of Havel and Lévinas too theological. James Bohman worried that while "existential revolution" could be used descriptively, it is dangerous to speak of it normatively. Martin Löw-Beer found it difficult to discourse within Lévinas's metaphysics. Habermas's point is best answered by Kierkegaard's nuanced distinction between immanent (A) and transcendent–Christian (B) religiosity. Neither (A) nor (B) assume the traditionalist authority of the sacred but require existential pathos. Havel's posture, while oriented to the wholly other, stands for this existential passion; its communication depends neither on the domains of atheism nor on the contents of prayer. Bohman's objection mistakenly blurs the ungrounded choice of values in cultural spheres with Havel's existential self-choice of a way of thinking and living within the community of the shaken. But we cannot judge the irresolution of the Kierkegaardian existential drama from a monological and decisionist political stance of propaganda or catechism. Löw-Beer's difficulty should be cured by Havel's existentially performative reading of Lévinas.

CHAPTER 9

1. See Luigi Pirandello, *Six Characters in Search of an Author*, trans. Frederick May (London: Heinemann, 1958); Havel, H; and Kierkegaard, Pr, the foreword by Marc C. Taylor and the translator's intro. by William McDonald. On postmodern uses of Kierkegaard, see also James L. Marsh, John D. Caputo, and Merold Westphal, Eds., *Modernity and Its Discontents* (New York: Fordham University Press, 1992).

2. On Havel's "nonpolitical politics" see Chap. 8 above.

3. Kierkegaard, Pr 22–28/SV 5:10–15. I am not assuming any positive binary

opposition between the "feminine" and the "masculine". I wish to retrieve Kierkegaard's critique of a "masculinist" way of being an author which stands in the way of existential authoring. (On this, see also Chap. 6, section 6.1.B, above.)

4. Kierkegaard, Pr 29–99/SV 5:16–71; on Hegel's Preface to the *Phenomenology of Spirit*, see CUP 251f./SV 7:212.

5. See Jacques Derrida, *The Postcard: From Socrates to Freud and Beyond*, trans. Alan Bass (Chicago: University of Chicago Press, 1987), and McDonald's translator's intro. to Kierkegaard's Pr, n. 14. For an excellent analysis of the Prefaces in Kierkegaard's FT, see Edward F. Mooney, *Knights of Faith and Resignation: Reading Kierkegaard's "Fear and Trembling"* (Albany: SUNY Press, 1991), chap. 2.

6. Kierkegaard, CUP 252ff./SV 7:213.

7. Kierkegaard, CUP 260/SV 7:220.

8. Kierkegaard, CUP 263f., 270/SV 7:223, 229.

9. Kierkegaard, CUP 276f., 280ff./SV 7:236, 238ff. Cf. SLW.

10. Kierkegaard, CUP 251f./SV 7:212. See Taylor's foreword and McDonald's translator's intro. to Kierkegaard's Pr. See also John D. Caputo, *Radical Hermeneutics: Repetition, Deconstruction, and the Hermeneutic Project* (Bloomington: Indiana University Press, 1987); I disagree with Caputo that "the book is an illusion" (293, cf. 294), because this is an abstract observation that cannot be strictly redeemed in his own book. Climacus's disclaimer raises an existential–performative claim, whereas Caputo's standpoint of a textual observer blurs the horizontal starts/endings of the authorship with the existential difficulty of authoring. But Kierkegaard shows that one can begin/conclude a book, disclaim the authority of its authorship, and yet need neither inscribe a closure into authoring, reading, or acting nor vanish in textuality without ever facing the difficulty of responsible authoring.

11. Kierkegaard, CUP 289/SV 7:247f.

12. Kierkegaard, CUP 617, 619ff./SV 7:537, 539f. See the start of Chap. 5 above.

13. Kierkegaard, CUP 625/SV 7:545f.; cf. PVA.

14. Kierkegaard, PVA 107f., 143n., 147/SV 13:589f., 494n., 497; and COR. See Bruce H. Kirmmse, ""This Disastrous Confounding of Politics and Christianity': Kierkegaard's Open Letter of 1851," in Robert L. Perkins, ed., *International Kierkegaard Commentary*, Vol. 13, *The Corsair Affair* (Macon, Ga.: Mercer University Press, 1990) 179–184.

15. See Kierkegaard, PVA 93–103/SV 13:576–582.

16. Kierkegaard, CUP 625f./SV 7:546.

17. Kierkegaard, CUP 626f., 629f./SV 7:546f., 548f.

18. Kierkegaard's Prefaces to EUD/SV 4:7, 73, 121; SV 5:79, 175; cf. SV 8:117, 247.

19. Kierkegaard, AUCH 95f./SV 14:117f.

20. Kierkegaard, PVA 107f./SV 13:589f.

21. Kierkegaard, PVA 112f./SV 13:593f.

22. Kierkegaard, PVA 115–118/SV 13:595ff. Imagination fails some Kierkegaard scholars—for instance, Jeremy Walker, "Communication and Community," in Alastair McKinnon, ed. and intro., *Kierkegaard: Resources and Results* (Montreal: Wilfrid Laurier University Press, 1982): "I now believe that Kierkegaard ... had no pattern of a social and political existence to recommend. . . . A proper under-

standing of Kierkegaard's position, I now believe, shows that it could not possibly yield any social and political recommendations. Kierkegaard thought constantly about 'the crowd' and 'the individual.' There is no third concept within his writings which might identify the way in which individuals can exist together in this world. Nor in the other world either" (70).

23. Kierkegaard, PVA 124/SV 13:601.

24. Kierkegaard, PVA 126f./SV 13:603f.; cf. JP 1843:5664/P IV A107.

25. Kierkegaard, PVA 128ff./SV 13:604f.

26. Kierkegaard, PVA 156 and n./SV 13:507f. and n.

27. Kierkegaard, PVA 157/SV 13:508. See Albert Camus, *The Rebel: An Essay on Man in Revolt*, trans. Anthony Bower (New York: Knopf, 1956).

28. Kierkegaard, CUP 585/SV 7:510; cf. JP 1851:6780/P X^4 A383.

29. C. Stephen Evans, *Kierkegaard's Fragments and Postscripts: The Religious Philosophy of Johannes Climacus* (Atlantic Highlands, N.J.: Humanities Press, 1983) 162f. On permanent revolution, see Karl Marx, "Address to the Communist League" (1848), in David McLellan, ed., *Karl Marx: Selected Writings* (London: Oxford University Press, 1977) 277, 280, 285, and "The Class Struggle in France" (1848) 296.

30. Kierkegaard, PVA 157f./SV 13:508f.

31. Kierkegaard, CUP 518/SV 7:509. I respond here to Habermas's ambiguous use of Kierkegaard in replying to the theological reception of communicative ethics (see Chap. 1 above). On Nietzsche, Marx, and Freud as hermeneuts of suspicion, see Paul Ricoeur, *Freud and Philosophy: An Essay on Interpretation*, trans. Denis Savage (New Haven, Conn.: Yale University Press, 1970) 32. On Kierkegaard as a hermeneut of suspicion, see Merold Westphal, *Kierkegaard's Critique of Reason and Society* (Macon, Ga.: Mercer University Press, 1987), chap. 7, 105–125. On Peter Berger's *methodological atheism* and its use in describing religious acts apart from truth questions about whether religious projection fabricates or discovers, hallucinates or reveals, see Westphal, *God, Guilt, and Death: An Existential Phenomenology of Religion* (Bloomington: Indiana University Press, 1984) 18ff., with reference to Peter L. Berger, *The Sacred Canopy* (Garden City, N.Y.: Doubleday, 1967) 100, 193 n. 33. Westphal, following Berger and Ricoeur, allows for both "methodological theism" that is receptive to and "methodological atheism" that scrutinizes the believer in order to "enter into a conversation devoid of the assuring assumption that their own stances are justified." This conversation is admittedly more just than Habermas's, who excludes from communicative ethics all religious claims on the Feurbachean basis of equating religiosity with ideology. Habermas's posture betrays a projection of that belief affirmation which itself has not been purified by methodological atheism (i.e., by suspicion of all deification). In my portrayal of Kierkegaard's religious point of view as posttraditional, I have been appealing to something which Ricoeur notes in a psychoanalytic critique of religious projection—"that . . . 'destruction' of religion can be the counterpart of a faith purified of all idolatry." Habermas privileges the nonfaith interpretations over the possibility of ideology-free faith, and thus his "destruction of idols" abrogates for itself a dogmatic claim that excludes a priori that other receptivity. Ricoeur, *The Symbolism of Evil*, trans. Emerson Buchanan (New York: Harper and Row, 1967) 230, 235; cf. Westphal, *God, Guilt, and Death* 20 n. 33, here in sympathy with Habermas.

32. Kierkegaard, PVA 130, 132/SV 13:605, 607; cf. TA.
33. Kierkegaard, PVA 134ff./SV 13:608ff.
34. Kierkegaard, PVA 143 n., 147/SV 13:494f., n., 497.
35. Kierkegaard, PVA 148f. and 149 n./SV 13:498f. and 499 n.
36. (See Chap. 6, section 6.3.B, and Chap. 7, section 7.2.B, above.)
37. Kierkegaard, PVA 117f., 151, 5/SV 13:597, 501, 517.
38. Kierkegaard, PVA 6–9/SV 13:518–520.
39. Kierkegaard, PVA 10–14, 31–34/SV 13:522–524, 535ff.
40. Kierkegaard, PVA 17/SV 13:525.
41. Kierkegaard, PVA 38ff./SV 13:540ff.
42. Kierkegaard, PVA 44f./SV 13:544.
43. Kierkegaard, PVA 45–53/SV 13:545–549.
44. Kierkegaard, PVA 53–60/SV 13:549–554.
45. Kierkegaard, PVA 61ff./SV 13:555f.
46. Kierkegaard, PVA 64–74/SV 13:556–563.
47. Kierkegaard, PVA 75/SV 13:563.
48. Kierkegaard, PVA 84–88/SV 13:569–572; cf. WOL.
49. Kierkegaard, PVA 93–103/SV 13:576–582.
50. Kierkegaard, TA 5–23/SV 8:5–22; JP 1846:5873, 5877/P VII[1] A4, A9.
51. Habermas, TCA 2:396, cites Claus Offe, "Konkurenzpartei und kollektive politische Identität," in R. Roth, ed., *Parlamentarisches Ritual und politische Alternative* (Frankfurt a/M: Suhrkamp, 1980). See Havel, PH.
52. See Ivan Vejvoda, "Loss and Construction of Identity: Democracy Revisited," paper presented at the Dubrovnik's Inter-University Center International Seminar on "Identity and Civil Society," Ischia, Italy (2 April 1992).
53. For a summary of the latter issue, see Jeri Laber, "Witch Hunt in Prague," *New York Review of Books* (23 April 1992) 5–8, and Stephen Engelberg, "The Velvet Revolution Gets Rough," *New York Times Magazine* (31 May 1992) 31–33, 49, 54.
54. Cf. Havel, Lp 94–115. Ralf Dahrendorf, "In Politics Begin Responsibilities" (review of Havel's Lp) *New York Times Book Review* (7 June 1992) 1, 29.
55. On this addendum to Lp, see Havel, PL 8.
56. See Havel, AH and Ss. In Np, Havel speaks about writing a play about the lustration fever. Yet one wonders if in the moment when he signed the purgation law this well-meant dramatic irony did not mask mere abstract inaction, whether the author was not suddenly bereft of any existential resistance to power.
57. See Francis Fukuyama, "Rest Easy. It's Not 1914 Anymore," *New York Times* (9 Feb. 1992), E-17 and Chap. 1 above; Habermas VaZ 9–44.

CHAPTER 10

1. See Karl Jaspers, *Die geistige Situation der Gegenwart* (Berlin Gruyter, 1931), published two years before Hitler's rise to power; trans. by Eden and Cedar Paul as *Man in the Modern Age* (New York: Henry Holt, 1933). My commentary on Habermas's intro. to OSSA 1–28 develops my review of it in *Auslegung* 14/2 (1988) 225–228.
2. Habermas, OSSA 2ff.

3. Habermas, OSSA 3. Johann Baptist Metz's "Productive Noncontemporaneity" is the most Kierkegaardian contribution (169–177).

4. The exception to this conspiracy of silence is Andrew Buchwalter's translator's intro. to the American edition of Habermas's OSSA, which mentions in n. 3 Karl Löwith's *From Hegel to Nietzsche* (1941), trans. David E. Green (New York: Holt, Rinehart & Winston, 1964). Löwith notes how the French Revolution problematized traditional claims under the notion of "the spirit of the age." This refers no longer to "the spirit of the ages" but to one's own particular epoch as the last court of appeal. It was not, however, Hegel but Fichte, Kierkegaard, Nietzsche, and Marx who attended "to temporal terms of the spirit as such." Fichte's criterion in his lectures on the "Characteristics of the Present Age" (1804) lies in the role of the present for the future. Marx radicalizes the left Hegelianism in "the political eschatology of the *Communist Manifesto*." At the same time, Kierkegaard issues a call to a decisive moment that harnesses all dimensions of time in the signification of eternity. "Time as such has no real present; it exists only in the moment, as the salient point of decision" Löwith 201–207.

5. Jaspers, *Man in the Modern Age* 10f.

6. Jaspers, *Man in the Modern Age* 23.

7. Jaspers, *Man in the Modern Age* 123f., 129.

8. Löwith, *From Hegel to Nietzsche* 151, 158, 249; cf. 321. On the legacy of TA in Heidegger, Jaspers, Löwith, Lukács, and Adorno, and in the typical leftist caricatures of Kierkegaard's critique of mass society, see John M. Hoberman, "Kierkegaard's *Two Ages* and Heidegger's Critique of Modernity," in Robert L. Perkins, ed., *International Kierkegaard Commentary*, Vol. 14, *Two Ages: The Age of Revolution and the Present Age. A Literary Review* (Macon, Ga: Mercer University Press, 1984) 254ff.

9. Perkins, *Commentary*, Vol. 14, *Two Ages: xiii–xxiv* and "Envy as Personal Phenomenon and as Politics" 107–132.

10. Anton Hügli, "Kierkegaard und der Kommunismus," in Michael Theunissen and Wilfried Greve, eds., *Materialien zur Philosophie Sören Kierkegaard* (Frankfurt a/M: Suhrkamp, 1979) 532–538.

11. Merold Westphal, *Kierkegaard's Critique of Reason and Society* (Macon, Ga.: Mercer University Press, 1987) 43–59. James L. Marsh, "Interiority and Revolution," *Philosophy Today* (Fall 1985) 191–202; Marsh "Praxis and Ultimate Reality: Intellectual, Moral, and Religious Conversion as Radical Political Conversion," *Ultimate Reality and Meaning*, 13 (September 1990) 222–240.

12. Bruce H. Kirmmse, *Kierkegaard in Golden Age Denmark* (Bloomington: Indiana University Press, 1990) 264, 245ff. Contrast this antimandarin position with that of Heidegger or Schmitt in the climate of prefascist Germany: see Hauke Brunkhorst, *Der Intellektuelle im Land der Mandarine* (Frankfurt a/M: Suhrkamp, 1988). (Cf. n. 35 below.)

13. Kierkegaard, TA 62/SV 8:59 for the first four quotations below.

14. Kierkegaard, 62f./SV 8:59.

15. This notion of the wholly other is that formal requirement by which the later Max Horkheimer defined critical theory. See his *Gesammelte Schriften*, Vol. 7 (Frankfurt a/M: Fischer, 1985), "Die Sehnsucht nach dem ganz Anderen" (1970) 387, 398. The wholly other does not negate the normative search for a just society. Horkheimer insists that a critical theorist must resist any identification of searching

with an ultimate achievement. His corrective effects Habermas's fallibilism and qualifies his consensual ideal of critical theory.

16. Kierkegaard, TA 63/SV 8:59.

17. Kierkegaard, TA 63f./SV 8:60 for the quotations below.

18. Kierkegaard, TA 90–93/SV 8:84–87—for the quotations below.

19. Kierkegaard, TA 103f./SV 8:96f.—for the quotations below.

20. See Walter Kaufmann's Intro. to Kierkegaard's *Present Age*, trans. Alexander Dru (New York: Harper & Row, 1962) 20ff.

21. Kirmmse, *Kierkegaard* 266–271. Kierkegaard writes not as an author of a political novel but, though in his name and within the secular medium, as a reviewer—of an anonymously published book (Fru Gyllembourg, 1845) by the mother of Johan Ludvig Heiberg, Thomasine Bentzen (TA 5/SV 8:5).

22. Kierkegaard, TA 74ff./SV 8:70f.

23. Kierkegaard, TA 110, 76/SV 8:102, 72.

24. Kirmmse, *Kierkegaard* 270f. See Kierkegaard, E/O I 281–300/SV 1:257–272.

25. Kirmmse, *Kierkegaard* 278; cf. 273, 275f., and 246.

26. Kierkegaard, JP 1848:no English trans. is published/P IX B8, B10, B22, B24; see Malantschuk's commentary in JP, Vol. 4: 664ff. See also Max Horkheimer and Theodor W. Adorno, *Dialectic of Enlightenment* (1944) trans. John Cumming (New York: Continuum, 1987); Michel Foucault, *Discipline and Punish: The Birth of the Prison*, trans. Alan Sheridan (New York: Random House, 1977).

27. Kierkegaard, TA 81–84/SV 8:76–79.

28. Kierkegaard, TA 79, 81f./SV 8:74, 76f.; on Foucault, see n. 26 above.

29. Kierkegaard, JP 1848:4128/P VIII^1 A551.

30. Kierkegaard, TA 84f./SV 8:79f.

31. Kierkegaard, TA 84, 86/SV 8:79, 81.

32. Kierkegaard, TA 86f./SV 8:80ff.; JP 1847:4121/P VIII^1 A245; JP 1848:4127/P VIII^1 A531; JP 1848:4129/P VIII^1 A552.

33. Kierkegaard, JP 1850:4171/P X^2 A356 and JP 1850:4137/P X^2 A609 for the quotations below.

34. See Kierkegaard, TA 63/SV 8:59; JP 1848:4127/P VIII^1 A531.

35. Kierkegaard, TA 106/SV 8:99. See my critique of Best's and Kellner's reading of Kierkegaard's politics in my review of Perkins, ed., *International Kierkegaard Commentary*, Vol. 13, *The Corsair Affair*, in *Man and World* 26 (1993) 93–97. (See also n. 12 above and Chap. 7, n. 10.)

36. Kirmmse, *Kierkegaard* 277f. See Kierkegaard, TA 87f., 78–110/SV 8:82f., 74–102.

37. Kierkegaard, TA 88f./SV 8:82ff.; JP 1850:6604/P X^2 A622.

38. Kierkegaard, TA 107f./SV 8:99f.

39. Kierkegaard, TA 108f./SV 8:101f.

40. Kierkegaard, JP 1848(?)–1849:6256/P X^6 B40.

41. Kierkegaard, JP 1851:4198/P X^4 A41; TA 110/SV 8:102; JP 1848:2933/P VIII^1 A538.

42. See Frederick Douglass, *Narrative of the Life of Frederick Douglass, An American Slave* (1845) (New York: New American Library, 1968).

43. On Habermas, see Chap. 1, section 1.2.B, above; on Havel, Chap. 8 above.

44. Václav Havel, "Šifra socialismus" (1988), in Drs 202ff., cf. 51, 67; Dv 12–

15, 147; on "inter-existential" communication, DO, letters 142f. Perhaps it is not wholly fair and accurate to connect, like Seyla Benhabib, Havel's and Rorty's reasons for their disenchantment with "socialism." Havel is concerned with existentially communicating individuals; Rorty's play of edifying discourse requires neither existential edification in communication nor responsible speakers. For Benhabib's point and last citation, see her editor's intro., *Praxis International* 11/1 (April 1991) 5, 2 with an indirect reference to my earlier essay, "Havel and Habermas on Identity and Revolution," *Praxis International* 10/3–4 (1990–1991) 261–277 (see Chap. 8 and Chap. 1, n. 7, above).

45. Havel, Lp 44–60, 95.

46. Havel, Sos. On "ptydepe," see his drama *Vyrozumění* [Notice], in H; on other examples of beautiful words that nevertheless—when spoken by some dramatic masks—sound like phrases, see his LD and his *Pokoušení* [Tempting], in H.

47. Havel, AH 118–123/Vo 19–22. Cf. Herbert Marcuse's critique of the present age in *One-Dimensional Man: Studies in the Ideology of Advanced Industrial Society* (Boston: Beacon Press, 1964, 1991) and Douglas Kellner, who in his new Introduction (1991) portrays Marcuse as "a radical individualist who is deeply disturbed by the decline of the traits of authentic individuality" (*xxviii*).

48. Havel, AH 125–129/Vo 23–26. This analysis offers a plausible interpretation of the ferocity with which nationalist conflicts erupt in the former Yugoslavia or the former Soviet Union.

49. Havel, Cs 11/Vo 81–85 for all quotations from this lecture.

50. To be fair to Habermas, in his "Peirce and Communication" (only in the English trans. of ND), he critiques Peirce for rendering the individual as "something merely subjective and egoistic." Against Peirce's logical socialism, Habermas defends individuals who become accountable in the process of their "unforced agreement." They are to resist "the leveling force of a universalism," sustain "the multivocal character of intersubjectivity," and "encounter in communication" the other "as contradiction and difference." But Habermas's model never provides the sufficient conditions of this resisting possibility (108–111).

51. Havel, Ss; see Chap. 8 above. On Habermas, cf. Chap. 1 above. Both Habermas's Brussels proposal and Derrida's post-modern yet Enlightenment ideal of socially just and multicultural community, *The Other Heading: Reflections on Today's Europe*, trans. Pascale-Anne Brault and Michael B. Nass, (Bloomington: Indiana University Press, 1992), lack an attention to existential politics.

52. Havel's Jerusalem speech, in AF 52–55/P 100–103.

53. Havel, Ps 41–59. Cf. Habermas, TCA 2: chap. 8.

54. Havel, Lp 89, 94–115. See also Havel, PCN.

55. Herbert Marcuse, "Über konkrete Philosophie" (1929), in *Schriften*, Vol. 1 (Frankfurt a/M: Suhrkamp, 1978) 385–406. See Douglas Kellner, *Herbert Marcuse and the Crisis of Marxism* (Berkeley: University of California Press, 1984) 63–68.

56. Kellner, *Marcuse* 66, 98ff., 409 n. 22, and 410 nn. 26, 29, 31. On philosophical existentialism (Kierkegaard) versus political existentialism (Schmitt), see Herbert Marcuse, *Negations: Essays in Critical Theory*, trans. Jeremy J. Shapiro (Boston: Beacon Press, 1968) 31, 274 n. 68; "Philosophie des Scheiterns: Karl Jaspers Werk," *Unterhaltungsblatt der Vossichen Zeitung* (14 December 1933); and Preface, n. 8, above.

57. Richard Wolin, "Carl Schmitt, Political Existentialism, and the Total State,"

Theory and Society 19 (1990) 396f. In all the positions—from nationalism, to decisionist politics, to the uses of war—ascribed by Wolin to Schmitt ("Schmitt" 397, 393ff., 401, 404, 406, 409, 412, n. 8, and n. 21), Kierkegaard sharply dissents. See Wolin for the secondary literature, nn. 4–5, and for his discussion of the *Telos* issue 72 (1987) on Schmitt; see also Habermas's review, "The Horrors of Autonomy: Carl Schmitt in English," in EAS 115–158/NC 128–139. Cf. György Lukács, *Werke*, Vol. 9 (Neuwied: Luchterhand, 1974) 219, 264.

    58. Marcuse, *Negations* 32–42.

    59. Kellner, *Marcuse* 410 n. 29, notes that Marcuse bypassed Jaspers's view of existence as communication, yet that there is an affinity between Jaspers and Habermas's communicative model of critical theory.

    60. Cf. Metz, "Productive Noncontemporaneity," in Habermas OSSA 169.

    61. Kierkegaard, JP 1850:4175f./P X² A478f.

    62. See the following "obituaries" of the "velvet revolution": Havel, IHW; Paul Wilson, "The End of the Velvet Revolution," *New York Review of Books* (13 August 1992) 57f., 60–64; George F. Kennan, "Keeping the Faith" [review of Paul Wilson's English trans. of Havel's Lp], *New York Review of Books* (24 September 1992), 3f.; Henry Brandon, "Who Split Czechoslovakia?" *New York Times*, Op-Ed (24 September 1992) A-29; and Henry Kamm, "Czech Regrets the Rift with Slovakia," *New York Times* (29 September 1992) A-7, and Kamm, "Nation Split, Havel Aspires to a New Political Life," *New York Times* (30 September 1992) A-3. Brandon is right that Vladimír Mečiar, Václav Klaus, and Václav Havel share some responsibility for the breakup of Czecho-Slovakia, but his point is too simplistic. Besides other politicians and the deadlocked Parliament, these three are not the only ones to bear some blame. The transition to democracy in Czechoslovakia is frustrated by the historical longing after a benevolent philosopher–king, a popular desire characteristic for central European anxieties. These expectations placed on Havel more burden than any finite human could bear. True, both Czechs and Slovaks do not wish the divorce (the politicians Mečiar and Klaus cooked this up for their power designs, and so it is they who should bear the primary blame). Yet people did not press their representatives for the passage of those constitutional proposals that could have prevented the present split. Slovaks have democratically elected the populist Prime Minister, Mečiar, who has a totalitarian past and possible ties to the state secret police (Stb), and who in his campaign stirred nationalist passions. Czechs have chosen a right-wing market conservative Prime Minister, Klaus, who had little patience for the Slovak economic and social specificum. Czechs in their beer pubs have arrogantly concluded that this is for the better—"Let Slovaks go"—and have all but disregarded the democratic and profederation forces in Slovak culture. Slovaks have rallied behind the Pyrrhic victory of their nationalist yet not so democratic sovereignty, while they have helplessly watched the split of the country, and in Slovakia imminent economic debacle and rising repression—on good national grounds, of course, of freshly won freedom. Perhaps Havel was politically too naïve and not ready for the forces that 1989 unleashed: even moral leadership should not want to remain above party politics. But blaming Havel for failing to be an enlightened god-like monarch who governs by decrees in place of fostering deliberative democracy is just a convex mirror of all revolutionary desires, whether left- or right-wing, for a strong hand. The morally fallible leader can practice only the politics of the possible. Thus, people need to take responsibility for

their own "velvet revolution" in which both Havel and they played equal parts. Let's not blame anyone else but ourselves, the people, for the politicians and directions we choose for our countries. Theodor Draper and Rita Klimová, the former Czechoslovak Ambassador to the United States, exchanged a series of observations on the root reasons for the breakdown of Czechoslovakia. [See Draper, "A New History of the Velvet Revolution," *New York Review of Books* XI/1–2 (14 January 1993) 14–20; "The End of Czechoslovakia," *New York Review of Books* XI/3 (28 January 1993) 20–26 and the letters by Klimová and Draper, "'The End of Czechoslovakia': An Exchange," *New York Review of Books* XI/7 (8 April 1993) 50–52.] The contention between them is whether or not the referendum about the split should have been called after the parliamentary elections of Klaus and Mečiar. Klimová argues that to say it should have been overlooks the desire of the Czech and Slovak governments to settle the national question without force. To call for a referendum in the fall of 1992, she insists, would have been irresponsible given the fact that Yugoslavia is not far from Central Europe. And, she points out, a peaceful divorce is a mark of Czech and Slovak civility. Yet a hurried divorce as such is not necessarily a guarantee of anything (i.e., of democracy). Draper correctly states that there was a rather low popular support for the split and a strong popular opposition to it. Thus, contrary to Klaus, whom Klimová defends in her reply to Draper, the results of the June 1992 elections do not seem to be a sufficient ground for avoiding the referendum which Havel advocated in 1991. There was no valid reason to think that the vote against the split would necessarily lead to violence unless of course the politicians planned to exploit this fear before such a referendum could take place and/or stir up nationalist passions after a possible vote against the split, i.e., to follow the Yugoslav political practices. It was a peaceful divorce, all right, but in cabinet secrecy and without any "marriage counseling" with the people. Thus, unfortunately, Draper might after all be correct in his observation that Klaus and Mečiar did not want the referendum both because they did not trust the democratic voice of the people and because it could have gone against the split and embarrassed them for their unwillingness to find a political compromise. While Draper is right that this mistrust sets a bad precedent when it comes to the future democratic deliberations, neither he nor Klimová pay much attention to existing democratic and pro-federation forces in Slovakia, such as represented by the journal *Kultúrny život*, that found themselves doubly abandoned by the authoritarian Mečiar government and counted out by the defeatist Czech intellectuals.

63. See Ivan Vejvoda, "Loss and Construction of Identity: Democracy Revisited," paper presented at the Dubrovnik's Inter-University Center Seminar in "Identity and Civil Society," Ischia, Italy (2 April 1992), manuscript. See also Chap. 9, section 9.2, above.

APPENDIX A

1. 1. This conversation transpired in Frankfurt a/M, Germany, on 22 May 1990. (For further references, see Chap. 1 and Part I *passim* above.) I am thankful to Jürgen Habermas for reading through my reconstruction of his replies and for suggesting some minor corrections.

2. See Habermas, TCA 2:96–106/147–163.

3. I critique Habermas's explanation in Chap. 4, section 4.1.B, above.)

4. Habermas, TCA 2:96ff./147ff.

5. Habermas, TCA 2:109/167.

6. Habermas's Copenhagen essay, NC 260ff./EAS 172ff.; see Chap. 1 above.

7. Habermas, ND 149–204/187–241.

8. See Habermas, AG, Part I on Kierkegaard; and n. 6 above, and Ernst Tugendhat, *Selbstbewusstsein und Selbstbestimmung: Sprachanalytische Interpretationen* (Frankfurt a/M: Suhrkamp, 1979).

9. Habermas, TCA 2:109/167.

10. Habermas, NR 179–224; on constitutional patriotism and revolutionary melancholy, see Habermas VV.

11. On permanent democratic revolution, see Habermas, VV; on existentential revolution, see Chap. 8 and Part III *passim* above and Havel, uR.

12. See Habermas, "Transzendenz von innen, Transzendenz ins Diesseits," in TuK 138ff.; see also Edmund Arens, ed., *Habermas und die Theologie: Beiträge zur theologischen Rezeption, Diskussion und Kritik der Theorie kommunikativen Handelns* (Düsseldorf: Patmos, 1989).

13. On existential pathos, see Chap. 6 above; on the ideal community, see Chap. 7 above.

14. Habermas, NR 144, 220; NC 260f./EAS 172f.

15. On Horkheimer, see Habermas, TuK 91–126.

16. For the definitions of these terms, see Part III above.

17. See Max Horkheimer, *Gesammelten Schriften*, Vol. 7 (Frankfurt a/M: Fischer, 1985): "Theismus und Atheismus" (1963) 182–186 and "Zur Zukunft der kritischen Theorie" (1971) 429–434.

18. Habermas, NR 188ff.

19. See Habermas, NR, VV, and his reply to question 3 above.

20. *Post scriptum*: my last questions to Habermas occurred long before he, along with many Frankfurt academic leftists, justified the 1991 American-led allied intervention against Iraq on the grounds that there was a legitimate rational core in the consensus reached by the United Nations (Habermas, VaZ 9–44).

Bibliography of Secondary Works

Adorno, Theodor W. *Gesammelte Schriften*. Frankfurt a/M: Suhrkamp, 1984.

_____. *Kierkegaard: Construction of the Aesthetic*. Trans. Robert Hullot-Kentor. Minneapolis: University of Minnesota Press, 1989.

Agger, Ben. *The Discourse of Domination: From the Frankfurt School to Post-modernism*. Evanston, Ill.: Northwestern University Press, 1992.

Ames, Van Meter. "Mead and Sartre on Man." *Journal of Philosophy* 53 (1956) 205–219.

_____. "Buber and Mead." *Antioch Review* 27 (1967) 181–191.

Apel, Karl-Otto. *Der Denkweg von Ch.S. Peirce*. Frankfurt a/M: Suhrkamp, 1967, 1975.

_____. *Transformation der Philosophie*. Frankfurt a/M: Suhrkamp, 1973.

_____. *Diskurs und Verantwortung: Das problem Des Übergangs zur Post-konventionellen Moral*. Frankfurt a/M: Suhrkamp, 1988.

Appiah, Anthony. "The Uncompleted Argument: Du Bois and the Illusion of Race." In Henry Louis Gates, Jr., Ed., *Race, Writing, and Difference*. Chicago: University of Chicago Press, 1986, 21–37.

Arendt, Hannah. "What Is Existenz Philosophy?" *Partisan Review* 2/1 (Winter 1946) 34–56.

Arens, Edmund. Ed. *Habermas und die Theologie: Beiträge zur theologischen Rezeption, Diskussion und Kritik der Theorie kommunikativen Handelns*. Düsseldorf: Patmos, 1989.

Arnason, Johann P. "Nationalism, Globalization, and Modernity." *Theory, Culture and Society* 7/2–3 (June 1990) 207–236.

Ash, Timothy Garton. *The Uses of Adversity: Essays on the Fate of Central Europe*. Baltimore: Penguin Books, 1983; Cambridge: Granta Books, 1991.

Augustine. *The City of God*. Ed. David Knowles. Trans. Henry Bettenson. Baltimore: Penguin Books, 1981.

Austin, J. L. *How to Do Things with Words* (1962). Cambridge, Mass.: Harvard University Press, 1975.

Avineri, Shlomo. "Hegel and Nationalism." *Review of Politics* 24 (1962) 461–484.

_____. *The Social and Political Thought of Karl Marx*. Cambridge: Cambridge University Press, 1968.

_____. *Hegel's Theory of the Modern State*. Cambridge: Cambridge University Press, 1972.

Balibar, Etienne, and Immanuel Wallerstein. *Race, Nation, Class: Ambiguous Identities* (1988). Trans. Chris Turner. New York, London: Verso, 1991.

The bibliography of primary works appears as Appendix B.

Bataille, Georges. *Visions of Excess: Selected Writings, 1927–1939.* Ed. A. Stoekl. Minneapolis: University of Minnesota Press, 1985.

Bayard, Caroline. "The Intellectual in the Post Modern Age: East/West Contrasts." *Philosophy Today* 34/4 (Winter 1990) 291–302.

Baynes, Kenneth. *The Normative Grounds of Social Criticism: Kant, Rawls, and Habermas.* Albany: SUNY Press, 1992.

Becker, Ernest. *The Denial of Death.* New York: Free Press, 1973.

_____. *Escape from Evil.* New York: Free Press, 1975.

Bělohradský, Václav. *Krize eschatologie neosobnosti* [The Crisis of the Eschatology of Nonpersonality]. London: Rozmluvy, 1983.

Bělohradský, Václav. "Je Masarykovo pojetí Německa ještě aktuální?" [Is Masaryk's Understanding of Germany Still Actual?] *Přítomnost* (Praha, 4 June 1990) 16–17.

Benhabib, Seyla. *Critique, Norm, and Utopia: A Study of the Foundation of Critical Theory.* New York: Columbia University Press, 1986.

_____. "Feminism and Postmodernism: An Uneasy Alliance." *Praxis International* 11/2 (July 1991) 137–149.

_____, and Drucilla Cornell. Eds. *Feminism as Critique.* Minneapolis: University of Minnesota Press, 1987.

_____, and Fred Dallmayr. Eds. *The Communicative Ethics Controversy.* Cambridge, Mass.: MIT Press, 1990.

Benhabib, Seyla. Ed.'s Intro. *Praxis International* 11/1 (April 1991) 1–6.

_____. *Situating the Self: Gender, Community and Postmodernism in Contemporary Ethics.* New York: Routledge, 1992.

Benjamin, Walter. *Gesammelten Schriften.* Vol. 3. Frankfurt a/M: Suhrkamp, 1972.

Berger, Peter L. *The Sacred Canopy.* Garden City, N.Y.: Doubleday, 1967.

Bergman, Paul. Ed. *Debating P. C.: The Controversy over Political Correctness on College Campuses.* New York: Laurel Books, 1992.

Bernasconi, Robert, and David Wood. Eds. *The Provocation of Levinas: Rethinking the Other.* London: Routledge, 1988.

Bernstein, Richard J. *Beyond Objectivism and Relativism: Science, Hermeneutics, and Praxis.* Philadelphia: University of Pennsylvania Press, 1985.

_____. Ed. *Habermas and Modernity.* Cambridge, Mass.: MIT Press, 1985.

Bigelow, Pat. *Kierkegaard and the Problem of Writing.* Tallahassee: Florida State University Press, 1987.

Bloch, Ernst. *Das Prinzip Hoffnung.* Vols. 1 and 3. Frankfurt a/M: Suhrkamp, 1977.

Bolte, Gerhard. Ed. *Unkritische Theorie: Gegen Habermas.* Lüneburg: zu Klampen, 1989.

Bourgeois, Patrick L., and Sandra B. Rosenthal. "Role Taking, Corporeal Intersubjectivity, and Self: Mead and Merleau-Ponty." *Philosophy Today* 34/2 (Summer 1990) 117–128.

Brandon, Henry. "Who Split Czechoslovakia?" *New York Times*, Op-Ed, 24 September 1992, p. A-29.

Brown, Norman O. *Life against Death: The Psychoanalytical Meaning of History.* Middletown, Conn.: Wesleyan University Press, 1959, 1985.

_____. *Love's Body.* New York: Vintage Books, 1966.

Browning, Don S., and Francis Schüssler Fiorenza. Eds. *Habermas, Modernity, and Public Theology.* New York: Crossroad, 1992.

Brunkhorst, Hauke. *Der Intellektuelle im Land der Mandarine*. Frankfurt a/M: Suhrkamp, 1988.

Buber, Martin. *Werke*. Vols. 1–3. München: Kösel, 1962–1964.

––––––––. *Between Man and Man*. With an afterword by the author on "The History of the Dialogical Principle." New York: MacMillan, 1978.

Bubner, Rüdiger. "Brauchen wir einen Begriff der Nation?" Paper presented in the Philosophy Department of J. W. Goethe-Universität, Frankfurt a/M (June 1991). Manuscript.

Bühler, Karl. *Sprachtheorie*. Jena: Gustav Fischer, 1934.

Camus, Albert. *The Rebel: An Essay on Man in Revolt*. Trans. Anthony Bower. New York: Knopf, 1956.

––––––––. *The Fall*. Trans. Justin O'Brien. New York: Vintage Books, 1960.

––––––––. *The Myth of Sisyphus and Other Essays*. Trans. Justin O'Brien. New York: Knopf, 1960.

Caputo, John D. *Radical Hermeneutics: Repetition, Deconstruction, and the Hermeneutic Project*. Bloomington: Indiana University Press, 1987.

Clement, Grace. "Is the Moral Point of View Monological or Dialogical? The Kantian Background of Habermas's Discourse Ethics." *Philosophy Today* 33 (Summer 1989) 159–173.

Cohen, Richard A. Ed. *Face to Face with Levinas*. Albany: SUNY Press, 1986.

Collins, James. *The Mind of Kierkegaard*. Chicago: Henry Regnery, 1953, 1965.

Connell, George B., and C. Stephen Evans. Eds. *Foundations of Kierkegaard's Vision of Community: Religion, Ethics, and Politics in Kierkegaard*. Atlantic Highlands, N.J.: Humanities Press, 1992.

Dahrendorf, Ralf. "In Politics Begin Responsibilities" [review of Havel's Lp (q.v.)]. *New York Times Book Review*, 7 June 1992, pp. 1, 29.

Dauenhauer, Bernard P. "Taylor and Ricoeur on the Self." *Man and World* 25 (1992) 211–225.

de Candole, James. "Václav Havel jako konzervativní myslitel." Trans. Z. *Proglas*, No. 1 (Brno, 1990) 52–57. ["Václav Havel as a Conservative Thinker." *Salisbury Review* (December 1988).]

Dérer, Miroslav. "Obrana Václava Havla" [Defending Václav Havel.] *Kultúrny život* (Bratislava), 4 April 1991, p. 4.

Derrida, Jacques. *The Postcard: From Socrates to Freud and Beyond*. Trans. Alan Bass. Chicago: University of Chicago Press, 1987.

––––––––. "The Politics of Friendship." *Journal of Philosophy* 85 (November 1988) 632–644.

––––––––. *L'autre cap*. Paris: Gallimard, 1991. [*The Other Heading: Reflections on Today's Europe*. Trans. Pascale-Anne Brault and Michael B. Naas. Bloomington: Indiana University Press, 1992.]

Deuser, Hermann. *Sören Kierkegaard: Die paradoxe Dialektik des politischen Christen. Voraussetzungen bei Hegel: Die Reden von 1847/48 in Verhältnis von Politik und Ästhetik*. München: Kaiser/Grünewald, 1974.

––––––––. *Dialektische Theologie: Studien zu Adornos Metaphysik und zum Spätwerk Kierkegaards*. München: Kaiser/Grünewald, 1980.

––––––––. "Kierkegaard in der Kritischen Theorie." *Text & Kontext* 15 (1983) 101–113.

Dienstbier, Jiří. Interview on PBS television (29 February 1990).

_____. *Snění o Evropě: Politický esej* [Dreaming about Europe]. Praha: Lidové noviny, 1990.

Douglass, Frederick. *Narrative of the Life of Frederick Douglass, an American Slave* (1845). New York: New American Library, 1968.

Draper, Theodore. "A New History of the Velvet Revolution." *New York Review of Books* XI/1–2 (14 January 1993) 14–20.

_____. "The End of Czechoslovakia." *New York Review of Books* XI/3 (28 January 1993) 20–26.

Dubiel, Helmut. "Linke Trauerarbeit." *Merkur* 44/6 (June 1990) 482–491. ["Beyond Mourning and Melancholia on the Left." Trans. Don Reneau. *Praxis International* 10/3–4 (October 1990–January 1991) 241–249.]

Du Bois, W. E. B. "The Conservation of Races." In Howard Brotz, Ed., *African-American Social and Political Thought, 1850–1920.* New Brunswick, NJ: Transaction Publishers, 1992, 483–492.

Durkheim, Emile. *The Elementary Forms of the Religious Life.* Trans. J. W. Swain. New York: Free Press, 1965.

Dussel, Enrique. *Ethics and Community.* Trans. Robert R. Barr. New York: Maryknoll, 1988.

Ebeling, Hans. *Neue Subjektivität: Die Selbstbehauptung der Vernunft.* Würzburg: Köningshausen und Neumann, 1990.

Edelstein, Wolfgang, and Gertrud Nunner-Winkler. Eds. *Zur Bestimmung der Moral: Philosophische und sozialwissenschaftliche Beiträge zur Moralforschung.* Frankfurt a/M: Suhrkamp, 1986.

Elrod, John W. *Being and Existence in Kierkegaard's Pseudonymous Works.* Princeton, NJ: Princeton University Press, 1975.

Engelberg, Stephen. "The Velvet Revolution Gets Rough." *New York Times Magazine,* 31 May 1992, pp. 31–33, 49, 54.

_____. "Careful Breakup in Czechoslovakia." *New York Times,* 21 June 1992, p. A-7.

_____. "Havel calls for Preservation of United Czechoslovakia." *New York Times,* 26 June 1992, p. A-2.

_____. "Leaders Drive Apart Czech and Slovak: Schism at the Top." *New York Times,* 28 June 1992, p. E-3.

_____. "Václav Havel: Still Puckish, Still a Politician, No Longer President." *New York Times,* 21 July 1992, p. A-5.

English, Jane. "Justice between Generations." *Philosophical Studies* 31 (1977) 91–104.

Erikson, Erik H. *Identity and the Life Cycle: Selected Papers.* New York: International University Press, 1959.

_____. *Insight and Responsibility: Lectures on the Ethical Implications of Psychoanalytic Insight.* New York: Norton, 1964.

Evans, C. Stephen. *Kierkegaard's Fragments and Postscript: The Religious Philosophy of Johannes Climacus.* Atlantic Highlands, N.J.: Humanities Press, 1983.

Farias, Viktor. *Heidegger und der Nationalsozialismus.* Frankfurt a/M: Fischer, 1989.

Ferrara, Alessandro. "Postmodern Eudaimonia." *Praxis International* 11/4 (January 1992) 387–411.

_____. *Modernity and Authenticity: A Study in the Social and Ethical Thought of Jean-Jacques Rousseau.* Albany: SUNY Press, 1993.

Foucault, Michel. *Discipline and Punish: The Birth of the Prison*. Trans. Alan Sheridan. New York: Random House, 1977.

Frank, Manfred. *Die Unhitergehbarkeit von Individualität: Reflexionen über Subjekt, Person und Individuum aus Anlaß ihrer 'postmodernen' Toterklärung*. Frankfurt a/M: Suhrkamp, 1986.

_____, Gérard Raulet, and Willem van Reijen. Eds. *Die Frage nach dem Subjekt*. Frankfurt a/M: Suhrkamp, 1988.

Fraser, Nancy. *Unruly Practices: Power, Discourse and Gender in Contemporary Social Theory*. Minneapolis: University of Minnesota Press, 1989.

Fukuyama, Francis. *The End of History and the Last Man*. New York: Free Press, 1992.

_____. "Rest Easy. It's Not 1914 Anymore." *New York Times*, 9 February 1992, p. E-17.

Gadamer, Hans-Georg. *Truth and Method*. Ed. Joel Weinsheimer. Trans. Donald G. Marshall. New York: Crossroad, 1989.

Gellner, Ernest. *Nations and Nationalism*. Ithaca, N.Y.: Cornell University Press, 1983.

Gilligan, Carol. *In a Different Voice*. Cambridge, Mass.: Harvard University Press, 1982.

Goldmann, Robert B. "Havel's Message Deserves Hearing." *International Herald Tribune*, 15 August 1990, p. 6.

Gould, Carol C. *Rethinking Democracy: Freedom and Social Cooperation in Politics, Economy, and Society*. Cambridge: Cambridge University Press, 1988, 1990.

Grathoff, Richard. "Zur gegenwärtigen Rezeption von Georg Herbert Mead" [Review of new literature on Mead]. *Philosophische Rundschau* 34, 1/2 (1987) 131–145.

Gray, John. (Review of Liah Greenfield's *Nationalism: Five Roads to Modernity*.) *New York Times Book Review*, 27 December 1992, pp. 6–7.

Greve, Wilfried. *Kierkegaards maieutische Ethik: Von "Entweder/Oder II" zu den "Stadien."* Frankfurt a/M: Suhrkamp, 1990.

Grondin, Jean. "Habermas und das Problem der Individualität." *Philosophische Rundschau* 36/3 (1989) 187–205.

Günther, Klaus. *Der Sinn für Angemessenheit: Anwendungsdiskurse in Moral und Recht*. Frankfurt a/M: Suhrkamp, 1988.

_____. "Ein Normativer Begriff der Kohärenz für eine Theorie der Juristischen Argumentation." *Rechtstheorie* 20 (1989) 163–190.

Hall, Ronald L. *Word and Spirit: A Kierkegaardian Critique of the Modern Age*. Bloomington: Indiana University Press, 1993.

Hanzel, Vladimír. *Zrychlený tep dějin: realné drama o deseti jednáních*. [The Speeded Up Pulse of History: The Realistic Drama in Five Acts. Documents of the political discussions between the state and the democratic opposition in November and December of 1989.] Praha: OK Centrum, 1991.

Harris, Leonard. "The Horror of Tradition or How to Burn Babylon and Build Benin While Reading 'A Preface to a Twenty-Volume Suicide Note.'" *Philosophical Forum* 24/1–3 (1992–1993) 94–118.

"Havel Mahnt Waldheim indirect: Rede in Salzburg—Ohne Volle Wahrheit Keine Volle Freiheit." *Frankfurter Rundschau*, 27 July 1990, p. 1.

"Havel über die Anatomie des Hasses: Eine Konferenz der Stiftung Elie Wiesel in Oslo." *Neue Zürcher Zeitung* ["Hinweise" section], 3 September 1990, p. 4.

Hegel, Georg Wilhelm Friedrich. *Hegel's Philosophy of Right*. (1952). Trans. T. M. Knox. London: Oxford University Press, 1967.

_____. *Werke*. Vols. 1–20. Eds. E. Moldenhauer and K. M. Michel. Frankfurt a/M: Suhrkamp, 1970–1971.

Heidegger, Martin. *Was ist Metaphysik?* (1929). Frankfurt a/M: Klostermann, 1955.

Henrich, Dieter. Ed. *Kant oder Hegel? Über Formen der Begründung in der Philosophie*. Stuttgart: Klett-Cotta, 1983.

Hobsbawm, Eric J. *Nations and Nationalism since 1780: Programme, Myth, Reality*. Cambridge: Cambridge University Press, 1990.

Honneth, Axel. *Kritik der Macht: Reflexionsstufen einer kritischen Gesellschaftstheorie*. Frankfurt a/M: Suhrkamp, 1986, 1989.

_____. "Integrität und Mißachtung: Grundmotive einer anerkennungstheoretischen Moralkonzeption." Inaugural lecture presented at the Habilitation proceedings, Frankfurt a/M (28 June 1990). Manuscript.

_____. *Kampf um Anerkennung: Zur moralischen Grammatik sozialer Konflikte*. Frankfurt a/M, Suhrkamp, 1992.

_____, and Hans Joas. Eds. *Kommunikatives Handeln: Beiträge zu Jürgen Habermas' "Theorie des kommunikativen Handelns."* Frankfurt a/M: Suhrkamp, 1986.

_____, Thomas McCarthy, Claus Offe, and Albrecht Wellmer. Eds. *Zwischenbetrachtungen: Im Prozeß der Aufklärung*. Frankfurt a/M: Suhrkamp, 1989.

Hooks, bell, and Cornel West. *Breaking Bread: Insurgent Black Intellectual Life*. Boston: South End Press, 1991.

Horkheimer, Max. *Kritische Theorie* (1968). Ed. Alfred Schmidt Vols. 1 and 2. Frankfurt a/M: Fischer, 1977.

_____. *Gesammelte Schriften*. Vols. 1–14. Frankfurt a/M: Fischer, 1985.

_____, and Theodor W. Adorno. *Dialectic of Enlightenment* (1944). Trans. John Cumming. New York: Continuum, 1987.

Ingram, David. *Habermas and the Dialectic of Reason*. New Haven, Conn.: Yale University Press, 1987.

Jaspers, Karl. *Die geistige Situation der Gegenwart*. Berlin: Gruyter, 1931.

_____. *Man in the Modern Age*. Trans. Eden and Cedar Paul. New York: Henry Holt, 1933.

_____. *Philosophie*. Vol. 1. Berlin: Springer, 1956.

_____. *Vernuft und Existenz*. München: R. Piper, 1960.

Jay, Martin. *The Dialectical Imagination: A History of the Frankfurt School and the Institute of Social Research, 1923–1950*. Boston: Little, Brown, 1973.

_____. *Adorno*. Cambridge, Mass.: Harvard University Press, 1984.

_____. *Marxism and Totality: The Adventures of a Concept from Lukács to Habermas*. Berkeley: University of California Press, 1984.

Joas, Hans. *Praktische Intersubjektivität: Die Entwicklung des Werkes von G. H. Mead*. Frankfurt a/M: Suhrkamp, 1980.

_____. Ed. *Das Problem der Intersubjektivität: Neuere Beiträge zum Werk George Herbert Meads*. Frankfurt a/M: Suhrkamp, 1985.

Kamm, Henry. "Havel's Lesson for Austria: Don't Fear the Past." *International Herald Tribune*, 27 July 1990, p. 1.

_____. "Czech Regrets the Rift with Slovakia." *New York Times*, 29 September 1992, p. A-7.

_____. "Nation Split, Havel Aspires to a New Political Life." *New York Times*, 30 September 1992, p. A-3.

Kalberer, Guido. "Ein denker zwischen Husserl und Heidegger: Jan Patočkas Habilitationsarbeit in deutscher Übersetzung." *Neue Zürcher Zeitung* ["Hinweise" section] 11 September 1990, p. 35.

Kaufmann, Walter. Introduction to Kierkegaard's *Present Age*. Trans. Alexander Dru. New York: Harper & Row, 1962.

Kellner, Douglas. *Herbert Marcuse and the Crisis of Marxism*. Berkeley: University of California Press, 1984.

Kelly, Michael. Ed. *Hermeneutics and Critical Theory in Ethics and Politics*. Cambridge, Mass.: MIT Press, 1990.

Kennan, George F. "Keeping the Faith" [review of the English trans. of Havel's Lp (q.v.)] *New York Review of Books*, 24 September 1992, pp. 3–4.

Kirmmse, Bruce H. *Kierkegaard in Golden Age Denmark*. Bloomington: Indiana University Press, 1990.

Klimová, Rita, and Theodore Draper. "'The End of Czechoslovakia': An Exchange." *New York Review of Books* XI/7 (8 April 1993) 50–52.

Kohl, Helmut. An interview with Austrian national television (16 February 1991).

Kohlberg, Lawrence. *Essays on Moral Development*. Vol. 1. San Francisco: Harper & Row, 1981.

Kriseová, Eda. *Václav Havel: Životopis* (Authorized biography). Brno: Atlantis, 1991.

Kristeva, Julia. *Nations Without Nationalism*. Trans. Leon S. Roudiez. New York: Columbia University Press, 1993.

Kuhlmann, Andreas. "Der Kerker als Front: Jan Patočka's existentialistischer Begriff des Politischen." *Frankfurter Allgemenine Zeitung* ["Geisteswissenschfaten" section], 23 May 1990, p. N-3.

_____. "Kommt die europäische Staatsbürgernation: Ein Kongreß in Brüssel über die Identität und die Vielfalt Europas." *Frankfurter Rundschau*, 29 May 1991, p. 9.

Kuhlmann, Wolfgang. Ed. *Moralität únd Sittlichkeit: Das Problem Hegels und die Diskursethik*. Frankfurt: Suhrkamp, 1986.

Kundera, Milan. *The Unbearable Lightness of Being*. Trans. Michael Henry Heim. New York: Harper & Row, 1984.

_____. *The Art of the Novel*. Trans. Linda Asher. New York: Grove Press, 1988.

Kymlicka, Will. "Two Theories of Justice." *Inquiry* 33/1 (March 1990) 99–119.

Laber, Jeri. "Witch Hunt in Prague." *New York Review of Books*, 23 April 1992, pp. 5–8.

Langsdorf, Lenore, and Stephen Watson, Eds. *Political Theory: The Selected Studies in Phenomenology and Existential Philosophy*. Vol. 20. Albany, NY: SUNY Press, in press.

Lapointe, Francois. *Søren Kierkegaard and His Critics: An International Bibliography of Criticism*. Westport, Conn.: Greenwood Press, 1980.

Levin, David Michael. *The Body's Recollection of Being: Phenomenological Psychology and the Deconstruction of Nihilism*. London: Routledge & Kegan Paul, 1985.

_____. Ed. *Pathologies of the Modern Self: Postmodern Studies on Narcissism, Schizophrenia, and Depression.* New York: New York University Press, 1987.

Lévinas, Emmanuel. *Totality and Infinity: An Essay on Exteriority.* Trans. Alphonso Lingis. Pittsburgh: Duquesne University Press, 1969.

_____. *Otherwise Than Being or Beyond Essence.* Trans. Alphonso Lingis. Hague: Martinus Nijhoff, 1981.

_____. *Collected Philosophical Papers.* Trans. Alphonso Lingis. Hague: Martinus Nijhoff, 1987.

List, Elisabeth, and Herlinde Studer. Eds. *Denkverhältnisse: Feminismus und Kritik.* Frankfurt a/M: Suhrkamp, 1989.

Lonergan, Bernard. *The Subject.* Milwaukee: Marquette University Press, 1968.

Lorraine, Tamsin E. *Gender, Identity, and the Production of Meaning.* Boulder, Colo.: Westview Press, 1990.

Löwith, Karl. *From Hegel to Nietzsche* (1941). Trans. David E. Green. New York: Holt, Rinehart & Winston, 1964.

Lukács, György. "Das Zerschellen der Form am Leben: Sören Kierkegaard und Regine Olsen" (1909). In *Die Seele und die Formen.* ["Sammlung Luchterhand" series]. Neuwied: Luchterhand, 1971, 44–63.

_____. *Werke.* Vols. 1–17. Neuwied: Luchterhand, 1962–1975.

MacIntyre, Alasdair. *After Virtue: A Study in Moral Theory.* 2nd ed. London: Duckworth, 1985–1987.

_____. *Whose Justice? Which Rationality?* Notre Dame, Ind.: University of Notre Dame Press, 1988.

Mackey, Louis. *Kierkegaard: A Kind of Poet.* Philadelphia: University of Pennsylvania Press, 1971.

Macpherson, C. B. *The Political Theory of Possessive Individualism: Hobbes to Locke.* Oxford: Clarendon Press, 1962.

Malantschuk, Gregor. *Kierkegaard's Thought.* Eds. and Trans. Howard V. Hong and Edna H. Hong. Princeton, N.J.: Princeton University Press, 1971.

_____. *The Controversial Kierkegaard.* Trans. Howard V. Hong and Edna H. Hong. Waterloo, Ontario: Wilfred Laurier University Press, 1978.

Marcuse, Herbert. "Beiträge zu einer Phänomenologie des Historischen Materialismus," *Philosophische Hefte* 1/1 (1928) 45–68.

_____. "Über konkrete Philosophie." *Archiv für Sozialwissenschaft und Sozialpolitik* 62 (1929) 111–128.

_____. "Transzendentaler Marxismus?" *Die Gesellschaft* 7 (part 2)/10 (1930) 304–326.

_____. "Zum Problem der Dialektik." *Die Gesellschaft* 7 (part 1)/1 (1930) 15–30 and 8 (part 2)/12 (1931) 541–557.

_____. *Hegels Ontologie und die Grundlegung einer Theorie der Geschichtlichkeit.* Frankfurt: a/M. Klostermann, 1932.

_____. "Neue Quellen zur Grundlegung des Historischen Materialismus." *Die Gesellschaft* 9 (part 2)/8 (1932) 136–174.

_____. "Philosophie des Scheiterns: Karl Jaspers Werk." *Unterhaltungsblatt der Vossichen Zeitung*, 339 (14 December 1933).

_____. *Eros and Civilization* (1955). New York: Vintage Books, 1962

_____. *Negations: Essays in Critical Theory* (1963). Trans. Jeremy J. Shapiro. Boston: Beacon Press, 1968.

_____. *Schriften.* Vols. 1–5. Frankfurt a/M: Suhrkamp, 1978–1992.

_____. *One-Dimensional Man: Studies in the Ideology of Advanced Industrial Society* (1964). New Intro. Douglas Kellner. Boston: Beacon Press, 1991.

Marquard, Odo, and Karlheinz Stierle. Eds. *Identität, Poetik und Hermeneutik*. Vol. 8. München: Wilheln Fink, 1979.

Marsh, James L. "Interiority and Revolution." *Philosophy Today* 29 (Fall 1985) 191–202.

_____. *Post-Cartesian Meditations: An Essay in Dialectical Phenomenology*. New York: Fordham University Press, 1988.

_____. "Praxis and Ultimate Reality: Intellectual, Moral, and Religious Conversion as Radical Political Conversion." *Ultimate Reality and Meaning* 13 (September 1990) 222–240.

_____, John D. Caputo, and Merold Westphal. Eds. *Modernity and Its Discontents*. New York: Fordham University Press, 1992.

Martin, Bill. *Matrix and Line: Derrida and the Possibilities of Postmodern Social Theory*. Albany: SUNY Press, 1992.

Marx, Karl. *The Economic and Philosophic Manuscripts of 1844*. Trans. Martin Milligan. New York: International Publishers, 1964.

_____. *Early Writings*. Trans. Rodney Livinstone and Gregor Benton. New York: Vintage Books, 1975.

Matthiesen, Ulf. *Das Dickicht der Lebenswelt und die Theorie des kommunikativen Handelns*. München: Wilhelm Fink, 1983–1985.

Matuštík, Martin J. (Review of Habermas's *Observations on the "Spiritual Situation of the Age"*). *Auslegung* 14/2 (Summer 1988) 225–228.

_____. "Habermas on Communicative Reason and Performative Contradiction." *New German Critique* no. 47 (Spring/Summer 1989) 163–192.

_____. "Transcendental–Phenomenological Retrieval and Critical Theory." *Method: Journal of Lonergan Studies* 8/1 (March 1990) 94–105.

_____. "Jürgen Habermas at 60." *Philosophy and Social Criticism* 16/1 (1990) 61–80 and 16/2 (1990) 159–60.

_____. "Havel and Habermas on Identity and Revolution." *Praxis International* 10/3–4 (October 1990–January 1991) 261–277.

_____. "Post/Moderní Pokoušení." *Tvar*, No. 36 (Prague), 8 November 1990, pp. 1, 4–5.

_____. [Review of Bubner's *Essays in Hermeneutics and Critical Theory*]. *Auslegung* 16/1 (Winter 1990) 116–123.

_____. "Merleau-Ponty on Taking the Attitude of the Other." *Journal of the British Society for Phenomenology* 22/1 (January 1991) 44–52.

_____. "Merleau-Ponty's Phenomenology of Sympathy." *Auslegung* 17/1 (January 1991) 41–65.

_____. "Identita a moc: k debatě mezi postmodernou Michela Foucaulta a kritickým modernismem Jürgena Habermase." *Filosofický časopis* 39/2 (February 1991) 177–198.

_____. "Kierkegaard a existenciálna revolúcia." *Kultúrny život* (Bratislava, June 1991) 6–7.

_____. "Habermas's Reading of Kierkegaard: Notes from a Conversation." *Philosophy and Social Criticism* 17/4 (August 1991) 313–323.

_____. [Reviews of Perkins, Ed., *International Kierkegaard Commentary: Vol. 13. The Corsair Affair* (q.v.)]. In *Man and World* 26 (1993) 93–97; and *International Philosophical Quarterly* 23/4 (December 1992) 524–526.

_____. "Post-National Identity: Habermas, Kierkegaard, and Havel." *Thesis Eleven* no. 34 (March, 1993) 89–103.

_____. "Kierkegaard as Socio-Political Thinker" (Review of recent secondary Kierkegaard literature) *Man and World* (in press).

McCarthy, Thomas. *The Critical Theory of Jürgen Habermas*. Cambridge, Mass.: MIT Press, 1978.

_____. "Philosophical Foundations of Political Theology: Kant, Peukert, and the Frankfurt School." In Leroy S. Rouner, Ed., *Civil Religion and Political Theology* (pp. 23–40). Notre Dame, Ind.: University of Notre Dame Press, 1986.

_____. "On the Margins of Politics." *Journal of Philosophy* 85 (November 1988) 645–48.

McDonald, William. Introduction to Kierkegaard's Pr (q.v.), 1989. 1–13.

McKinnon, Alastair. Ed. and Intro. *Kierkegaard: Resources and Results*. Waterloo, Ontario: Wilfrid Laurier University Press, 1982.

McLellan, David. Ed. *Karl Marx: Selected Writings*. London: Oxford University Press, 1977.

Mead, George Herbert. *Mind, Self, and Society*. Chicago: University of Chicago Press, 1934. [*Geist, Identität, und Gesellschaft*. Trans. Hans Joas. Frankfurt: a/M Suhrkamp, 1968.]

_____. *Philosophie der Sozialität*. Frankfurt a/M: Suhrkamp, 1969.

_____. *Gesammelte Aufsätze* (1980). Vols. 1–2. Frankfurt a/M: Suhrkamp, 1980.

Merleau-Ponty, Maurice. *The Primacy of Perception*. Trans. James M. Edie. Evanston, Ill.: Northwestern University Press, 1964.

_____. *Phenomenology of Perception*. Trans. Colin Smith. London: Routledge & Kegan Paul, 1965, 1986.

_____. *Adventures of the Dialectic*. Trans. Joseph Bien. Evanston, Ill.: Northwestern University Press, 1973.

Michnik, Adam. "Bojím sa antikomunistov s tvárami bol'ševikov" [I Am Afraid of the Anticommunists with the Faces of Bolseviks] (Interview). *Kultúrny život* (Bratislava), 11 June 1992, p. 3.

Misgeld, Dieter. "Critical Hermeneutics versus Neoparsonianism?" *New German Critique* no. 35 (1985) 55–87.

Mooney, Edward F. *Knights of Faith and Resignation: Reading Kierkegaard's "Fear and Trembling."* Albany: SUNY Press, 1991.

Mueller, Howard R. "The Dialectic of Self-Transformation: A Study in the Structure and Development of the Historical Consciousness in the Thought of Søren Kierkegaard." Ph.D. dissertation, University of London, Heytrop College, 1977.

Mueller, Robert William. "A Critical Examination of Martin Buber's Criticism of Søren Kierkegaard." Ph.D. dissertation, Purdue University, 1974.

Murphy, John Michael, and Carol Gilligan. "Moral Development in Late Adolescence and Adulthood: A Critique and Reconstructions of Kohlberg's Theory." *Human Development* 23 (1980) 77–104.

"Nationen in schlechter Verfassung: Nationalismen nach der Perestrojka." A series of presentations at Palais Jalta (Frankfurt a/M, 21 April–30 June 1991).

Nietzsche, Friedrich. *Twilight of the Idols* (1889). Trans. R. J. Hollingdale. Baltimore: Penguin Books, 1968.

_____. *Beyond Good and Evil* (1886). Trans. R. J. Hollingdale. Baltimore: Penguin Books, 1973.

Okin, Susan. "Gender and Justice." *Philosophy and Public Affairs* 16 (Winter 1987) 42–72.

_____. *Justice, Gender and the Family*. New York: Basic Books, 1989.

Outlaw, Lucius. "Lifeworlds, Modernity, and Philosophical Praxis: Race, Ethnicity, and Critical Social Theory." In Eliot Deutsch, Ed., *Culture and Modernity: East–West Philosophic Perspectives*. Honolulu: University of Hawaii Press, 1991, 21–49.

_____. "Against the Grain of Modernity: The Politics of Difference and the Conservation of 'Race.'" *Man and World* 25/3–4 (October 1992) 443–468.

Parfit, Derek. *Reasons and Persons*. Oxford: Clarendon Press, 1984.

Patočka, Jan. *Ausgewählte Schriften*. Ed. Klaus Nellen and Jiří Němec. Trans. Eliška and Ralph Melville. Stuttgart: Klett-Cotta, 1987.

_____. *Kacířské eseje o filozofii dějin* [Heretical Essays about the Philosophy of History]. Intro. Ivan Dubský. Praha: Academia, 1990.

Peirce, Charles Sanders. *Collected Papers*. Eds. Charles Hartshorne and Paul Weiss. Cambridge, Mass.: Harvard University Press, 1931–1958.

"The Perils of Lustration" (Editorial). *New York Times*, 7 January 1992, p. A-12.

Perkins, Robert L. Ed. *International Kierkegaard Commentary. Vol. 14. Two Ages: The Age of Revolution and the Present Age. A Literary Review*. Macon, Ga.: Mercer University Press, 1984.

_____. *International Kierkegaard Commentary: Vol. 13. The Corsair Affair*. Macon, Ga.: Mercer University Press, 1990.

Peukert, Helmut. *Science, Action, and Fundamental Theology: Towards a Theology of Communicative Action*. Trans. James Bohman. Cambridge, Mass.: MIT Press, 1984–1986.

Pfuetze, Paul. *Self, Society, Existence: Human Nature and Dialogue in the Thought of George Herbert Mead and Martin Buber*. New York: Greenwood Press, 1961.

Pippin, Robert, and Andrew Feenberg, Charles P. Webel, and contributors. *Marcuse: Critical Theory and the Promise of Utopia*. South Hadley, Mass.: Bergin & Garvey, 1988.

Pirandello, Luigi. *Six Characters in Search of an Author*. Trans. Frederick May. London: Heinemann, 1958.

Plato. *Great Dialogues of Plato*. Trans. W. H. D. Rouse. New York: New American Library, 1956.

Plekon, Michael. "Kierkegaard and the Interpretation of Modernity." *Kierkegaard-Studiet* no. 11 (1981) 3–12.

_____. "Moral Accounting: Kierkegaard's Social Theory and Criticism." *Kierkegaardiana*, No. 12 (1982) 69–82.

Polanyi, Michael. *Personal Knowledge: Towards a Post-Critical Philosophy*. Chicago: University of Chicago Press, 1958.

Přečan, Vilém. Ed. *Charta 77: 1977–1989. Od morální k demokratické revoluci* [From Moral to Democratic Revolution]. Bratislava: ARCHA, 1990.

Rabinow, Paul. Ed. *The Foucault Reader*. New York: Pantheon Books, 1984.

Raiser, Konrad. *Identität und Sozialität: Georg Herbert Meads Theorie der Interaktion und Ihre Bedeutung für die theologische Anthropologie*. München, Kösel: 1971.

Rasmussen, David M. *Reading Habermas*. With a bibliography by René Görtzen. Oxford: Blackwell, 1990.

_____. Ed. *Universalism vs. Communitarianism: Contemporary Debates in Ethics*. With a bibliography by Michael Zilles. Cambridge, Mass.: MIT Press, 1990.

Rawls, John. *A Theory of Justice*. Cambridge, Mass.: Harvard University Press, 1971.

Ricoeur, Paul. "Philosopher après Kierkegaard." *Revue de théologie et de Philosophie* 3/13 (1963) 303–316. ["Philosophieren nach Kierkegaard." Trans. Reinhild Weskott. In Theunissen and Greve, Eds., *Materialien* (q.v.), 1979.].

_____. *The Symbolism of Evil*. Trans. Emerson Buchanan. New York: Harper & Row, 1967.

_____. *Freud and Philosophy: An Essay on Interpretation*. Trans. Denis Savage. New Haven, Yale University Press, 1970.

_____. *Soi-même comme un autre*. Paris: Éditions du Seuil, 1990.

Riedel, M. Ed. *Materialien zu Hegels Rechtsphilosophie*. Vol. 2. Frankfurt a/M: Suhrkamp, 1974.

Rockmore, Tom. *Habermas on Historical Materialism*. Bloomington: Indiana University Press, 1989.

Rorty, Richard. *Philosophy and the Mirror of Nature*. Princeton, N.J.: Princeton University Press, 1979.

Rosenthal, A.M. "Havel and Waldheim." *New York Times*, 29 July 1990, p. E-19.

Rothschild, Thomas. "Der Schriftsteller als Politiker: Bücher über und von Václav Havel." *Frankfurter Rundschau*, 26 June 1991, p. 12.

Ruddick, Sara. "Maternal Thinking." *Feminist Studies* 6 (1980) 342–367.

Sandel, Michael. *Liberalism and the Limits of Justice*. Cambridge: Cambridge University Press, 1982.

_____. *Liberalism and Its Critics*. New York: New York University Press, 1984.

Sartre, Jean-Paul. *Being and Nothingness* (1948). Trans. Hazel E. Barnes. New York: Citadel, 1964.

Scheller, Wolf. "Versuch, in der Wahrheit zu leben: Gespräch mit dem Staatspräsidenten und Dramatiker Václav Havel." *Stuttgarter Zeitung* ["Feuilleton" section], 11 May 1991.

Schleicher, Harry. "An 'Jedermann' kommt keiner vorbei: Václav Havel und Kurt Waldheim, die Unperson aus der Wiener Burg." *Frankfurter Rundschau*, 27 July 1990, p. 3.

Schlesinger, Arthur M., Jr. *The Disuniting of America*. New York: Norton, 1992.

Schmitt, Carl. *The Crisis of Parliamentary Democracy*. Trans. E. Kennedy. Cambridge, Mass.: MIT Press, 1985.

_____. *Political Theology*. Trans. C. Schwab. Cambridge, Mass.: MIT Press, 1985.

_____. *Political Romanticism*. Trans. Guy Oakes. Cambridge, Mass.: MIT Press, 1986.

Schoolman, Morton. *The Imaginary Witness: The Critical Theory of Herbert Marcuse*. New York: New York University Press, 1984.

Schrag, Calvin O. *Communicative Praxis and the Space of Subjectivity*. Bloomington: Indiana University Press, 1986, 1989.

Selman, R., and R. Yando. Eds. *Clinical-Developmental Psychology*. ["New Directions for Child Development" series]. No. 7. San Francisco: Jossey-Bass, 1980.

Siebert, Rudolf J. *From Critical Theory to Communicative Political Theology*: *Universal Solidarity*. New York: Peter Lang, 1989.

Springe, T. L. S. "The Satanic Novel: A Philosophical Dialogue on Blasphemy and Censorship." *Inquiry* 33/4 (December 1990) 377–400.

Stern, Paul. "On the Relation between Rational Autonomy and Ethical Community: Hegel's Critique of Kantian Morality." *Praxis International* 9/3 (October 1989) 234–248.

Strawson, Peter. *Individuals*. London: Methuen, 1959; Garden City, N.Y.: Doubleday, 1963.

Taylor, Charles. *Human Agency and Language: Philosophical Papers*. Vol. 1. Cambridge: Cambridge University Press, 1985.

_____. "Cross-Purposes: The Liberal-Communitarian Debate." In Nancy Rosenbaum, Ed., *Liberalism and the Moral Life* (pp. 159–182). Cambridge, Mass.: Harvard University Press, 1989.

_____. *Sources of the Self: The Making of the Modern Identity*. Cambridge: Cambridge University Press, 1989.

Taylor, Marc C. *Journeys to Selfhood: Hegel and Kierkegaard*. Berkeley: University of California Press, 1980.

_____. *Altarity*. Chicago: University of Chicago Press, 1987.

_____. Foreword to Kierkegaard's Pr (q.v.), 1989.

Theunissen, Michael. *Der Andere: Studien der Sozialontologie der Gegenwart*. Berlin: Gruyter, 1965, 1972.

_____, and Wilfried Greve. Eds. *Materialien zur Philosophie Sören Kierkegaard*. Frankfurt a/M: Suhrkamp, 1979.

_____. *Negative Theologie der Zeit*. Frankfurt a/M: Suhrkamp, 1991.

_____. *Der Begriff der Verzweiflung: Korrekturen an Kierkeaard*. Frankfurt a/M: Suhrkamp, 1993.

Thompson, Josiah. *Kierkegaard: A Collection of Critical Essays*. Garden City, N.Y.: Doubleday, 1972.

_____. *Kierkegaard*. New York: Knopf, 1973.

Thyen, Anke. *Negative Dialektik und Erfahrung: Zur Rationalität des Nichtidentischen bei Adorno*. Frankfurt a/M: Suhrkamp, 1989.

Tucker, Aviezer. "Václav Havel's Heideggerianism." *Telos* no. 85 (Fall 1990) 63–78.

Tugendhat, Ernst. "Das Sein und das Nichts." In V. Klostermann. Ed. *Durchblicke: Festschrift Martin Heidegger zum 80. Geburtstag*. Frankfurt a/M: Klostermann, 1970.

_____. *Vorlesungen zur Einführung in die sprachanalytische Philosophie*. Frankfurt a/M: Suhrkamp, 1976.

_____. *Selbstbewusstsein und Selbstbestimmung: Sprachanalytische Interpretationen*. Frankfurt: Suhrkamp, 1979. [*Self-Consciousness and Self-Determination*. Trans. Paul Stern. Cambridge, Mass.: MIT Press, 1986].

Vejvoda, Ivan. "Loss and Construction of Identity: Democracy Revisited." Paper presented at the Dubrovnik's Inter-University Center International Seminar on "Identity and Civil Society," Ischia, Italy (2 April 1992). Manuscript.

Wahl, Jean. *Etudes Kierkegaardiennes*. Paris: Fernand Aubier, 1938.

Waldenfels, Bernard. *Der Spielraum des Verhaltens*. Frankfurt a/M: Suhrkamp, 1980.

Wallulis, Jerald. *The Hermeneutics of Life History: Personal Achievement and His-*

tory in Gadamer, Habermas, and Erikson. Evanston, Ill.: Northwestern University Press, 1990.

Warren, Mark. "Liberal Constitutionalism as Ideology: Marx and Habermas." *Political Theory* 17 (November 1989) 511–534.

Washington, James Melvin. Ed. *A Testament of Hope: The Essential Writings of Martin Luther King, Jr.* New York: Harper & Row, 1986.

Weiss, Peter. *The Persecution and Assassination of Jean-Paul Marat as Performed by the Inmates of the Asylum of Charenton under the Direction of the Marquis de Sade.* Trans. Geoffrey Skelton. Intro. Peter Brook. Verse adapt. Adrian Mitchell. New York: Atheneum and Pocket Books, 1965.

Wellmer, Albrecht. *Ethik und Dialog: Elemente des moralischen Urteils bei Kant und in Diskursethik.* Frankfurt a/M, Suhrkamp, 1986.

Westphal, Merold. *History and Truth in Hegel's Phenomenology.* Atlantic Highlands, N.J.: Humanities Press, 1978.

_____. *God, Guilt, and Death: An Existential Phenomenology of Religion.* Bloomington: Indiana University Press, 1984.

_____. *Kierkegaard's Critique of Reason and Society.* Macon, Ga.: Mercer University Press, 1987.

_____. "Taking Suspicion Seriously: The Religious Uses of Modern Atheism." *Faith and Philosophy* 4/1 (January 1987) 26–42.

Wiggershaus, Rolf. *Die Frankfurter Schule: Geschichte, Theoretische Entwicklung, Politische Bedeutung.* München: Deutsche Taschenbuch, 1989.

Wilson, Paul. "The End of the Velvet Revolution." *New York Review of Books*, 13 August 1992, pp. 57–58, 60–64.

Wittgenstein, Ludwig. *On Certainty.* (1969). Ed. G. E. M. Anscombe and G. H. von Wright. Trans. Denis Paul and G. E. M. Anscombe. Oxford: Blackwell, 1974.

Wolin, Richard. "Carl Schmitt, Political Existentialism, and the Total State." *Theory and Society* 19 (1990) 389–416.

_____. *The Terms of Cultural Criticism: The Frankfurt School, Existentialism, Poststructuralism.* New York: Columbia University Press, 1992.

Wyschograd, Michael. *Kierkegaard and Heidegger.* London: Routledge and Kegan Paul, 1954.

INDEX